CARDANO FOR THE MASSES

A financial operating system for people who don't have one

John Greene BSc, MSc, CISSP, C|EH

kindle direct publishing

Cardano for the Masses: A financial operating system for people who don't have one
By John Greene

Cover:
credit *Heisenbird* (twitter @EyeOfTheKing1)

Proofreaders:
Oussama Benmahmoud
Dr Lingling Liu
Diarmuid Buckley
Kevin Pendred

About the Author

John Greene has a background in cloud infrastructure and security with an MSc in Digital Currencies from the University of Nicosia. This is his 'difficult second book' after *AWSoeasy* in 2015 (outdated now). He lives in Dublin and enjoys Cardano for the mind, mountain running for the body, and playing the bodhrán for the soul.

Contact:

twitter.com/CardanoBook,
john@cardanobook.com

Preface 9

Chapter 1: In the beginning 12

Origins of blockchain and cryptocurrencies 13

Charles Hoskinson's early days in crypto 20

Cardano is born 27

Cardano Timeline.. 31

Chapter 2: What is Cardano?.. 33

Foundational concepts.. 35

Why is Cardano different?... 38

Why choose Cardano?... 46

Cardano roadmap 48

How does Cardano work? 50

Cardano design decisions.. 53

Behind the names.. 62

Chapter 3: Proof of Stake.. 68

What is proof of stake?.. 69

'The green blockchain' 71

Philosophy of POS 74

Stake Pool Personas.. 76

Setting up and running a stake pool................................. 77

Cardano network 78

How to Research Stake Pools 80

Stake Pool Performance.. 81

Ranking Stake Pools 82

Types of Addresses in Cardano.. 82

Pledging... 84

Delegation 87

Pledging and rewards 89

Pledging and Delegation Options...................................... 90

Types of Keys in Cardano 91

Cardano RTView...94

Cardano tracking tools...95

Chapter 4: Shelley (Consensus).............................97

The Scalability Challenge...98

What is a Consensus Protocol?..99

Ouroboros..99

The different implementations of Ouroboros......................100

How the Consensus Layer Works.......................................107

Hard Forking Business..111

Path to Full Decentralization...116

Ouroboros lays the foundation for the Basho Era...............123

Chain v transaction confirmation.......................................126

P2P (peer-to-peer)...127

Cardano Entropy (Randomness)...132

Fees on Cardano..134

The 3 different sides of full Decentralization......................136

Edinburgh Decentralization Index.......................................139

Chapter 5: Goguen (Smart Contracts).....................142

Extended UTXO...143

'Neither smart nor a contract'..151

Metadata on Cardano..152

Token Locking on Cardano...156

Native Tokens...158

Multi-Asset Support (MAS)..163

Creating native tokens on Cardano....................................169

The lifecycle of native tokens on Cardano..........................172

Min-ada-value requirement..173

Native Token FAQ...174

Multi-assets on Exchanges..179

Smart Contracts Rollout..184

The concurrency non-issue...186

UTXO alliance...190

Chapter 6: Plutus 194

What is Plutus?...195

Plutus Scripts 201

Plutus Versions..203

Typical Plutus Use Cases 209

Plutus Tools..210

Writing Plutus transactions 216

Collateral mechanism..220

Learning Plutus...222

Chapter 7: Marlowe...227

What is Marlowe?..228

Marlowe Language Structure 232

Marlowe Playground 235

Using Blockly with Marlowe 236

Using the Editor for Haskell or JavaScript 241

Marlowe Run..244

Actus Smart Contracts...251

Marlowe for P2P Finance 254

Marlowe Playground evolves 258

Marlowe FAQs...261

Chapter 8: Basho (Scalability) 264

Scalability Defined 265

Ongoing enhancements 267

Pipelining...272

On-disk storage 275

Off-chain computing..276

Mithril...276

Hydra 279

Sidechains 287

Midnight in the Garden of Good and Evil 289

Milkomeda 292

Input Endorsers 295

Chapter 9: Voltaire (Governance) *302*

Money is social 303

Cardano Improvement Proposals (CIPs) 305

What is Project Catalyst? 309

Catalyst's early funds 313

Catalyst Circle 316

Catalyst Natives 318

Later Funds 319

The Cardano cFund 321

dReps 323

Tactical Pause for Catalyst 324

The Age of Voltaire 326

Chapter 10: RealFi on Cardano *335*

The DeFi Revolution 336

~~DeFi~~ RealFi for the Masses 340

Atala Prism Decentralized IDs 342

Babel Fees 343

Stablefees 348

Tiered Pricing as the network scales 351

Djed stablecoin 354

Djed FAQ 360

How EUTXO copes with impermanent loss 365

ERC20 Converter 369

Certified DApps on Cardano 373

Oracles on Cardano 376

Cardano in Africa 377

Outlook...**380**

Preface

I discovered Cardano while researching a college project in 2018. Ever since I asked a question of Cardano co-founder Charles Hoskinson in one of his AMAs[1] I had intended to write a book of some sort. I tried different ideas, gave up, and returned several times. On hearing that the much-anticipated *Mastering Cardano* book would be delayed, I felt there might be a space for a 'can opener' in the meantime.

Writing about cryptocurrencies is challenging. Most of the best-selling crypto books have 'Flesch reading ease scores' in the 50s. I wanted this book to be more inclusive.

With so much jargon in the blockchain space, I decided to arm the reader with explainers throughout. However, I didn't want to obstruct the flow either. As Kindle automatically converts footnotes to a popup format, explainers are accessible by clicking on superscripts in the text. The explainers also form a glossary at the end of the book. I added excerpts from Charles Hoskinson's various updates to interweave his perspective throughout the book. I felt they add context to many technology decisions while painting a vision for the overall project and industry.

I made every effort to be accurate, however, Cardano is evolving rapidly. There has probably been a change, or update of some sort, as you read this. I intend to update the book regularly in cadence with Cardano updates, improving readability with each edition.

For e-readers, graphics are best viewed in 'landscape' mode.

Intended audience

This book is mainly for Cardano newcomers. It does not focus on specific projects built on Cardano. The inaugural *Essential Cardano Guide to the Ecosystem* report[2] covers that. It does not go deep into the weeds of the technical research papers,[3] nor explore concepts in detail. The goal is to give a broad overview of Cardano. Each chapter can be read on its own, however, it's best to read from start to finish if you are new to Cardano. OGs[4] can browse and read sections independently. Nothing within these covers is financial advice.

Chapter 1 is a high-level overview of blockchain and how Cardano started. Chapter 2 goes through foundational concepts and Chapter 3 addresses proof of stake and

---

[1] Sunday AMA 05/17/2020, youtube.com/watch?v=-CJ5pcullgg&t=690s

[2] The Essential Cardano Guide to the Ecosystem, services.iohk.io/guide-to-the-ecosystem

[3] IOHK Library, iohk.io/en/research/library/

[4] **OG** (crypto Original Gangster) is slang for a founder of any early crypto blockchain such as Vitalik Buterin, who invented Ethereum. A crypto OG can also refer to an early investor in Bitcoin or Ethereum.

Cardano's differentiators. The remaining chapters walk through different aspects of the Cardano roadmap (roadmap.cardano.org). The final Chapter 10 is about the end product: RealFi on Cardano.

IOG and IOHK

Input Output was founded in Hong Kong, hence the abbreviation IOHK. However, the company has since moved its base to Wyoming, US and is rebranding itself as Input Output Global (IOG). At some stage, the website will probably migrate from iohk.io to iog.io.

Acknowledgments

It's best to come clean at the outset and admit I'm not Satoshi Nakamoto, nor did I invent the *Ouroboros* consensus protocol or think up Babel fees.

This book was inspired by the brilliant minds at IOG and the Cardano ecosystem. For some of the technical concepts and features still in research, I did not stray far from the documentation. I have tried to reference all sources.

Chapter 1: In the beginning

'The best prophet of the future is the past'

— Lord Byron

Origins of blockchain and cryptocurrencies

Anyone who doubts the adage 'the truth is stranger than fiction' should look at the history of money.[5] From the round stones on Yap island, to the Irish 'paying through the nose' to the Danes, to the peace and prosperity of the Belle Époque era, to the adoption and abandonment of the gold standard…cryptocurrencies, and the blockchains[6] they run on, are just the latest twist in a long and colorful story.

To understand a third generation blockchain such as Cardano, we must first review its predecessors. The first generation is Bitcoin,[7] whose goal was to create decentralized money. Could there be a scarce, tradable token that lives on some sort of decentralized blockchain maintained by people all around the world?

This wasn't a new pursuit. Bitcoin happened to be the breakthrough, but it was built on previous attempts. The idea of Bitcoin started in the 1980s, with a lot of ideas coming from the 'cypherpunk' movement.[8] Ecash preceded DigiCash with pioneering work from Hal Finney and David Chaum. During the 1990s and into the early 2000s, Nick Szabo proposed the 'bitgold' system. There were other contributing factors like the technological advances of the Arm chip powering smaller devices, making processing possible.

In 2008, Bitcoin was just a pipe dream in the form of a white paper.[9] Satoshi Nakamoto is the pseudonym for whomever it was who wrote this paper. The Bitcoin founder has remained anonymous, even after their email account was compromised and emails publicly shared. Since the beginning, Bitcoin has been shrouded in mystery. It is an experiment born out of discontent with the way things are, and idealism for how things should be. On January 3, 2009, Satoshi Nakamoto mined the first block – the genesis

---

[5] 'A brief (and fascinating) history of money', britannica.com/story/a-brief-and-fascinating-history-of-money

[6] A **blockchain** is a continuously growing list of records, called blocks, which are linked and secured using cryptography. Each block typically contains a link to a previous block, a timestamp and transaction data. By design, blockchains are inherently resistant to modification of the data. A blockchain is 'an open, distributed ledger that can record transactions between two parties efficiently and in a verifiable and permanent way.'

[7] **Bitcoin (BTC)** is a cryptocurrency and a payment system that uses a public distributed ledger called a blockchain. Invented by a single (or potentially a group) under the Satoshi Nakamoto alias. On 31 October 2008, Bitcoin was introduced to a cryptography mailing list and released as open-source software in 2009. There have been various claims and speculation concerning the identity of Nakamoto, none of which has been confirmed. The system is peer-to-peer, so transactions take place between users directly, without an intermediary. These transactions are verified by network nodes and recorded in the blockchain, which uses bitcoin as its unit of account.

[8] A **cypherpunk** is any activist advocating widespread use of strong cryptography and privacy-enhancing technologies as a route to social and political change. Originally communicating through the cypherpunks email list, informal groups aimed to achieve privacy and security through proactive use of cryptography. Cypherpunks have been engaged in an active movement since the late 1980s.

[9] Satoshi Nakamoto (2008) 'Bitcoin: A Peer-to-Peer Electronic Cash System', bitcoin.org/bitcoin.pdf

block[10] – for Bitcoin. These 100,000 lines of mediocre C++ code[11] attracted a lot of brilliant minds.

From early supporters such as Hal Finney to Martti Malmi, many others flocked over the years as Bitcoin grew from a few crypto anarchists on a mailing list, to a global movement. All this despite no marketing budget, with a logo provided by a forum user with the name Bitboy.[12] Bitcoin has since proven its resilience. It has been declared dead countless times and endured many crashes. It has lost many of its early contributors. Developers such as Mike Hearn and Gavin Andresen fell out and left. Satoshi Nakamoto, the pseudonymous founder, vanished. Despite these obstacles and setbacks, the dream has persisted.

Within a few years, Bitcoin accrued thousands of users who could send and receive value without a trusted third party, or intermediary. The price of bitcoin went from less than a penny to $1 in 2011, to $1,000 in 2013, $17,000 in 2018 and a peak of $67,000 in 2021. Amid this, there were the crashes, such as the 'crypto winter' of 2017, when the bitcoin price fell from about $20,000 to $6,000 within weeks. There was a similar crash in early 2022, with two-thirds of the price again being lost.

The idealism of Bitcoin is about creating better money, or 'sound money[13] in a digital age' as described by the economist Saifedean Ammous in *The Bitcoin Standard*. Bitcoin appeared after the 2008 financial meltdown, the worst global financial crisis since the Great Depression. Many people were starting to go back to first principles, questioning whether central banks could be trusted to create 'sound money'? Can other people create better money? Does the world really need banks to act as middlemen? Can't I just be my own bank? Questions like these, along with a mistrust of institutions, were the seeds from which Bitcoin grew.

What are the properties of sound money?

Money is usually defined as having three primary properties:

1) Unit of account
2) Medium of exchange
3) Store of value.

Money being a **unit of account** means we have the ability to measure prices in a consistent way. We should be able to compare goods and services in dollars, euros or sterling. Without it, it might be like prison where you compare and trade cigarettes for

---

[10] A **genesis block** is the first block of a block chain. The genesis block is almost always hardcoded into the software of the applications that utilize its block chain. It is a special case in that it does not reference a previous block.

[11] Bitcoin Source Code Walkthrough, drnealaggarwal.info/bitcoin-source-code-walkthrough/

[12] Bitcoin's logo, decrypt.co/43923/bitcoins-logo-the-story-of-the-big-orange-b

[13] **Sound money** is money that is not liable to sudden appreciation or depreciation in value.

bread, books, baseball cards, or whatever is lying around. It would obviously be chaotic, making price discovery[14] next to impossible.

Medium of exchange, means the token should be widely accepted. For a proposed money to function, it should be able to be exchanged for goods and services and act as an intermediary instrument. Being a valid means of exchange avoids the limitations of the barter system, where what one wants must be exactly matched with what the other has to offer.

Finally, a **store of value** is the property, whereby when you get money, it doesn't fade, doesn't evaporate into thin air, spoil or rot. Many goods have some of the properties of money. For example, if you were in prison, bananas or tinned food may be a viable means of exchange. But, in general, food can't be used as a store of value because it perishes. For money to be a store of value, it must be durable in value over time. It should be physically durable also. Even if you forget to empty your pockets before washing your clothes, euro notes and coins are usually usable afterwards. There are plenty of coins still around from Roman times and earlier.

There are many other properties. Like is it transportable? Gold is often said to be a poor means of exchange because it's difficult to haul over long distances. Would a large store of gold in a basement be valuable to someone fleeing war? **Transportability** of money may supersede all other properties in such a scenario.

Fungibility was a term familiar only to commodity traders until the 2021 craze for NFTs (non-fungible tokens).[15] It's a measure of *sameness*, of whether two things are identical, or whether each is unique. If fungible, then there is no practical difference between two things. For business to flow smoothly, there must be consistency in that a dollar is a dollar, is a dollar. This could be in digital form in a credit card payment, a loan, or a physical note handed over. This is what you would expect with two units of the same currency. However, if you buy an expensive painting from a gallery, you want it to be non-fungible, a unique object.

Divisibility is another important property. You can try, but a coffee shop is unlikely to accept seashells as payment. So it is convenient to replicate a 'cash in, cash out' system. Digital currencies facilitate divisibility in a mathematical sense very well by design. However, some are more intuitive in practice. For example, paying a $10 equivalent for this book in different cryptocurrencies (July 2022) would work out as follows:

---

[14] **Price discovery** is the process of determining the price of an asset in the marketplace through the interactions of buyers and sellers.

[15] **Non-fungible token (NFT).** Such a token proves ownership of a digital item in the same way that people own crypto coins. However, unlike crypto coins, which are identical and worth the same, an NFT is unique. A craze started with the Christie's auction of *Everydays: the First 5,000 Days*, a collage of 5,000 digital pieces on March 11, 2021. Mike Winkelmann, known as Beeple, created the digital art and made an NFT of it. Bidding started at $100. It sold for $69.3m. Ten days later, Twitter co-founder Jack Dorsey sold an NFT of the first tweet for 1,630.5 ether ($2.9m) and donated the proceeds to charity. NFT became the Collins Dictionary's word of the year for 2021. However, when the buyer of Dorsey's NFT tried to sell it a year later, the highest bid was just $6,800. Ultimately, the value of an NFT is determined solely by what someone is willing to pay for it.

0.00043 Bitcoin (BTC)
0.0063 Ethereum (ETH)
20.01035705 Cardano (ADA)

Some real currencies are losing divisibility and there have been proposals to get rid of the penny, which is a fundamental unit of account. Rounding was introduced for cash transactions in Ireland in 2015, which means that the total amount of a bill will be rounded up or down to the nearest five cents.

How you might go about defining the different types of inflation and what exactly is 'sound money' is worthy of a book of its own. Bitcoin takes a stance on how to provide the properties required for a form of money. It is scarce, with just 21m bitcoins in existence. One bitcoin is divisible into 100,000,000 satoshis. Bitcoin is digital, so regards itself as durable. Bitcoin is portable as a monetary asset. In April 2020, a crypto exchange transferred coins worth $1.1bn in a single transaction in a matter of minutes at a cost of 68 cents.[16] Bitcoins are fungible, but not perfectly so, because anyone can trace transfers between wallets on the blockchain.

At a high level, Bitcoin attains the above properties through decentralization.[17] Decentralization, at its core, is about removing, or 'killing' the middleman but there is no set definition the industry agrees upon. This has been a bone of contention for some time, especially when it comes to proposing legislation. The term has also been misused as a marketing buzzword and more cynically as a smoke screen for flagrant misconduct by centralized entities posing as web3[18] idealists. This led to the establishment of the EDI 'Edinburgh Decentralization Index' which is an attempt bring clarity by developing a framework to evaluate blockchain decentralization. The index being developed by the University of Edinburgh[19] looks at objective measures like the distribution of the currency, the treasury, developer distribution, the level of decentralization of consensus, etc. More about the EDI later.

The haves and the have-nots

If we were to meet for a coffee in a developed country, the apparatus and mechanisms are in place to make payment seamless. Although paying with a credit card is effortless and instant as a consumer experience, there is a lot of 'centralized' activity behind the scenes. You, the card holder, got your credit card from an issuer. This issuer is typically a bank, or some financial institution, issuing credit cards on behalf of the big networks (Visa and Mastercard). The coffee shop is the merchant in this case. Then there is a fourth party involved, the acquirer. This is usually a bank, such as JP Morgan Chase or HSBC, where the coffee shop (merchant) has its account.

---

[16] 'Five biggest bitcoin transactions in history', cryptovantage.com/news/here-are-the-5-biggest-bitcoin-transactions-in-history/

[17] **Decentralization** is the process by which the activities of an organization, particularly those regarding planning and decision making, are distributed or delegated away from a central, authoritative location or group.

[18] Web3 (also known as Web 3.0) is an idea for a new iteration of the World Wide Web which incorporates concepts such as decentralization, blockchain technologies, and token-based economics

[19] The Edinburgh Decentralization Index, ed.ac.uk/informatics/blockchain/edi

This entire authorization process, from the time you tap your card for payment takes a few seconds. It doesn't matter if your bank is in Ireland and the merchant's bank is in Japan, the data flows quickly in real time. The full authorization and value transfer between banks can take several business days behind the scenes. The settlement process is heavily regulated, expensive and not inclusive.

Banks would not offer these services if it were not profitable for them. As a consequence, there are three billion people 'unbanked', mostly in the developing world, where such infrastructure doesn't exist. For these people, there are no banks, there are no accompanying services such as credit or insurance.

Any form of money is only as good as the trust people have in it. Trust is variable and affected by economic events large and small. People must have faith that the money they use is worth something, that it holds the properties and characteristics they expect.

So this is what Bitcoin set out to achieve. It was, and is, a very ambitious and idealistic goal to offer an online form of money that was not reliant on a central authority issuing it. People had to have faith in it as a viable form of money. There is no Federal Reserve or central bank involved. Nobody is in charge, but everyone is in charge. Bitcoin achieves this through cryptography (explained in later chapters) to preserve 'inclusive accountability', the notion that everyone can 'check each other's homework'.[20] Everyone can see and review the record to ensure transaction(s) are valid and nobody is telling fibs.

Another driving force behind Bitcoin was discontent and exasperation. People lost faith in institutions and their mechanisms. The genesis block of Bitcoin had embedded within it a reference to a headline from *The Times* newspaper of January 3, 2009, 'Chancellor on the brink of second bailout for banks', implying frustration with events of the time. The 2008 financial meltdown was just the latest in a line of institutional failings.

Most, if not all fiat currencies[21] eventually lose their value and/or collapse. Power corrupts. There are so many political and moral temptations to debase the currency for short-term benefits, at the expense of long-term gains. You don't have to look far back in history for examples. The Weimar Republic in Germany, Venezuela, Argentina and Zimbabwe have all suffered from hyperinflation.[22] The effects of the 2008 financial crisis are still rippling and have been compounded by the costs of keeping people in jobs during the Covid-19 pandemic, with trillions of US dollars printed out of nowhere.

---

[20] Addressing Blockchain's Hidden Trade-Off, youtube.com/watch?v=FSByg_sdjaM

[21] **Fiat money** has been defined variously as:
Any money declared by a government to be legal tender
State-issued money which is neither convertible by law to any other thing, nor fixed in value in terms of any objective standard
Intrinsically valueless money used as money because of government decree
An intrinsically useless object that serves as a medium of exchange, also known as fiduciary money.

[22] In economics, **hyperinflation** quickly erodes the real value of a local currency as the prices of all goods rise. This causes people to minimize their holdings in that currency as they switch to more stable foreign currencies (hard currency).

What is blockchain?

Bitcoin runs on a blockchain. However, cryptocurrency is just one application of blockchain. If creating and trading digital tokens, they reside on a ledger somewhere. This ledger is often compared to a database. Some crypto skeptics claim, 'It's just a database! What is the point?' Blockchain has the potential to remove the need for a central authority in many scenarios. That is a pretty compelling selling point. You can think of blockchain as a 'trust broker' where separate parties, who don't trust each other, need to work together. Blockchain is also commonly referred to as a distributed ledger technology (DLT).[23]

So it's a special kind of database; it stores a record of events and all sorts of metadata (data about data) related to transactions. Normally an intermediary such as Revolut, or Bank of Ireland, would verify and hold all your banking history on behalf of Visa or Mastercard. What if you don't trust them anymore? Or if you don't want to pay transaction processing fees? This is the core innovation of Bitcoin, to provide an alternative system with a blockchain that acts as a 'trust broker'. So, succinctly, a blockchain is simply a ledger and it stores transactions and associated data so anyone can verify claims.

Blockchains achieve this using cryptographic methods and a consensus protocol.[24] Think of it as using mathematics and computer science to create a type of database in the cloud. Once a record is written, it's immutable, it's a fact that cannot be altered. So once there is a decentralized trust broker that eliminates the need for a centralized authority, it can be used for many other things. If the human element can be removed by creating decentralized money, the obvious next question was 'can the same mechanisms be used for decentralized authentication? ...for decentralized voting, and so on?'

Blockchain use cases

Voting can be recorded on a blockchain and be immutable, transparent, tamper-resistant, inexpensive and convenient (vote with a mobile app). Is democracy safe when such a high percentage of an electorate don't believe in the outcome of an election? Should a country's leader be able to decide unilaterally to invade another country without a public vote? Without passing a high majority threshold?

Property rights are currently managed by some form of central registry. So if you have a title, or deeds to a house, a central actor has to maintain that database. What happens if that actor can manipulate or edit that database? What happens if there is a change of government? Like when Isis took over Syria, or the turmoil in Ukraine. If the central

---

[23] **Distributed ledger technology (DLT)** is a protocol or database that is consensually shared and synchronized across many sites, institutions, or geographies, accessible by many people, and enables the secure functioning of a decentralized digital database.

[24] A **consensus protocol** is a fault-tolerant mechanism that is used in blockchain systems to achieve the necessary agreement on a single data value or a single state of the network among distributed processes or multi-agent systems, such as with cryptocurrencies.

actor(s) can just decide to update the history, then it becomes very difficult, after peace returns, to decide who actually owns what and where. Millions of people throughout the world live on disputed land. A blockchain could provide a more just system, without the presence of a central authority.

Along with Banking, **Publishing** is one of the oldest industries around. Although e-readers and online book shops disrupted the model to some extent, most companies operate in a centralized manner. You are typically buying a license to view an eBook, without ever owning the product. *Book* (book.io) is an innovative new platform that aims to disrupt the publishing space by bringing books ('decentralized encrypted assets') to the blockchain. Under this model, the buyer owns the digital asset, can resell the book after reading it, and 'read to earn' rewards to buy other books or engage with the platform in other ways, such as AMAs (ask-me-anything) with the author. There are all sorts of implications for readers, authors and publishers outlined in Book's whitepaper.[25]

Supply chains are another ideal use for blockchains. During the Covid-19 pandemic, supply chains for personal protective equipment and vaccines were critical for millions of people. These goods were handled by many companies, and people were making life-and-death decisions based upon the stability of these supply chains and the reliability of the information in them. With blockchain technology, you don't have to trust a central authority or third parties to make sure that the records were accurate.

Identity itself is a critical personal asset that is essential for many services to function inclusively for all. Traditionally you would need a passport or driver's license for know-your-customer (KYC) checks or just get a credit score to be eligible for a loan. Many people's identity has become linked with personally identifiable information (PII) in online profiles held by Facebook, Google and other centralized behemoths.

Today, your identity is at the mercy of third parties. Statements and claims are then made about that identity, again by credit agencies and government services. You, the subject, don't actually own your own identity online. You're not in control, and your identity – usually in the form of many identities online – is typically managed by middlemen and third parties who have the potential to manipulate the records against your best interest. Decentralized identity made possible by decentralized IDs (DIDs)[26] and DID documents,[27] resolves many of these issues and provides greater privacy to the user.

Decentralized finance (DeFi) is about blockchain disrupting traditional banking services. Banking customers in the developed world are not in dire need of DeFi. In the

---

[25] BOOK Token : The Path to Decentralize Knowledge, book-token.medium.com/book-token-the-path-to-decentralize-knowledge-1ee651d657c3

[26] **Decentralized identifiers (DIDs)** are a type of identifier that enables verifiable, decentralized digital identity. A DID refers to any subject (such as a person, organization, thing, data model or abstract entity) as determined by the controller of the DID. In contrast to typical, federated identifiers, DIDs have been designed so that they may be decoupled from centralized registries, identity providers, and certificate authorities.

[27] **DID document**: a set of data describing the DID subject, including mechanisms, such as cryptographic public keys, that the DID subject or a DID delegate can use to authenticate itself and prove its association with the DID. A DID document might have one or more different representations.

developing world, where you might pay up to 80% interest on a microfinance loan, it's easy to see why DeFi is starting to be accepted. That's an important potential aspect of blockchain and cryptocurrencies – bringing three billion 'unbanked' people into the economy, liquefying trillions of dollars of illiquid wealth.

The above examples only scratch the surface. There are many other platforms that we use daily that can be improved with decentralized alternatives. So the point of these systems is to find a way to build them in a way where they work for the small guy in Africa, as much as they do the affluent banker sitting in a Manhattan skyscraper.

Charles Hoskinson's early days in crypto

Charles Hoskinson is a Colorado-based technology entrepreneur and mathematician. He studied analytic number theory before he discovered cryptography. He was a supporter of the Ron Paul campaign for the US presidency campaign in 2008 and often speaks glowingly of how Paul inspired him.[28] Hoskinson was involved with Bitcoin from the early days:[29]

> So, the 2008 financial crisis happened and then I just kept seeing political failure after political failure. I said, there's got to be a different way and then when Bitcoin came out, it was a marriage of a lot of things I loved. I love open-source[30] software and I love cryptography and the real hard science stuff, but then at the same time, there's kind of this political undercurrent of anarcho-capitalism and libertarian ethics and these things that lived in the Bitcoin space and there was a completely different monetary policy. I said, 'wow that's really cool, it'll never work ... but it's really cool', because it was one of those 'chicken and the egg' type of ecosystems where you say, 'Well, for it to work, a lot of people have to take it seriously, but people only take it seriously if it works. How do you get that critical mass?' Everybody said, 'Oh, deflationary money can't work ... We tried that in the 19th century, and it was a miserable failure so, yeah, don't even think about it.' All the economists said Bitcoin would die.
>
> I was a speculator. I bought a lot of Bitcoin and I was a miner. I had an AMD CrossFire set-up, and I was on Slush Pool[31] ... 1.2 giga hashes of mining power, which was quite a lot back in those days and I made a lot of Bitcoin, but I didn't take the space too seriously. Then right around 2013, I noticed an inflection

---

[28] Charles Hoskinson on How did Ron Paul inspire you, youtube.com/watch?v=jqiLVxSAt8w

[29] Slot Leader Episode 1: Interview with Charles Hoskinson, youtube.com/watch?v=YT0PXYBEnuE, Charles Hoskinson: The Future of Blockchain in Africa, youtube.com/watch?v=m3eSEPrJ-1A

[30] **Open-source** software (OSS) is software in which source code is released under a license in which the copyright holder grants users the rights to study, change, and distribute the software to anyone and for any purpose.

[31] Slush pool, slushpool.com/home/

point; it was after the Cypriot crisis[32] where the government said, 'Okay, it's alright for us to just start taking money out of other people's bank accounts to pay for things.' Whoa! That's probably going to happen here if we're not so careful, and lo and behold bitcoin went from $4 to, I think $263. It was just a crazy surge and so, I said this will probably be a big thing. I need to get on the ship and if I don't get on the ship, it will sail right by me.

I had the analytic skills from the math world, and I programmed a lot, so I had cryptography skills and I've known about a lot of the stuff because there's a strong overlap between number theory and cryptography. And then I also had all this monetary policy knowledge, so I got excited about the cryptocurrency space, but I didn't know anybody. I didn't know what to do in the space.

So, I said, 'All right, well, I'll go talk to one of my old professors and ask his advice' and that's Karl Gustafson over at the University of Colorado Boulder … Karl said, 'Charles, those who cannot do… teach.' So I created a free course on Udemy about Bitcoin. It was called 'Bitcoin or how I learned to stop worrying and love crypto'[33] and I got 70,000 students and thousands of emails and I met everybody. I met Roger Ver, Erik Voorhees and Andreas Antonopoulos and all the big names in the cryptocurrency space, before they were big.

Bitcoin was ahead of its time in 2009. It allowed for the creation of decentralized value, and for it to be sent and received like an email. It wasn't long until people wanted more. Just like when the web browser evolved from static to dynamic pages, programmability[34] was required to meet the demand for more applications.

As well as moving value, there's also a story behind every financial transaction, because there are terms and conditions. For example, if you want to buy a book online, there will be a check to see if you have enough funds. If you pay the required amount, the book is sent to your Kindle if, and only if, payment is received. This is a contract; this is the story of a simple transaction. The first-generation blockchain, Bitcoin, wasn't equipped for this. Hoskinson, and others such as Vitalik Buterin, another future co-founder of Ethereum,[35] wanted to improve Bitcoin. But they were met with resistance, and it wasn't easy to reach agreement on how to proceed.

Invictus Innovations & BitShares

---

[32] Cypriot Financial Crisis, theatlantic.com/business/archive/2013/03/everything-you-need-to-know-about-the-cyprus-bank-disaster/274096/

[33] Charles Hoskinson and Brian Göss, 'Bitcoin or how I learned to stop worrying and love crypto', udemy.com/course/bitcoin-or-how-i-learned-to-stop-worrying-and-love-crypto/

[34] **Programmability** is the capability within hardware and software to change; to accept a new set of instructions that alter its behavior. Programmability generally refers to program logic (business rules), but it also refers to designing the user interface, which includes the choices of menus, buttons and dialogs.

[35] **Ethereum** is a decentralized, open source blockchain with smart contract functionality. Ether is the native cryptocurrency of the platform. Ethereum was conceived in 2013 by programmer Vitalik Buterin. Additional founders of Ethereum included Gavin Wood, Charles Hoskinson, Anthony Di Iorio and Joseph Lubin.

Hoskinson met many people through his Udemy course. One of his students was Li Xiaolai who had founded *Bitfund.*[36] Xiaolai offered funding to start a business together, so in June 2013, Hoskinson started a thread on Bitcointalk called *Project Invictus,*[37] named after a [William Ernest] Henley poem. The post asked what could be done to make Bitcoin 'undefeatable' and solve existing problems. The feedback focussed on two industry needs. First was the need for a stablecoin,[38] to limit exposure to volatility. The second was a need for a decentralized exchange.[39] This was around the time of the Mt Gox[40] collapse, so centralized exchanges were deemed a single point of failure. CH:[41]

> *I said 'alright, well is there a way we can bundle both solutions together?', and of all people, the very first person who replied on the thread was Dan Larimer,[42] and he said, 'I'm in!' ...and he had this paper called BitShares.[43] So I read the paper, we rewrote it together, his dad (Stan) was involved. Stan, Dan and I, we started a company called Invictus together. [...]it ended up being two Larimers and one Hoskinson, so I took a buyout.*

Around the same time, Buterin grew frustrated trying to expand Bitcoin's functionality with colored coins[44] and Mastercoin.[45] Trying to augment Bitcoin proved to be more effort than it was worth. CH:[46]

> *Let's be honest here, it (Bitcoin) is the least sophisticated ledger, the least sophisticated consensus algorithm and it consumes more power than the country of Sweden or Switzerland. It is the least sophisticated scripting language, it is not useful at the moment, and it requires enormous effort to innovate.*

---

[36] Bitfund, crunchbase.com/person/xiaolai-li

[37] Project Invictus, bitcointalk.org/index.php?topic=229315.0

[38] **Stablecoins** are cryptocurrencies designed to minimize the volatility of its price, relative to some 'stable' asset or a basket of assets. A stablecoin can be pegged to another cryptocurrency, fiat money, or to exchange-traded commodities. Stablecoins redeemable in currency, commodities, or fiat money are said to be backed, whereas those tied to an algorithm are referred to as seigniorage-style (not backed).

[39] **Decentralized Exchanges (DEX)** are peer-to-peer (p2p) online services that allow direct cryptocurrency transactions between interested parties. ErgoDEX and WingRiders are just two of many on Cardano.

[40] **Mt Gox** was a bitcoin exchange based in Tokyo. Launched in 2010, three years later it was handling 70% of all bitcoin transactions worldwide. In February 2014 Mt Gox suspended trading, closed its website and exchange service, and filed for bankruptcy protection from creditors. In April 2014, the company began liquidation proceedings.

[41] Cardano, Crypto Toxicity, & Institutional Collapse, youtu.be/5-vsuU-OIhI?t=1405

[42] Dan Larimer, iq.wiki/wiki/dan-larimer

[43] The History of BitShares, how.bitshares.works/en/master/technology/history_bitshares.html

[44] **Colored coins** are a class of methods for associating real-world assets with addresses on the Bitcoin network. Examples could be a deed for a house, stocks, bonds or futures.

[45] Omni (formerly **Mastercoin**) is a digital currency and communications protocol built on the bitcoin blockchain. It is one of several efforts to enable complex financial functions in a cryptocurrency.

[46] Charles Hoskinson Interview 'Ivan on Tech', youtu.be/dWW_RRgAxKI?t=3500

We created Ethereum on the bones of colored coins and Mastercoin. We didn't just go create Ethereum. Everybody in that damn project was trying to do something useful with Bitcoin and they couldn't! They spent millions of dollars, and months and months to do basic things like issue an asset, and then suddenly with Ethereum around, you could do it with a few lines of code that we could put on a f$$king t-shirt!

So this is my counterpoint to Bitcoin, and my primary issue with Bitcoin, is of the insular nature of the community, especially the maximalists,[47] the inability to adapt and grow and adopt new technology, even when it's obvious that that tech is good like NIPoPoWs,[48] the fact that they brutally attack people who are innovating and call those people criminals and scammers for having the audacity to try different things.

The fact that the monetary policy can never be updated or evolved, that's both a blessing and a curse, and the ignorance of science, especially when it comes to proof of stake,[49] and this belief that what they've done is perfect and never can be changed and that cult of personality around the cult of Satoshi. That said, its digital gold, it's a standard, I think it'll always have value. It's done a huge amount of good. Bitcoin is why we're all here, it's why I'm here. So I never will say it's a bad project and I'll never say it's not worth holding BTC.

Origins of Ethereum

Hoskinson met Anthony Di Iorio through a contact of his. Di Iorio ran the Bitcoin Alliance of Canada (BAC)[50] and asked him if they could use some of his educational material on Udemy. Hoskinson agreed and they started working together. Di Iorio shared Vitalik Buterin's white paper and Hoskinson read it and provided feedback. The white paper went through several iterations, the group converged together, and the result was Ethereum, deemed now to be the second-generation blockchain. Gavin Wood was credited by Hoskinson as the person who built it in a proper way that actually would work. Hoskinson helped set up the initial legal structure. The main point of Ethereum was to add programmability to cryptocurrencies. CH:[51]

---

[47] A **maximalist** is a person who holds extreme views and is not prepared to compromise.

[48] **Non-Interactive Proofs of Proof-of-Work (NIPoPoWs)** are short stand-alone strings that a computer program can inspect to verify that an event happened on a proof-of-work-based blockchain without connecting to the blockchain network and without downloading all block headers. For example, these proofs can illustrate that a cryptocurrency payment was made.

[49] **Proof of stake (PoS)** is a type of algorithm by which a cryptocurrency blockchain network aims to achieve consensus. In PoS-based cryptocurrencies the creator of the next block is chosen via various combinations of random selection and funds committed (ie, the **stake**). In contrast, the algorithm of **proof-of-work**-based (PoW) cryptocurrencies such as bitcoin uses mining; that is, the solving of computationally intensive puzzles to validate transactions and create blocks.

[50] Bitcoin Alliance Canada, coindesk.com/bitcoin-alliance-launches-canada

[51] The Erica Show EP9 - Charles Hoskinson, youtu.be/l35h0xW47-Y?t=904

So in 2009, to about 2013, that was the experimental phase of Bitcoin and then in 2013, Bitcoin got to about a billion dollars, a stable industry formed around it and I said, 'Alright, well, it's not going anywhere.' Bitcoin is here to stay. The problem with Bitcoin though, is it's blind, deaf and dumb, and what I mean by that is that you can't do much with it other than just push bitcoins around. You can't issue your own currency; you can't write applications.

It was similar to when JavaScript was introduced to the web browser. Before that, the web browser worked, but websites were dull and static. JavaScript allowed for the likes of YouTube, Facebook and Google to offer dynamic content with videos and e-commerce. Similarly, with Bitcoin, you could send, receive, and display transactions, you could use metadata for interesting things but DApps weren't possible, ICOs[52] weren't possible, you couldn't issue your own custom token … all the interesting and useful features that now make up the DeFi landscape of the industry.

Ironically, Ethereum was announced at the January 2014 North American Bitcoin conference. Bitcoin had just surged from $100 to $1,000, so the event was boisterous and rowdy. The first Ethereum t-shirt, made for the conference, had source code on the back of it for issuing your own token. It was so awkward to do that with Mastercoin and colored coins. So ironically, Ethereum was also born out of frustration, frustration with Bitcoin's rigidness and poor developer experience. By bringing a programming language to a blockchain, this allowed smart contracts[53] to be written to have customizable transactions. So now when Alice sent value to Bob, terms and conditions could be embedded within the transaction, bespoke to her particular needs.

---

[52] **Initial coin offering (ICO)** is a means of crowdfunding via use of cryptocurrency, which can be a source of capital for start-up companies and open-source software projects. In an ICO, a percentage of the newly issued cryptocurrency is sold to investors in exchange for legal tender or other cryptocurrencies such as bitcoin or ether.

[53] A **smart contract** is a computer protocol intended to facilitate, verify, or enforce the negotiation or performance of a contract. Smart contracts were first proposed by Nick Szabo in 1996. Proponents of smart contracts claim that many kinds of contractual clauses may be made partially or fully self-executing, self-enforcing, or both. The aim with smart contracts is to provide security that is superior to traditional contract law and to reduce other transaction costs associated with contracting.

Figure 1: Ethereum T-shirt at January 2014 launch

Hoskinson wanted to set up a proper company, a for-profit and have Founders Agreements.[54] After looking at the project's structure and direction, he was worried nobody had any incentive to stay involved after the project was launched. He wanted 'golden handcuffs', vesting, and standard things a normal company would have. There was a disagreement as Buterin wanted it to remain an open-source project. Hoskinson argued that if everyone was paid upfront, nobody would be motivated to commit long term. It didn't work out, Hoskinson left in June 2014.

There were no egos, or books written at that point. The group just wanted to produce 'something interesting and cool' to extend the functionality of cryptocurrencies. Ethereum went on to be a huge success. The term 'the Flippening' was even coined. It referred to the hypothetical moment of Ethereum overtaking Bitcoin as the biggest cryptocurrency. The main problem was scalability, it can't handle millions of users, and billions of transactions. Bitcoin could only manage 7 transactions per second, Ethereum 10-20.

Governance was also a problem. It became a victim of its own success. Every single time there was a major debate, instead of resolving it amicably, there were messy hard forks.[55] Ethereum split in two, with one half forming Ethereum Classic. Likewise Bitcoin had a breakaway faction forming Bitcoin Cash.[56] Sustainability problems emerged. After the

---

[54]A **Founders' Agreement** is a contract that a company's founders enter into that governs their business relationships. The Agreement lays out the rights, responsibilities, liabilities, and obligations of each founder.

[55] **Hard fork**: a total overhaul of the network's protocol, resulting in a shift in operational flow from one model to another. Cardano has a unique mechanism, called the hard fork combinator, for executing hard forks with minimal disruption. See Chapter 4.

[56] **Bitcoin Cash** is a cryptocurrency created in mid-2017. A group of developers wanting to increase Bitcoin's block size limit prepared a code change. The change, called a hard fork, took effect in August 2017 and the

ICO money runs out for a project, or its venture capital funds run out, who will step in and fund things? These gaping holes in Ethereum's design would be addressed by third-generation blockchains such as Cardano and Polkadot (founded by Gavin Wood).

The Ethereum platform forked into two versions: 'Ethereum Classic' (ETC) and 'Ethereum' (ETH). Prior to the fork, the token had been called Ethereum. After the fork, the new tokens[57] kept the name Ethereum (ETH), and the old tokens were renamed Ethereum Classic (ETC). Ethereum Classic formed as a result of disagreement with the Ethereum Foundation regarding The DAO Hard Fork.[58] Some people wanted to reimburse the funds. Others united under the 'code is law' philosophy, rejected the hard fork and split into Ethereum classic. Users that owned ETH before the DAO hard fork owned an equal amount of ETC after the fork.

Re: time at Ethereum. CH:[59]

> *I don't imagine Vitalik has a super high opinion of me, and it is what it is. The reality is that we have very big philosophical disagreements about how things ought to be run. When I was there, I said, 'look if we are taking other people's money, we have to put that money into a structure that creates accountability. Furthermore, we have to put golden handcuffs on the founders and keep them loyal to the project, because there's too many of them. There are eight founders and if they're not locked into something, then what's going to happen is they're all going to run away and create their own ventures.'*
>
> *Which is what they did, Anthony (Di Iorio) did 'Decentral', Gavin (Wood) did PolkaDot[60] and Parity, I did Cardano. Seven of the eight are gone, and furthermore the incentives were set up that we got paid up front, with a founder reward, which I didn't take, the other seven did... basically if the projects successful, hallelujah, if it fails, hallelujah... but you've already got your maximum reward up front, whereas in an equity finance model, you have to build value over time, and you have a venture capital arm keeping you accountable.*

---

cryptocurrency split in two. At the time of the fork anyone owning bitcoin was also in possession of the same number of Bitcoin Cash units.

[57] **Crypto tokens** are digital assets that are built on a cryptocurrency blockchain. A blockchain is a digital ledger that stores information in blocks that are linked. This information can be transaction records or full-fledged programs that operate on the blockchain, which are called smart contracts. The 'coin' of a cryptocurrency is a token. In effect, it's the digital code defining each fraction, which can be owned, bought and sold.

[58] The **DAO** was a decentralized autonomous organization (DAO) that was launched in 2016 on Ethereum. After raising $150 million USD worth of ether (ETH) through a token sale, The DAO was hacked due to vulnerabilities in its code base.

[59] Charles Hoskinson on leaving Ethereum, youtube.com/watch?v=AWSI78nh6jc

[60] **Polkadot** is a blockchain network being built to enable Web3, a decentralized and fair internet where users control their personal data and markets prosper from network efficiency and security. Polkadot is the flagship project of the Web3 Foundation.

So first, there was a fundamental disagreement about business strategy and execution vision. I felt a for-profit model with VC money, to build the protocol, made a lot more sense and then when the protocol was done, spin it out and have a governing foundation run it would be probably a much better approach.

That's one dimension, the other dimensions are interpersonal reasons. We had, for six months, been living like hippies in the Switzerland house and he was traveling around the world, and communication was very siloed, and paranoia and fear started building up. There are three books now written about this, and those books paint a portrait that there was a bunch of very brilliant people, that got two doses of brains and half a dose of social skills, myself included, and when you put them into a high-stress hippie-like situation, it breeds a lot of conspiracy theories and fear and these types of things.

...and frankly, there were just too many founders. So at some point you have to consolidate and there were really two different paths that Vitalik could choose, he was sitting in the middle, he could pick the business side, which is what I was advocating, and Anthony Di Iorio and Joe Lubin were advocating, or he could pick the tech, crypto anarchy, not-for-profit, egalitarian, meritocratic, open-source world.

Cardano is born

Now 0-2 as a crypto entrepreneur, Hoskinson felt disillusioned, but another door was to open. CH:[61]

> *After Ethereum I took some time off, about six months, and I was actually going to leave the space. I did a TED Talk,[62] and I said 'alright, this is my exit point, I'm going to tell everybody what the space is all about and then I'm just going to go do something else.'*

Hoskinson's talk focused on the matter closest to his heart, making finance universally accessible to everyone. He proffered that the main point of blockchain technology is about economic identity. That it should be geared towards the three billion people in the world without access to a bank account, who don't have identity systems nor property systems and therefore, live in perpetual poverty as victims of geopolitical circumstance.

The talk was well received. Jeremy Wood, who had managed operations at Ethereum and stayed in touch with Hoskinson, invited him to Japan to talk about a new venture with local businesspeople. Negotiations went back and forth for a few months on the proposed structure, how funds could be raised, and they reviewed Hoskinson's unused roadmap from Ethereum. Eventually a deal was reached with Japanese investors to start the 'Ethereum of Japan' which would become Cardano.

---

[61] Cardano, crypto toxicity, & institutional collapse, youtu.be/5-vsuU-OIhI?t=21

[62] The future will be decentralized | Charles Hoskinson | TEDxBermuda, youtube.com/watch?v=97ufCT6lQcY

The Cardano Foundation (cardanofoundation.org), now based in the Swiss canton of Zug, was set up as a governance body and is the legal custodian of the brand. The Japanese people formed a company which later became Emurgo (emurgo.io), the commercialization arm of Cardano. In 2015, Hoskinson and Wood co-founded Input Output Global (iog.io), formerly IOHK (iohk.io). IOG is the development and science arm for Cardano. The rest of 2015 was focused on protocol development and a team of scientists were hired. The Cardano crowdsale[63] ran from late 2015 to January 2017, managed by a Japanese company called Attain[64] who aggregated all the funds. IOG got a 5-year contract to build Cardano.

Right from the start, their mission was clear: 'using peer-to-peer innovations to provide financial services to the three billion people who don't have them'. IO believed in the founding principle of 'cascading disruption' – the idea that most of the structures that form the world's financial, governance and social systems are inherently unstable and thus minor perturbations can cause a ripple effect that fundamentally reconfigures the entire system. The company committed to identifying and developing technology to force these perturbations in order to push towards a more fair and transparent order.

All of 2016 was devoted to science and research. The initial small team with massive ideas was Charles Hoskinson, Chief Executive; Jeremy Wood, strategy chief; Nikos Bentenitis, operations chief; Chikara Wakae, communications chief; Richard Wild, design chief; and Tomas Vrana, full stack developer.

November 4, 2020. What is IOG? CH:[65]

> *With input output, what I wanted to do there was marry two things simultaneously. One, I wanted to have a company with a very strong philosophy about how to build products. I said, 'these products are born as a scientific method and of evidence, and we need to follow formal methods[66] and evidence-based software and we need to follow a rigorous academic approach to protocol development'.*
>
> *So that was one thing, the other thing was the types of products I wanted to build. What I believe in is the philosophy of cascading disruption. So basically what that means is that you're like the first domino, you're like the little pebble on the top of the hill that when you push it, it creates an avalanche. So you build*

---

[63] A **crowdsale** is a type of crowdfunding that issues tokens that are stored on the user's device. The tokens can function like a share of stock and be bought and sold ("equity tokens"), or they can pay for services when the service is up and running ("user tokens").

[64] Cardano CrowdSale, nasdaq.com/articles/iohk-launches-cardano-blockchain-ada-now-trading-on-bittrex-2017-10-02

[65] The Erica show EP9 - Charles Hoskinson, CEO of Input Output, youtu.be/l35h0xW47-Y?t=611

[66] In computer science, **formal methods** are a particular kind of mathematically based techniques for the specification, development and verification of software and hardware systems. The use of formal methods for software and hardware design is motivated by the expectation that, as in other engineering disciplines, performing appropriate mathematical analysis can contribute to the reliability and robustness of a design.

a product, you embed in it all these processes and rules and then after a while, maybe a few years… you can actually walk away, and the product becomes self-evolving.

Back in 2015, IOG stepped back and asked a very simple question which was 'What is the consequence of Ethereum's success? If it works, what's going to happen to the industry?'

They identified three problems that were inevitable if Ethereum was to succeed.

1) **Scalability.** The problem with the way Bitcoin and Ethereum were designed, and Vitalik Buterin has basically admitted this by building Eth 2 (Ethereum 2.0),[67] is that Ethereum can only get to a certain capacity, and at that point, it becomes untenable. Transactions get too expensive, system bloat sets in. A different protocol stack was needed so that, as you gain users, performance level is consistent. It needs to work similarly to centralized systems like Facebook or amazon where it can handle millions to billions of people. IOG sought to figure out how to solve that problem.

2) **Interoperability.** The world is made up of many standards, varying for different industry verticals and jurisdictions. It's likely legacy financial systems aren't going away, so it's best to work with them on bridging where possible. Wi-Fi standards would never work if they were tied to manufacturers. If your Huawei mobile could only talk to a Huawei router, it wouldn't be practical to roam anywhere. The reason Wi-Fi works is because it works for everybody regardless of your mobile manufacturer. Similarly, like with your funds and your identity, it would make life easier if information could flow seamlessly between the thousands of cryptocurrencies and legacy systems.

3) **Governance**, sometimes referred to as sustainability. Bitcoin and Ethereum have both encountered problems as they scale. There were no governance mechanisms to drive change. When they grew to millions of users, eventually it became impossible to make controversial decisions without fracturing the project. For example, Bitcoin had the 'Big blocks versus SegWit' debate which led to it splitting in two, Bitcoin Cash and Bitcoin. Ethereum had similar upheaval with the DAO hack. This divisiveness is a big obstacle to government adoption, Fortune 500 adoption and mainstream adoption because everyday users and corporations fear more infighting and hard forks every time a controversy, or hard decision arises.

Governance is not a sexy topic on Crypto twitter,[68] but it's arguably the most important for a project's long-term viability. Who decides how to change the system? How and when should an update be executed? A blockchain needs to have a short-range

---

[67] **Ethereum 2.0** is a new version of the Ethereum blockchain that will switch to a proof of stake consensus mechanism, moving from the original, existing proof of work mechanism.

[68] **Crypto Twitter** is a term to describe the Twitter subculture and community that surrounds the topics of blockchain and cryptocurrency.

microscope for near and present dangers, and a long-range telescope for technical challenges on the horizon. For example, if all hell breaks loose when debating a parameter change, what happens when quantum computers arrive? It is inevitable somebody in the next few decades will produce a commercializable quantum computer that can break cryptography. We know it's coming, so how does a fledgling protocol deal with this? IOG has had quantum resistance planned since the early days of the project and will implement it when appropriate.

There are also funding problems with first- and second-generation cryptocurrencies. There's a tragedy of the commons[69] scenario where most people agree essential infrastructure, or critical updates, are required but there's no mechanisms to apply for, or approve, funding for development.

From 2015 to 2017, IOG took a big step back and just did academic research and asked foundational questions, without deciding on anything. They asked, 'what is a blockchain?' They didn't even decide on proof of work or proof of stake. They just tried to create definitions and models and understand enough foundations so they could reasonably approach these problems.

Professor Aggelos Kiaysis[70] came onboard in 2016. IOG invented a new proof-of-stake protocol called *Ouroboros*, and proved it was possible and secure. They invented a whole gamut of interoperability protocols like NIPoPoWs (Non-Interactive Proofs of Proof-of-Work) and sidechain[71] protocols, as well as a governance stack. IOG staff have written and published over 170 academic papers (latest count) cited countless times throughout the space, often by competitors. IOG staff have appeared at most major Cryptography conferences in the world.

As well as seeking out the best academics, IOG also reached out to the best engineering teams at companies such as WellTyped, Tweag, and Runtime Verification, for people like Duncan Coutts, and Edsko de Vries, whose work includes the hard fork combinator discussed later. IOG (IOHK) feature prominently on Google Scholar, many of whom are professors or have professor-level citations, such as Dionysis Zindros, Kevin Hammond among many others.

IOG uses formal methods to implement rigorous security in theory and in development. All of IOG's research papers go through some form of peer review. The goal is always to eventually implement high assurance code, using the same techniques one would see with the Shinkansen,[72] or in aircraft engines, where system failure results in human death.

---

[69] The **tragedy of the commons** is a situation in a shared-resource system where individual users, acting independently according to their own self-interest, behave contrary to the common good of all users, by depleting or spoiling that resource through their collective action.

[70] Prof. Aggelos Kiayias, iohk.io/en/team/aggelos-kiayias

[71] A **Sidechain** is a blockchain that runs in parallel to the main blockchain. Tokens can be transferred and synchronized between the main chain and the sidechain.

[72] The **Shinkansen** is a high-speed railway in Japan. Initially, it was built to connect distant Japanese regions with Tokyo, the capital, to aid economic growth and development.

These techniques are applied to IOG's protocols, engineering and development, to garner a high level of trust in the quality of the code to avoid such debacles as the DAO attack, the Parity Wallet hack or the Solana Wormhole hack.[73]

IOG chose one of the most scientifically oriented programming languages, Haskell,[74] in use and stress-tested since the 1980s. Prof Phil Wadler,[75] one of the creators of Haskell, led Plutus[76] development alongside Manuel Chakravarty, Prof Elias Koutsoupias and Prof Simon Thompson. IOG has funded research and development at the Blockchain Technology Lab at Edinburgh University as well as University of Athens, Tokyo Institute of Technology, Stanford University, and the University of Wyoming. Plutus and Marlowe[77] were launched at PlutusFest in December 2018 by this cutting-edge research team.

Cardano Timeline

Sep 2015	Crowdsale funded development and treasury.
Aug 2017	Ouroboros paper accepted at Crypto 17[78]
Sep 2017	Byron release
Dec 2018	Launch of Plutus and Marlowe at PlutusFest
Dec 2018	Sidechains paper[79] published
Dec 2019	Shelley Incentivized Testnet (ITN)[80]
Mar 2020	Byron Reboot, first Hard Fork Combinator event
July 2020	Shelley release (decentralization)
Mar 2021	Full decentralization (d=0)
Sep 2021	Goguen release (smart contracts, Plutus V1)
Sep 2022	Vasil release (Plutus V2)
Nov 2022	Launch of *Age of Voltaire* at ScotFest
Feb 2023	SECP upgrade

---

[73] Solana's Wormhole Hack Post-Mortem Analysis, extropy-io.medium.com/solanas-wormhole-hack-post-mortem-analysis-3b68b9e88e13

[74] **Haskell** is a general-purpose, statically typed, purely functional programming language with type inference and lazy evaluation. Designed for teaching, research and industrial applications, Haskell has pioneered a number of programming language features.

[75] Prof Phil Wadler, iohk.io/en/team/philip-wadler

[76] **Plutus** is a suite of programming tools for creating Cardano smart contracts.

[77] **Marlowe** is a programming language created specifically for the creation of financial smart contracts. It is restricted to financial applications and is intended for finance professionals rather than programmers.

[78] Crypto 17, iacr.org/conferences/crypto2017/

[79] Gazi1, Kiayias, Zindros (2018), 'Proof-of-Stake Sidechains', eprint.iacr.org/2018/1239.pdf

[80] Dynal Patel, 'Incentivized Testnet: what is it and how to get involved', iohk.io/en/blog/posts/2019/10/24/incentivized-testnet-what-is-it-and-how-to-get-involved

Note that there was no white paper in all this time, instead IOG focused on building on principles. In the next chapter we'll delve into more technical details and explain Cardano's roadmap and naming scheme.

Hoskinson often laments at being introduced as a former co-founder of Ethereum. He prefers to be known for his work at IOG:[81]

> *I have six (in 2021) years of history at IOG, and I have six months of history at Ethereum. What's so disheartening is that Ethereum is the big project and Cardano isn't quite there yet, so Ethereum is what everybody knows me for. So they only had six months of data, where I had limited ability to influence and control things, and I was just one brick in the wall amongst many, and then at IOG, I've been the CEO, the big guy, so I've had the ability at my company to demonstrate what a vision would look like.*

> *...and a lot of people often ask well what would have happened with Ethereum had you stayed? So we've already run that experiment. It would look a lot like Cardano, so how we built Cardano, the approach we took, that's exactly what Ethereum would look like. Similarly, they asked what would have happened to Ethereum had Gavin Wood had more say. Well, we already ran that experiment, we have PolkaDot.*

---

[81] Charles Hoskinson on leaving Ethereum, youtube.com/watch?v=AWSI78nh6jc

Chapter 2: What is Cardano?

'We tell you what we're going to do, we write it down, we go do it, and then we tell you that we did it, and we show you the evidence and proof ... it's the Paul Halmos way of doing things'

— Charles Hoskinson

Alex Hammer
@AlHammer

Replying to @IOHK_Charles

Charles, please explain the essential value proposition of Cardano in one sentence.

Charles Hoskinson ✔
@IOHK_Charles

Replying to @AlHammer

Cardano is an open platform that seeks to provide economic identity to the billions who lack it by providing decentralized applications to manage identity, value and governance

Cardano is a decentralized, third-generation, proof-of-stake blockchain platform. It is the first blockchain to emerge from a scientific ethos and a research-driven methodology. Ada (₳, or ADA is the 'ticker' used on cryptocurrency exchanges) is the first cryptocurrency built on Cardano.

December 12, 2020. How do you explain the Cardano project and its mission in a few minutes to someone not engaged in the cryptocurrency space or even the financial sector? CH:[82]

> *The easiest way of explaining it is that the world is going through an upgrade, where we will go from a split system to a unified system. Right now, we have two systems, the developed world and developing world system. The developed world system has banks, insurance, credit; it has identity, you can do business online. You can build trust with people, manage risk and be able to grow wealth. So, any person born in a developed world country, if they work hard, has a good chance of getting to a point where they can retire and have a good life. That means a life where they have food, water, shelter, etc. They're able to pursue things that make them happy and have enough left over that when they become weak and vulnerable, their savings can cover them to pay for those infirmities.*
>
> *When you look at the developing world, for no fault of their own, they live in systems where wealth creation is very difficult. Even if you have some of it, you can't insure it and hedge it, so when an event happens, be it a war or natural event like a hurricane or a tsunami, they get wiped out. So, the world is upgrading so that we'll have a unified system where all 7-8 billion people live under one financial operating system. So, your identity is interoperable and universal. You can get a loan no matter who you are or where you are. You can*

---

[82] Surprise AMA! 12/12/2020, youtube.com/watch?v=GlVU8ZiVUL0

get insurance no matter where you're at. You can do business with anyone in the world in a friction-free way.

The point of Cardano is to acknowledge this must be done with principles. So, what are we trying to accomplish? We're trying to push power to the edges, and put you in charge of your own money, put you in charge of your own identity, put you in charge of your own voice and give you governance and these types of things. So that when we get to that universal system we get to an open, decentralized, principled system that can't be co-opted. Highly resilient to people trying to come and tamper with it, and then suddenly the richest people in the world, the Jeff Bezos's of the world, will use the same system as the poorest people in the world, and both will have a better system than the system that came before it, in both of those old systems. That's what we're trying to accomplish.

Foundational concepts

As discussed in Chapter 1, a blockchain has some features of a database, in this case an accounting ledger,[83] that is copied and distributed to all users of the blockchain. The blockchain consists of a network of nodes[84] linked across the internet that store data or valuable digital files in blocks.[85] Transactions verify these blocks, which are then connected in a chain in chronological order. The details of these transactions are etched forever in the block and cannot be changed.

This blockchain technology, also known as distributed ledger technology (DLT), offers a decentralized and accessible data structure for digital files and documents. Financial payment and transaction data, as well as other sorts of information such as commercial records and information for supply chain management, might be included.

A decentralized blockchain is independent of centralized, controlling companies, institutions, or intermediaries because it keeps data in a decentralized way. This increases the visibility of data storage and administration. A fundamental aspect of blockchain is that records are stored immutably, which means they cannot be modified, falsified, or destroyed without causing the chain of records to be broken.

---

[83] **Ledger**: a distributed ledger (also called a shared ledger or referred to as distributed ledger technology) is a consensus of replicated, shared, and synchronized digital data geographically spread across sites, countries, or institutions. There is no central administrator or centralized data storage.

[84] In telecom networks, a **node** is either a redistribution point or a communication endpoint. The definition of a node depends on the network and protocol layer referred to. A physical network node is an active electronic device that is attached to a network, and is capable of creating, receiving, or transmitting information over a communications channel.

[85] **Block**: a record of recent network transactions. Each block also includes the data necessary for blockchain management, such as an encrypted record of the preceding block. Each finished block is followed by the creation of the next block to continue the chain.

A blockchain may be likened to a book of permanent records, with each page serving as a data storage device.

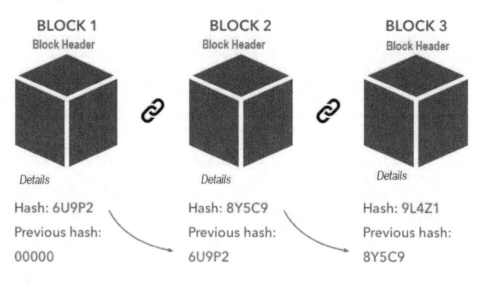

Figure 2: Infographic of blockchain blocks linked by hash[86] pointers

Networks can be configured in several ways (see Figure 3):

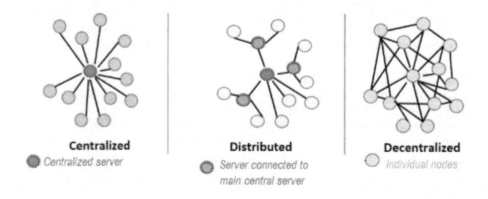

Figure 3. Three types of network structures.

With decentralized blockchains, users can deal with each other directly – peer to peer – without having to go through a central, controlling system

---

[86] A **cryptographic hash** is a math algorithm that maps data of an arbitrary size (often called the 'message') to a bit string of a fixed size (the 'hash value', 'hash', or 'message digest'). It is a one-way function, that is, a function that is practically impossible to invert. Cryptographic hash functions are a basic tool of modern cryptography.

- Centralized systems: in most cases, a single central server manages all data and actions. This raises the possibility of a single point of failure while also implying that the controlling organization (typically a bank or a government agency) makes all the decisions.

- Distributed systems: these depend on several server nodes, each of which serves a portion of the total number of users.

- Decentralized systems: all data and transaction records are encrypted and kept over a network of linked, independent nodes and terminals, rather than on a single server. This assures security, transparency, and independence from centralized institutions.

In addition to providing an immutable and secure database, blockchains serve as a functional environment for transmitting cash, creating digital currencies, and processing complicated transactions, including smart contracts (automated digital agreements).

What is a cryptocurrency?

A cryptocurrency is a digital asset that is recorded on a ledger and is usually intended to be used as a form of payment for products or services.

In a decentralized setting, blockchain ledgers serve as the foundation technology for cryptocurrencies. To allow the minting (creation) of cryptocurrencies and to safeguard and validate crypto ownership and money movement records, blockchain systems use stringent cryptography methods. A government, or centralized financial institution, has no influence on the protocol level of a cryptocurrency. They can certainly influence price indirectly through rumor, threat (enactment) of legislation. A cryptocurrency's worth, links to real-world data, market supply and demand are what define it.

When transmitting crypto payments, addresses[87] are used. Each address is a one-of-a-kind identifier made up of a string of numbers and letters derived from each user's public keys.

Each blockchain ledger has its own cryptocurrency that provides the 'oil' to run the system. This cryptocurrency is 'native' to the blockchain because it interacts directly with the blockchain. Cardano's founding native currency, ada (₳), is the blockchain's primary payment unit. Ada may be used to pay fees, make deposits, and is the sole currency in which rewards[88] are given out. This will change with sidechains (discussed later in Chapter 8).

---

[87] **Address**: a data structure used to express different types of information in transaction outputs. To identify between various networks (eg, mainnet or testnet), each address has a network discriminant tag and a proof of ownership (who owns the transaction output). Delegation options and script references are also included in some addresses.

[88] **Reward**: an amount contained in each new block that is paid out to the stakeholder by the network.

The smallest ada denomination is a lovelace. 1,000,000 lovelaces = 1 ada. Because transactions are calculated to six decimal places, it is easy to divide a single ada into fractions.

What is a native token?

Cardano allows users to generate (mint), or delete (burn), their own tokens. These are digital assets, each of which is minted for a particular purpose. On Cardano, tokens are native assets, meaning that they interact directly with the blockchain, rather than being generated using a smart contract. This means that users, developers, and companies may create tokens that reflect a value footprint on the Cardano blockchain (as defined by the community, market state, or self-governed entity). A token may be fungible (replaceable) or non-fungible (unique), and it can be used as a payment unit, a reward, a trade asset, or a holder of information.

Why is Cardano different?

Cardano is a durable blockchain that is designed to be secure, scalable, and interoperable.[89] Importantly, Ouroboros, Cardano's proof-of-stake consensus protocol, has been shown to provide the same security assurances as proof-of-work blockchains such as Bitcoin.

Cardano is described as a 'third-generation' blockchain:

- first generation: Bitcoin, a proof-of-work blockchain;

- second generation: Ethereum brought programmable capabilities and smart contracts to blockchain. However, it was flawed because, like Bitcoin, it originally used a proof-of-work system that wasted huge amounts of energy to solve ever-more-complex mathematical puzzles that have no purpose apart from validating transactions. It is also not very scalable, so the more transactions are performed the slower the blockchain becomes, and the more expensive it is to make a transaction. In September 2022, Ethereum finally transitioned from proof of work to proof of stake, but this is only a step on long, convoluted Ethereum 2.0 roadmap. Transaction (gas) fees remain high, and there are unattractive features like slashing[90] and uncertainty around users' stakes being

---

[89] Coined by Vitalik Buterin, who led the creation of Ethereum, the **'blockchain trilemma'** sets out the challenges developers face in creating a blockchain that is scalable, decentralized and secure, without compromising on any facet. Blockchains are forced to make trade-offs between these three aspects:
- decentralization: creating a blockchain system that does not rely on a central point of control.
- scalability: the ability of a blockchain to handle a growing number of transactions.
- security: the ability of a blockchain to operate as expected, and defend itself from attacks, bugs, and other unforeseen issues.

[90] **Slashing** is a mechanism used by some PoS protocols (but not Cardano) to discourage harmful behavior and make validators more responsible. They help keep the network secure because, without slashing penalties, a validator can use the same node to validate blocks on more than one chain or do so on the wrong chain.

locked up indefinitely.[91]

- third generation: Cardano uses proof of stake, which uses trivial amounts of energy, to provide all the capabilities of Ethereum. It is also designed to grow, work with other blockchains, and has a treasury built in, and a structure for managing change in the future.

The engineers who wrote the open-source code for Cardano decided that the best way to produce high assurance software systems that users could trust to handle digital currencies was to employ formal methods such as mathematical specifications, property-based tests, and proofs. Cardano was designed using formal methods to get strong guarantees on the functional correctness of the system's basic components.

One of Cardano's central tenets is security. Haskell, a secure functional programming language, is used in its development. A functional language like Haskell promotes the use of pure functions[92] in system design, resulting in an architecture that is easily tested in isolation. Furthermore, Haskell's sophisticated capabilities provide powerful ways to ensure the code's correctness, such as basing the implementation on formal and executable specifications, thorough property-based testing, and simulation testing.

Cardano must be able to grow and interact with traditional finance systems to provide a robust infrastructure on a global scale. Despite the fact that Cardano was built with resource efficiency in mind, scale is still an issue, as it is for all blockchain protocols. To address the problem of growth, IOG researchers developed Hydra,[93] a protocol that can be run on top of Cardano[94] and allows transaction and smart contract processing off the main chain. Hydra, and many more scalability solutions discussed in Chapter 8.

Performance engineering techniques were used to test which design choices helped IOG achieve resilience, performance, and scalability. Another important goal of Cardano's architecture is to prevent centralization by using economic incentives that encourage decentralization. Stake pools[95] have an economic incentive to expand as soon as they are created, so it was critical to make it less appealing for a stake pool to become too large.

---

[91] Nobody Knows When Ethereum Stakers Will Be Able to Withdraw Their ETH, beincrypto.com/nobody-knows-when-ethereum-stakers-will-be-able-to-withdraw-their-eth/

[92] A **pure function** is a function that has the following properties: first, its return value is the same for the same arguments (no variation with local static variables, non-local variables, mutable reference arguments or input streams from input-output devices); second, its evaluation has no side effects (no mutation of local static variables, non-local variables, mutable reference arguments or inputs and outputs).

[93] MMT Chakravarty, S Coretti, M Fitzi, P Gazi, P Kant, A Kiayias, and A Russell (2020) 'Hydra: fast isomorphic state channels'. eprint.iacr.org/2020/299.pdf

[94] In the decentralized ecosystem, a **Layer 1** refers to the blockchain protocol itself. **Layer 2** refers to a technology that operates on top of a blockchain to improve its scalability and efficiency. For example, Bitcoin is a Layer 1 network, and the Lightning Network is a Layer 2 to improve transaction speeds. Hydra is a layer 2 protocol built on top of Cardano, layer 1.

[95] **Stake pool**: a stable, block-producing server node that aggregates the stakes of several stakeholders (in Cardano's case, ada holders) into a single entity, or pool.

However, a balance has to be struck because a limited number of big pools is more cost-effective than a large number of tiny pools.

A balance was accomplished by altering the reward formula. In a basic system, a pool's total rewards are simply proportional to its stake, hence the larger the stake, the better. With Cardano, if a pool collects more stake than a given threshold ($1/k$, where k is an adjustable parameter), the pool's payout will no longer rise. The pool is said to be saturated,[96] and delegating more ada stake will not increase the rewards. The result is k pools of nearly equal size if everyone acts in their own self-interest to maximize their rewards.

Interoperability, or the capacity to communicate with other systems, is a fundamental architectural component of Cardano. The use of sidechains is one of Cardano's innovations. The design means that the system can be compartmentalized, and it enables interoperability inside the blockchain platform. A sidechain holds and manipulates data off the main chain. Many sidechains may function at the same time, and if one fails, the rest of the system remains operational. As a consequence, the blockchain has more certainty and trustworthiness. Assets can be moved between separate blockchains that run under distinct rules, procedures, or languages, as well as various methods of accessing the network, by using sidechains.

Cardano's architecture also prioritizes governance[97] to maintain the system's long-term viability and flexibility. A well-developed governance structure allows Cardano's long-term development to be funded effectively and democratically. Cardano's treasury system is a long-term financing source for the protocol and projects building on it. It will be run by the community and will allow for a decentralized, collaborative decision-making mechanism to ensure Cardano's continued growth and upkeep. Various financing sources can be used to top up the treasury, such as the aggregation of newly minted coins, a portion of stake pool rewards, transaction fees, and donations. It will be able to support project development and pay for improvement recommendations using the funds earned. Additionally, Cardano improvement proposals (CIPs) are issued to stimulate and codify community conversations about new features and their development.

A voting system is at the heart of the treasury, allowing ada holders to decide on funding proposals and determine how funds are spent. This will guarantee that choices are taken democratically rather than by a small group of people. This voting method will decide on choices such as financing projects, allowing protocol upgrades, and implementing any constitutional changes such as decision-making process modifications. Project Catalyst[98]

---

[96] **Saturation**: a stake pool is saturated when it has more stake delegated to it than is optimal for the network. The saturation level is expressed as a percentage. When a stake pool achieves 100% saturation, the rewards start to shrink. The saturation mechanism was created to avoid centralization by encouraging ada owners to delegate to several stake pools, and operators to build more pools to keep receiving maximum rewards. Saturation aims to safeguard both the interests of ada holders delegating their stake and the interests of stake pool operators (SPOs).

[97] Blockchain **governance** brings together norms and culture, laws and code, and the people and the institutions that are needed to run a system and ensure its stability in the long term. Governance, including voting and a treasury for long-term funding, is the focus of the Voltaire stage of the Cardano roadmap.

is evolving into a fully on-chain democratic governance mechanism that will enable the project to expand over time while also allowing it to support itself in a sustainable manner through a visionary treasury system.

20 January, 2021. What is Project Catalyst? How can people get involved for future funds? CH:[99]

> *So we're building a whole stack of voting into Cardano and we're partnered with a lot of great companies and think tanks. For example, we're partnered with an innovation management company called IdeaScale… they've been around for almost a decade. They work with Pfizer and Boeing … so, yes, how'd Pfizer come up with that vaccine so quickly? They use IdeaScale. So we basically brought them in along with some decentralized tooling and we created a whole new voting system. We spent four years researching how to do a private blockchain-based voting system out of Lancaster University that can scale to lots of users.*
>
> *Basically, what we've been doing is systematically launching funds… so the treasury of Cardano takes some of the inflation that normally you'd give to stake pool operators or miners… and it gives it to a decentralized account and then people submit ballots to get funded. Over time, people can vet those ballots and it goes through a process, like a gauntlet… and if they survive, they can vote… and if enough votes come in you get funded.*

Cardano differentiators

The following aspects of Cardano are outlined in detail in later chapters, but here is a summary of the blockchain's innovations.

Academic research: formal methods, including mathematical specifications, property-based tests, and proofs, are the most effective means of delivering high-assurance software systems. They also provide users with trust in the management of digital assets. Cardano was created with formal methods to obtain strong assurances on the functional correctness of the system's key components. The research that supports Cardano is published at academic conferences and in journals, papers are available to the public and all Cardano development activity is documented on GitHub.[100]

Only when the Ouroboros consensus algorithm had been proven to be mathematically secure by an academic team led by Prof Aggelos Kiayias at the University of Edinburgh did the software engineering work begin on implementing the blockchain in code. IOG are rightly proud of their growing presence in academia around the globe.[101] The

---

[98] **Project Catalyst** is a series of experiments that seek to encourage the highest levels of community innovation. Catalyst is bringing on-chain governance to Cardano by allowing the community to determine priorities for growth (see Chapter 9).

[99] Let's talk Cardano - Interview with Charles Hoskinson, youtube.com/watch?v=NX3fGKMd004

[100] IOG GitHub: github.com/input-output-hk/

significance of these partnerships and investments will come up again later in Chapter 9 (Voltaire).

System design: Cardano is built in Haskell, a secure functional programming[102] language that facilitates the creation of systems using pure functions, resulting in a design that is easy to test in isolation. Furthermore, Haskell's sophisticated capabilities include powerful ways to ensure the code's correctness, such as basing the implementation on formal and executable specifications, thorough property-based testing, and simulation testing.

Security: Ouroboros[103] (Cardano's proof-of-stake protocol) offers strict security assurances; it is based on peer-reviewed papers presented at top-tier cybersecurity and cryptography conferences and publications. Only around half of the users who are active in the network are required to follow the protocol; in fact, momentary rises beyond the 50% threshold can be accepted. As a result, Ouroboros is much more robust and adaptive than traditional Byzantine fault tolerance (BFT)[104] protocols, which must forecast the degree of expected involvement and may shut down if the prediction is incorrect.

Cardano's network protocol uses a pull communication method. If a node tries to push information, it is automatically disconnected.

- Unique built-in security capabilities:

    ○ VRF (verifiable-random function): used to prove that a node has the right to create a block in a given slot.[105]
    ○ VRF[106] use makes the consensus difficult to attack because it's impossible to predict the next producing nodes.

---

[101] How IOG's research spans the academic world, iohk.io/en/blog/posts/2022/10/25/how-iog-s-research-spans-the-academic-worl

[102] **Functional programming** is a rigorous style of building the structure and elements of computer programs that treats computation as the evaluation of mathematical functions and avoids changing the properties of the data being processed. It is a 'declarative' paradigm in that programming is done with expressions or declarations instead of statements. In functional code, the output value of a function depends only on its arguments, so calling a function with the same value for an argument always produces the same result. This is in contrast to imperative programming where, in addition to a function's arguments, the global state of a program can affect a function's resulting value. Eliminating side-effects, that is, changes in state that do not depend on the function inputs, can make understanding a program easier, which was one of the motivations for the development of functional programming.

[103] Prof Aggelos Kiayias, 'The Ouroboros path to decentralization', iohk.io/en/blog/posts/2020/06/23/the-ouroboros-path-to-decentralization/

[104] **Byzantine fault tolerance (BFT)**: A Byzantine fault is a condition of a computer system, particularly distributed computing systems, where components may fail and there is imperfect information on whether a component has failed. The term takes its name from an allegory, the 'Byzantine Generals Problem', developed to describe a situation in which, to avoid catastrophic failure of the system, the system's actors must agree on a concerted strategy, but some of these actors are unreliable.

[105] Slot: Within an epoch, a set duration of time. Time is separated into numbered slots for each epoch. Active slots are those that are occupied by blocks.

○ KES (key-evolving signature): keys are rotated after a certain number of epochs.[107]

- Plutus, Cardano's native scripting language,[108] uses a formal methodology to bring advanced smart contract capabilities to the blockchain without compromising security.
- DApp[109] certification program to be rolled out in 2023.

As is best practice, IOG rotates between various security auditors such as Bcryptic, R9B (root9b), Grimm, rpisec and Kudelski. The reports are available on the IOG GitHub page.[110]

February 4, 2020. Re: security. CH:[111]

> So, when we started the Cardano project we said, 'well let's write software differently and let's think about science a little differently than how our industry thinks about it ...as opposed to writing some white paper or just writing ideas down or saying here's the code, enjoy it'. We said we will start with the peer-reviewed scientific process. So, the first thing we did is that we hired a large group of scientists, and we asked a lot of hard questions, and they thought deeply about security proofs, adversaries and security models and deeply about what had been done and where original innovation needed to exist.
>
> Now that alone, at the time, was a major step forward because it had not simply been done at a large commercial scale by anyone in our industry. Now we're starting to see that with David Chaum and Silvio Micali entering the space, and others actually hiring real scientists, writing real papers, including Ethereum, that that's no longer a core distinction, but we didn't stop there.
>
> In 2015, we also aspired to have this concept of formal methods, and this is something that very few software engineers in our space fully understand or appreciate the value of. So basically, what a formal methodology is, it's where you say, 'okay let's write down in a very specific, detailed, rigorous, mathematical way what we intend on doing ...what is what'.

---

[106] In cryptography, a **verifiable-random function (VRF)** is a pseudo-random function that provides publicly verifiable proofs of its outputs' correctness.

[107] **Epoch:** a set group of slots that constitute a period of time (currently 5 days).

[108] A **script** is a generic term for an executable program used in the ledger. In the Cardano blockchain, these are written in Plutus Core.

[109] A **decentralized application** (DApp, dApp, or Dapp) is an open-source project that runs on a blockchain network. The distributed nature of these networks provides users with transparency, decentralization, and resistance to attacks.

[110] IOG audits, github.com/input-output-hk/external_audits

[111] Some Brief Comments on Process, youtube.com/watch?v=T4hjGjredpw

So, we have this concept of Ouroboros, there's many flavors of it, but what does it actually mean to go from these dry, dead papers that our academics have written to something that an engineer can look at, and know with absolutely no ambiguity, that what they have created matches the intent of the authors of the system? So basically, you have to write a specification for this, and specifications can then be analyzed in a rigorous way for correctness. You can use all kinds of techniques like model checking and SAT solving[112] and so forth to verify that your specification meets some sort of collection of design requirements or tests.

So, we chose to go down this road and unfortunately most of the time, when you write software in this way, it adds years to your roadmap and that's exactly what happened with us. When we went down this road we had to hire, in addition to a bunch of scientists, a bunch of formal methods experts and then we had to figure out how to do formal methods with cryptocurrencies. At the time, no one had actually done that before.

Power consumption: Cardano is a proof-of-stake blockchain. It requires far less power to operate than proof-of-work chains. The Bitcoin network grows by computers doing energy-intensive calculations – a process known as proof of work – which is unsustainable in the long run. According to the Cambridge Bitcoin Electricity Consumption Index,[113] the machines that run Bitcoin use as much energy each year as a country such as Norway or Sweden. Ouroboros identifies the participants' leverage in the system using stake as the primary resource. Despite 'costless simulation' and 'nothing at stake' attacks,[114] which were previously regarded to be fundamental hurdles to stake-based ledgers, no physical resource is spent in the process of ledger maintenance. This distinguishes Ouroboros from proof-of-work methods, which need exorbitant energy consumption to establish consensus.

Seamless upgrades: in older blockchains, upgrades were done via hard forks. When a hard fork occurs, the existing protocol is disabled, new rules and modifications are introduced, and the chain is restarted – with all the history destroyed. Hard forks are handled differently by Cardano. Rather than making drastic changes, the Cardano hard fork combinator[115] (HFC) allows for a seamless transition to a new protocol while preserving the history of blocks and causing minimal inconvenience to users.

---

[112] The Boolean satisfiability problem (abbreviated **SATISFIABILITY** or **SAT**) is the problem of determining if there exists an interpretation that satisfies a given Boolean formula. It asks whether the variables of a given Boolean formula can be consistently replaced by the values TRUE or FALSE in such a way that the formula evaluates to TRUE. If this is the case, the formula is called satisfiable. On the other hand, if no such assignment exists, the function expressed by the formula is FALSE for all possible variable assignments and the formula is unsatisfiable.

[113] 'Country ranking',ccaf.io/cbeci/index/comparisons

[114] Oettler (2022), 'Nothing at stake / Costless Simulation', blockchain-academy.hs-mittweida.de/courses/game-theory-blockchain/lessons/attacks-on-proof-of-stake-pos/topic/nothing-at-stake-costless-simulation/

[115] Anthony Quinn, 'Combinator makes easy work of Shelley hard fork', iohk.io/en/blog/posts/2020/05/07/combinator-makes-easy-work-of-shelley-hard-fork/

Decentralization: Cardano is managed via a community-run network of over 3,000 distributed stake pools. Without relying on a centralized authority, network members verify all blocks and transactions.

Ouroboros includes a reward-sharing system to encourage participants to form operational nodes, known as stake pools, that can provide quality service regardless of how stake is divided among the user population. As a result, all stakeholders contribute to the system's operation, guaranteeing resilience and democratic representation, while the expense of ledger maintenance is dispersed effectively across the user community. The system's features discourage centralization. As a result, Ouroboros is inherently more inclusive and decentralized than other protocols, which either end up with a small number of actors accountable for ledger maintenance or give no incentives for stakeholders to join and deliver quality service.

Ouroboros also provides a better staking[116] experience. Cardano doesn't impose penalties such as stake slashing or lock-up (bonding). When you delegate ada to a stake pool from your wallet, it isn't locked up. Rewards are distributed every epoch (about 4% of the ada in circulation) and you can access or withdraw the stake at any time. Plus, staking on Cardano is non-custodial which means there's no risk of slashing either. As a delegator, your staked funds are never at risk of being taken by the stake pool.

- The Ouroboros protocol is highly efficient meaning that stake pool operators can run their nodes on low spec hardware, with less hardware investment required than other blockchains.

- Over 80% of tokens are held by the public and more than 70% of ada is staked in millions of wallets.

Websites such as AdaPools (adapools.org) and PoolTool (pooltool.io) give information about stake pools.

A functional environment for business: Cardano is laying the groundwork for global, decentralized finance by allowing developers to create decentralized applications (DApps) that run on functional and domain-specific smart contracts and provide multi-asset[117] tokens for any need. Two smart contract language platforms are provided: Plutus,[118] which is 'Turing complete',[119] so can be used for any purpose; and Marlowe, a specialized language for banking and financial services.

---

[116] **Staking** involves holding funds in a cryptocurrency wallet to support the security and operations of a blockchain network, and in return receive staking rewards. In other words, staking is the process of actively participating in transaction validation (similar to mining) on a proof-of-stake (PoS) blockchain.

[117] A **multi-asset (MA)** ledger can do the accounting for or interact with more than one type of asset. Cardano uses native tokens to provide this feature.

[118] **Plutus:** a Turing-complete programming framework for constructing functional smart contracts. Plutus is a Haskell-based programming language.

[119] A system is said to be **Turing complete** if it can be used to simulate any Turing machine. This means that this system is able to recognize or decide other data-manipulation rule sets. Turing completeness is used as a

Cardano adds programmability to Bitcoin's proven UTXO model[120] with its extended UTXO (EUTXO) ledger model, offering smart contracts with increased scalability, while maintaining security. With EUTXO, metadata[121] and scripts are bundled together in a single transaction for greater throughput. Transaction verification is simpler, so you can predict what's going to happen, including how much a transaction will cost. And if a transaction fails, no fee is charged. The testing features provided in Plutus and Marlowe mean that developers can ensure their smart contract scripts operate as intended.

Fungible and non-fungible tokens (NFTs) are treated as native tokens, so no smart contracts are needed. This reduces complexity, making it easier for developers, and opens up new uses – and a superior gaming and metaverse experience.

Why choose Cardano?

Of the 18,000 cryptocurrencies[122] around today, trying to grasp what differentiates one from another can be overwhelming. Are cryptos actually ranked on their merits? How is something as trite as Doge[123] in the top 20 while a technical marvel like Ergo[124] languishes outside the top 200? If you look at it long enough, CoinMartketCap begins to look like the odds for a horse race, and just as unpredictable.

---

way to express the power of such a data-manipulation rule set. Virtually all programming languages today are Turing complete. The concept is named after English mathematician and computer scientist Alan Turing.

[120] The **Unspent Transaction Output (UTXO)** model is commonly used in the field of Distributed Ledger Technology (DLT) to transfer value between participants. A UTXO is the technical term for the amount of digital currency that remains after a cryptocurrency transaction. You can think of it as the change you receive after buying an item. Much more on this later, Chapter 5.

[121] **Metadata**: a collection of extra data expressing transaction circumstances or owner information. Metadata is used in smart contracts to indicate the circumstances under which a transaction should take place.

[122] Adam Hayes, (2022) '10 important cryptocurrencies other than Bitcoin', investopedia.com/tech/most-important-cryptocurrencies-other-than-bitcoin

[123] **Dogecoin** is a cryptocurrency featuring a likeness of the Shiba Inu dog from the 'Doge' internet meme as its logo. Introduced as a 'joke currency' in 2013, Dogecoin quickly developed its own online community and reached a capitalization of US$1bn in 2018.

[124] **Ergo** (ergoplatform.org) is a proof-of-work smart-contract platform that enables new models of financial interaction, underpinned by a safe and rich scripting language built with flexible and powerful zero-knowledge proofs (Σ-protocols).

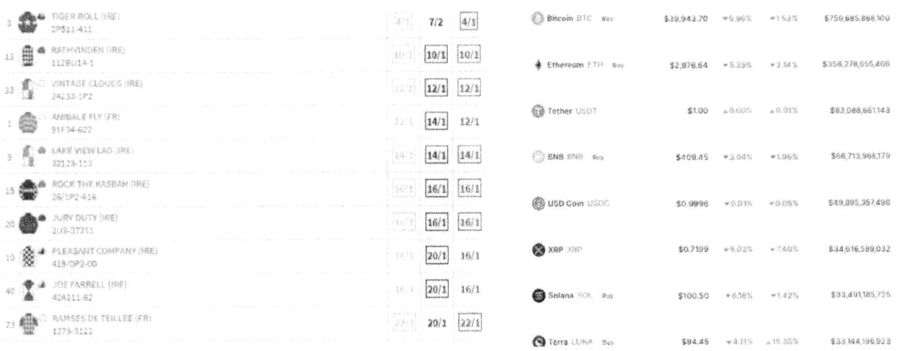

Figure 4. Horse racing odds vs Coincap.io

So what is so special about Cardano? The first generation of blockchains (Bitcoin) provided safe cryptocurrency transmission via decentralized ledgers. However, such blockchains did not offer a suitable environment for the settlement of complicated transactions or the creation of decentralized applications (DApps). The second generation of blockchain technology (Ethereum) brought more advanced solutions for writing and executing smart contracts, application development, and the creation of tokens as blockchain technology evolved. However, second-generation blockchains were also built using energy-hungry proof-of-work mining and face scalability challenges.

Cardano is regarded as a 'third generation' blockchain platform because it incorporates the characteristics of previous generations but avoids their pitfalls and can adapt to meet all user demands. It is built on Ouroboros, a peer-reviewed[125] proof-of-stake blockchain protocol that was published at the world's top cryptology research conference (the International Association for Cryptologic Research 37th International Cryptology Conference – Crypto 2017).

The Cardano papers are open-access, patent-free, and give all the technical information necessary for anybody with the appropriate technical skills to verify the accuracy of the performance, security, and functionality claims (iohk.io/research). Other projects have borrowed heavily from IOG's research, for example, Polkadot's hybrid consensus protocol was inspired by Ouroboros.[126] You can inspect the citations on Google Scholar: a search produces about 1,500+ citations.[127] Similarly, the 'Bitcoin backbone protocol'

---

[125] **Peer review** is the evaluation of work by one or more people with similar competences as the producers of the work (peers). It functions as a form of self-regulation by qualified members of a profession within the relevant field. Peer review methods are used to maintain quality standards, improve performance, and provide credibility. In academia, scholarly peer review is used to determine an academic paper's suitability for publication.

[126] 'Polkadot consensus', wiki.polkadot.network/docs/learn-consensus

[127] A Kiayias, A Russell, B David, R Oliynykov (2017) 'Ouroboros: A provably secure proof-of-stake blockchain protocol' citations, scholar.google.com/scholar?cites=9760004817031418890&as_sdt=2005&sciodt=0,5&hl=en

(GKL) paper, which has been the foundation for much of Cardano has more than 1,800 citations.[128]

The ideal solution should offer the greatest levels of security, scalability (transaction speed, data scale, network capacity), and functionality to handle all aspects of business deal settlement, not just transaction processing. Furthermore, it is critical to guarantee that blockchain technology continues to evolve in terms of sustainability and interoperability with other blockchains and financial institutions.

To meet these demands, Cardano focuses on principles such as:

Scalability: assures that the Cardano ledger can handle a huge number of transactions without slowing down the network. Higher bandwidth possibilities are also provided through scalability, allowing transactions to transport a sizable quantity of supporting data that can be handled simply inside the network. IOG is gradually introducing Hydra along with other solutions such as sidechains. dcSpark (third party development company) launched the first sidechain, Milkomeda and IOG will launch their own soon. (More on this later in Chapter 8).

Interoperability: guarantees a multi-functional environment for financial, business, or commercial processes by allowing users to engage with numerous currencies across multiple blockchains. Interoperability with centralized financial bodies is also critical for ensuring legitimacy and ease of use.

Sustainability: building a proof-of-stake blockchain necessitates ensuring that the system is self-sufficient. Cardano is designed to enable the community to sustain its development by engaging in, submitting proposals, and implementing system innovations to promote growth and maturity in a fully decentralized way. To maintain long-term viability, the community controls the treasury system, which is regularly supplied from various sources such as freshly minted coins held back as financing, a portion of stake pool rewards, and transaction fees.

Cardano roadmap

Cardano's development roadmap[129] has been divided into five eras, each focusing on a different feature set:

- Byron focused on establishing a foundation.
- Shelley focused on network decentralization.
- Goguen is all about smart contracts.
- Basho is the drive to attain true scalability.
- Voltaire is based on implementing decentralized governance.

---

[128] J Garay, A Kiayias, N Leonardos (2014) 'The bitcoin backbone protocol: analysis and applications', eprint.iacr.org/2014/765.pdf

[129] Cardano roadmap, roadmap.cardano.org/en/

Each era is built around a collection of features that are implemented and improved over many code releases. While the work for each of these development streams is delivered in order, it is typically done simultaneously, with research, prototyping, and development happening at the same time throughout.

Figure 5. from roadmap.cardano.org

Byron

Byron laid the groundwork for the creation of Cardano. It enabled users to purchase and trade ada on a proof-of-stake blockchain network. Initially, the Cardano ledger was set up as a federated network, with stake pools run by Input Output Global and Emurgo handling block generation and transaction validation. Byron saw the release of the Daedalus and Yoroi wallets,[130] as well as a block explorer for examining the blockchain.[131]

Shelley

The Shelley development era offered a decentralized ledger, resulting in a new economic structure that propels network growth and optimization. In the run-up to decentralization, an Incentivized Testnet (ITN) was set up to demonstrate that Cardano would be viable in the long term with only community-managed pools.

Shelley emerged from Byron's federated network, with the dispersed stake pool operator (SPO) community producing an increasing number of blocks until the network was fully decentralized in 2021. In terms of stake pool operation, delegation[132] preferences, and

---

[130] A **cryptocurrency wallet** stores the public and private keys which can be used to receive or spend a cryptocurrency. A wallet can contain many public keys but only one private key, which must be kept safe from loss or theft. Once a private key is lost that ends the life of that wallet. The cryptocurrency itself is not in the wallet. The cryptocurrency is decentrally stored and maintained in a publicly available ledger called the blockchain. Every piece of cryptocurrency has a private key. With the private key, it is possible to digitally sign a transaction and write it in the public ledger, in effect spending the associated cryptocurrency.

[131] Cardano Explorer, explorer.cardano.org/en

[132] **Delegation**: By delegating the stake related to their ada holdings to a stake pool, ada owners participate in the network and collect rewards each epoch (five days). Delegators are rewarded in proportion to the amount of stake delegated.

incentives, Shelley focuses on essential processes that provide an improved user experience.

Goguen

The development of Goguen focuses on the creation of a worldwide, financial, and multi-functional system for the creation of decentralized applications (DApps), smart contract support, and custom token issuing. Goguen is a fundamental component in establishing a flexible platform for developing applications in areas such as supply chain, track and trace, finance, medical records, identity voting, property registration, and peer-to-peer payments.

Basho

Basho concentrates on Cardano's optimization in terms of network scalability and interoperability. While past rounds of development concentrated on decentralization and new features, Basho is all about enhancing the Cardano network's fundamental performance to facilitate growth and uptake for busy applications.

Voltaire

Voltaire is built on decentralized governance and decision-making, allowing the Cardano community to vote on network development updates, technological advancements, and project finance. To be truly decentralized, the Cardano network needs not just the distributed architecture developed during Shelley, but also the capacity to be maintained and enhanced in a decentralized manner over time. Project Catalyst is about putting the mechanisms in place so people can apply for funding and vote on proposals.

How does Cardano work?

The Cardano node is the network's top-level component that powers the blockchain. The networking layer, which is the driving force for supplying information exchange needs, connects network nodes to one another. For enhanced data flow, this provides new block diffusion and transaction metadata. Cardano nodes keep in touch with each other using a peer-selection method. You participate in and contribute to the Cardano network by hosting a node. As with every aspect of Cardano, security is paramount. The network protocol uses a pull communication method so if a node tries to push information, it is automatically disconnected.

Stake pools are responsible for transaction processing and block generation and use the Cardano node to check how the pool interacts with the network. They operate as secure server nodes, storing and maintaining the pooled stakes of several stakeholders in a single entity.

Block production

The purpose of blockchain technology is to create a cryptographically connected, independently verifiable chain of records (blocks). A network of block producers collaborates to enhance the blockchain as a whole. A consensus protocol ensures that the chain is transparent and determines which candidate blocks should be chosen to expand it.

Valid transactions that have been submitted may be included in any new block. A block's producer signs it cryptographically and links it to the preceding block in the chain. This makes it hard to erase transactions from a block, change the order of the blocks, remove a block from the chain (if it has a lot of other blocks following it), or add a new block to the chain without notifying all network members. This protects the blockchain expansion's integrity and accountability.

Slots and epochs

The Ouroboros protocol is used by the Cardano blockchain to support chain consensus. Time is divided into epochs. An epoch is made up of slots, each of which lasts one second. There are currently 432,000 slots (five days) in a Cardano epoch. Slot leaders[133] are elected randomly from among the stake pools. One node should be nominated every 20 seconds on average, for a total of 21,600 nominations every epoch. One of the randomly drawn slot leaders will be added to the chain if they create blocks. A node that goes offline will miss its chance, and another node will be chosen. This means stake pools have to be very reliable and be online all the time. The remainder of the candidate blocks will be discarded.

There are several versions of Ouroboros: Classic, Byzantine Fault Tolerance (BFT), Genesis, Praos, and Hydra. More about this in Chapter 3.

Slot leader election

The Cardano network is made up of a number of stake pools, or delegators, that govern the aggregated stake of their owners and other stakeholders. The slot leaders are chosen at random from the stake pools. The bigger a pool's stake, the more likely it is to be chosen as a slot leader and generate a new block that is accepted into the blockchain. This is the foundation of Cardano's proof-of-stake (PoS) approach. Cardano includes an incentive scheme that discourages delegation to pools that already control too much of the overall stake, to preserve a level playing field and avoid a small number of extremely large pools controlling most of the stake.

Transaction validation

A slot leader must confirm that the sender has included enough resources to pay for the transaction and that the transaction's requirements are satisfied while validating a

---

[133] **Slot leader**: an elected node that has been chosen to construct a block in the current slot. An arbitrary election takes place based on the proportionate stake.

transaction. The slot leader will record the transaction as part of a new block, which will subsequently be joined to other blocks in the chain, if it fits all these conditions.

How to purchase ada?

Most people buy ada via centralized exchanges such as Kraken, Coinbase or Binance. The steps are documented in Cardano Docs and via a plethora of blogs and YouTube videos.[134] Centralized exchanges are no longer the only fiat onramps available with wallets such as *eternl* and vendors like nmkr.io offering the user the ability to buy Ada with their local currency.

How to Delegate and earn rewards

The number of ada you hold determines the size of your stake. Cardano users may receive passive rewards for verifying blocks if they have a stake in the protocol.

Because not everyone has the time, skills, or money to operate a stake pool, ada holders may delegate their stake to a chosen pool and have it managed on their behalf by an operator. This enables everyone to contribute to the consensus and receive rewards without having to keep a node online all of the time. The bigger the stake in a pool, the greater the rewards for its owners. You can spend your ada whenever you choose, regardless of whether it has been delegated.

Ada holders initially relied on the *Daedalus* wallet from IOG (full node, desktop wallet) or *Yoroi* from Emurgo (light, mobile client) to delegate their share. But as Cardano matures, there are now many more options. In June 2022, IOG announced a new light wallet, *Lace* will be one-stop shop for everything in the Cardano ecosystem. Meanwhile dcSpark's (dcSpark.io) *Flint* and *eternl* are just two of the many wallets available.[135] Here are a few guides recommended in Cardano Docs:

- How to choose a stake pool[136]
- How safe is it to delegate to a stake pool?[137]
- How to delegate to a stake pool[138] (Daedalus)
- Staking and delegating for beginners[139] (Daedalus)
- How to delegate from the Yoroi wallet[140]

---

[134] How to buy Cardano ada cryptocurrency for beginners, youtube.com/watch?v=3MEO-Im6OSg

[135] Cardano wallets, cardanocube.io/collections/wallets

[136] How to choose a stake pool, iohk.zendesk.com/hc/en-us/articles/900002174303-How-to-choose-a-stake-pool

[137] How safe is it to delegate to a stake pool?, iohk.zendesk.com/hc/en-us/articles/900002046123-How-safe-is-it-to-delegate-to-a-stake-pool-

[138] How to delegate to a stake pool, iohk.zendesk.com/hc/en-us/articles/900005718683-How-to-Delegate-to-a-stake-pool

[139] Staking and delegating for beginners, forum.cardano.org/t/staking-and-delegating-for-beginners-a-step-by-step-guide/36681

Cardano-node, originally developed by IOG, is now an open-source project in its own right. IOG are placing more and more of an emphasis on their open-source credentials. You can review the repository on GitHub[141] to understand how you can contribute, codes of conduct, benchmarking results, etc. and visit CardanoUpdates.com for roadmap details.

Cardano design decisions

Many people discovered Cardano by watching Charles Hoskinson's Whiteboard YouTube presentation[142]. However, Cardano didn't start out with a detailed plan or even a white paper, as many open-source initiatives do. IOG explored the cryptocurrency landscape by adopting a 'first principles' approach.[143] The Scorex project[144] and IOG's vault of research papers[145] were the product of this study.

Unlike successful protocols such as TCP/IP,[146] most cryptocurrencies have no layering in their architecture. Regardless of whether it makes sense, there has been a desire to retain a single concept of agreement around facts and occurrences recorded in a single ledger.

For example, Ethereum has accumulated vast complexity in its quest to become a world computer, yet it is plagued by minor issues that might jeopardize the system's capacity to function. Should every DApp, regardless of its economic worth, maintenance costs, or regulatory implications, be treated as a first-class citizen?

Layered architecture

The focus of IOG's design is to accommodate the social features of cryptocurrencies, to create layers by separating value accounting from computation, and to answer the demands of regulators while adhering to the founding principles.[147] IOG also assessed

---

[140] How to delegate from the Yoroi wallet, forum.cardano.org/t/cardano-shelley-how-to-delegate-from-the-yoroi-wallet/38230

[141] cardano-node, github.com/input-output-hk/cardano-node

[142] IOHK | Cardano Whiteboard; overview with Charles Hoskinson, youtube.com/watch?v=Ja9D0kpksxw

[143] **First-principles thinking** is one of the best ways to reverse-engineer complicated problems and unleash creative possibilities. Sometimes called 'reasoning from first principles,' the idea is to break down complicated problems into basic elements and then reassemble them from the ground up.

[144] Scorex project, iohk.io/projects/scorex/

[145] IOHK research papers, iohk.io/research/library/

[146] The **Transmission Control Protocol (TCP)** is one of the main protocols of the **Internet Protocol (IP)** suite. Therefore, the entire suite is commonly referred to as TCP/IP. TCP provides reliable, ordered, and error-checked delivery of a stream of octets (bytes) between applications running on hosts communicating via an IP network. Major internet applications such as the World-Wide Web, email, and file transfer rely on TCP.

[147] Why Cardano?, why.cardano.org/

protocols via peer review and inspected code against formal specifications[148] whenever possible.

February 8, 2019, Charles Hoskinson: In Defense of Peer Review[149]

> *...unlike journals, which sometimes take years for research to actually get published, fully peer-reviewed and get through the system, conferences are very frequent. If you look at the cryptographic world you have Eurocrypt, CCS, Real World Crypto and dozens of other conferences every year. Almost every month there's some form of conference going on. So it doesn't slow you down to write a paper, in a very structured, thoughtful way, get it into a conference and then get some review from the community. Suddenly, now you have some of the brightest people in the world waking up trying to destroy your argument, because they know that it benefits their academic career if they can find a flaw in your paper.*

Cardano is a cryptocurrency that acknowledges that 'money is social'. A social construct is something that comes through human interaction rather than objective reality. It exists because people acknowledge and believe in it. Countries and currencies are two examples of social constructs.

Flexibility and the capacity to handle complexity in any transaction are critical. If the Cardano project is successful in scaling up to be used by billions of people, massive computing, storage, and network resources will be required to handle billions of concurrent transactions. Cardano's architecture inherits the notion of separation of concerns[150] from TCP/IP.

Blockchains are, at their core, databases that arrange facts and events based on timestamps and immutability to record asset ownership. It's non-trivial then to add complicated computation for storing and executing DApps. Do we need to know how much money someone is sending? Do we want to become engaged in deciphering the transaction's whole narrative?

To figure out what's happening, a single protocol must be able to comprehend arbitrary events, script arbitrary transactions, allow for fraud arbitration, and even reverse transactions when new information becomes available.

Then there's the issue of deciding what information to retain for each transaction, which is a challenging design choice. What components of a transaction narrative are relevant? Are they going to be significant in the future? When will it be safe to discard certain

---

[148] Duncan Coutts, 'Cryptocurrencies need a safeguard to prevent another DAO disaster', iohk.io/blog/cryptocurrencies-need-a-safeguard-to-prevent-another-DAO-disaster/

[149] In defense of peer review, youtube.com/watch?v=3-rbn73cUEk

[150] **Separation of concerns** is a design principle for separating a computer program into distinct sections, so that each section addresses a separate concern. A concern is a set of information that affects the code of a computer program.

data? Is it illegal in certain jurisdictions to do so? Certain computations are by their very nature secret.[151] It's always good to remember the difference between confidentiality and privacy.

Privacy and confidentiality are two separate concepts that protect different types of data. 'Privacy' is used in relation to data that is protected by law, whereas 'confidentiality' refers to different data contained in valid contracts and agreements.

A transaction consists of two parts: the mechanism for sending and recording token flows, as well as the reasons and circumstances for transferring tokens. The latter may be very complicated, including gigabytes of data, signatures, and the occurrence of unforeseen scenarios. With a single signature moving value to another address, it can also be straightforward.

Modeling the motives and circumstances of value movement is difficult because they are personal to the parties involved in the most unanticipated ways. Contract law creates an even more complex picture, in which the actors may not even be aware that the transaction does not match commercial reality.[152] This concept is known as the 'semantic gap'.[153]

The general lack of legal clarity around protocol participants' legal safeguards is another gray area. There is no limit to what a sophisticated cryptocurrency may do. A blockchain such as Cardano can unwittingly facilitate all sorts of crime and malfeasance. Just how complex this is in practice is discussed in various academic papers, including *The Ring of Gyges:*[154] *using smart contracts for crime.*[155]

Cardano and Bitcoin have an advantage in that they have opted to split into layers. Bitcoin gave us Rootstock (rsk.co),[156] while the Cardano Computation Layer is Cardano's proposal.

---

[151] Hoskinson announces a new system to tackle both security & privacy concerns, ambcrypto.com/hoskinson-announces-a-new-system-to-tackle-both-security-privacy-concerns/

[152] Wet code and dry, unenumerated.blogspot.com/2006/11/wet-code-and-dry.html

[153] The **semantic gap** characterizes the difference between two descriptions of an object by different linguistic representations, for instance languages or symbols. According to Hein, the semantic gap can be defined as "the difference in meaning between constructs formed within different representation systems". In computer science, the concept is relevant whenever ordinary human activities, observations, and tasks are transferred into a computational representation.

[154] The **Ring of Gyges** is a mythical, magical artifact mentioned by the philosopher Plato in his *Republic*. It grants its owner the power to become invisible at will. Through the story of the ring, *Republic* considers whether an intelligent person would be just, if they did not have to fear reputational damage if they committed injustices.

[155] Ari Juels, Ahmed Kosba, and Elaine Shi, 'The Ring of Gyges: using smart contracts for crime', arijuels.com/wp-content/uploads/2013/09/Gyges.pdf

[156] **RootStock** is a smart-contract peer-to-peer platform built on top of the Bitcoin blockchain. Its goal is to add value and functionality to the core Bitcoin network by the implementation of smart contracts as a sidechain.

IOG provides a reference library of Plutus code for application developers to use in their projects, similar to the Solidity-based[157] Zeppelin project.[158] IOG also created a set of tools for formal verification based on the Liquid Haskell project.[159]

The 'Why Cardano' essay from 2017 describes the vision[160] for The Cardano Settlement Layer (CSL) vs Cardano Computation Layer (CCL). The same functionality exists today, but it is implemented differently than outlined back then.

The layered approach was kept but computation is done on the main chain, Layer 1. This was implemented very carefully as the development of Plutus relied on formal methods and a secure design that would not endanger 'simple' non-script assets on the chain.

The code base was totally rewritten in a modular[161] format in preparation for the implementation of the hard fork combinator (HFC)[162] in March 2020. The modular approach made it far easier to make changes with the HFC. The 'Byron reboot' and HFC in 2020, with the move to Ouroboros Praos, were fundamental in implementing code that would support the future of the blockchain. This was a watershed in the efficiency of the chain and for the productivity of IOG. It made possible the move to the quarterly update schedule in place today. Nobody had done anything like the HFC before; it made upgrades easy, another advantage of the third-generation approach.

---

[157] **Solidity** is an object-oriented programming language for writing smart contracts. It is used for implementing smart contracts on various blockchain platforms, most notably, Ethereum.

[158] Jeevak Kasarkod, 'Zeppelin: a secure smart contracts open-source framework for blockchain applications', infoq.com/news/2016/10/zeppelin-secure-smart-contracts/

[159] Liquid Haskell, ucsd-progsys.github.io/liquidhaskell-blog/

[160] Why Cardano? CCL, why.cardano.org/en/introduction/cardano-computation-layer/

[161] Broadly speaking, **modularity** is the degree to which a system's components may be separated and recombined, often with the benefit of flexibility and variety in use. The concept of modularity is used primarily to reduce complexity by breaking a system into varying degrees of interdependence and independence across and 'hide the complexity of each part behind an abstraction and interface.'

[162] A combinator is a technical term used to indicate the combination of certain processes or things. In the case of Cardano, a **hard fork combinator** combines protocols, thereby enabling the Byron-to-Shelley transition without system interruption or restart. It ensures that Byron and Shelley ledgers appear as one ledger.

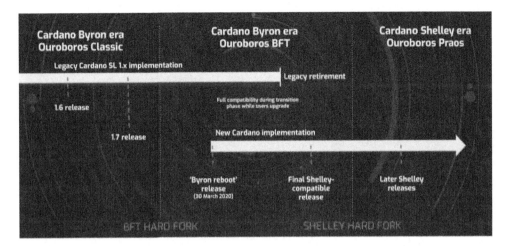

Figure 6: Mainnet Byron to Shelley Roadmap

Charles Hoskinson has explained the layered approach in many of his YouTube AMAs (ask-me-anything). Excerpts from some of these are included below for clarity.

April 21, 2019. Is Cardano going to be more of a sidechain host model? CH:[163]

> *Cardano has always been a two-layer system, so this concept of the settlement system and a control layer idea ...so the control layers are either permissioned or permissionless[164] and they can have arbitrary complexity. The settlement system has basically everything that you would need for a long-term cryptocurrency ...so basically Cardano, at the settlement layer, is kind of like what I would like Bitcoin to look like. [...]*
>
> *In terms of the conceptual design and actually the formal specification, we have a total understanding of what ledgers need to look like, the accounting systems behind them... we have an incredibly intricate understanding of what consensus looks like and the tradeoffs of consensus. We have a detailed understanding of interoperability; we understand how to extend the UTXO model to include pretty much as much scripting as you want... but do this in a very safe way where you have predictable gas cost*

July 9, 2020. Thoughts on Cross Chain Communication, Sidechains, NiPoPoWs and Litecoin[165]

---

[163] Post Conference recap, thoughts and an AMA 04/21/2019, youtu.be/pBXZVrBQ6U8?t=3325

[164] **Permissioned v permissionless**. At the simplest level, the distinction lies in whether the design of the network is open for anyone to participate – permissionless – or limited only to designated participants, or permissioned.

[165] Thoughts on cross chain communication, sidechains, NiPoPoWs and Litecoin, youtube.com/watch?v=HvIAgDEUC4o,

You can have a maximalist model ...and if they (Bitcoin) ever actually implemented this technology, it actually would be competitive. They've had since 2014 to do it but they haven't done it. This is this concept of primary - secondary chains. Used to be called master – slave, but that language is rapidly falling out of use even in different context. Basically, we did this in our original white paper, we said SL (settlement layer) and the CL (computation layer) concept... so the idea is that there's one primary chain and that's where the token lives, ADA. Then that token ADA can be used to power different chains, that have different network logic, it has different consensus rules, it has different ledger rules, a different computational model and somehow these chains don't have their own native token ...rather they are at the service of the primary chain. So, let's look at this in the context of the ITN (incentivized testnet).

So let's say that we modify Ouroboros....and Ouroboros now when you're a stake pool operator, instead of just getting one block, you get block Cardano... but then you'd also get block CL1, block CL2... block CLn... and so if you're a stake pool operator, when your job comes up to expand the state of the chain, you'll actually do that for each of these networks in addition to SL. So you'll generate the normal Cardano block, like all the stake pool operators do, but then you'll make the block for the next network, the block for the next network ... and you'll look up that network logic and those consensus rules and the ledger logic and you'll follow the computational model, and these will all be different.

[...] This was kind of an envisioned model that came out of Blockstream[166] when they were talking about sidechains. They said Bitcoin can be that version of SL, and it could be very simple and safe and secure, and then you could have Ethereum as a sidechain of Bitcoin, send your Bitcoin into that sidechain, operate and then send your Bitcoin back when you're done.

December 30, 2020. Is the distinction between the Cardano computation layer and the Cardano's settlement layer still relevant? CH:[167]

Yes, and in fact the sidechains that we're going to run are examples of what I call the computation layer. The difference is they're not ephemeral, they're actually permanently there ...but yeah that's exactly what we intended. You have a very stable secure settlement system which is the primary network with the stake pool operators ...and you have this collection of sidechains which do different things and have different computational models than the main chain.

Regulatory landscape

---

[166] **Blockstream** is a blockchain technology company led by co-founder Adam Back. Blockstream intends to develop software to 'break off' transactions from the bitcoin network and charge a fixed monthly fee to allow people to use alternative 'sidechains'. Blockstream employs a large number of prominent Bitcoin Core developers.

[167] Special Edition New Year's AMA 2020, youtu.be/GtWt68kp1dg?t=777

If a financial system grows and achieves adoption, it develops a need for regulation, or at the very least a desire for it. This is usually the consequence of periodic market breakdowns caused by the incompetence of some actor(s).

The Knickerbocker Crisis of 1907, for example, led to the establishment of the Federal Reserve System as a lender of last resort in 1913. Another example is the excesses of the United States in the 1920s, which ended in the Great Depression, a devastating financial catastrophe. The Securities Exchange Commission was established in 1934 as a result of this collapse in an attempt to avoid a repeat of the incident or at the very least hold unscrupulous actors responsible. The Bitcoin Genesis block referred to 'Chancellor on the Brink of Second Bailout for Banks'[168] implying some inspiration from the events of the time.

One might question the need, breadth, and usefulness of regulation, but one cannot deny that it exists and that major governments have implemented it with enthusiasm, with many subsequently performing an about-turn once they realize the consequences.[169] Cardano, like other financial systems, must have a viewpoint on what is fair and acceptable in its design. Cardano opted to distinguish between individual rights and market rights.

Individuals should always have complete control over their finances, free of coercion or civil asset forfeiture. This principle must be enforced because, as crises like Venezuela, Zimbabwe and Cyprus have shown previously, and the ongoing war in Ukraine shows today, not all governments can be trusted not to misuse their sovereign authority for the personal enrichment of corrupt leaders. Cryptocurrencies must be designed with the lowest common denominator in mind.

There should never be any tampering with history. Immutability is promised by blockchains. Introducing the ability to rewrite history or the official record offers much too much temptation to change the past to favor a certain actor(s).

There should be no restrictions on the movement of wealth. Human rights are harmed by capital restrictions and other artificial barriers. Aside from the impossibility of enforcing them, in a global market where many residents in developing countries migrate outside of their jurisdiction in search of a livable income, limiting capital flows frequently harms the world's poorest.

According to these concepts, markets are separate from people. While Cardano believes in individual rights, markets also have the right to publicly express their terms and conditions. If a person decides to conduct business inside this market, they must be held to those T&Cs for the sake of the system's integrity.

---

[168] Chancellor on the brink of second bailout for banks, coindesk.com/podcasts/the-breakdown-with-nlw/13-years-on-the-meaning-of-chancellor-on-the-brink-of-second-bailout-for-banks/

[169] 'Now that India has pulled back from banning crypto, here's how it plans to develop digital currency on its own terms', fortune.com/2022/02/02/india-crypto-ban-plans-develop-digital-currency-taxes-regulation-bitcoin/

December 30, 2020. Is the SEC (Securities & Exchange Commission) the enemy of Crypto? CH:[170]

> *No…the regulators are not the enemy of crypto … let's be honest here our space created Bitconnect,[171] OneCoin,[172] Mount Gox,[173] Bitmex[174]… thousands of scams that have hurt people. Regulators are like vampires, in a good way. They come in when you invite them. Okay, a vampire standing at the door says, 'can I come in?' …what brings a regulator into an industry? Happy well-functioned industries where everything is going right? … like how many regulators are there for mathematics? Is there a mathematics exchange commission? …that sits down and says 'we really need to look into those topologists? …. they're slippery people, we are deeply concerned about statistics. Yeah, there's some problems there man, serious problems, 64% of people know that…'*

> *No! because it's like… what scandals occur in the mathematical world? Occasionally we have an older fields medalist who claims he proved the Riemann hypothesis and turns out his brain's baked and it is a garbage paper! Okay we're pretty good at self-regulating in that industry. On the other hand, why is the pharmaceutical industry regulated? Because they make stuff that you put into people's bodies, and if they they that up they break your penis, they break your brain, they break your eyes, you go deaf …. okay more than one person has gone deaf from the first reaction to an antibiotic. There are all kinds of bad things that can occur …so you need to regulate it! Because there are perverse incentives against your health!*

> *…*

> *So let's look at crypto, you have the ICO (Initial Coin Offering) boom, you have tons of scandals and scams, you have rampant insider trading, you have wash trading on exchanges, you have exchanges failing and the principals of the exchange are stealing the money and fleeing abroad, you have software flaws that were made on purpose to steal people's money, you have massive misrepresentations… you have impersonations… you have people claiming they're using project capital for something but they're actually using to buy yachts and Miami houses and prostitutes and… rah-rah-rah*

> *That is a big neon sign at the front of your door…. 'Vampire come in!' …our industry did that, we didn't self-regulate, we didn't stop the agency failures, we*

---

[170] Special Edition New Year's AMA 2020, youtu.be/GtWt68kp1dg?t=7282

[171] BitConnect Founder Indicted in Global $2.4 Billion Cryptocurrency Scheme, justice.gov/opa/pr/bitconnect-founder-indicted-global-24-billion-cryptocurrency-scheme

[172] What We Can Learn From OneCoin, Crypto's Biggest Scam, fool.com/the-ascent/cryptocurrency/articles/what-we-can-learn-from-onecoin-cryptos-biggest-scam/

[173] Payments for $9 billion bitcoin settlement from Mt. Gox collapse could start in months, markets.businessinsider.com/news/currencies/mt-gox-bitcoin-settlement-payouts-9-billion-dollars-early-2022-2021-11

[174] Federal Court Orders BitMEX to Pay $100 Million for Illegally Operating a Cryptocurrency Trading Platform and Anti-Money Laundering Violations, cftc.gov/PressRoom/PressReleases/8412-21

created a neon sign and welcomed a vampire and now they're here! ...and we're going to complain that they're doing stuff... filing lawsuits, getting involved like a bull in a China shop... of course they are, and their ability to act is proportional to the sophistication of the tools and the modernity of the laws. The Howey test[175] is an artifact of the 1940s ...it cannot work in 'stem cell' finance, where an asset can be everything... it can be a currency, a commodity and a security all at the same time, could be everything and nothing...

In June 2022, Charles Hoskinson spoke[176] before Congress on the 'The Future of Digital Asset Regulation'. He didn't focus attention on Cardano, and instead spoke for the industry. The main message he delivered to representatives was cryptocurrencies, in general, should be treated as financial stem cells rather than be rigidly defined as a security, currency or a commodity. Future legislation should be based on principles, not focused on individual jurisdictions or bodies. His contribution was broadly well received.[177]

Cardano Vision

Cardano is a long-term project that has benefited from the input of hundreds of the world's brightest minds, both within and outside the cryptocurrency sector. It entails constant iteration, active peer review, and leverages the findings of open-source research.

While no project can meet all goals or please all users, IOG intends to present a vision for what a self-evolving financial stack should look like for countries that don't have one. Realistically, cryptocurrencies will not replace current financial institutions. Legacy financial systems have always been able to absorb change. Instead, it's more fruitful to focus on jurisdictions where deploying the old banking system is just too costly, where many people survive on less than a few dollars a day, have no fixed identification, and credit is difficult to come by.

The ability to combine a payment system, property rights, identification, credit, and risk protection into a single mobile app is not just beneficial, but life-altering in these regions.

---

[175] **Howey Test**: Securities and Exchange Commission (SEC) v. W. J. Howey Co. (1946). The case resulted in a test, known as the **Howey test**, to determine whether an instrument qualifies as an 'investment contract' for the purposes of the Securities Act: 'a contract, transaction or scheme whereby a person invests his money in a common enterprise and is led to expect profits solely from the efforts of the promoter or a third party. The Howey Test has remained a notable determiner of regulatory oversight for many decades. In the past few years, it has been called into question, most frequently in conjunction with discussions about Cryptocurrencies and Blockchain technology'.

[176] The Future of Digital Asset Regulation, youtube.com/watch?v=K4ZM2AlGT-s

[177] Cardano founder steals the show at Congressional hearing on crypto regulation, cryptoslate.com/cardano-founder-steals-the-show-at-congressional-hearing-on-crypto-regulation/

IOG believes Cardano can build on the successes of projects like M-pesa[178] and Kiva.[179] If Cardano can transform the way cryptocurrencies are conceived, developed, and financed, then we are heading towards Dr Pangloss's 'best of all possible worlds.'[180]

Behind the names

Why is it called Cardano? CH explains:[181]

> *Girolamo Cardano was the ultimate Renaissance guy, he was a doctor, a lawyer, he was a mathematician, he was a gambler, a complete scoundrel. He was the personal physician of the Pope but then excommunicated but still hung out with the Pope even after being excommunicated, because the Pope liked him. He nearly killed one of his sons in a sword duel because they were sleeping with the same woman. Then he was also a gambler, and he invented a lot of probability theory just so he could be a better gambler. So, he created all this advanced mathematics just so he could count cards and roll dice properly and so forth. And he had a habit of getting kicked out of cities… And he also was a cryptographer because in Renaissance Italy, they had a lot of intrigue between the banking families. So, he invented this wheel device to encrypt messages, so they kept secret communication between the families. So, I just read about him years ago and thought he's one of the most interesting people I've ever read about in my life. So, I was thinking of a cryptocurrency, it could do both good things and bad things, and it also does a little bit of everything and it's just all-around an interesting system, and I thought it'd be cool to name it after Cardano.*

> *He was just one of those guys that lived a life that was unbelievably rich, wasn't nice, wasn't evil, he was somewhere in between. He basically built out modern probability theory because he wanted to be a better gambler. He also inadvertently created the Italian peer review process because, at the time, he was around most of the scientists in Italy who would guard their knowledge and not publish anything because it was a way to maintain employment. So how you would get a professorship in an Italian university is, you would go and present to the students and if they felt you were knowledgeable, they'd say yes, this person should be part of our system, so people didn't want to publish anything because it would ruin their brand, they kept things secret.*

---

[178] **M-Pesa** (M for mobile, pesa is Swahili for money) is a mobile phone-based money transfer, financing and microfinancing service, launched in 2007 by Vodafone for Safaricom and Vodacom, the largest mobile network operators in Kenya and Tanzania. It has since expanded to Afghanistan, South Africa, India and in 2014 to Romania and in 2015 to Albania. M-Pesa allows users to deposit, withdraw, transfer money and pay for goods and services (Lipa na M-Pesa) easily with a mobile device.

[179] **Kiva** (commonly known by its domain name, Kiva.org) is a non-profit organization, the world's first online lending platform connecting online lenders to entrepreneurs across the globe. Kiva's mission is 'to expand financial access to help underserved communities thrive.'

[180] Best of all possible worlds, everipedia.org/wiki/lang_en/Best_of_all_possible_worlds

[181] Some Random Thoughts and Updates, youtu.be/ttFptsL5hN0?t=4353

So what Cardano would do, he would get people very drunk and learn all of their secrets and he wrote them all down and then he eventually published books about this, which was super taboo and included how to factor quartic polynomial ...he got that from Tartaglia[182] ...which means the stutterer. So he was a legendary guy and I think he was even a contemporary of DaVinci and I figured it'd be the perfect name for a cryptocurrency because the cryptocurrency is not good or bad, it's a neutral thing, it's brilliant and inspired, it's a bit of a polymath and everybody has an opinion about it and you'll never get a clear and concise way, but it certainly has a huge impact and it's a man of its time.

But then the other thing is that when you have cryptocurrency, you have the protocol name, then you have the currency name. In Bitcoin, it's Bitcoin, it's the same, but in other systems they're different. So, what I decided to do with Cardano is I named the currency, Ada, after Ada Lovelace.[183] She was a pioneering figure in the 19th century, the first female programmer of note, good friends with Charles Babbage, and left a great legacy and inspired generations of women that came after her to enter into the sciences and become developers. I'd like to say the 20th century spiritual successor to Ada Lovelace is Grace Hopper, creator of COBOL (Common business-oriented language) and also the gal responsible for the computer bug, there's a great legacy there as well.

When we were naming the Cardano ecosystem and thinking carefully about the name, the protocol, and what to name the currency, I wanted to connect every part of Cardano to historical figures who did something unique and special in their lives, not necessarily the best of people. Like for example, Cardano himself was a polymath and a brilliant mathematician, but he was also a little bit of a scoundrel from time to time. In fact, if you read his biography, it's a surprise to me that Hollywood hasn't made a book or a movie yet about Cardano, because he's an incredible guy, but Ada is one of the good ones and she lived an incredible life and left an incredible legacy.

And then I named every major release of Cardano after, either a famous poet or famous computer scientist, or somebody I was inspired by. So, for example, Byron was after Lord Byron. Then the next thing, Goguen is a world-famous computer scientist, who did a lot of work I admire.

Lord Byron is one of my favorite poets, he wrote She Walks in Beauty.[184] So I said it'd be cool to get a Byron connection and bring this in. I also wanted a balance, if I named something after a guy, I'd like to name something after a girl. So always have a nice balance between the feminine and masculine inside the system. That's where that came from.

---

[182] Tartaglia, everipedia.org/wiki/lang_en/Niccol%25C3%25B2_Fontana_Tartaglia

[183] Happy Birthday ADA!, youtu.be/hhAOJyi_3lA?t=27

[184] She Walks in Beauty, poetryfoundation.org/poems/43844/she-walks-in-beauty

Where did the naming scheme come from in Cardano? CH explains:

> *They're just all people that I admired in my life… Voltaire's work, and I read Shelley's work, and some of the things were cautionary tales, - like Percy Shelley wrote Ozymandias[185] for example.*
>
> *The name Shelley is interesting, there's actually two famous Shelleys. There's Mary Shelley and Percy Shelley. A lot of people think it's Mary Shelley because she's the more famous of the two. She wrote Frankenstein and a lot of other books, and her husband Percy was a famous poet, he was also a member of the Illuminati, and he traveled the world and was an artist. He did a lot of cool things, so actually, I named Shelley after Percy, but at this point so many people confuse it for Mary. I say take your pick. The point of it was, that no matter how great a centralized system is, there's this concept that eventually time takes its place and so Shelley wrote a very famous poem called Ozymandias about a traveler who went to Egypt, and he saw all these ruined monuments from long long ago, and he was just commenting on the fact that they're all decaying now.*
>
> *So, I kind of looked at it the same way, that all things must change no matter how great your original ideas are. Time takes its place, so it's kind of a reminder these systems require constant vigilance, updates, and maintenance to actually sustain themselves. It's now in the hands of not a leader, but the community to do that with Shelley. So, I felt that was a proper way of naming it, but when I said the release was named Shelley, everyone just assumed it was Mary and they were quoting Frankenstein when it came out and I said, 'damn it. Okay, it's Mary if you want, they were married, so it kind of works.' Anyway, it's been overwhelmingly well received.[186]*

Why the bull's head symbol for the Daedalus wallet? CH:[187]

> *That is not a bull's head, that is a minotaur's head. The minotaur was a mythological creature that lived in the labyrinth. We named Daedalus after Daedalus the historical figure, or mythological figure, the father of Icarus and the creator of the maze. The labyrinth was built because no chains could bind the minotaur and so, by basically building a giant maze and putting the minotaur in it, he couldn't escape the maze. So Daedalus is the name of the Cardano wallet. Daedalus is the creator of the labyrinth, and the minotaur is the most prominent creature within the labyrinth, that's why the symbol is a minotaur.*

Byron is named after the Romantic poet who was the father of Ada Lovelace. The British

---

[185] Ozymandias, poetryfoundation.org/poems/46565/ozymandias

[186] Charles Hoskinson - Building a Better World with the Blockchain, podcasts.apple.com/us/podcast/charles-hoskinson-building-a-better-world/id1553861681?i=1000517944232

[187] Special Edition New Years AMA 2020, youtu.be/GtWt68kp1dg?t=8496

Library[188] described him as 'Dedicated to freedom of thought and action, and anarchic in his political views and personal morality, the poet and adventurer Lord Byron was the personification of the Romantic hero.'

Lord Byron was an English poet, peer, and politician who became a revolutionary in the Greek War of Independence and is considered one of the historical leading figures of the Romantic movement of his era. He is regarded as one of the greatest English poets and remains widely read and influential. Among his best-known works are the narrative poems *Childe Harold's Pilgrimage* and *Don Juan*, a lengthy satiric poem where Byron portrayed Juan as someone easily seduced by women, reversing the legend of Don Juan as an actual womanizer.

He traveled extensively across Europe, especially in Italy, where he lived for seven years in the cities of Venice, Ravenna, and Pisa. During his stay in Italy, he frequently visited his friend and fellow poet, Percy Shelley. Later in life, Byron joined the Greek War of Independence fighting the Ottoman Empire and died of disease leading a campaign during that war, for which Greeks revere him as a national hero. Often described as the most flamboyant and notorious of the major Romantics, Byron was considered a celebrity in his era both for his success as a romantic poet and for his aristocratic excesses, which included huge debts and many sex scandals – numerous love affairs with both men and women. One of his lovers, Lady Caroline Lamb, summed him up in the famous phrase 'mad, bad, and dangerous to know'. His only legitimate child, Ada Lovelace, is regarded as a foundational figure in the field of computer programming. Cardano ticker, ADA, is named after her first name, and her surname Lovelace is used to describe smaller units of ada tokens. 1m lovelaces = 1ada

Goguen: Joseph Goguen was a US computer scientist. He was a professor of Computer Science at the University of California and the University of Oxford and held research positions at IBM and SRI International. Goguen's work was one of the earliest approaches to the algebraic characterization of abstract data types and he originated and helped develop the OBJ[189] family of programming languages. Goguen studied the philosophy of computation, formal methods, and functional programming. He inspired Cardano with his work to build the K framework to verify the code of smart contracts, so they can be automatically checked for errors. Goguen was and advisor to Grigore Roşu[190] when Grigore was at University of California. Grigore is chief executive of Runtime Verification who continue much of this work[191] today. CH:[192]

> *By the way, I really regret this one. I shouldn't have named it Goguen, this should have been called Hopper after Grace Hopper. I like Goguen, he's a good guy, but there's not enough women here (on the roadmap).*

---

[188] Lord Byron, bl.uk/people/lord-byron

[189] OBJ programming language, everipedia.org/wiki/lang_en/OBJ_%28programming_language%29

[190] Grigore Rosu, runtimeverification.com/blog/author/grigore-rosu/

[191] Cardano360 - March 2021, youtu.be/ULBLgPgxtN8?t=1571

[192] IO ScotFest Keynote with Charles Hoskinson, youtu.be/tbtkClr3Y3I?t=356

Basho: Matsuo Basho was the most famous poet from Japan's 17th century Edo period. He wrote short 3 sentence poems. One of his most famous poems is called *Old Pond* which describes how a frog, by doing small jumps, can reach the big ocean. The analogy being, as Cardano grows and new users onboard, the system will scale and be seaworthy for the 'ocean'. CH:

> *Basho went on this crazy journey during the Edo period in Japan when everybody lived in their silos there, you weren't allowed to travel, but he was a guy who traveled and somehow didn't get killed, and he wrote about all these crazy journeys.*

Voltaire: Named after the French philosopher who prized criticism and argued for the separation of church and state. Voltaire, one of Charles Hoskinson's favorite poets, was a versatile and prolific writer, producing works in almost every literary form, including plays, poems, novels, essays, and historical and scientific works. He wrote over 20,000 letters and over 2,000 books and pamphlets. He was an outspoken advocate of civil liberties; despite the risk this placed him in under the strict censorship laws of the time. As a satirical polemicist, he frequently made use of his works to criticize intolerance, religious dogma, and the French institutions of his day.

Yoroi is a 'light client' mobile wallet[193] for Cardano. In Japanese, Yoroi means armor. It was built to protect the integrity of the samurai back in the Middle Ages.

Ouroboros is the name of Cardano's network consensus protocol. The Ouroboros is an ancient symbol ('tail devourer' in Greek) depicting a snake or a dragon, eating its own tail, a fertility symbol also representing eternity and endless return.

Jörmungandr[194] is a node implementation, written in Rust,[195] with the initial aim to support the Ouroboros type of consensus protocol on the incentivized testnet in 2019, then subsequently repurposed to be part of Catalyst. A node is a participant of a blockchain network, continuously making, sending, receiving, and validating blocks. Each node is responsible to make sure that all the rules of the protocol are followed. Jörmungandr refers to the Midgard Serpent in Norse mythology. It is an example of an Ouroboros, the Ancient Egyptian serpent, who eat its own tail, as well as the IOG paper[196] on proof-of-stake.

---

[193] Yoroi mobile wallet, yoroi-wallet.com/

[194] Jormungandr, everipedia.org/wiki/lang_en/J%C3%B6rmungandr

[195] **Rust** is a lightweight, portable programming language from Mozilla that compiles to the web, iOS and Android. Rust is a multi-paradigm, general-purpose language designed for performance and safety, especially safe concurrency.

[196] Kiayias, Russell, David, Oliynykov (2019) 'Ouroboros: A Provably Secure Proof-of-Stake Blockchain Protocol', eprint.iacr.org/2016/889.pdf

Plutus is the Greek god of wealth. He was made blind by Zeus, because Zeus wanted him to be able to disperse his gifts without any prejudices and discrimination. Plutus[197] is the smart contract platform for Cardano. Plutus contracts consist of parts that run on the blockchain (on-chain[198] code) and parts that run on a user's machine (off-chain or client code). Plutus draws from modern language research to provide a safe, full-stack programming environment based on Haskell, the leading functional programming language.

Marlowe. Named after Christopher Marlowe, an Elizabethan 'forger, a brawler, a spy, but above all a playwright, a poet and the most celebrated writer of his generation'[199] who was killed at the age of 29 in a drunken brawl over a bill but might have been assassinated. Marlowe, also known as Kit Marlowe, was an English playwright, poet and translator. He greatly influenced William Shakespeare, who was born in the same year as Marlowe. He was for anti-intellectualism, which is a form of hostility and mistrust of intellectuals.

In Cardano, Marlowe is a new domain-specific language[200] (DSL) for modeling financial instruments as smart contracts on a blockchain. It is embedded in the Haskell language, which has its own established ecosystem and testing framework. You do not need programming expertise to use Marlowe and you can explore your Marlowe financial contracts with a browser-based contract editor and simulator.

---

[197] Plutus, developers.cardano.org/en/programming-languages/plutus/overview/

[198] **Off-chain code**: The part of a contract application's code which runs off the chain, usually as a contract application. **On-chain code**: The part of a contract application's code which runs on the chain (i.e. as scripts).

[199] Marlowe, bbc.co.uk/programmes/p003k9d6

[200] A **domain-specific language (DSL)** is a computer language specialized to a particular application domain. This is in contrast to a general-purpose language (GPL), which is broadly applicable across domains.

Chapter 3: Proof of Stake

'He who has a why to live for can bear almost any how'

— Friedrich Nietzche

What is proof of stake?

Proof of stake (PoS) is a consensus protocol, or methodology, that determines consensus based on the amount of stake (or value) retained in the system. A consensus protocol, in essence, is what governs the laws and parameters that regulate the behavior of blockchains, similar to a set of rules that each network member follows. Because blockchains aren't controlled by a single, central authority, a consensus protocol is employed to enable dispersed network users to agree on the network's history as recorded on the blockchain - to achieve agreement on what's occurred and move forward from a single source of truth.

Cardano is based on Ouroboros, an innovative proof-of-stake consensus system that was created via peer-reviewed research. Stake pools, which are server nodes maintained by a stake pool operator (SPO) to whom ada holders may delegate their stake, are at the core of this PoS technology. Stake pools are used to guarantee that everyone may participate in the protocol, regardless of technical expertise or availability to maintain a node. These stake pools are focused on upkeep and hold the pooled stakes of several stakeholders in one place.

Proof of stake vs proof of work

Proof of work (PoW), on the other hand, is a synchronous system[201] that encourages miners to compete to solve problems inside the block first. This problem-solving is rewarded via a system of incentives. This strategy, however, comes at a cost: higher power consumption and longer time span to handle issues within the chain. These issues might cause the network to slow down dramatically, making it expensive to maintain.

One of the most important elements of proof of stake (PoS) is that as a user's funds grow, so does their ability to maintain the ledger. ie. the ability to create new blocks that can be put to the blockchain and timestamped correctly. A mix of random selection and a determination of their stake, or money, determines who creates a new block. Within the chain, a form of leader election takes place. Under a proof-of-stake system, users earn transaction fees as they go, increasing their balance with passive income (staking). This strategy promotes the blockchain's steady and consistent expansion in line with the goal of the network becoming stronger as participants join.

Benefits of proof of stake

The following are some of the main benefits of PoS versus PoW:

- A proof-of-stake protocol incorporates stringent security procedures
- Decentralization - the danger of centralization is lowered by imposing penalties for selfish behavior inside the network

---

[201] In a **synchronous system**, operations are coordinated by one, or more, centralized clock signals. An asynchronous digital system, in contrast, has no global clock. Asynchronous systems do not depend on strict arrival times of signals or messages for reliable operation. Coordination is achieved via events such as: packet arrival, changes (transitions) of signals, handshake protocols, and other methods.

- Energy efficiency - energy consumption is incredibly efficient since the blockchain requires less power and hardware resources to operate. For example, 'Berry' is a Cardano Stake pool[202] running on a Raspberry Pi.[203] Markus Gufler[204] ran a Cardano node on a Rock Pi (single-board computer made by Radxa) at the IOHK Summit in 2019. A Rock Pi uses as little as 10W to function.
- Cost-effectiveness - proof-of-stake currencies are considerably more cost-effective than proof-of-work currencies.

Although using proof of stake for a cryptocurrency was a contentious design decision, IOG chose to embrace it since it offers a method for introducing safe voting, has more scaling capacity, and allows for more complex incentive schemes.

The Ouroboros protocol was developed by a skilled group of cryptographers from five academic institutions headed by Professor Aggelos Kiayias of the University of Edinburgh. Beyond being verified secure using a rigorous cryptographic model, the fundamental innovation it delivers is a modular and adaptable architecture that allows for the combination of multiple protocols to boost functionality.

Delegation, sidechains, subscribable checkpoints, improved data structures for light clients,[205] multiple types of random number generation, and even alternate synchronization assumptions are all possible thanks to this flexibility. The needs of a network's consensus algorithm will alter as it grows from hundreds to millions and ultimately billions of members. As a result, it's critical to have enough flexibility to handle these changes and, as a result, future-proof the cryptocurrency's core.

---

[202] Berry Pool, github.com/alessandrokonrad/Pi-Pool

[203] **Raspberry Pi**: computer on a credit-card-sized board. Idea developed by Eben Upton and others from Cambridge University's Computer Lab and launched by their Raspberry Pi Foundation. Taking inspiration from the 1980s BBC Computer Literacy Project, the single-board computer running Linux with open-source software was launched in 2012 costing £22 to encourage computing in schools and the developing world.

[204] Cardano on the Rocks: energy efficient proof-of-stake stake pools, youtube.com/watch?v=kXR1UXkM46s

[205] A **light client**, or thin client is a lightweight computer that has been optimized for establishing a remote connection with a server-based computing environment. The server does most of the work, which can include launching software programs, performing calculations, and storing data. This contrasts with a fat client or a conventional personal computer; the former is also intended for working in a client–server model but has significant local processing power, while the latter aims to perform its function mostly locally.

'The green blockchain'

The environmental effect of proof-of-work mining became a hot topic in 2021. Yahoo Finance,[206] EuroNews[207] and the Independent Newspaper[208] were just some of those to dub Cardano the 'green blockchain'. Cardano's staking mechanism avoids Bitcoin mining's huge energy consumption and hardware pollution. Bitcoin has been the subject of debate since Satoshi Nakamoto released the Bitcoin whitepaper[209] in 2008. Cryptocurrency has been in the news a lot of times for all the wrong reasons. The most common objection is that Bitcoin mining, and other cryptos based on proofs of useless work[210] protocols are harmful to the environment.

TABLE II: Ranking of Bitcoin and Ethereum among countries based on annual carbon footprint as of July 2021 [23, 26, 27, 30].

Rank	Country	Population (Millions) [26]	Emission ($MtCO_2$)	Share (%)
0	World	7,878.2	37,077.40	100.00
1	China	1,444.9	10,060.00	27.13
2	U.S.A	332.9	5410.00	14.59
3	India	1,336.4	2,300.00	6.2
38	Nigeria	211.3	104.30	0.28
39	Czech Republic	10.7	100.80	0.27
40	Belgium	11.6	91.20	0.24
41	Bitcoin + Ethereum	N.A.	90.31	0.24
42	Kuwait	4.3	87.80	0.23
43	Qatar	2.9	87.00	0.23
49	Oman	5.2	68.80	0.18
50	Bitcoin	N.A.	64.18	0.17
51	Greece	10.3	61.60	0.16
76	Tunisia	11.94	26.20	0.07
77	Ethereum	N.A.	26.13	0.07
78	SAR	17.9	25.80	0.06

Figure 7. Table from Cornel University Paper

According to a paper[211] published by Cornell University, Bitcoin and Ethereum's combined carbon footprint would rank 41st in the world.

---

[206] Take the green blockchain to the next level with Cardano, finance.yahoo.com/news/green-blockchain-next-level-cardano-192654597.html

[207] Could Cardano's 'green' cryptocurrency ADA take over Bitcoin and Ethereum?, euronews.com/next/2021/08/23/could-cardano-s-green-cryptocurrency-ada-take-over-bitcoin-and-etherium

[208] What is Cardano? The 'green' crypto that defied Musk's bitcoin crash – and hopes to surpass Facebook and Netflix, independent.co.uk/space/cardano-crypto-bitcoin-elon-musk-b1849021.html

[209] Satoshi Nakamoto, 'Bitcoin: A Peer-to-Peer Electronic Cash System', bitcoin.org/bitcoin.pdf

[210] Dotan and Tochner, 'Proofs of Useless Work: Positive and Negative Results for Wasteless Mining Systems', arxiv.org/pdf/2007.01046.pdf

[211] An Analysis of Energy Consumption and Carbon Footprints of Cryptocurrencies and Possible Solutions, arxiv.org/pdf/2203.03717.pdf

Algorithms for mining take a lot of power. This problem was exacerbated until recently by the fact that 70% of mining took place in China, where energy is generated using fossil fuels, notably coal. A crackdown by Chinese authorities has resulted in a crypto mining migration, which only shifted the issue to other nations. And the problem has ramifications in other areas. Concerns over energy use, for example, led to the banning of mining in Inner Mongolia.[212]

Bitcoin's proof-of-work algorithm is it's Achilles heel, yet essential to its operation. Mining rigs that are powerful and state-of-the-art create higher yields, but the quicker they are, the more energy they use. This raises the issue of long-term viability. According to a recent article on the Ethereum Foundation blog,[213] 'Ethereum's power-hungry days are limited,' and that the long-awaited switch to proof of stake would require 99.95% less energy.[214] 'The Merge' finally took place in September 2022, however, the move to proof-of-stake has been anything but smooth with stakes locked up indefinitely and centralization concerns.[215] It's also just the first step on a convoluted roadmap to Eth 2.0. Since 'the Merge' was delayed for several years, it's difficult to forecast when the rest of the roadmap will happen.

As Ethereum's proof of work miners were effectively fired as a result of 'the Merge', an interesting discussion is 'When Ethereum goes Proof of Stake, is Ergo likely to absorb most of the hash power?'[216]

But what distinguishes proof of stake from other blockchains in terms of environmental impact? Because miners must answer increasingly sophisticated mathematical problems to produce blocks, proof of work is resource intensive. They're on a high-energy race across the world to solve meaningless, randomly generated problems. This vast amount of computing power might be put to better use like programming wind turbines or solar cells. This PoUW (Proof-of-useful-work) paper[217] discusses alternatives to proof of work. This squandered digital effort has real-world ramifications.

The need for powerful hardware creates a further issue: e-waste. Miners must continually stay up with their competitors, which necessitates the purchase of increasingly powerful mining equipment. 'Old' equipment, which is typically only fit for mining, soon becomes outdated. It is wasted, and Bitcoin's e-waste is a growing problem. Because only 20% of electronic trash is recycled worldwide, the rigs' plastics and dangerous elements, such as

---

[212] Major bitcoin mining region in China sets tough penalties for cryptocurrency activities, cnbc.com/2021/05/26/major-china-bitcoin-mining-hub-lays-out-harsher-crackdown-measures.html

[213] Ethereum's energy usage will soon decrease by ~99.95%, blog.ethereum.org/2021/05/18/country-power-no-more/

[214] This breakthrough could make Ethereum more environmentally friendly than Bitcoin, fortune.com/2021/05/24/ethereum-bitcoin-buterin-carbon-footprint-proof-of-stake/

[215] What Does the Ethereum Merge Mean for Crypto?, builtin.com/blockchain/ethereum-merge

[216] Roundtable with Charles Hoskinson and Alex Chepurnoy | Ergo Pulse, youtu.be/k9a3SYV6FJA?t=3182

[217] A novel proof of useful work for a blockchain storing transportation transactions, sciencedirect.com/science/article/pii/S0306457321002302

heavy metals, may wind up in landfills. By 2050, the United Nations predicts that the globe will create up to 120m tons of e-waste each year. This paper 'Bitcoin's growing e-waste problem'[218] goes into greater detail.

So why is Cardano being dubbed the 'green blockchain'? Cardano offers two distinct benefits when it comes to sustainability and environmentally friendly cryptocurrencies: considerably reduced energy use and staking. Network users run nodes in proof of stake, and the chain chooses a node to add the next block depending on the stake and other attributes of the node. The fundamental difference between these two algorithms (and hence their energy needs) is that block producers in proof of stake do not need to spend a lot of time and compute power solving random problems. Cardano's energy consumption is projected to be 0.01% of Bitcoin's.[219]

In a meaningless, energy-intensive arms race, proof-of-work cryptos need compute power to create blocks. A Cardano node, on the other hand, may operate on a low-power CPU like a Raspberry Pi. More than 40 million of these have been created, many of which are destined for schools in underdeveloped nations due to their low cost of $40-$70. This simplicity also cuts down on plastic and electronic waste.

Extreme weather and forest fires seem to increase each year, with the warnings from UN Climate reports becoming starker and starker. The latest report in April 2022[220] insists it's 'now or never'. Society is aware of deforestation, ice shelf depletion, and global warming. Heatwaves are wreaking havoc on the ecosystem in many regions of the globe, and forest fires are ravaging numerous places. As a result, everything that contributes to the sustainability issue is scrutinized. This encompasses the expanding cryptocurrency market.

When it comes to solving environmental issues, there are no simple solutions. Cardano is a decentralized platform that can replace older and legacy systems' inefficiencies. Cardano, and other proof-of-stake protocols, are considered to be contributing to the solution because of their sustainability credentials.

Although Cardano is a proof-of-stake blockchain and the focus of much of IOG's work, they do research other protocols and have published extensively on Proof of work also. Their latest paper[221] *Ofelimos: Combinatorial Optimization via Proof-of-Useful-Work: A Provably Secure Blockchain Protocol* was presented at Crypto 2022.

---

[218] Bitcoin's growing e-waste problem, sciencedirect.com/science/article/abs/pii/S0921344921005103

[219] What is Cardano? The 'green' crypto that defied Musk's bitcoin crash – and hopes to surpass Facebook and Netflix, independent.co.uk/life-style/gadgets-and-tech/cardano-crypto-bitcoin-elon-musk-b1849021.html

[220] UN climate report: It's 'now or never' to limit global warming to 1.5 degrees, news.un.org/en/story/2022/04/1115452

[221] Fitzi, Kiayias, Panagiotakos, Russell (2022), 'Ofelimos: Combinatorial Optimization via Proof-of-Useful-Work: A Provably Secure Blockchain Protocol', iohk.io/en/research/library/papers/ofelimos-combinatorial-optimization-via-proof-of-useful-work-a-provably-secure-blockchain-protocol/

Philosophy of POS

Decentralization is arguably Cardano's most important and fundamental goal. The basis of every blockchain is protocols and parameters. However, the community itself, how it perceives itself, acts, and establishes shared norms, is a major influence on the project's success. Cardano has been meticulously architected to have 'by design' all of the qualities required for a successful blockchain system. Cardano is a social construct, and as such, adherence, interpretation, and social conventions all have a part in determining its robustness and long-term viability.

Staking Principles

Since the debut of the Bitcoin blockchain, consensus-based on a *resource* that is disseminated over a population of users – rather than identity-based participation – has been the hallmark of the blockchain ecosystem. Proof-of-stake systems are distinct in this space because they employ a *virtual resource* called stake that is recorded in the blockchain itself.

Pooling resources for participation is unavoidable; some amount of pooling is generally advantageous in terms of economics; therefore resource holders will find a means to make it happen. Given this inevitability, the challenge is then to avoid the emergence of a dictatorship, large entity, or oligarchy[222] controlling too much stake.

Goal of Staking Rewards System

Unlike previous blockchain systems, Cardano employs a reward sharing mechanism that (a) permits staking without unnecessary inconvenience and (b) incentivizes resource pooling in such a manner that system-wide decentralization develops spontaneously through resource holders' rational engagement.

The mechanism's two main goals are as follows:

- Involve all stakeholders - The more people who are involved in the system, the more secure the distributed ledger becomes. This also means that the system should have no participation barriers and should not cause friction by necessitating off-chain coordination amongst stakeholders to participate with the mechanism.

- Keep individual stakeholders' power to a minimum - For certain stakeholders, pooling resources increases their influence. The power of pool operators on the system is proportional to the resources managed by their pool, not to their own. Without pooling, all resource holders have a leverage of one. The stronger the system's leverage, the less secure it is (a 51% attack[223] on the system is more likely).

---

[222] **Oligarchy**, meaning 'few', and 'to rule or to command', is a form of power structure in which power rests with a small number of people.

A large pool size is not the sole cause of increased leverage; stakeholders may also gain leverage by forming several pools, either publicly or secretly (known as a Sybil attack[224]). The greater the degree of decentralization of a blockchain system, the lesser its leverage.

From Theory to Practice

So, how does Cardano's reward-sharing mechanism achieve the aforementioned goals? Staking with Cardano allows for two options: pledging[225] and delegating. Stake pool operators use pledged stake; pledged stake is committed to a stake pool and is expected to remain there for the duration of the pool's operation. Consider pledge to be a 'commitment' to the network. It's a way to 'lock up' a specific amount of stake to help protect and secure the protocol.

Delegating, on the other hand, is for individuals who don't want to be hands-on. Instead, individuals are encouraged to evaluate the stake pool operators' offers and delegate their stake to one or more pools that, in their judgment, best serve their and the community's interests. There is no reason to refrain from staking in Cardano since delegation does not involve the locking up of money; all stakeholders are welcome to do so. This is not a given with other proof-of-stake blockchains.

For example, with Polkadot,[226] your funds are 'bonded', which is a fancy word for 'locked'. It takes a full 28 days to 'unbond' or 'unlock' your funds. That is generous compared to Ethereum, where stakers may not be able to withdraw staked Ether until the *Shanghai* (Sept 2023) upgrade or later. Staking on Cardano is non-custodial, so there are no slashing[227] penalties imposed. As a delegator, your staked funds are never at risk of being taken by the SPO, significantly adding to delegator participation.

Cardano's incentive model is based on Nash equilibrium.[228] The idea is that when stake pool operators and delegators are properly incentivized, then a Nash equilibrium will be reached based on their rational and honest behavior. The goal of the incentive mechanism is to achieve a high level of decentralization, security and participation.

---

[223] A **51% attack** is a hostile takeover of a Cryptocurrency validated via proof-of-work Algorithms through the acquisition of the majority of the network's hashing power.

[224] In a **Sybil attack**, the attacker subverts the reputation system of a peer-to-peer network by creating a large number of pseudonymous identities and uses them to gain a disproportionately large influence. It is named after the subject of the book *Sybil*, a case study of a woman diagnosed with dissociative identity disorder.

[225] **Pledging**: when a stake pool operator assigns their own ada stake to support their stake pool. This provides protection against Sybil attacks by preventing pool owners from creating a large number of pools without themselves owning a lot of stake.

[226] Polkadot staking, wiki.polkadot.network/docs/learn-staking

[227] **Slashing** is a mechanism used by PoS protocols to discourage harmful behaviors and make validators more responsible. They help keep the network secure since, without slashing penalties, a validator can use the same node to validate blocks on multiple chains or do so on the wrong chain.

[228] **Nash equilibrium** is used in game theory for modeling and defining the solution in a game where players do not cooperate together.

Two parameters, *k* and *a0* (/*a naught*/), are crucial to the mechanism's operation. Pool rewards are limited to 1/k of the amount available thanks to the k-parameter. Adding X amount of pledge to a pool boosts its rewards by up to a0*X, thanks to the *a0* option. This isn't at the expense of other pools; any rewards that go unclaimed due to inadequate pledging will be restored to Cardano's reserves and distributed in the future.

Creating a stake pool necessitates operators (aka stake pool operators, aka SPOs) declaring their profit margin[229] and operating expenditures[230] in addition to agreeing on an amount to pledge. The operating expenses are withheld first when the pool payouts are distributed at the conclusion of each epoch, ensuring that stake pools stay sustainable. Following that, the operator profit is determined, and all pool delegators are compensated in accordance with their investment.

This approach, when combined with the delegates' evaluation of stake pools, offers the correct set of restrictions for the system to converge to a configuration of k equal-sized pools with the largest amount of pledge.

Cardano's blockchain architecture, like many others, has an innovative and well-researched mechanism. The rewards system has been mathematically shown to provide an equilibrium that matches its goals. But, in the end, arithmetic alone will not be enough; only humans will be able to make it happen. The future of Cardano lies in the hands of the community.

Stake Pool Personas

A stake pool is a server node that aggregates and maintains the stakes of several stakeholders into a single entity. Stake pools oversee transaction processing and block production, and they monitor their interactions with the network via the Cardano node.

To manage a stake pool effectively, you'll need a stake pool operator and one or more stake pool owners. There are conceptual differences between these two jobs:

- A stake pool operator is in charge of setting up and managing the stake pool, which means they own or rent a server, manage and monitor the node, and have access to the stake pool. Stake pool operators may sign blocks, register, re-register, and retire stake pools, as well as upload updated certificates, using their key

---

[229] **Profit margin**: The stake pool operator takes a portion of total ada rewards before dividing the remainder of the rewards with all of the pool's delegators. If the operator's profit margin is low, they're taking less risks, which means delegators should anticipate reaping more of the rewards for their delegated stake. A private pool is one with a profit margin of 100%, indicating that the operator receives all of the rewards and the delegators get none.

[230] **cost per epoch:** The stake pool operator deducts a predetermined charge from the pool payouts every epoch to cover the expenses of maintaining a stake pool. Before the operator collects their profit margin, the cost per epoch is removed from the total ada that is awarded to a pool. Whatever is left is divided evenly among the delegators.

- A stake pool owner is someone who offers their stake to the pool to boost the pool's reward earning capability and appeal. Sybil attacks are mitigated by the owner's capacity to pledge stake.

The stake pool operator and owner are normally the same person, although a stake pool might have several owners who commit their share to establish a larger pool and maintain it competitively. Stake pool activities are still managed by a single stake pool operator in this case.

The stake pool operator must have the trust of all stake pool owners. All operator and owner rewards are placed into a single shared reward account linked to the pool's reward address, and the protocol distributes them among the owner accounts. The reasoning for this is because if everyone could become a co-owner of a stake pool rather than delegating, the process would be rendered obsolete.

It's advisable to have a contract to specify when and how the collected incentives in a shared account should be divided. They can, for example, agree to have the operator manage the shared account, or they can use a multisig[231] account.

A bidirectional relationship and trust are required to run a pool properly. If this trust is betrayed, other parties may suffer losses in terms of accumulated or projected benefits, as well as the operator's reputation.

The **controlled stake** is the entire amount of stake held by a stake pool. It combines the pool operator's stake and any stakes that have been delegated to the pool by other ada holders. It may be expressed as a total quantity of ada (e.g., 2M ada) or as a percentage of the network's total ada supply (e.g., 2%).

Setting up and running a stake pool

Stake pools are an important aspect of the decentralized Cardano network, since they enable the procedures that assure the network's long-term health and viability. Stake pool operators allow other users to participate in the system and earn rewards without having to host an active node all of the time. The scope of this book is to address the theoretical. More in-depth practical details are out of scope and covered in the following Cardano documentation sections:

- Creating a stake pool[232]
- Establishing connectivity between core and relay nodes[233]

---

[231] **Multisignature** (multi-signature) is a digital signature scheme which allows a group of users to sign a single document. Usually, a multisignature algorithm produces a joint signature that is more compact than a collection of distinct signatures from all users. Multisignature can be considered as generalization of both group and ring signatures providing additional security for cryptocurrency transactions.

[232] Creating a stake pool, docs.cardano.org/getting-started/operating-a-stake-pool/creating-a-stake-pool

- Operational certificates and keys[234]
- Public stake pools and metadata management[235]
- SMASH metadata management[236]
- Stake pool performance[237]
- Stake pool ranking[238]

Cardano network

Federated nodes were solely responsible for block production and network connectivity in the Byron era. The Byron network was made up of federated core nodes, which were static nodes that created blocks and kept the Cardano network running. With the launch of Shelley, the network transitioned to a hybrid mode, with IOG-operated federated nodes (which configure connection between various stake pool operators) and SPO (stake pool operator)-operated nodes. The percentage of blocks produced by decentralized nodes steadily increased, while federated nodes progressively ceased operations, distributing network maintenance equitably across all stake pool operators. Using ongoing automated discovery and selection of peers, Shelley's network migrated to complete decentralization.

Nodes linked to other nodes using a static configuration established in a topology file during the startup phase. It is critical to connect to dependable relay nodes to avoid a situation where relay nodes fall offline, rendering block-producing nodes unreachable. IOG provided SPOs with a list of all registered relays[239] organized by geographical location for connecting reasons. SPOs should additionally produce a configuration that includes 20 other SPOs as peers. Many SPOs can employ more than 20 peers for connection reasons in practice. The list lets you choose peers both close and far away, ensuring inter-region connection.

The node's network layer was altered to employ continuous automated discovery and peer selection as the network was shifted from federated to completely decentralized. Upgrades to the network stack were used to accomplish this. Initially, this allowed for enhanced automation of connecting SPO relays to one another, reducing the requirement

---

[233] Establishing connectivity between the nodes, docs.cardano.org/getting-started/operating-a-stake-pool/node-connectivity

[234] Operational certificates and keys, docs.cardano.org/getting-started/operating-a-stake-pool/creating-keys-and-certificates

[235] Public stake pools and metadata management, docs.cardano.org/getting-started/operating-a-stake-pool/public-stake-pools

[236] SMASH metadata management, docs.cardano.org/getting-started/operating-a-stake-pool/SMASH

[237] Stake pool performance, docs.cardano.org/getting-started/operating-a-stake-pool/performance

[238] Stake pool ranking, docs.cardano.org/getting-started/operating-a-stake-pool/ranking

[239] List of registered relays, explorer.cardano-mainnet.iohk.io/relays/topology.json

for static setup. It will eventually allow all Cardano nodes to have a full peer-to-peer (P2P)[240] architecture, eliminating the network's need for IOG-run relays.

More information regarding the Cardano network, node communication, and mini protocols that allow this capability may be found in the docs.[241]

Core and Relay Node Connections

As a stake pool operator, you are concerned with two node types: core nodes and relay nodes. One or more relay nodes must accompany each core node. Core nodes are in charge of creating blocks, whilst relays are in charge of connecting with other relays in the network as well as broadcasting blocks. This distinction influences how they are set up and linked to the network.

For block generation, a core node is set up with several key pairs[242] and an operational certificate. It only communicates with the relay nodes it has set up.

Instructions to configure a node and create an operational certificate:

- About node configuration files[243]
- Configuring topology files for block-producing and relay nodes[244]
- Creating an operational certificate with key evolving signature (KES)[245]

Because a relay node does not need any keys, it is unable to create blocks. It communicates with its core node, relays, and external nodes.

---

[240] **Peer-to-peer (P2P):** distributed application architecture that partitions tasks or workloads between peers. Peers are equally privileged, equipotent participants in the application. They are said to form a peer-to-peer network of nodes. In Cardano this involves sending transactions (or files) directly between nodes in a decentralized system without relying on a centralized authority.

[241] About the Cardano network, docs.cardano.org/explore-cardano/cardano-network/about-the-cardano-network

[242] **Key pair:** Public-key cryptography, or asymmetric cryptography, is a cryptographic system that uses pairs of keys: public keys which may be disseminated widely, and private keys which are known only to the owner. The generation of such keys depends on cryptographic algorithms based on mathematical problems to produce one-way functions. Effective security only requires keeping the private key private; the public key can be openly distributed without compromising security. Within the blockchain, these keys are used to process and authorize transactions.

[243] About node configuration files, github.com/input-output-hk/cardano-node/blob/master/doc/getting-started/understanding-config-files.md

[244] Configuring topology files for block-producing and relay nodes, github.com/input-output-hk/cardano-node/blob/master/doc/stake-pool-operations/core_relay.md

[245] Creating an operational certificate with key evolving signature (KES), github.com/input-output-hk/cardano-node/blob/master/doc/stake-pool-operations/KES_period.md

Each node should operate on its own server, with the firewall on the core node server set to only accept connections from its relays.

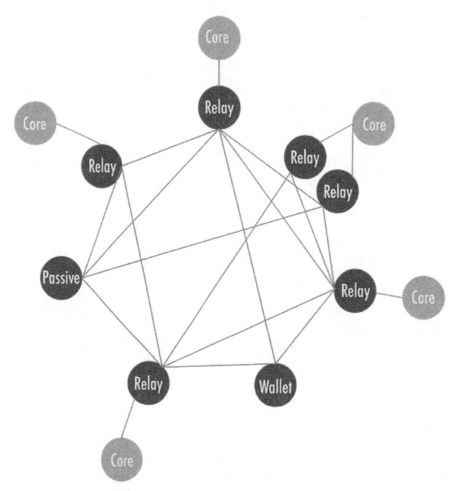

Figure 8: Core and Relay nodes

How to Research Stake Pools

SPOs (Stake pool operators) may be interested in getting specific information regarding their pools' activities after a successful stake pool registration and operation. pooltool.io, which gives confirmed stake pool facts, may be used to get information about those pools that are active on mainnet.[246]

---

[246] **Mainnet**: The blockchain that has been deployed and is now in use. Assets stored on the mainnet have value, but assets held on the testnet do not.

Exchanges and stake pool operators, in particular, are on the lookout for detailed information regarding their mainnet and testnet pools in certain circumstances. It's advisable to use cardano-node, cardano-db-sync,[247] and a cardano-graphql[248] to access data stored on the Cardano blockchain.

GraphQL is an open-source data query and manipulation language for APIs, and a runtime for fulfilling queries with existing data. GraphQL was developed internally by Facebook in 2012 before being publicly released in 2015. On 7 November 2018, the GraphQL project was moved from Facebook to the newly established GraphQL Foundation, hosted by the non-profit Linux Foundation. Here is a short video I recorded explaining *GraphQL in 6 mins*.[249]

Docker[250] may be used to install and deploy each of the integration components described above.

Another alternative is the public Cardano Explorer (explorer.cardano.org), which is likewise built on the cardano-graphql instance and is often used by exchanges and stake pool operators who want to test stake pool functionality on testnet.[251] There are a growing number of third-party alternatives like *cexplorer.io*

Stake Pool Performance

The creation of new blocks for the Cardano network is the responsibility of a stake pool designated as a slot leader.[252] The slot will stay unfilled if the stake pool does not create a block, and the blockchain will not be extended. Although the Cardano blockchain may accept a few missing blocks, the bulk of expected blocks (at least 50% + 1) must be created within an epoch. Although missing blocks do not affect the blockchain's overall extension, an unresponsive elected stake pool reduces the network's overall speed.

The ratio of the number of blocks a stake pool generates in a particular epoch versus the number it was capable of producing is used to measure stake pool performance. For example, if a stake pool could create 100 blocks in an epoch (depending on its stake and likelihood of being elected), but only produced 50 blocks, its performance would be 50%. Poor stake pool performance reduces the quantity of rewards received by a pool and its

---

[247] cardano-db-sync, github.com/input-output-hk/cardano-db-sync

[248] cardano-graphql, github.com/input-output-hk/cardano-graphql

[249] GraphQL in 6 mins, youtube.com/watch?v=Ys-aox3oOD8

[250] **Docker** is a software tool that makes it easier to deploy applications by using 'containers', each of which holds all the parts, such as libraries, that the application needs to run.

[251] A **testnet** is an alternative blockchain used by software developers to check that their code runs properly before they make possibly costly deployments to a **mainnet**. The testnet uses identical technology and software as the 'mainnet' blockchain, in other words a parallel network, except the testnet doesn't make 'actual' transactions with 'value' and is intended for testing purposes. Testnet coins are distinct from actual coins on a mainnet, as testnet coins do not have any monetary value.

[252] Slot leader, developers.cardano.org/docs/stake-pool-course/introduction-to-cardano/

members, making it less appealing to delegators. A stake pool should have adequate network connectivity, be run on a dependable system, and engage in block generation and verification to increase its performance.

The stronger the pool's performance, the more appealing it will be to delegators, since higher rewards will be offered. Setting up and running a stake pool is not too challenging from a technical perspective. Marketing and attracting delegation to your pool is a competitive sport.

Ranking Stake Pools

Stake pools are ranked in the Daedalus wallet and Cardano Explorer depending on the amount of rewards users will get if they opt to delegate to them. The ranking indicates the saturation[253] level of the pool, making pool selection easier. From the standpoint of a delegator, once a pool reaches a specific saturation threshold, delegating to it is no longer profitable. The most desirable stake pools are shown first, and they are sorted from top to bottom.

The ranking system is intended to let users pick the best stake pool for a greater return on investment (ROI), so that dependable stake pool owners can keep the system running and maximize decentralization.

Ranking parameters

The cost and margin of a pool, as well as the pool's performance and the amount of stake it has previously attracted, all factor towards its rating. These variables encourage the creation of dependable stake pools that are not yet saturated and provide low cost and margin.

The Cardano Docs includes guidelines for operating large stake pools[254]

Types of Addresses in Cardano

The addresses are a blake2b-256 hash of the related verifying/public keys combined with some metadata stored on the Cardano blockchain.

Shelley introduced four different types of addresses:

---

[253] **Saturation**: a word that refers to a stake pool that has more stake delegated to it than is optimal for the network. The saturation level is expressed as a percentage. When a stake pool achieves 100% saturation, the rewards start to shrink. The saturation mechanism was created to avoid centralization by encouraging delegators to delegate to multiple stake pools and operators to build up alternative pools in order to keep receiving maximum rewards. Saturation aims to safeguard both the interests of ada holders delegating their stake and the interests of stake pool operators.

[254] Guidelines for large SPOs, github.com/input-output-hk/cardano-documentation/blob/staging/content/02-getting-started/04-guidelines-for-large-spos.mdx

- base addresses
- pointer addresses
- enterprise addresses
- reward account addresses

Aside from those addresses, Byron-era bootstrap[255] and script addresses are still supported by Shelley. Only the new base and pointer addresses have stake rights. Addresses, such as a UTXO[256] address, are made up of serialized data described in the ledger specification stored in the blocks of the blockchain.

There are two pieces to the serialized data (address):

- Metadata for interpreting.
- Payload: raw or encoded data

Base Address

The staking key that should manage the stake for that address is explicitly specified in a base address. The owner of the staking key can exercise the staking rights connected with funds kept at this address. Without first registering the staking key, base addresses may be used in transactions. Only by registering the stake key and delegating to a stake pool[257] can the stake rights be exercised. After the stake key has been registered, stake rights can be exercised for base addresses used in transactions before or after the key registration.

Pointer Address

A pointer address indirectly specifies the staking key that should control the stake for the address. They are quite nuanced, and their practical use is open to question. They are not discussed in detail here because they are not intuitive to understand, but also because removing pointer addresses is a dependency for implementing a future version of Ouroboros. To dig into the technical reasoning, see the ongoing discussion on *CPS-0002 Pointer Address Removal*.[258] CPS stands for 'Cardano Problem Statement,' a governance mechanism for proposing change. More on this later.

Enterprise Address

Because enterprise addresses don't come with stake rights, adopting them implies you're opting out of the proof-of-stake protocol. Stake rights may not be exercised by exchanges

---

[255] In general, **bootstrapping** usually refers to a self-starting process that is supposed to proceed without external input. In computer technology the term (usually shortened to booting) usually refers to the process of loading the basic software into the memory of a computer after power-on or general reset, especially the operating system which will then take care of loading other software as needed.

[256] An **unspent transaction output (UTXO)** is the technical term for the amount of digital currency that remains after a cryptocurrency transaction.

[257] Stake Pools, docs.cardano.org/core-concepts/stake-pools

[258] CPS-0002 Pointer Address Removal, github.com/cardano-foundation/CIPs/pull/374

or other entities that control substantial quantities of ada on behalf of other users. Exchanges may indicate that they observe this guideline by utilizing enterprise addresses. Enterprise addresses are automatically removed from the process that determines the slot leadership schedule since they are not connected with any staking key. Employing addresses with no stake rights reduces the overall amount of stake, which aids a prospective attack.

Reward Account Address

A reward address[259] is a cryptographic hash of the address's public staking key. To pay rewards for participating in the proof-of-stake protocol, reward account addresses are used (directly or via delegation).

They possess the following characteristics:

- Account-style accounting is employed rather than UTXO-style
- Transactions cannot be used to receive funds. Instead, when rewards are paid, their balance[260] is just raised
- Registered staking keys and reward account addresses have a one-to-one relationship.

When funds are removed from the address, this key is used. Additionally, the stake connected with the funds in the address contributes to the stake of this key. The staking object for a reward address does not have to include any information, just as with enterprise addresses.

Pledging

Decentralization became a point of contention as Shelley approached on the Cardano mainnet. Proof-of-work cryptocurrencies like Bitcoin have grown increasingly centralized over time, regardless of their original founding aim. The days of Bitcoin fanatics mining blocks on AWS EC2 spot instances[261] are long gone, and today's mining networks are dominated by a tiny handful of specialized, professional mining companies.

This isn't inherently a negative thing in and of itself, but it would go against Cardano's idea of a decentralized, proof-of-stake system if it occurred. Cardano was built from the bottom up with decentralization in mind, especially in terms of stake delegation and

---

[259] **Rewards Wallet:** a wallet that contains ada and may be used to delegate stakes. A stake may only be delegated to a single stake pool from a single Rewards wallet. You'll need to construct numerous Rewards wallets and divide ada across them if you want to delegate to more than one stake pool. Split pool delegation has been promised by IOG for some time but has been postponed, to allow focusing resources on other roadmap priorities.

[260] **Balance wallet:** your original testnet ada balance, copied from the mainnet through the balance snapshot, is stored in this wallet. This wallet's stake is not transferable, although it may be moved to and delegated from a Rewards wallet.

[261] Can we use AWS spot instances for guaranteed mining profits?, stackoverflow.com/questions/51665962/can-we-use-aws-spot-instances-for-guaranteed-mining-profits

reward systems. Pools larger than a certain size will not be competitive on the Cardano network, and delegation rewards for everyone will be ideal when there are numerous medium-sized pools. Diversity is beneficial to all ecosystems. Similarly, this method strikes the optimal mix between promoting grassroots participation from experienced community members and assisting individuals looking to start commercial stake pool firms.

How Pledging Works

A pool operator might pledge a personal investment in their pool upon registration to make it more appealing. The pledged sum may be modified epoch by epoch and will be refunded when the pool closes.

On the Cardano blockchain, anybody may run a pool. There is no minimum pledge. To make their pool more appealing, pool managers might pledge some or all of their stake to the pool. The more ada pledged, the more rewards will be given to the pool, which will attract more delegators.

It's also worth noting that there's also no maximum pledge, so a pool operator with a lot of ada to stake may maximize their own profits by filling up the pool with pledges and avoiding attracting any delegation. Of course, only a few operators will be able to do so; most will attempt to entice delegation with a mix of pledge, cheap costs, low profit-taking, and strong performance.

The appeal of a pool to delegators is determined by four interconnected factors:

- operating costs (lower the better)
- operator margin (lower the better)
- performance (higher the better)
- pledge (higher the better).

The pool operator might request a bigger operator margin while remaining desirable to delegators by offering a larger pledge.

Pledging rewards

Given two similar stake pools, the one with the higher pledge will receive more rewards and hence be more appealing to other delegators. The SPO (Stake pool operator) or other pool owners should work together to fulfill the pledge by delegating themselves. It's also crucial to make sure there's enough funds in the accounts that utilize the pool owner's address(es) as stake reference. Failure to meet the pledge will result in no rewards for the pool being earned by any owner or delegators. This will almost always result in a loss of delegation and, in the worst-case scenario, pool collapse.

Unlike delegation, the SPO is in charge of all pledge rewards distribution. This may be done in any way that is mutually agreed upon and is not governed by the blockchain.

Why do we need pledging?

Pledging on the Cardano blockchain is a technique for promoting a healthy economic environment. The pledge mechanism is also required to prevent Sybil attacks[262] on the system. In such an attack, someone with very little personal stake establishes hundreds or thousands of pools with tiny margins and attempts to draw the bulk of stake to their pools. They can influence consensus and engage in double-spending[263] attacks, create forks, censor blocks, and harm or even collapse the system if this succeeds. Such attacks are stopped by making pools with greater pledges more appealing, since an attacker must now divide their stake over many pools, making those pools less desirable and raising the inherent cost of executing a Sybil attack.

How to measure the impact of Pledging

Prior to the launch of Shelley on the Cardano mainnet, the parameter that affects pledging needed to be set. The parameter was created to be flexible and adaptable over time. The Shelley Haskell testnet[264] was an excellent resource for fine-tuning this parameter and determining which values worked and which didn't. IOG also created a calculator[265] to assist pool operators estimate alternative pledge quantities and figure out how delegation could be affected.

Reasonable values are determined by a variety of variables, including: What percentage of a pool operator's interest does he or she own? How much does it cost to run a node? How many people want to run a staking pool? During the Incentivized Testnet, a lot of data was acquired.

IOG is committed to the scientific approach and that their architecture will result in a decentralized, stable, and secure blockchain— yet science and mathematics can only take you so far. Modeling assumptions must always be made, and no model will ever be as complex and colorful as what happens in practice.

On Reddit[266] and on a 'Cardano Effect' episode,[267] there was heated discussion on the matter. The Shelley Haskell testnets provided the ideal environment for continued debate.

---

[262] Lars Brünjes, 'Preventing sybil attacks', iohk.io/en/blog/posts/2018/10/29/preventing-sybil-attacks/

[263] **Double-spending** is a potential flaw in a digital cash scheme in which the same single digital token can be spent more than once. Unlike physical cash, a digital token consists of a digital file that can be duplicated or falsified. As with counterfeit money, such double-spending leads to inflation by creating a new amount of copied currency that did not previously exist. This devalues the currency relative to other monetary units or goods and diminishes user trust as well as the circulation and retention of the currency. Fundamental cryptographic techniques to prevent double-spending, while preserving anonymity in a transaction, are blind signatures and, particularly in offline systems, secret splitting.

[264] Kevin Hammond, 'From Byron to Shelley: Part one, the testnets', iohk.io/en/blog/posts/2020/04/29/from-byron-to-shelley-part-one-the-testnets/

[265] Cardano Calculator, cardano.org/calculator/?calculator=operator

[266] Cardano Mainnet: Pledge Influence Factor Analysis, reddit.com/r/cardano/comments/gfed1l/cardano_mainnet_pledge_influence_factor_analysis/

[267] Pledge Influence Factors, Effects on Operators and Stakers, with Umed Saidov | TCE 88, youtube.com/watch?v=ubWIytFZYGE

IOG evaluated, iterated and cooperated with stake pool managers to determine what is best for everyone. IOG enlisted the community's support to put their findings into effect, much as they did with the Incentivized Testnet and Daedalus Flight[268] user testing.[269]

Delegation

The practice of assigning individual stakeholders' ada to collective stake pools is known as stake delegation. Delegation is used in block production to guarantee that the block is created in accordance with the proof-of-stake consensus. Stakeholders do not transfer stake ownership, voting rights, or other rights when they delegate.

To maintain confidence in the blockchain, large SPOs will often own a considerable amount of third-party stake, making them accountable for:

- block production
- transaction processing
- Cardano network maintenance
- ensuring the owner makes a pledge
- pool security (protecting its private keys.etc)
- updating the community about anything related to the pool.

The blockchain handles the distribution of block production rewards to delegators, so large operators aren't concerned with it. SPOs are also not in charge of procuring delegated keys or acting on behalf of stakeholders in terms of delegation, voting, or other activities. Individual stakeholders must assume personal responsibility for their own security and make their own judgments on delegation, voting, and other matters.

Because Cardano is a proof-of-stake system, having ada gives you the right, and duty, to participate in the protocol and build blocks in addition to allowing you to purchase products and services. Delegation of stake is a technique built into the Cardano proof-of-stake (PoS) protocol that enables it to grow even in the face of a widely dispersed group of stakeholders.

Anyone with ada may take part in the stake delegation process while keeping their spending power. Note that regardless of how you delegated your ada, you may spend it at any stage. In each epoch, the protocol allows stakeholders to engage in the slot leader election process.

Stake delegation creates 'stake pools,' which function similarly to the Bitcoin protocol's mining pools. When they are chosen as slot leaders, stake pool operators must be online in order to create blocks.

Stake delegation requirements

---

[268] **Daedalus Flight** is a 'pre-release' version of the Daedalus wallet.

[269] Anthony Quinn, 'We need you for a Daedalus testing program!', iohk.io/en/blog/posts/2020/04/01/we-need-you-for-the-daedalus-flight-testing-program/

Delegating stake involves uploading of two certificates to the chain: a staking address registration and a delegation certificate. Because posting certificates necessitates funds, a user who is just getting started with their wallet needs a bootstrapping method. This approach is based on the ability of base addresses using staking keys before publishing the key's registration certificate. The stake address can be based on a single key or a script like multi-sig.

Delegation Scheme

With the notion of delegation, any stakeholder may authorize a stake pool to create blocks for the Cardano network, and the protocol will subsequently distribute the rewards to all participants, including the stake pool operators' fees. A stakeholder is assigned to a specific pool ID, which is a hash of the operator's verification key.

The stakeholder may restrict the proxy signing key's[270] valid message space to strings ending with a slot number in a certain range of values to limit the delegate's block generating capability to a specific range of epochs and slots. Due to the verifiability and abuse prevention qualities of proxy signature[271] schemes, this basic scheme is reliable. This guarantees that every stakeholder can verify that a proxy signing key was granted to a particular delegate by that stakeholder and that the delegate may only use these keys to sign messages inside the key's valid message space.

A single transaction with a delegation certificate is required to post funds belonging to one staking key of a user's wallet. Only the standard transaction fees will apply. A stakeholder must pay a deposit to register a stake address, not for the stake delegation itself. After registering a stake address, the stakeholder will simply have to pay fees for their chosen delegation. During the rewards process, the stakeholders' stake will be considered part of the pool's stake.

Stake Delegation Example

Consider a user who is set to get their first ada, whether via redemption, an exchange transaction, or some other means. They'll generate a new wallet and an address for receiving the payments. This address will be a base address that will be used with a staking key created by the wallet but not yet registered on the Cardano blockchain.

---

[270] Cardano founder shares proxy keys idea to implement, coinregwatch.com/cardano-founder-shares-proxy-keys-idea-to-implement/

[271] **Proxy signature** is a special type of digital signature which allows one user (original signer) to delegate his/her signing right to another signer (proxy signer). The latter can then issue signatures on behalf of the former.

The user may then engage in staking by posting a staking key registration certificate and a delegation certificate for their staking key. Newly created addresses may be pointer addresses to the staking key registration certificate after the key has been registered.

Pledging and rewards

Pledging is a critical method for fostering the development of a healthy ecosystem on the Cardano blockchain. You may pledge part or all of your ada to a stake pool when you register it to make it more appealing to others who wish to delegate. Although pledging is not mandatory when creating a stake pool, it may make it more desirable to delegators since the bigger the quantity of ada pledged, the higher the rewards given out. The $a0$ protocol parameter specifies how the pledge affects the pool reward. There is no optimal pledge amount, it depends on the pool and personal preference. The more you pledge the higher the rewards.

Rewards Distribution

Rewards are issued to all stakeholders who have delegated to a stake pool, either their own or another pool, at the end of each epoch. The protocol generates these rewards and does not rely on the stake pool operators to administer them. There are two types of rewards:

- All transaction fees: compiled from the collection of transactions contained in a block minted (generated) in that epoch

- Monetary expansion entails determining the difference between the total and maximal supply of ada. All ada now in circulation, as well as ada held in the treasury, make up the total supply. The maximal supply refers to the most ada that can ever exist (45 billion ada). The reserve is the difference between these two amounts. A predetermined proportion of the remaining reserve is withdrawn during each epoch and used for epoch rewards and treasury, with the amount transferred to the treasury being a set percentage of the amount taken from the reserve.

IOG's chief scientist Professor Aggelos Kiayias discusses more in this *Rewards sharing and pledge on Cardano* video.[272]

Remember that the pledge is expressed (together with the cost and margin amounts) during pool registration and must be fulfilled by the pool owners who are delegating to the pool: Pool rewards for that epoch will be 0 if they collectively delegate less than the specified pledge. If the pool's operator margin is set to less than 100%, the pool will be public.

---

[272] Rewards sharing and pledge on Cardano, youtube.com/watch?v=EAzyN3H8MOA

Pledging and Delegation Options

On the Cardano network, ada reflects a user's stake in the protocol, with the amount of the stake proportional to the number of ada possessed. Cardano users may receive passive rewards for verifying blocks if they have a stake in the cryptocurrency. The quantity of ada they pledge or delegate to a stake pool determines the amount of rewards they may receive.

Ada holders have 3 options when it comes to delegating their stake:

1. They are in charge of their own stake pool.
2. Rely on third party to manage a private stake pool on their behalf, such as Kraken,[273] one of the oldest Crypto exchanges.
3. Delegate to other stake pools

See the create transaction instructions[274] for advice on how to set up a stake pool, pledge, delegate and earn ada rewards.

Stake pools must maintain high availability, which means they must be accessible to verify and produce new blocks at all times. The quantity of ada committed or delegated, as well as the number of blocks a stake pool may build in a particular epoch, determine the rewards a stake pool can get. Based on the aforementioned criteria, Ouroboros, the backbone of the Cardano protocol, elects the slot leader that grants permission to process transactions and mint new blocks.

Note: Before deploying to the mainnet, all stake pool functionality should be thoroughly tested on the testnet.

Pledging

When a stake pool is launched, the stake pool operator's pledge is the amount of ada that they 'delegate' to their own pool. The operator's commitment to maintain their pool and promote network activity can be seen in the pledge. It is not necessary to make a pledge, however it is suggested that you do so before starting the stake pool. The greater the pledge, the more rewards for the pool which is contingent on the pool's uptime and performance.

Delegation

Delegating to any stake pool accessible on the network might yield incentives for ada holders who do not have technical knowhow in operating a stake pool. The Daedalus

---

[273] Earn 4-6% Staking Cardano (ADA), Available on Kraken Now!, blog.kraken.com/post/8891/earn-4-6-staking-cardano-ada-available-on-kraken-now/

[274] Create a simple transaction, developers.cardano.org/docs/stake-pool-course/handbook/create-simple-transaction/

wallet has a user interface that lets users start delegating to any registered stake pool straight away. *Lace* light wallet (lace.io) is a more user friendly option for beginners.

Note: holders of ada and SPOs (stake pool operators) who pledge, or delegate will always have access to their ada. The rewards drop proportionately when the delegated ada is spent or withdrawn from the pool.

Rewards

For engaging in staking (either pledging or delegating), delegators earn rewards, which are immediately divided among the participants according to the rewards plan. Cardano's reward system is decentralized, meaning there is no one governing entity. Rewards are calculated by the Ouroboros protocol and generally are about 4-6% assuming you have delegated to an unsaturated stake pool. If the amount of ada delegated to a given stake pool is over a set amount, the pool is deemed to be oversaturated. The delegating tab in Daedalus will display useful stats and details on each of the stake pool delegation candidates.

Rewards are distributed each epoch to stake pools for validating blocks. In 2022, about 4% of the amount staked is distributed. The staking and rewards should not be confused with *earning interest*. Interest is a fixed sum promised to a recipient, whereas there is a random element in distributing rewards, with the onus on the ada holder to delegate to a pool that is not saturated. Pooltool.io has a column 'return on stake'; this varies between 0% and 18% for the 2,978 pools listed.

Types of Keys in Cardano

Asymmetric cryptography[275] key pairs known as keys are used for:

- Securing payments and staking certificates by signing and verifying them
- Identifying and defining addresses.

---

[275] Public-key cryptography, or asymmetric cryptography, is a cryptographic system that uses pairs of keys: public keys which may be disseminated widely, and private keys which are known only to the owner. Effective security only requires keeping the private key private; the public key can be openly distributed without compromising security.

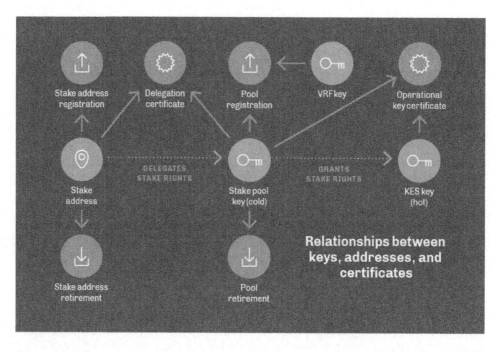

Figure 9. The link between keys, addresses, and certificates:

There are two main types of keys in Cardano:

- Node keys
- Address keys

Node Keys

The following keys make up the node keys, which constitute the blockchain's security.

- Operator/operational key
- KES key pair
- VRF keys

Operator/operational key

These are offline key pairs for operators that include a certificate counter for new certificates. The operator is responsible for managing both the hot (online) and cold (offline) keys for the pool. Cold keys must be kept secure and should not be stored on a device that has internet access. Cold key backups should be kept in several locations.

KES key pair

A Key Evolving Signature[276] (KES) key pair, which authenticates who you are, is required to establish an operational certificate for a block-producing node.

A KES key can only evolve for a set amount of time (a certain number of epochs) before becoming worthless. This is important because, even if an attacker compromises the key and has access to the signing key, he can only use it to sign blocks going forward, not blocks from previous epochs, preventing the attacker from rewriting history.

The node operator must produce a new KES key pair, issue a new operational node certificate with the new key pair, and restart the node with the new certificate when the specified number of epochs have elapsed.

VRF keys

Ouroboros Praos (Ouroboros versions are explained later, in Chapter 4) provided an additional degree of protection by using Verifiable Random Function (VRF) keys in block production. VRF makes the consensus protocol difficult to attack because it's impossible to predict the next producing nodes.

Because the slot leader schedule is known in other proof-of-stake blockchain protocols (such as Ouroboros Classic or BFT), it's known who has the authority to create the block in each slot. In this instance, you have to establish that you are who you claim you are, and anybody can verify this by looking at the public slot leader schedule. This process was subsequently improved in the Feb 2022 release,[277] with a new CLI tool for SPOs to check their own slot leadership schedule.

Ouroboros Praos' slot leader schedule, on the other hand, is kept private, which means that no one knows who the slot leader in advance will be, but once they are, they can verify to everyone else that they are using the VRF key.

The VRF key is a signature verification key that is recorded in the operating certificate. It establishes a node's permission to produce a block in a certain slot.

Address keys

The purposes of address keys are derived from the keys for identifying ada on the blockchain, which include the following keys:

- Payment key: a single address key pair that is often used to create UTXO addresses
- Staking key: a key pair consisting of a stake and a reward address that is typically used to generate account and reward addresses.

---

[276] Why use key evolving signatures, forum.cardano.org/t/why-use-key-evolving-signatures/11133/4

[277] Tim Harrison, 'From node enhancement to block leadership... Cardano's February release', iohk.io/en/blog/posts/2022/02/28/from-node-enhancement-to-block-leadership-cardano-s-february-release

Signatures

If a cryptocurrency uses a single signature scheme, it must accept the risk that the scheme may be broken in the future, and that at least one entity will be unable to utilize the cryptocurrency owing to legal or industry constraints. However, a cryptocurrency cannot support all signature schemes since each client would have to comprehend and verify each scheme.

For Cardano, IOG chose to start with elliptic curve encryption, specifically the Ed25519 curve.[278]

Cardano will enable additional signature systems post 'Vasil' hard fork. Quantum computer-resistant signatures will be included into the system. Cardano was built with specific features that enable a soft fork and the addition of new signature schemes. They will be included when required and as part of the roadmap's major releases.

March 19, 2020, in response to the US Senate bill and prose to outlaw encryption. CH:[279]

> *I think that's equivalent to the ability to outlaw gravity or to change Pi to 3. I mean people can certainly say stuff and try to do things, but you cannot enforce something as crazy as outlawing encryption ...it's like how would the internet even work? SSL (secure sockets layer)[280] is now illegal? You have to have certificate authorities ...put a man-in-the-middle attack for every single website? Does the US government enforce that? It's old people who have no clue how the internet works, or technology works, playing and fiddling with things ...and they should be in diapers instead of voting.*

Cardano RTView

RTView[281] is a real-time monitoring application that shows the status of Cardano nodes in real time. Even if the nodes are on separate computers, it offers multiple node monitoring.

Developers, testers, and end users with nodes connected to the actual cluster may use RTView to view what's going on and how the nodes are doing. It shows how much memory and CPU are being utilized, the status of the blockchain, how many blocks a specific node has forged, how many transactions have been handled, and so on.

---

[278] In public-key cryptography, Edwards-curve Digital Signature Algorithm (**EdDSA**) is a digital signature scheme using a variant of Schnorr signature based on Twisted Edwards curves. It is designed to be faster than existing digital signature schemes without sacrificing security.

[279] Surprise AMA 03/19/2020, youtu.be/9rClM2pLNmo?t=2406

[280] Transport Layer Security (TLS) and its predecessor, **Secure Sockets Layer (SSL)**, are cryptographic protocols that provide communications security over a computer network.

[281] Install RTView, github.com/input-output-hk/cardano-rt-view/blob/master/doc/getting-started/install.md/

It's a cross-platform program that works with Windows, Linux, and macOS, and it features a web-based user interface that lets you use any browser.

The key advantage of RTView is its ease of use. It's easy to set up; theoretically, there's no installation required; all you have to do is unpack the archive and run an executable. It's very straightforward to set up since it has an interactive setup popup that tells the user which modifications to make in the node configuration files. It may also be used with any browser.

How to set up RTView

Follow the installation instructions to download, unpack, and launch RTView. RTView will be launched and ready to use after you've finished these steps.

Cardano tracking tools

Because Cardano is a public blockchain ledger, many tools may be used to conveniently follow all recent transactions, block information, and epoch data.

Exploring transactions and blocks

Cardano Explorer is a user-friendly application that pulls information from the main database and displays it in an easy-to-use online interface.

By selecting a single block, you may discover more about it, including its ID, size, epoch, and block data, as well as the number of transactions and confirmations contained. You may also use the search area to look for certain epochs, transactions, or blocks by pasting their IDs.

There's a whole gamut of tools such as *cardanoscan.io*, *cexplorer.io* and many more listed under IOG's Essential Cardano,[282] the Cardano Developer Portal,[283] as well as third party sites like *CardanoCube* (cardanocube.io) and *BuiltOnCardano* (builtoncardano.com).

Exploring assets

Multi-asset generation and administration are supported by Cardano. You may use tools such as Cardano Assets (cardanoassets.com) and Cardanoscan (cardanoscan.io/tokens) to view a list of assets and tokens. Everyone has their favorite, mine is taptools.io

Exploring stake pools

---

[282] Essential Cardano, github.com/input-output-hk/essential-cardano/blob/main/essential-cardano-list.md

[283] Cardano developer portal, developers.cardano.org/showcase

You can use these tools like Adapools (adapools.org) and Pool.pm (pool.pm/search) to get a list of all active stake pools, their tickers, pool names, and IDs. IOG has created a stake pool metadata aggregation server (SMASH) to give a list of validated stake pools with proper information to the community. Smash is connected with the Daedalus wallet, and under the delegation center page, users may view a list of eligible stake pools.

Chapter 4: Shelley (Consensus)

'If winter comes, can spring be far behind?'

— Percy Bysshe Shelley

The Scalability Challenge

Distributed systems are made up of a group of servers[284] (nodes) that have agreed to execute a protocol, or a collection of protocols, to achieve a shared purpose. This objective might be as simple as distributing a file using the BitTorrent protocol,[285] or decentralized storage.[286]

As more nodes join the network, the most efficient protocols acquire resources. If several peers are simultaneously downloading a movie file provided by BitTorrent, for example, it may be downloaded substantially quicker on average. Because peers both contribute and use up resources, the speed increases. When someone says a distributed system scales, they're usually referring to this feature.

The problem with most existing blockchain protocols is that they were not built to be scalable in the first place. Blockchains, for example, are often a linked list of blocks that can only be added to. A blockchain protocol's security and availability are dependent on numerous nodes having a complete copy of the blockchain data. As a result, N nodes must copy a single bit of data. Additional nodes place a burden on resources required.

This is true for both transaction processing and gossip protocol[287] across the system. Increasing the number of nodes in the consensus system does not increase transaction processing power. It simply indicates that more resources are required to do the same task. More network relaying means that more nodes must send the same messages to keep the whole network in sync with the most recent block.

Cryptocurrencies cannot grow to a worldwide network, comparable to older financial systems, due to their structure. Legacy infrastructure, on the other hand, is scalable and can handle orders of magnitude greater processing and storage power. Bitcoin is a relatively tiny network in comparison to its payment counterparts such as Visa, Mastercard, PayPal, etc and it is currently struggling to handle its present load.

The Ouroboros consensus protocol boosts scalability for Cardano. It allows for the decentralized election of a quorum of consensus nodes, which may then execute more conventional protocols to meet the demands of huge infrastructure providers like AWS, Google and Facebook.

---

[284] A server is a computer program or device that provides a service to another computer program and its user, also known as the client.

[285] **BitTorrent** is a communication protocol for peer-to-peer (P2P) file sharing which is used to distribute data and electronic files over the Internet. BitTorrent is one of the most common protocols for transferring large files, such as digital files containing movies or music.

[286] Comparing 4 decentralized data storage offerings, techtarget.com/searchstorage/tip/Comparing-4-decentralized-data-storage-offerings

[287] A **gossip protocol** is a procedure or process of computer peer-to-peer communication that is based on the way epidemics spread. Some distributed systems use peer-to-peer gossip to ensure that data is routed to all members of an ad-hoc network. Some ad-hoc networks have no central registry and the only way to spread common data is to rely on each member to pass it along to their neighbors.

For example, electing a quorum for an epoch implies there is a trustworthy group of nodes to keep the ledger up to date for a specified length of time. It is simple to elect many quorums at the same time and divide transactions among them.

What is a Consensus Protocol?

A consensus protocol is a collection of rules and parameters that regulate the behavior of distributed ledgers: a set of rules that each network member must follow. There is no one central authority in charge of public blockchains. Instead, a consensus mechanism is employed to enable dispersed network users to agree on the network's history as recorded on the blockchain - to achieve agreement on what has occurred and proceed from a single source of truth.

A single record is provided by that one source of truth. This is why blockchains are frequently referred to as 'trustless,' since trust is built into the protocol rather than needing users to trust one another. Unknown actors may communicate and trade with one another without requiring the mediation of a third party or the sharing of personal data.

Consensus is the method through which everyone participating in the blockchain's operation comes to an agreement. There must be unanimity on which blocks to generate, which chain to use, and how to establish the network's single state. Individual nodes examine the current state of the ledger and form a consensus using the consensus protocol Ouroboros. It has three key responsibilities: doing a leader check and deciding whether a block should be created, handling chain selection, and verifying blocks that have been produced.

Blockchains achieve consensus by enabling users to group transactions submitted to the system into blocks and add them to their own chain (sequence of blocks). The objective of the various consensus protocols is to determine who is permitted to generate a block? When? …and what to do in the event of a disagreement? For example, what if two participants add different blocks at the same time? There are many different types of consensus protocols,[288] the main two being proof of work and proof of stake. Ouroboros is a consensus mechanism based on proof of stake that has been shown to have the same level of security as proof of work.

Ouroboros

Ouroboros is a mythological creature represented as a snake, or dragon, devouring its own tail in a closed circle. The name 'Ouroboros' comes from Ancient Greek and literally means 'tail eater' or 'tail devourer.'

Ouroboros is a symbol for infinity of time flowing back into itself in an endless circle, as if trapped in an unending loop. The first appearance of the Ouroboros was in Egypt in the 13th century BC. Alchemists later used Ouroboros in their mystical symbolism.

---

[288] 6 types of blockchain consensus mechanisms, essentialcardano.io/article/6-types-of-blockchain-consensus-mechanisms

Ouroboros has been understood and employed in a number of ways by many civilizations throughout history. One of the most prevalent interpretations of the symbol is that it signifies the Universe's interconnection and infinity.

Charles Hoskinson named Cardano's proof-of-stake consensus Ouroboros in 2017. In this sense, Ouroboros reflects the blockchain's potential for endless growth and scalability. The core theme of Ouroboros is the provision of expanded possibilities for the planet, as well as its preservation through drastically decreased energy usage.[289]

Ouroboros was the first blockchain consensus system to be created via peer-reviewed research as a more energy efficient and sustainable alternative to proof of work, which is the foundation of previous cryptocurrencies such as Bitcoin and, until recently, Ethereum. Ouroboros and its various iterations give a new foundation for solving some of the world's toughest issues safely and at scale.

Ouroboros ensures the security and sustainability of any blockchain that uses it by combining unique technology and mathematically validated methods (including behavioral psychology and economic philosophy ideas). Ouroboros has demonstrated to be secure and capable of facilitating the spread of global, permissionless networks with little energy consumption. Cardano is the first network of its kind. Ouroboros enables users - in this example, stake pools[290] - to establish new blocks based on the amount of stake they own in the network, and thus enables the creation of a distributed, permissionless network.

The different implementations of Ouroboros

May 25, 2020. re: Ouroboros. CH:[291]

> *So if I had to succinctly say ..'well what is Ouroboros?'... I'd say it's a first principles-based, new way of doing consensus that keeps the stuff we've come to know and love from Bitcoin, that's very useful and great, but then does it in a much more sustainable energy-friendly way, that also allows you to layer on many more utilities than just mining to the system. It does so in a way that attracts lots of competition, lots of decentralization and lots of businesses. Mining tends to centralize to a small group of actors because of economy of scale*

Ouroboros Classic

Ouroboros Classic was the first implementation released in 2017. It established the

---

[289] Fernando Sanchez, 'Why They're Calling Cardano the Green Blockchain', iohk.io/en/blog/posts/2021/08/17/why-they-re-calling-cardano-the-green-blockchain/

[290] About stake pools, docs.cardano.org/getting-started/operating-a-stake-pool/about-stake-pools

[291] Lark Davis interview, youtu.be/BptZkkNN3tw?t=575

protocol as an energy-efficient alternative to proof of work, provided a mathematical framework for analyzing proof of stake, and presented a unique incentive mechanism for proof-of-stake users.

What set Ouroboros apart from previous blockchains and other proof-of-stake protocols was its capacity to provide unbiased randomness in the protocol's leader selection method, as well as the security guarantees that came with that. Randomness prevents patterns from forming and is an important aspect of the protocol's security. When a behavior can be expected, it may be manipulated — and although Ouroboros assures transparency, it prevents coercion. Ouroboros is notable for being the first blockchain technology to undergo such thorough security testing.

The research paper on Ouroboros has in depth explanations of its functionality. The blockchain is divided into slots and epochs by Ouroboros. Each slot in Cardano lasts 1 second, and each epoch (which is a collection of slots) comprises five days' worth of slots.

The awareness that attacks are unavoidable lies at the heart of Ouroboros' design. As a result, the protocol includes tolerance to prevent attackers from spreading other copies of the blockchain, and it assumes that an opponent may transmit arbitrary messages to any member at any moment. In reality, the protocol is guaranteed to be safe as long as honest players hold more than 51% of the stake.

Each slot has a slot leader who oversees adding blocks to the chain and passing them on to the next slot leader. To prevent hostile efforts to undermine the protocol, each new slot leader is obliged to treat the final few blocks of the incoming chain as transitory, with only the chain before the predetermined number of transient blocks being deemed resolved. This is also known as the settlement delay. This means, among other things, that a stakeholder may be offline and still be synchronized to the blockchain, as long as the latency isn't longer than the settlement delay.

Each network node in the Ouroboros protocol keeps a copy of both the transaction mempool,[292] where new transactions are inserted if they are consistent with current ones, and the blockchain. When a node becomes aware of a newer, more legitimate chain, the locally stored blockchain is replaced.

The disadvantages of Ouroboros Classic were that it was vulnerable to adaptive attackers — a real-world danger that was addressed in Ouroboros Praos – and that there was no safe means for a new member to bootstrap from the blockchain, which is addressed with Ouroboros Genesis.

Ouroboros BFT[293]

---

[292] Mempool role in multiple transactions, docs.cardano.org/core-concepts/multiple-transactions

[293] Kiayias, Russell (2018) 'Ouroboros-BFT: A Simple Byzantine Fault Tolerant Consensus Protocol', eprint.iacr.org/2018/1049.pdf

Following 'Classic' was the Ouroboros BFT paper in 2018 (deployed in May 2020). Cardano employed the Ouroboros BFT (Byzantine Fault Tolerance) protocol during the Byron reboot, which was the transfer of the old Cardano codebase to the new. Ouroboros BFT aided in the preparation of Cardano's release of Shelley, with it, decentralization.

Rather than needing all nodes to be always available, Ouroboros BFT assumes a federated network of servers and synchronous communication between the servers, allowing for easier and more predictable ledger consensus.

Other advantages include immediate evidence of settlement, transaction settlement at network speed (i.e., the speed of your network connection to an OBFT node determines transaction settlement), and instant confirmation in a single round trip of communication. Each of these has a substantial impact on performance.

Ouroboros Praos[294] (current protocol at time of writing, Jan 2023)

The Ouroboros Praos paper dropped in 2018 (deployed in August 2020) and is based on Ouroboros Classic, but with significant security and scalability enhancements. Ouroboros Praos, like Ouroboros Classic, divides transaction blocks into slots, which are then aggregated into epochs. Praos, on the other hand, is inspected in a semi-synchronous context and is safe against adaptive attackers, unlike Ouroboros Classic.

It presupposes two things: that adversaries may transmit arbitrary messages to any participant at any time, and those adversaries can delay honest participant communications for more than one slot. Praos assures that a powerful attacker cannot guess the next slot leader and conduct a targeted attack (like a DDoS attack) to pervert the protocol by using private-leader selection and forward-secure, key-evolving signatures. Praos can also tolerate adversarial controlled message delivery delays and gradual corruption of individual participants in an evolving stakeholder population, which is critical for maintaining network security in a global setting, as long as an honest majority of stakeholder population is maintained.

Ouroboros Genesis[295] (paper 2018, not deployed at time of press, but in development)

Ouroboros Genesis was the fourth version of the protocol and built on Ouroboros Praos by including a unique chain selection mechanism that allows parties to bootstrap from a genesis block — without the requirement for trusted checkpoints or assumptions about prior availability. Genesis also proves the protocol's universal composability,[296]

---

[294] David, Gazi, Kiayias, Russell (2017) 'Ouroboros Praos: An adaptively-secure, semi-synchronous proof-of-stake blockchain', eprint.iacr.org/2017/573.pdf

[295] Badertscher, Gazi, Kiayias, Russell, Zikas (2019), 'Ouroboros Genesis: Composable Proof-of-Stake Blockchains with Dynamic Availability', eprint.iacr.org/2018/378.pdf

[296] The framework of **universal composability** is a general-purpose model for the analysis of cryptographic protocols. It guarantees very strong security properties. Protocols remain secure even if arbitrarily composed with other instances of the same or other protocols. Security is defined in the sense of protocol emulation. Intuitively, a protocol is said to emulate another one, if no environment (observer) can distinguish the

demonstrating that it may be used with other protocols in real world configurations without weakening its security posture. This boosts its security and long-term viability, as well as that of the networks that use it. Genesis is in development and will allow the IOG relays to finally be turned off, which along with the peer-to-peer deployment, will complete the decentralisation of the physical network.

Ouroboros Hydra

Hydra is an off-chain scaling architecture that tackles three major scalability issues: large transaction output, low latency, and lightweight storage per node. The Hydra whitepaper proposes and details the inclusion of multi-party state channels,[297] which provide parallel transaction processing to greatly boost Cardano's transaction-per-second (TPS) output, as well as speedy confirmation of transactions. The paper refers to off-chain ledger siblings — state channels – as heads, reflecting the implementation's namesake. This makes the ledger multi-headed.

Instead of scaling vertically by adding more powerful hardware, Ouroboros Hydra allows Cardano to expand horizontally, enhancing performance by including extra nodes. Early testing indicates that each head is capable of 1,000 TPS. Hydra is being developed in collaboration with the Ouroboros protocol and the Cardano ledger, although it may be used with other systems as long as they have the same properties as Cardano. Hydra was later decoupled from Ouroboros and became an open-source project[298] in its own right. More about Hydra later in Chapter 8.

Consensus Redux

The Consensus Redux[299] paper was published August 2020. This paper discusses the concept of a self-healing ledger. How does the ledger recover when it's been attacked? How does a network recover when it's been attacked? The paper outlines solutions in both categories.

Ouroboros Crypsinous[300]

The Crypsinous paper was published in 2019 but has yet to be implemented. Crypsinous is the first privacy-preserving proof-of-stake protocol. It boasts increased security features to protect against adaptive attacks including a coin evolution technique based on SNARKS[301] and key-private forward-secure encryption.

---

executions. Literally, the protocol may simulate the other protocol (without having access to the code). The notion of security is derived by implication.

[297] **State channels** refer to the process in which users transact with one another directly outside of the blockchain, or 'off-chain,' and greatly minimize their use of 'on-chain' operations.

[298] Hydra Head GitHub, github.com/orgs/input-output-hk/projects/21

[299] Badertscher, Gazi, Kiayias, Russell, Zikas (2020), 'Consensus Redux: Distributed Ledgers in the Face of Adversarial Supremacy', eprint.iacr.org/2020/1021.pdf

[300] Kerber, Kohlweiss, Kiayias, Zikas (2019), 'Ouroboros Crypsinous Privacy-preserving proof-of-stake', eprint.iacr.org/2018/1132.pdf

Ouroboros Chronos[302] (Paper 2021, not deployed at time of press)

Chronos will deliver greater security and network resilience to communication delays by providing more accurate global timekeeping. To maintain the robustness of any dispersed network, global time synchronization is required. Time synchronization is critical in smart contract implementation, from guaranteeing up-to-date information amongst all participants to maintaining correct transaction processing and block construction.

IOG discovered a means to synchronize clocks across a blockchain in conjunction with experts from the Universities of Edinburgh, Purdue, and Connecticut to create a more secure and tamper-proof global time source. This includes time synchronization from internet of things (IoT)[303] devices, such as supply chain monitoring tools, and general distributed systems, especially if a central clock failure poses a security issue. The research is implemented as Ouroboros Chronos (Greek for 'Time').

Chronos is a cryptographically secure blockchain protocol that also offers an accurate source of time thanks to an innovative time synchronization technique that avoids the flaws of externally maintained clocks. This also enables blockchain to precisely time-stamp transactions, making the ledger more resistant to time-based attacks.

By syncing local time to a uniform network clock with no single point of failure, the new protocol may greatly improve the resilience of essential telecoms, transportation, trade systems, and infrastructures. This scientific accomplishment also represents a huge step toward building completely auditable and fraud-proof financial systems by providing exact time and hence full traceability of all transactions.

September 22, 2020, re: Chronos. CH:[304]

> *Ouroboros Chronos was a special paper. Leslie Lamport[305] was one of the first guys to do major work in distributed systems and he wrote this beautiful paper on clocks and time in the distributed system from the 1960s or 1970s. It's one of the most cited papers of all time in the systems world... 'Time, clocks, and the ordering of events in a distributed system'[306] and Chronos was like unfinished*

---

[301] **SNARK** stands for 'Succinct Non-Interactive Argument of Knowledge.' A (zero knowledge) zk-SNARK is a cryptographic proof that allows one party to prove it possesses certain information without revealing that information. This proof is made possible using a secret key created before the transaction takes place.

[302] Badertscher, Gazi, Kiayias, Russell, Zikas (2019),'Ouroboros Chronos: Permissionless Clock Synchronization via Proof-of-Stake', eprint.iacr.org/2019/838.pdf

[303] The **Internet of Things (IoT)** is a system of interrelated computing devices, mechanical and digital machines, objects, animals or people that are provided with unique identifiers (UIDs) and the ability to transfer data over a network without requiring human-to-human or human-to-computer interaction.

[304] Slot Leader Episode 1, youtu.be/YT0PXYBEnuE?t=2218

[305] Leslie Lamport, everipedia.org/wiki/lang_en/Leslie_Lamport

[306] Leslie Lamport, 'Time, clocks, and the ordering of events in a distributed system', dl.acm.org/doi/10.1145/359545.359563

business in that respect. It's fun to write papers like that and it has real use. You can completely decouple a dependency on NTP[307] and these types of things, there's a lot of theory there.

Timing is everything

Within computer systems and applications, the idea of time is critical. You wouldn't be able to access any transport layer security (TLS)-based websites, exchange data, or use other cryptographic techniques without this notion.

Time tracking, on the other hand, is a challenging issue to tackle. Accurate time synchronization requires data transfer throughout the whole internet, which costs time as well. It's also difficult to forecast how long a particular data transfer will take since the network status is continually changing and is influenced by variables like congestion and data size, among others. As a result, discrepancies are common, and it's critical to supply the tools and solutions necessary for accurate timekeeping.

It's easy to take timekeeping for granted with basic PCs. Behind the scenes, however, there is a strict protocol to follow. The Network Time Protocol[308] (NTP), for example, uses a worldwide hierarchy of servers to solve the timekeeping problem. This comprises up to 15 Stratums, each with its own routing designed to synchronize in the most efficient way possible. The development of a Bellman-Ford shortest-path spanning tree,[309] which reduces latency and transmission time inconsistencies, also helps.

Time synching on the Blockchain

For distributed ledger technology, the idea of timekeeping is different. The network cannot verify that a transaction being processed is genuine, and does not reverse the prior one, without a correct timestamp. Different timestamping algorithms are employed across a variety of blockchain ledgers; however, they aren't always reliable. Bitcoin, for example, employs timestamps for consensus security but not for timekeeping.

Timekeeping is also necessary for smart contract execution. Decentralized finance (DeFi) smart contract attacks are vulnerable to inaccuracy. Vulnerabilities in smart contracts aren't necessarily caused by bad code; time discrepancies should be fixed to prevent any potential attacks on the ledger. Some blockchains, such as Solana, have experienced critical 'clock drift' issues.[310]

---

[307] **Network Time Protocol (NTP)** is a networking protocol for clock synchronization between computer systems over packet-switched, variable-latency data networks. In operation since before 1985, NTP is one of the oldest Internet protocols in current use.

[308] Network time protocol, ntp.org/

[309] The **Bellman–Ford algorithm** computes shortest paths from a single source vertex to all of the other vertices in a weighted digraph. It is slower than Dijkstra's algorithm for the same problem, but more versatile, as it is capable of handling graphs in which some of the edge weights are negative numbers. The algorithm was first proposed by Alfonso Shimbel (1955), but is instead named after Richard Bellman and Lester Ford Jr., who published it in 1958 and 1956, respectively.

Time for reflection

Building complex trading platforms, such as Axo (axo.trade), is not trivial when calculating exact times on a decentralized blockchain. The topic has been debated in IOG's blogs, in the docs[311] and more heatedly on twitter. Although Cardano's current measure of time appears satisfactory to cover many use cases, it is not perfect. To dive deeper into the technical minutiae, it's best to take in the views of several experts. Axo chief Jarek Hirniak, an experienced developer in trading software, wrote *Time on Cardano*,[312] while Sebastien Guillemot has covered 'timing' comprehensively in several of his YouTube videos.[313]

December 12, 2020. Is Chronos implemented? CH:[314]

> *We'd like to be reliant on nothing and no one, and as decentralized as possible. So, we were the first to address this in the very first paper of its kind, with something called Ouroboros Chronos, but it would be an unnecessary diversion to just go and chase 3 months of implementation to pull Chronos in, when we don't need it as a system right now. [...]*
>
> *The other thing is that Chronos should be implemented with Consensus Redux, should be implemented with Genesis, and should be implemented with fast finality. and high throughput enhancements to the system, so Ouroboros 2 (subsequently named Ouroboros Omega) is a rollup of all the research that we've done which will make it considerably better than anything in market. So, the name of deployment execution is saying 'what is a problem today? What's a theoretical but unlikely issue? Versus what is a practical and certainly problematic issue to resolve?' ...and understand how to balance things and create a roadmap accordingly.*

Ouroboros Leios

The Leios paper[315] was published in November 2022 and is surprisingly readable. It was previewed in this video[316] by Professor Aggelos Kiayias. The focus of Leios is Input Endorsers which leverage the aforementioned foundational Ouroboros functionality as

[310] Solana Downtime Series Continues, Network Faces Serious Issues Again, u.today/solana-downtime-series-continues-network-faces-serious-issues-again

[311] Time handling on Cardano, docs.cardano.org/explore-cardano/time

[312] Jarek Hirniak on Cardano's timing issue, twitter.com/ravanave/status/1589241299667800065?s=20&t=tCzT7srtCJ362-aWyi-jYA

[313] MinSwap & Axo: sandwich attacks and timing in blockchain, youtube.com/watch?v=mGLm0QdVoNc

[314] Surprise AMA! 12/12/2020, youtu.be/GlVU8ZiVUL0?t=3061

[315] Coutts, Panagiotakos, Fitzi, (2022) 'Ouroboros Leios: design goals and concepts', iohk.io/en/research/library/papers/ouroboros-leios-design-goals-and-concepts/

[316] Advances in Ouroboros: Scaling for Future Growth, youtube.com/watch?v=xKv94MwSNBw

well as Mithril (See Chapter 8). As input endorsers are quite technical and based on concepts not discussed yet, they are covered in the last section of Chapter 8, *Basho (Scalability)*. From section 6.2 of the paper:

> *Just as Ouroboros Praos+Genesis is a valid combination, Ouroboros Leios+Genesis makes perfect sense too and provides the same benefits. Thus in some sense Leios and Genesis are independent features. In practice Genesis will be deployed by the time that Leios is available and so it would be a regression if the Genesis feature were not included.*

Ouroboros Omega[317] will be the capstone of all the proof-of-stake research IOG have accomplished since 2016. There should be a paper soon on the 'convergence of all the ideas.'

February 9, 2021. Can you talk about Ouroboros Omega? CH:[318]

> *Omega is the culmination of all of our research of the last 6 years for Ouroboros: no reliance on external clock, self-healing so it can gradually recover 51% attacks, the ability to bootstrap from Genesis, semi-synchrony, adaptive security, instant finality... all kinds of stuff...multi-validation per block... there's so much stuff .... Things like the consensus Redux paper, the Ledger Combiners paper[319] ... the Chronos paper, the Genesis paper, the Praos paper and then all the theory and then some of the engineering acumen, including an improvement to about a thousand TPS (transactions per second).*

How the Consensus Layer Works

Abstraction[320] is a key feature of the consensus layer.

The Cardano consensus layer is responsible for two major duties:

1. It uses the blockchain consensus mechanism to keep track of transactions. Consensus, or 'majority of opinion,' in the context of a blockchain, implies that everyone participating agrees on the one true chain. This means that the consensus layer is responsible for accepting blocks, selecting between rival chains if any exist, and determining when to create its own blocks.

---

[317] Ouroboros Omega, twitter.com/iohk_charles/status/1357364560504709120

[318] Surprise AMA 02/09/2021, youtu.be/K3l3_SAGXEE?t=1350

[319] Gazi, Kiayias, Russell, Zikas (2020) 'Ledger Combiners for fast settlement', eprint.iacr.org/2020/675.pdf

[320] **Abstraction** is used to make models that can be used and reused without having to re-write all the program code for each new application on every different type of computer. Abstraction is usually achieved by writing source code in some particular computer language which can be translated into machine code for different types of computers to execute. Abstraction allows program designers to separate a framework from specific instances which implement details.

2. It is in charge of preserving all of the information needed to make these judgments. The protocol must verify a block in relation to the state of the ledger before deciding whether to accept it. It must preserve enough history to be able to rebuild the ledger state on a different chain (a different point of a fork in the chain) if it chooses to move to a different chain. It must maintain a mempool[321] of transactions to be placed into those blocks to be able to create blocks.

The consensus layer sits between the network layer below it, which deals with communication protocols and peer selection, and the ledger layer above it, which defines how the ledger should be updated with each new block and how it should be updated. The ledger layer is completely stateless[322] and only contains pure functions. As a result, the consensus layer isn't necessary to understand the precise nature of the ledger state, or even the contents of the blocks (apart from some header fields required to run the consensus protocol).

The consensus layer makes extensive use of abstraction. This is significant for many reasons:

- When performing tests, it enables programmers to **simulate failures**. IOG may, for example, abstract the underlying file system and use it to stress-test the storage layer while simulating various disk errors. Similarly, they abstract across time and use this to see what happens to a node as the user's system clock advances or recedes.

- It enables IOG to **use a variety of ledgers** to create the consensus layer. They used it to run the consensus layer with the Byron ledger and the Shelley ledger for the Shelley Haskell testnet. They also utilized it to test the consensus layer using different types of ledgers developed expressly for testing, which are often simpler than 'real' ledgers, allowing IOG to concentrate their tests on the consensus layer itself.

- It **enhances compositionality**[323] by enabling IOG to construct bigger components from smaller ones. For example, the Shelley testnet ledger only includes the Shelley ledger; but, after Shelley was launched, the actual chain had both the Byron and Shelley ledgers up to the hard fork point. This necessitated the creation of a ledger layer that switched between two ledgers at a predetermined moment. Rather than creating a new ledger, IOG created a hard

---

[321] The **mempool (memory pool)** is a smaller database of unconfirmed or pending transactions which every node keeps. When a transaction is confirmed by being included in a block, it is removed from the mempool. You can think of a mempool as being like a 'waiting room' where a transaction sits before it is added to a block.

[322] **Stateful** services keep track of sessions or transactions and react differently to the same inputs based on that history. **Stateless** services rely on clients to maintain sessions and center around operations that manipulate resources, rather than the state.

[323] In mathematics, semantics, and philosophy of language, the principle of **compositionality** is the principle that the meaning of a complex expression is determined by the meanings of its constituent expressions and the rules used to combine them.

fork combinator that solely implements these features. This enhanced code reusability (no need to reimplement hard fork functionality for future hard forks), as well as separation of responsibilities (the hard fork combinator's development and testing aren't dependent on the details of the ledgers it flips between).

- The usage of abstraction **increases testability**. Combinators are variants of consensus methods that enable IOG to concentrate on certain areas. For example, IOG has a combinator that accepts an existing consensus protocol and merely alters the check to see whether a block should be produced. The consensus layer may then be used to establish testing scenarios in which many nodes produce a block in a particular slot or, conversely, no nodes at all, and verify that it performs properly.

Consensus Roles

The consensus protocol has three major roles:

1. Leader check (who should produce a block?)
2. Chain selection
3. Block verification

The protocol is designed to be independent of a specific block or ledger, allowing a single protocol to be used with a variety of blocks and/or ledgers. As a result, each of these three roles establishes its own 'picture' of the data.

Every slot has a **leader check** that determines whether the node should create a block. In practice, the leader check may need the extraction of certain information from the ledger state. The chance of a node being elected as leader (authorized to generate a block) in the Ouroboros Praos consensus protocol, for example, is dependent on its stake, the node's stake.

The process of selecting between two competing chains is known as **chain selection**. The chain length[324] is the most important selection criteria here, however other protocols may have extra requirements.

Blocks, for example, are usually signed using a 'hot' key that lives on the server and created by a 'cold' key that never appears on any networked device. If the hot key is compromised, the node operator may create a new one using the cold key and 'delegate' to it.

---

[324] **Block height** represents the number of blocks that were validated and confirmed in the entire history of a particular blockchain network, from the genesis block (or block zero) until the most recent one. Unlike the genesis block, all other blocks contain a reference, or hash, to the block that came immediately before it, and the block height is the number of each block in that sequence. So the block height of the genesis block is #0, and the block height of the first block is #1.

A consensus protocol will favor the newer hot key over two chains of similar length, ie. Each chain includes a tip[325] signed by the same cold key but a different hot key.

Block validation is primarily a ledger problem; checks such as ensuring all transaction inputs are accessible to prevent double spending are specified in the ledger layer. What's within the blocks is mainly unknown to the consensus layer; in fact, it may not even be a cryptocurrency, but a distinct use of blockchain technology. IOG used the example of a Pokémon ledger[326] on Ouroboros previously. However, block headers include a few items that are expressly designed to aid the consensus layer.

Node configuration

To execute, each protocol may need certain static data, such as keys to sign blocks, a unique id for the leader check, and so on. This is referred to as the 'node configuration.'

The ledger state

The consensus layer not only handles the ledger state but also operates the consensus protocol. It is unconcerned with the look of the ledger state; instead, it assumes that some form of ledger state is connected with a block type.

If a block is invalid, you may get an error while applying it to the ledger state. The ledger layer defines the precise kind of ledger errors, which are ledger specific. The Shelley ledger, for example, will have staking errors, but the Byron ledger would not since it does not enable staking; and ledgers that aren't crypto ledgers will have quite different errors.

The Cardano consensus layer was created with the Cardano blockchain in mind, which initially ran Byron and was updated to run Shelley. It's fair to ask why didn't IOG developers create for that particular blockchain first? Then generalize when utilizing the consensus layer for other blockchains? However, there would have been significant drawbacks in doing so:

- It would obstruct IOG's capacity to conduct tests. They wouldn't be able to choose which nodes create blocks when, they wouldn't be able to use a dual ledger, and so on

- It would entangle things that should be logically separate. The Shelley ledger, in the abstract method, is made up of three parts: a Byron chain, a Shelley chain, and a hard fork combinator that connects the two. Without abstractions, such separation of concerns would be more difficult to establish, resulting in code that was more complex to comprehend and maintain

---

[325] cardano-cli (command line interface) query command contains subcommand, one of which is tip:
tip: gets the node's current tip (slot number, hash, and block number)

[326] Anthony Quinn, 'Combinator makes easy work of Shelley hard fork',
iohk.io/en/blog/posts/2020/05/07/combinator-makes-easy-work-of-shelley-hard-fork

- Abstract code is less likely to include flaws. For example, since the dual ledger combinator is polymorphic [327] in the two ledgers it combines, and they are of different types, IOG couldn't construct type correct code that attempts to apply the main block to the auxiliary ledger

- When the time inevitably comes to instantiate the consensus layer for a new blockchain, writing it in an abstract manner from the start forces IOG to think carefully about the design and avoid coupling things that shouldn't be coupled, or making assumptions that may or may not be true in general. It might be difficult to fix such issues once the design has been implemented.

To achieve all of this, a programming language with exceptional abstraction capabilities is required, and Haskell is well equipped in this regard.

January 10, 2021. Please explain Cardano being 100x more decentralized than BTC or others, how is this calculated? CH:[328]

> *It's calculated by those who produce blocks, so if you have a hundred times the unique entities producing blocks, then we say it's a hundred times more decentralized, but there are many measurements of decentralization. You can look at network propagation, so how many full nodes you have. You can look at unique development entities responsible for it …you can look at the funding sources and see how many unique funding sources are there. You can see the totality of the user count….*

> *You can see it by the total applications on the system but usually when we say decentralization, we strictly mean the amount of nodes participating in the consensus process and how many unique people are making blocks. In the case of bitcoin, 3 to 5 usually make the same blocks again and again… and we consistently have 300 to 500 stake pools consistently making blocks that are unique. There's over 1200 registered* (currently over 3,000), *so I feel very comfortable in the 100x statement, but reasonable people can have different definitions, there's no consensus in the industry of what decentralization is.*

Hard Forking Business

In the context of the blockchain, a 'hard fork' refers to a significant change in the chain, such as switching from one protocol to another. A hard fork in most blockchains denotes block modifications or a change in their interpretation. Typically, when a hard fork is performed, the existing protocol is turned off, new rules and modifications are introduced, and the chain is restarted. A hard-forked chain will be distinct from the prior version, and that the pre-forked blockchain's history will no longer be accessible.

---

[327] Polymorphic: occurring in several different forms. In computing (feature of a programming language) allowing routines to use variables of different types at different times.

[328] Surprise AMA 01/10/2021, youtu.be/iLq6mRk2dyg?t=3926

The Cardano blockchain has hard forked from a federated Byron model to a decentralized Shelley model. This hard fork, on the other hand, was one-of-a-kind. IOG guaranteed a seamless transition to a new protocol while maintaining the history of earlier blocks, rather than making major modifications, the chain did not alter drastically. Instead, it included Byron blocks before adding Shelley blocks after a transition time. There was no 'turning it on and off again'. The entire history was retained. There has been no downtime or restarts with Cardano, which is not always the case with other chains.[329]

Hard Fork Combinator

In Cardano docs and blogs, you may have seen a hard fork referred to as an 'HFC' or a 'HFC event'. A combinator is a technical term that refers to the joining of two or more processes. In the context of Cardano, a hard fork combinator combines protocols, allowing the Byron-to-Shelley transition to be completed without the need for a system restart. It guaranteed that the ledgers of Byron and Shelley display as a single ledger. It was not necessary for all nodes to update at the same time when switching from Ouroboros BFT to Ouroboros Praos. Instead, nodes updated in stages; some running Byron blocks, others running Shelley blocks.

The hard fork combinator is intended to allow the integration of many protocols without requiring major changes. Byron and Shelley blocks are now combined in the Cardano chain. For future 'hard fork events', Basho and Voltaire blocks will be combined as well - all as a single property. By simplifying the prior Byron-to-Shelley evolution, this (HFC) hard fork combinator also made the transfer from Shelley to Goguen seamless with gradual, iterative upgrades rolled out as the *Allegra*, *Mary* and *Alonzo* updates.

HFC history to date

The Cardano platform entered a rapid development phase with the introduction of the Incentivized Testnet in 2019, which marked the beginning of the Shelley era. The Ouroboros Classic consensus system previously supported Byron and ada, and subsequently migrated to Ouroboros Praos. As Cardano decentralized, this was the version of proof-of-stake (PoS) protocol that first powered Shelley. It incorporated monetary rewards into the staking procedure for ada holders and stake pool owners.

In February 2020, IOG upgraded Cardano with a hard fork that moved the mainnet from Ouroboros Classic to Ouroboros BFT, an enhanced version of the original consensus mechanism. This BFT hard fork kicked off a transition phase under Ouroboros BFT, a pared-down version of the protocol aimed to ease the transfer to Praos while still avoiding malicious behavior. Users were unlikely to have noticed. It meant a routine software update for Daedalus wallet users. Exchanges were required to update manually, but they had many weeks to do it and IOG were available to assist.

The 'Byron reboot'[330] followed that in March 2020. Many Cardano components received

---

[329] Solana Sputters Back to Life Following Downtime, Network Restart, decrypt.co/81004/solana-back-online-following-downtime-network-restart

completely new code, including a new node to handle delegation and decentralization, as well as future Shelley features. The new code base was redesigned to be modular, which meant that many components could be updated without impacting the others.

In turn, the BFT served as a springboard for the Shelley hard fork, which happened after the Haskell testnet was complete. For exchanges, ada holders, and wallet users, this second hard fork was similar to the first, a non-event in terms of user disruption. However, although everything seems to be in order on the surface, there was a lot of activity going on behind the scenes. IOG's developers were hard at work making it a seamless, benign experience for the end user. IOG chief architect Duncan Coutts[331] explained at the time:

> *IOG's blockchain engineers believe in smooth code updates. Instead of trying to do the jump from Ouroboros Classic to Praos in a single update – which would be an incredibly complex task – it's been a two-stage approach using Ouroboros BFT as an intermediary. The BFT code is compatible with both the Byron-era federated nodes and the Shelley-style nodes released in the Byron reboot. It's like a relay race: one runner (in our case, running one protocol) enters the handover box where the other runner is waiting; they synchronize their speeds (so they're perfectly compatible with each other) and then hand over the baton (operating the mainnet), and then the new runner with the baton continues from the handover box for the next lap.*

IOG were able to swiftly design and test a new wallet using Daedalus *Flight*, and once everyone was using it on the mainnet, and IOG finished changing over the core nodes, the old code was obsolete. *Flight* is IOGs version of Chrome Canary for Daedalus.

In summary, the only real hard fork for Cardano was the switch from Ouroboros Classic to BFT (February 2020). The Byron mainnet was relaunched to run the BFT protocol, allowing for a smoother transition to Ouroboros Praos with fewer chain disruptions. The BFT protocol was meticulously built to preserve blockchain history and make the blockchain look as a single entity.

As IOG chief executive Charles Hoskinson discussed in his whiteboard video about the hard fork,[332] the goal was to have a 'graceful entry into Shelley.' The hard fork combinator was crucial in accomplishing this transition.

Goguen Era Updates

Allegra (Token Locking)

---

[330] Tim Harrison, 'What the Byron Reboot means for Cardano', iohk.io/en/blog/posts/2020/03/30/what-the-byron-reboot-means-for-cardano/

[331] Duncan Coutts, iohk.io/en/team/duncan-coutts

[332] How we will launch Shelley, youtube.com/watch?v=g7uySEgt06c

Token locking was a feature introduced to the Shelley protocol to allow a variety of smart contract use cases, such as generating and transacting with multi-asset tokens and adding support for the Voltaire voting mechanism. Token locking is the act of reserving a certain number of assets and agreeing not to sell them for a given length of time. This functionality was enabled in the *Allegra*[333] upgrade in December 2020. *Allegra* was named after Allegra Byron, Lord Byron's daughter and sister to Ada Lovelace.

Token locking allowed for more complicated deal settlement and fund accounting. It's used in the following scenarios:

- **Contractual agreement** - when someone engages into a contractual agreement, such as to sell an asset like a painting, it is essential to guarantee that the painting will not be sold to anyone else save the person who pays the money. The token may represent both the painting and the 'promise', the actual token locking in this example. The contract becomes invalid if the painting is sold to a different third party

- **Vote registry** - Token locking allows users to lock a set quantity of their tokens to reflect their voting rights inside the Voltaire voting system. Holders of ada tokens who participate in the voting process must 'lock' their tokens. This will reflect their voting rights in proportion to their investment and will prevent the hazards of double-counting votes, awarding more votes than is feasible, contradicting votes, or vote duplication

- **Multi-asset tokens** - In addition to ada, Cardano allows for multi-asset tokens, with the ledger supporting the creation and usage of several bespoke token types. Token locking enables ada tokens to be 'locked' to create a bespoke asset of equal value.

Mary (multi-asset support)

This then paved the way for the *Mary* (multi-asset support) upgrade in March 2021. It was named after Mary Shelley (the author and wife of Shelley). MAS (multi-asset support) means you can record that a particular token is being used for a specified purpose. The token may represent any object that is recorded on (native to) the blockchain ledger, such as ada, and other custom tokens. *Mary* enables users to generate (custom) tokens with unique characteristics and conduct transactions with them directly on the blockchain.

The ledger's accounting architecture now handles not just ada transactions, but also transactions that hold several asset types at the same time. Developers benefit from native support since they don't have to write smart contracts to handle bespoke token minting or transactions. Instead, the accounting ledger keeps track of asset ownership and transfers, minimizing unnecessary complexity and the risk of human error while also ensuring considerable cost savings.

---

[333] Cardano Allegra and Mary hard fork changes explained, youtube.com/watch?v=9mjvXjxTks8

To fulfill commercial or business goals, developers, enterprises, and apps can build general purpose (fungible) or specialized (non-fungible) tokens. Custom payment tokens or rewards for decentralized apps, stablecoins pegged to other currencies, and unique assets that represent intellectual property are just a few examples. All of these assets may then be traded, swapped, or used to purchase goods and services.

Alonzo (smart contracts)

Still part of the Goguen era, *Alonzo* was the next protocol update in Sept 2021. To enable functional smart contracts, *Alonzo* built on top of transaction metadata, token locking, and native asset functionality. By allowing the development of smart contracts and decentralized apps (DApps) for DeFi (decentralized finance), this update created a diverse platform that opened up options for enterprises and developers.

This functionality is available and enabled by the tools and infrastructure that make up the Plutus Platform. *Alonzo* enhanced Shelley's basic multi-signature (multisig) scripting language with a rigorous methodology based on formal methods and verification. For more sophisticated and secure scripting capabilities, Multisig was updated into the Plutus Core[334] language. *Alonzo* enables this through extended unspent transaction output (EUTXO) accounting. More on this later.

Alonzo was named after Alonzo Church (1903-95). Church was a logician and mathematician who worked on logic and the foundations of theoretical computer science in the US. He is also recognized for establishing lambda calculus,[335] a formal system that may be used to argue that the Entscheidungsproblem[336] is unsolvable. Later, when working with Alan Turing, they realized that the lambda calculus and the Turing machine[337] had equivalent capabilities, displaying numerous mechanical computing processes. Plutus Core (Cardano's smart contract language) is a variant of lambda calculus, which is one of the reasons for naming the smart contract upgrade after Church.

---

[334] **Plutus Core** is the programming language in which scripts on the Cardano blockchain are written. Plutus Core is a small functional programming language — a formal specification is available. Plutus Core is not read or written by humans; it is a compilation target for other languages.

[335] **Lambda calculus** (λ-calculus) is a formal system in math logic for expressing computation based on function abstraction and application using variable binding and substitution. It is a universal model of computation that can be used to simulate any Turing machine. It was introduced by the mathematician Alonzo Church in the 1930s as part of his research into the foundations of mathematics.

[336] In math and computer science, the ****Entscheidungsproblem**** (pronounced German for 'decision problem') is a challenge posed by David Hilbert and Wilhelm Ackermann in 1928. The problem asks for an algorithm that takes as input a statement of a first-order logic and answers 'Yes' or 'No' according to whether the statement is universally valid, i.e., valid in every structure satisfying the axioms. By the completeness theorem of first-order logic, a statement is universally valid if and only if it can be deduced from the axioms, so the Entscheidungsproblem can also be viewed as asking for an algorithm to decide whether a given statement is provable from the axioms using the rules of logic.

[337] A **Turing machine** is a mathematical model of computation that defines an abstract machine, which manipulates symbols on a strip of tape according to a table of rules. Despite the model's simplicity, given any computer algorithm, a Turing machine capable of simulating that algorithm's logic can be constructed.

Vasil

Named after a Bulgarian mathematician Vasil Dabov, who was also a Cardano community member, the *Vasil* hard fork in Sept 2022 brought five key features to boost performance. These were mainly focused on Plutus V2 after CIPs (Cardano Improvement Proposal) were submitted by the community. CIP-31 (Reference Inputs), CIP-32 (Inline Datums), CIP-33 (Reference Scripts), CIP-40 (Collateral Outputs), and diffusion pipelining are discussed later.

The terminology and the use of the same terms in different contexts can get quite confusing. Fear not, as there is page the documentation[338] explaining the difference between an 'era' and a 'phase', and how a 'hard fork' differs from an 'intra-era hard fork'. Starting with *Alonzo*, the 'ledger eras' are named after mathematicians and computer scientists, kind of like the hurricane naming system but in alphabetical ordering. The release dates are named in honor of Cardano community members.

Date	Phase	Era	Slot Number	Epoch Number	Protocol Version	Ledger Protocol	Consensus Mechanism	Notes
2017/09	Byron	Byron	0	0	0,0	-	Ouroboros Classic	
2020/02	Byron	Byron	3801600	176	1,0	-	Ouroboros BFT	
2020/07	Shelley	Shelley	4492800	208	2,0	TPraos	Ouroboros Praos	
2020/12	Goguen	Allegra	16588800	236	3,0	TPraos	Ouroboros Praos	
2021/03	Goguen	Mary	23068800	251	4,0	TPraos	Ouroboros Praos	
2021/09	Goguen	Alonzo	39916975	290	5,0	TPraos	Ouroboros Praos	
2021/10	Goguen	Alonzo	43372972	298	6,0	TPraos	Ouroboros Praos	intra-era hardfork
2022/09	Goguen	Babbage	72316896	365	7,0	Praos	Ouroboros Praos	Vasil HF

Figure 10: Cardano Phases, eras, and intra-era hard forks

The SECP update in Februrary 2023 was executed as an 'intra-era hard fork'. This brought new cryptographic primitives to Cardano. More about this update in chapter 6.

June 5, 2020. What is the best code in Cardano? CH:[339]

> *The hard fork combinator code is the second most elegant code we have; the most elegant code belongs to the network code. We have lots of crazy stuff there, very elegant, very academic scary code ...but beautiful.*

Path to Full Decentralization

Cardano hit a milestone at the end of March 2021 when *d*, the parameter that determines what proportion of transactions are processed by the genesis nodes, reached zero. The

---

[338] Development phases and eras on Cardano, docs.cardano.org/explore-cardano/eras-and-phases

[339] Surprise AMA 06/05/2020, youtu.be/6pQzQbVgX7c?t=2449

duty for block creation was totally decentralized at this time. Cardano's network of 1,800 (March 2021) community pools were fully responsible for the generation of blocks.

The day d reached 0 was a watershed point for Cardano. When IOG released the Shelley update in July 2020, they set d to 1.0, which meant that every block was generated by IOG's federated nodes. Of course, this was the opposite of decentralization, but it was a prudent (secure) strategy in the short term until the stake pool operator (SPO) network was set up and mature.

IOG steadily lowered d at a rate of 0.02 each epoch over time, an increase of two percentage points in community block production every 5 days. When d dropped, the community created more blocks, and more stake pools were able to generate blocks. The network's diversity and geographic dispersion grew as d decreased.

d hit zero on March 31, 2021, at the end of epoch 257. That day was memorable because, although d is a modest number, its importance is enormous. That zero was the most crucial external signal of decentralization, a parameterized symbol confirming a major principle of Cardano's ideology of pushing power to the edges.

Trickier parameter adjustments

Setting stable parameter settings, while still being flexible for the future, is critical to Cardano's continued development and decentralization. While the transitioning the d parameter was smooth and predictable, changing other parameters requires a more nuanced approach. IOG consulted with the community before setting initial values. Around 20 parameters[340] regulate network behavior, and settings had to be specified for all of them before the mainnet could be launched. The majority of these parameters are technical in nature, so although they must be set appropriately to ensure system safety and improve performance, their specific values have little impact on user experience. You can review the full list of current parameter settings on ADApools.org.[341]

June 4, 2019. Re: Ouroboros parameters. CH:[342]

> *What is the protection mechanism against too many stake pools? So, you have to delegate to the stake pools ...so there's only a finite amount of ada and the financial incentives are basically set up in a way where you will have a ceiling of stake pools, and if you have more than that, you actually make less money. So, I'd highly encourage you to read our paper, we wrote out of Oxford with Alexander Russel.[343] The paper covers how you parameterize that model and that's why we can believe that there'll be a stable thousand stake pools after a while.*

---

[340] Protocol Parameters, cips.cardano.org/cips/cip9/

[341] Current Cardano Parameter Settings, adapools.org/protocol-parameters

[342] Special 4th of July Surprise AMA, youtu.be/1qoeLinJ3rg?t=3278

[343] Alexander Russel, iohk.io/en/research/library/authors/alexander-russel/

K = number of stake pools

A crucial element is the desired number of stake pools, or the k parameter. k is the reward scheme parameter that determines the soft limit on the pool size. Cardano incentives have been intended to foster an equilibrium with k completely saturated pools, which means that when all stake is delegated equally to the k most appealing pools, rewards will be optimum for everyone. At equilibrium, assuming rational participants and no external influences, the mechanism is constructed such that the stakeholders' optimal response behavior converges to k pools of equal size, each delivering the same amount of rewards per unit of stake to their delegates.

The greater the value of k, the more decentralized the system. More k, on the other hand, results in a less efficient system (higher expenses, greater energy consumption) and fewer returns for both delegators and stake pool owners. IOG knew that the community would be motivated to build up pools based on what IOG learnt from both the Incentivized Testnet (ITN) and the Haskell Shelley testnet.

Decentralization occurred fast but decentralization alone is insufficient. Cardano requires long-term commitment from its operators, and operators must be appropriately rewarded for continuing to sustain the system. The initial proposal was $k=150$ for the mainnet deployment of Shelley, to be progressively raised to create a balance between decentralization and rewards for stake pool managers. This was a little improvement over the parameter choice in the incentive testnet (ITN), which was $k=100$. This was seen to be a cautious approach at the time, aimed to enable a seamless transition of the ITN environment to the mainnet. This guaranteed that the system was stable and efficient at first and could progressively evolve over time to become more decentralized, and secure, in the future.

Cardano is an order of magnitude more decentralized than any other blockchain due to k stake pools of roughly similar size. And this was only the start. Tiny, progressive increases in the k-parameter aren't possible (unlike, for example, the decentralization d parameter, which lent itself to a gradual reduction). Each rise in k necessitates action on the part of pools and delegators. For pool operators, this entails fine-tuning their settings, particularly their margin; for delegators, it entails selecting new pools to delegate their ada to, particularly if their existing selection becomes oversaturated.

As a result, the optimal method for increasing k is to do it in bigger, less frequent increments – and as quickly as realistic network dynamics and economics will allow. The optimum option is one that causes the least amount of disturbance to successful pools and their delegators while increasing the chance for medium and smaller pools to mint blocks and attract additional stake. It's also critical to have a long-term strategic aim in mind as a community: to spread decentralization as broadly as possible.

The $k = 500$ change

At epoch 234, an adjustment to $k=500$ was made on December 6, 2020. Small-to-medium-sized pools that were having trouble attracting delegation benefited from the change to $k=500$. It also restricted pool size to 64 million ada, meaning that more than 100 of the biggest pools would overfill.

It's always best practice for delegators to monitor their preferred pools. You should redelegate if you see your chosen pool becoming oversaturated. It's crucial to remember that rewards will still be paid out from relatively saturated pools, but they'll decrease when the pool's saturation rises. No one who delegated to an over-saturated pool ever lost any ada. It's only that if one remains in a saturated pool, the return on investment will be diminished.

Monetary Policy

Transaction fees and monetary expansion are used to fund staking rewards for both delegators and stake pool operators. Every epoch, all transaction fees from all transactions from all blocks created during that epoch are collected and placed in a virtual 'pot.' A predetermined proportion of the leftover ada reserves, ρ, is also contributed to the pot. Then a portion of the pot, τ, is paid to the Treasury, and the remainder is used as epoch rewards.

This approach guarantees that the share of rewards taken from the reserves is large in the beginning, when the number of transactions is still relatively modest since users are only starting to create their businesses on Cardano. Early adopters will be enticed to act swiftly to reap the benefits of the high initial payouts. The higher costs compensate for declining reserves over time as transaction volume grows.

This technique also guarantees that the rewards provided are predictable and evolve over time. There will be no 'jumps' like the bitcoin halving[344] occurrences that occur every four years. Instead, a steady exponential fall is guaranteed by a predetermined proportion deducted from residual reserves every epoch.

So, what kind of worth should ρ take? What percentage of the budget should go to the Treasury? This is also another trade-off: larger values of ρ indicate bigger rewards for everyone at first, as well as a faster-filling treasury. However, greater levels of ρ imply a quicker depletion of reserves. Paying big incentives and incentivizing early adopters is crucial, however, it is equally critical to present all stakeholders with a long-term view.

Cardano will never run out of reserves; instead, it will be an exponential decay. Calculate the 'reserve half-life,' or the time it takes for half of the reserve to be used up, to obtain a sense of the effect of a certain value of ρ. After careful consideration, 0.22% was the proposal for ρ. When the numbers are crunched, the 'reserve half-life' comes out to be roughly 4 to 5 years. In other words, half of the remaining reserve will be consumed every four to five years. Because this is near to the four-year 'bitcoin half-life,' Cardano holdings will diminish at a similar pace to bitcoin reserves.

---

[344] The Bitcoin halving is when the reward for Bitcoin mining is halved. Halving takes place every 4 years. The halving policy was written into Bitcoin's mining algorithm to counteract inflation by maintaining scarcity

It's worth mentioning that Bitcoin took almost eight years to attain its highest level of popularity and pricing. As a result, it is reasonable to anticipate Cardano transaction volume and exchange rate to rise substantially over the coming years to more than compensate for the reduction in monetary expansion.

Funding the Treasury

IOG also recommended a starting figure of 5% for τ, the proportion of rewards that are automatically sent to the Treasury at the end of each epoch. Over the following five years, at least 380m ada will be transferred from the reserves to the Treasury.

The actual amount coming to the Treasury will be much larger. To begin with, it's unrealistic to anticipate that all ada will be delegated based on learnings from the Incentivized Testnet, but also anticipating future usage of ada. Some of it will be stored on exchanges, traded, and used in smart contracts. Unclaimed rewards will result from the ada that is not delegated. The treasury will salvage these unclaimed rewards.

IOG doesn't anticipate most pools' pledges to be extremely large, just high enough to make launching a Sybil attack undesirable. The difference between prospective pool rewards with a very high pledge and pools with a more realistic pledge level, ends up in the treasury as well. For the foreseeable future, the total of all ada going to the Treasury indicates that there will be enough funds to pay for new features and upgrades.

Pledge Influence Factor (*a0*)

The ada pledged by pool owners protects against Sybil attacks by ensuring that delegated stake is not overly drawn to pools whose owners attempt to abuse the system by forming numerous pools without owning a substantial amount of stake themselves. There was a lengthy debate, at the time, on this episode of the Cardano Effect.[345] The debate has continued for some time about why, how and by whom, the parameters should be adjusted. Umed Saidov (who wrote this analysis[346] in 2020) and 'Big Pey' laid out their case for change in this passionate discussion[347] at the *Rare Bloom* event.

The pledge influence factor has a direct impact on a pool's rewards: the higher the influence factor, the greater the impact of a bigger pledge on rewards. A greater influence factor improves Sybil protection and makes the system safer and more secure, but it also offers stake pool owners who can afford a bigger pledge an advantage.

The initial value of 0.3 was intended to strike a compromise between the amount of Sybil protection and the pledge needed. However, there is no minimum pledge. The pledge may be made as low or as high as the pool operator decides. Their choices impact the

---

[345] Cardano Pledge, Rewards, and Network Security with Kevin, Lars, and Duncan | TCE 90, youtube.com/watch?v=X-ziLksiPOE

[346] Cardano Mainnet: Pledge Influence Factor Analysis, reddit.com/r/cardano/comments/gfed1l/cardano_mainnet_pledge_influence_factor_analysis

[347] Rare Bloom Day Two Cardano Livestream, youtu.be/eBH34WkU_2w?t=16180

rewards, but there is no 'hard' rule requiring them to pledge a certain amount. This means that pool pledges will eventually go as high as pool owners are willing to go, and it will be up to the community to strike a balance between security, economic concerns, and the desire for justice and equal opportunity.

Pledge deferred update

SPOs that concentrate their pledge into a limited number of pools are rewarded with the $a0$ parameter. This has worked well in encouraging pools with high levels of ada pledge to combine into big private pools (like IOG do), giving smaller pools a better chance to recruit delegators. However, IOG felt the existing method could be improved, therefore debated and modeled ideas to make pledge more successful at resolving pool splitting for lower pledge levels.

While there has been much internal debate, IOG came to the conclusion that any change in k should be only made after revising the formula for $a0$ to get the desired outcomes (especially encouraging stake to flow to smaller single pools rather than split pools). Because this was a complete formula change rather than just an epoch boundary change, it had to be issued as part of a hard fork. IOG planned to make this adjustment for some time but given their product pipelines and their team's focus on the Goguen rollout, the update has not occurred yet and pledge influence factor a0 remains at 0.3.

As things stand (Feb 2023)

Different parameters are used to as lever to control Cardano's protocol behavior. Some parameters are predictable and go unnoticed and largely left alone. Others are more prominent as they directly impact on-chain activities and need regular tuning as the protocol moves out of testnets and hard forks change the playing field conditions for stake pool operators and delegators.

Two variable parameters continue to divide opinion among the SPOs community as they relate to the core principle of Cardano, decentralization, and they impact their ability to earn a living. These are the k value (the number of stake pools who receive rewards), and the minimum pool fee, which is a set amount paid to a pool before rewards are split with delegators.

k (currently 500) impacts the max pool size, based on the equation: $= (45bn - reserves) / k = (35bn / 500) = 70m$

IOG conducted a community survey[348] to 'read the room' but there was not consensus on what changes to make, or how to implement them. IOG previously proposed raising k to 1000, but this was postponed as the survey was not clear cut, IOG were busy with the Vasil hard fork and it was decided more planning and discussion was required.

---

[348] Apr SPO Call - Discord Stage follow-up, input-output.typeform.com/report/Row2tnqQ/HSCUwpltfMyJ7yp7

The MinPool fee has also been an emotive topic. SPOs are the engine room for Cardano operationally. They produce new blocks and ensure a decentralized network grows. They are paid for their work in two ways:

- a fixed fee, a set amount taken if blocks are produced, and
- a variable fee, a percentage of the total rewards paid to a pool.

Staking pools can chose to set any variable fee they like, but the ledger rules has a *minimum* fixed fee in place. This was there originally as defence against Sybil attacks (an adversary might hijack the network by creating a lot of zero-fee pools). Many feel this protection is no longer needed, including IOG who admit this risk may be a more theoretical than practical at this stage as delegation is so decentralized.

A big reason to reduce, or remove it, is it is an obstacle for small new pools to compete with the bigger, more established stake pools. This can be a double whammy as the minimum fee can also incentivize larger SPOs to create new pools since there is a guaranteed profit from doing so.

To get a sense of how emotive these issues are, you should listen to the Twitter Space hosted by Bullish Dumpling[349] and read Adam Dean's twitter thread.[350] *Army of Spies* dedicated a video[351] to it and IOG have written a blog post[352] mapping out potential courses of action. We haven't even mentioned CIP 50 (Liesenfelt Shelleys Voltaire Decentralization Update) which is worthy of a book in itself. I suspect these decisions are deliberately being left to test-drive the new on-chain governance mechanisms in 2023. These new levers of power are explored in Chapter 9. Charles Hoskinson all but confirmed this on a recent AMA:[353]

> *It's not about IOG changing parameters, the system is stable at the moment, it be nice to get all the parameters and tune them on a regular basis, but that's the entire point of CIP 1694. You guys should be doing that. If you want to sign up and have a custodian sit down and think about how to tune the system every month, so that it promotes some outcome, I think that's not the point of Cardano, the point of Cardano is the Cardano community self-regulates Cardano. So what we did is we got the system to a stable state, with that stable state it's able to survive and thrive, the next step is to get the community to take that stable state and create a government on top of it. So if you want to change the system parameters, then go ahead and get something like CIP 1694 in. Obviously, there'll be some fine tuning throughout this year, there's some final things to do as things change, as peer-to-peer gets fully implemented and Genesis gets fully*

[349] Oct 25 2022: Cardano MinPool Fee Discussion, youtu.be/Gz8J5vX1Rnk

[350] @adamKdean, twitter.com/adamKDean/status/1612118333603860480?t=mM5focPvmY-GKax-lOkAPA

[351] Cardano (ADA) & Silver Bullets | Cardano Rumor Rundown #514, youtube.com/watch?v=yWRwncQd4Vs&t=28s

[352] Staking parameters and network optimization – where next for 'k' and 'min fee'?, essentialcardano.io/article/staking-parameters-and-network-optimization-where-next-for-k-and-min-fee

[353] Surprise AMA 01/07/2023, youtube.com/watch?v=djhKk-3rYhU&t=328s

implemented, but it defeats the entire purpose of decentralization to have a tuning committee that's federated

Ouroboros lays the foundation for the Basho Era

Cardano is built to service millions of users across a worldwide network. This means that, like any other decentralized blockchain, it must provide a predictable and steady supply of new blocks that collectively develop the chain and transparently record user transactions. It is critical that the system utilizes resources economically in order to guarantee that new blocks are propagated over the network in an effective and safe manner.

Because flexibility is so crucial, the Cardano protocol was built with genuine scalability in mind. Its parameterized technique is meant to bend and respond to price swings, network saturation and rising demand. There are a number of protocol options that may be used to fine-tune the system's behavior without requiring a hard fork. But even then, larger modifications that do need this may be handled neatly using the hard fork combinator (HFC). These are important differentiators for Cardano, since they provide it with durability and dependability, as well as very flexible upgrade options as the network develops and the user base grows.

Cardano's roadmap was similarly designed in eras, taking in one step at a time toward the final objective. Within a federated network, Byron was about fundamental transactional capacity. While working on the following phase, IOG were able to start establishing a community and relationships. The Byron reboot laid the groundwork for an increase in capabilities, while Shelley introduced stake pools, which helped to grow the community and enable 100% decentralized block production.

IOG debuted a slew of new, much-anticipated features in 2021. Cardano has enabled multi-assets and non-fungible token (NFT)[354] generation on the ledger since the 'Mary' upgrade. There was an explosion of activity in this field due to cheap fees and the lack of a requirement for smart contracts.

Support for Plutus smart contracts was added with the 'Alonzo' update in September 2021, allowing for the construction of a broad variety of decentralized apps (DApps). Smart contracts on Cardano are still in their infancy, but with many projects working on DApps and several already released, momentum is building. These additional features have an impact on how the ledger handles new scripts and transactions, as well as putting new demands on the system's resources. As the volume of activity increases, Cardano's design will enable it to bend and adapt as needed.

---

[354] The role of the blockchain is to prove uniqueness and ownership. **NFTs** came to prominence in 2017 with the CryptoKitties game, in which players buy and 'breed' limited-edition virtual cats. Game developers use NFTs to allow gamers to win in-game tools, and collectibles. Tokenization of such assets allows them to be transferred as tokens between games and players in NFT blockchain marketplaces. NFTs are now used to sell collectibles such as virtual trading cards, music, images and videos. A fractional NFT allows several people to hold (and trade) a share of an asset, for example a work of art.

Network bandwidth

All Cardano activities are built on top of networking. The Cardano network distributes transactions and blocks among nodes all around the globe that build and validate the blockchain. This is known as data diffusion, and it is necessary for the consensus protocol to make judgments by providing the necessary information to nodes. These choices move the chain forward, since node consensus guarantees that all transactions are confirmed and approved, allowing them to be included in a new block in a transparent manner.

The speed with which the system as a whole operates is influenced by network performance. This covers things like:

- *throughput* (amount of data transferred)
- *timeliness* (time for block adoption)

These two needs are in direct opposition to one another. When the created blocks are used as effectively as possible, throughput can be increased. This, in turn, requires adequate buffering to offset latency, reducing the negative effects of a globally distributed system. When the system is saturated, more buffering may frequently suggest greater block (and network) usage, but it comes at the expense of higher latency (time to adoption in the chain).

A block's budget

To comprehend how quickly Cardano transactions and scripts may be completed, the concept of the block budget is key. A block's total size strikes a balance between maximizing network use and reducing transaction latencies. A single block may include a variety of transactions, including smart contracts written in Plutus, native tokens, metadata, and straightforward ada transactions (payments).

Another attribute is the block time budget, which is a set amount of time allowed to complete all of the transactions in a single block. This is split between the amount of time available for Plutus script execution and the amount of time available for other transactions. This attribute guarantees that transactions containing Plutus scripts do not consume the available time budget, and that basic payments may always be processed in the same block as Plutus scripts.

The entire time budget for creating each block (including networking overhead) is set to 1 second, with a Plutus script execution budget of around 50 milliseconds. This is a reasonable provision; IOG's testing has demonstrated that many scripts on a testing environment will run in 1 millisecond or less.

The block time budget was set initially at 1 second. Due to security concerns, the Praos consensus process picks just a small proportion (1 in 20) of the blocks that might possibly be added to the chain. Obviously, the size and effective payloads of various transactions will change. A single transaction, for example, may close off an entire Catalyst voting round, moving millions of dollars in value.

As previously stated, each block contains a number of transactions submitted by end users through wallets, the command-line interface (CLI), and other means. These transactions are stored in the mempool, a temporary in-memory storage space, until they are ready to be processed and included in a block. As a block is minted, pending transactions are removed from the mempool, allowing new transactions to be added. The potential of nodes being overwhelmed during high-demand times was eliminated by employing a fixed-size mempool, although this meant that a wallet or application may have needed to re-submit transactions. The mempool size was determined using queueing models.

Stress testing the network

Ouroboros is built to manage massive amounts of data, as well as transactions and scripts of various sizes and complexity. With the settings in place the Cardano network was still only using around 25% of its capacity on average in October 2021. Of course, the most efficient option is for Cardano to operate at or near 100% capacity (network saturation). While many networking systems would suffer in such circumstances, Ouroboros and the Cardano network stack have been engineered to be fair and very durable even in the face of extreme saturation.

Benchmarking data reveals that even at 200% saturation, overall performance remains stable, and network failures occur. Even with stress tested at 44x, there were no problems in the entire network capacity (though some transactions may be slightly delayed). Backpressure[355] is used to regulate the overall system load, which is how the network is meant to function.

While certain users participating in a big NFT drop[356] may suffer lengthier wait times for their transactions or may need to resubmit the rare transaction from a large batch (or spread the drops over a longer time period), this does not indicate that the network is not coping. It really signifies that the network is working properly. It's referred to as 'graceful degradation,' and you can understand in more detail by reading the network design paper.[357] See 'Cardano Upcoming NFT drops.'[358]

Wallet types

End-user wallets submit payments and other transactions to the blockchain on their behalf, as well as monitor the blockchain's progress. One of the most important functions

---

[355] **Backpressure**: Cardano is designed to automatically deal with heavy traffic. Ouroboros and the network stack function even when saturated. If the network is saturated, Cardano can use the admission control method to regulate and restore normalcy. This is the term 'backpressure' mentioned in blogs and documentation, it is basically a strategy for network load management.

[356] An **NFT drop** is the release of a non-fungible token project. A drop refers to the exact date, time, and generally the minting price of the NFT. Many NFT drops have purchase limits that apply to the number of NFTs you are able to mint in one transaction.

[357] Coutts, Davies, Szamotulski, Thompson (2020) 'Introduction to the design of the Data Diffusion and Networking for Cardano Shelley', hydra.iohk.io/build/7249613/download/1/network-design.pdf

[358] Cardano Upcoming NFT Drops, nftcalendar.io/b/cardano/

of a wallet is to submit transactions on behalf of the user, validate that they have been approved into the blockchain, and retry them if the first attempt fails. That is, when the network saturates, the wallet should consider the implications of backpressure as well as other network effects (temporary disconnection, possible chain forks, etc). Wallets may be one of two types:

- Full-node wallets (like Daedalus), which operate a node that connects directly to the Cardano network using local compute and network resources

- Light wallets such as Yoroi and Flint, on the other hand, take advantage of pooled processing and networking resources to service a large number of users.

Both kinds of wallets may need to retry transactions during times of strong demand (e.g., an NFT drop). Light wallets may need to temporarily scale available compute and network resources to meet user demand since they share resources across numerous users. Full node wallets, on the other hand, may be unaffected. Transactions may be somewhat delayed, but each wallet will have the dedicated resources, including its own network connections, to attempt the submission. DApp providers should follow similar principles: if particular network endpoints are offered, system resources should be adjusted to match demand.

Chain v transaction confirmation

'What is Cardano's TPS (transactions per second)?' is one of the most common questions on Crypto Twitter. How many network confirmations does Cardano require before a transaction goes through? The solutions to these concerns necessitate a more in-depth examination of the principles of chain confirmation and transaction confirmation, as well as their relationship to the protocol.

Chain confirmation

This is the threshold at which the protocol guarantees that the chain will not change any further due to randomness or random occurrences. After enough future k blocks have been issued, chain confirmation happens at some point in the future. The stability window is the period between now and when chain confirmation for a certain transaction happens (that is, the number of slots required for a block to become stable, where stability is defined as a block that cannot be rolled back). The formula for calculating this window is:

$$3k/f$$

- where k is the parameter that restricts a pool's growth by lowering its rewards yield beyond a particular threshold,
- f is the parameter that determines a pool's maximum size

Transaction confirmation

When a transaction is accepted into the chain, it becomes immutable at this point. The terms 'block depth' and 'settlement window' are used here. If the block containing the transaction is deep enough in the chain, it is deemed confirmed. Deep enough is a relative term: the depth of a block shows how many further blocks have been added to the chain since that block was introduced. Because blocks have depth, the transactions included within them have depth as well.

The transaction is deemed verified when the depth of a specific block exceeds a certain threshold, and the assets in that transaction can be used 'safely' (i.e., the protocol can guarantee the transaction is immutable, so the assets can be traded, exchanged, etc).

The settlement window is the amount of time between when a transaction is confirmed and when the transaction's assets may be utilized to swap with other assets. A transaction becomes immutable as soon as its depth is greater than 3k/f slots (that is, 129600 slots on current mainnet, or 36 hours.

The chance of immutability

Another factor to examine when deciding whether or not a transaction is verified is its possibility of immutability. The likelihood of a transaction being immutable is proportional to the number of blocks added to the chain since the transaction was approved. The bigger the number of blocks added, the more likely the transaction will become immutable. When a transaction's depth exceeds 3k/f slots, it becomes immutable. The Ouroboros Praos protocol guarantees this.

In most cases, however, 3k/f slots surpass the criteria, therefore a more realistic way is to assess the likelihood of a transaction being immutable. In this scenario, we consider a transaction to be verified if the likelihood of it being immutable is sufficiently high.

Sebastien Guillemot covers transaction finality, amongst other in things, in this informative deep dive on *Cardano & Algorand: Leader Selection Explained*[359]

P2P (peer-to-peer)

The **networking layer** of Cardano is a physical infrastructure that unifies nodes and their interactions into a single system. The network disseminates transaction and block generation information to all active nodes. The system validates and adds blocks to the chain in this manner, as well as verifying transactions. As a result, a distributed network of nodes must have minimal communication latency and be robust enough to deal with outages, capacity restrictions, and hackers.

If there is to be complete decentralization in terms of block generation, it's also critical that there is decentralization of network connectivity as well. Cardano will do so by switching to peer-to-peer (P2P) networking.

---

[359] Cardano & Algorand: Leader Selection Explained, youtu.be/3k3ls7pzlKg

During the Byron era the P2P ran as a federated system, with nodes connected by a static configuration defined in a topology file. Since Shelley, the system moved to a hybrid mode. During this transition, IOG added added a manually constructed peer-to-peer (P2P) network of stake pool operator (SPO) relay nodes. SPO core nodes could now connect to both federated relay nodes and to other SPO-run relay nodes. This connectivity is not automated but still enables the exchange of block and transaction information without relying on federated nodes. The goal is to switch off all federated relay nodes so that SPOs can connect to each other's relays.

How it works

Cardano's network is a cutting edge, self-organizing network. It includes block producing nodes, relay nodes connecting the network and supporting nodes like Daedalus full node wallets, exchange nodes, etc. The network binds all these nodes together. The SPOs run the block producing nodes which isolate themselves from the network using relays, which talk directly with the rest of the network. The relays take care of the overall network connectivity.

A deeper dive into the intricacies around the techniques and mini-protocols involved is in the documentation.[360] Some of the innovative tools used by IOG include IOsim,[361] an open-source Haskell package which allows IOG to stress test the network with heavy network traffic to help them run simulations of rare large-scale events.

The network is also parametrically polymorphic,[362] meaning there is a degree of separation of the network layer from the rest of the cardano-node code. This allows the ledger and consensus layers to be developed independently of the node code, so critical updates to the network and node don't need to happen at the same time.

All connections are multiplexed[363] which means combining a series of mini protocols into a single Transmission Control Protocol (TCP) connection channel. This has three benefits: bidirectional peer communication (any peer may commence communication with no constraints since both parties have read and write rights inside the same channel), and improved node-to-node communication without compromising performance. It also makes troubleshooting easier as you have less connections.

The P2P governor[364] keeps track of connections and which peers are active and doing well. It optimizes network speed and reliability on an hourly basis. Peers are divided into three kinds:

---

[360] P2P networking docs, docs.cardano.org/explore-cardano/cardano-network/p2p-networking

[361] io-sim, github.com/input-output-hk/io-sim

[362] Polymorphism is the provision of a single interface to entities of different types.

[363] Multiplexing, docs.cardano.org/explore-cardano/cardano-network/networking-protocol/#multiplexing

[364] Ouroboros.Network.PeerSelection.Governor, input-output-hk.github.io/ouroboros-network/ouroboros-network/Ouroboros-Network-PeerSelection-Governor.html

- **cold peers**: peers that are known of, but where there is no established connection
- **warm peers**: where a connection is established but it is used only for network measurements and not for any application-level consensus protocols
- **hot peers**: peers where the connection is actively used for the application-level consensus protocols.

IOG's Technology Manager Kevin Hammond gave a clever analogy during his ScotFest talk:[365]

> *By hot connections, what I mean is me, and the people in this room are hot connections. Warm connections are the people watching me on YouTube, you're not active in this room at this point in time, but you could be very shortly, if you come to Edinburgh... Cold connections, those who are not yet connected, but we're aware of, people who aren't watching the YouTube video live but will watch it later. The cold connections may become (promoted) to warm connections when they watch the YouTube video, and then perhaps (promoted) to hot connections at some point in the future...this is the fundamental concept that we are using with the p2p governor system*

P2P roadmap

To get to a self-organizing, fully automated, decentralized P2P network, the network needs to pass through the following four phases. This strategy was not drawn up on the back of a beer mat but based on deep technical research[366] beyond the scope of this beginners' book.

---

[365] Kevin Hammond, P2P Network talk @ 2hr 30min,
twitter.com/InputOutputHK/status/1593884394715897858?s=20&t=0mPqLNPBdJ7vFHxTGFW6ew

[366] Kolyvas, Voulgaris (2022), 'CougaR: Fast and Eclipse-Resilient Dissemination for Blockchain Networks'
iohk.io/en/research/library/papers/cougar-fast-and-eclipse-resilient-dissemination-for-blockchain-networks/

Current "Hybrid" Mode

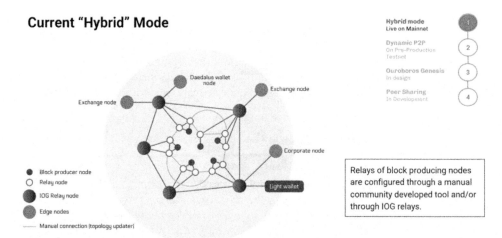

Figure 11: 'Hybrid' Mode, from Kevin Hammond ScotFest talk

Hybrid Mode is the current state of the network at time of writing. In this setup, the black nodes are block producing nodes, which connect via the red circles (relays). The community has produced a manual topology that allows block producing relays to connect with each other. The backbone, the outer ring, is the set of relays that is currently operated by IOG, which the exchanges, Daedalus wallets and light wallets connect with.

In Development: Dynamic Peer-to-Peer (P2P)

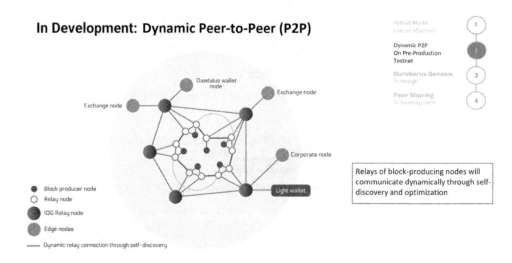

Figure 12: Dynamic p2p phase, from Kevin Hammond ScotFest talk

Stage 2 is being rolled out gradually over 2022-23. This phase introduces a dynamic self-discovery layer between the SPOs. Rather than having a manual configuration, there will be an automatic self-configuring, reconfiguring layer. SPOs won't have to go and download the latest list of relays, the relay nodes themselves will automatically reconfigure the network keeping it optimized and secure.

As always, it's best to check IOG's weekly dev updates[367] for the very latest. For those more technical, there are regular updates from engineering teams in the archive.[368]

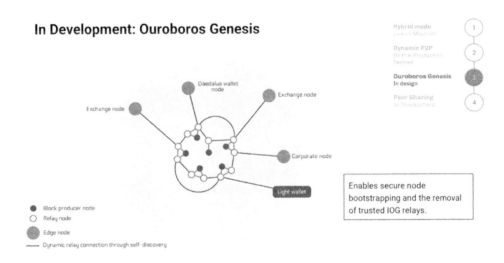

Figure 13: 'Genesis' phase, from Kevin Hammond ScotFest talk

The third stage is Ouroboros Genesis, which is in design and development. Genesis will enable secure node bootstrapping by removing the need for the IOG relays. The outer layer will be gone, leaving a completely peer-supported network.

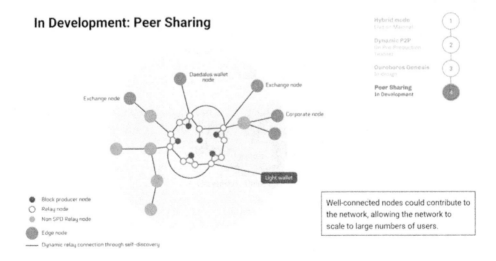

Figure 14: 'Peer sharing' phase, from Kevin Hammond ScotFest talk

---

[367] Cardano weekly dev updates, essentialcardano.io/development-update

[368] IOG Engineering updates, engineering.iog.io/archive/

The final stage 4 is 'peer sharing' when the orange nodes above will be introduced. These will be well connected nodes, run by the community, which will maintain and establish the network. So, then you will no longer have to go to a trusted sources to download the latest set of known relay peers, individual nodes will automatically reconfigure, and the network will be self-organizing.

Further Reading

You can read in much more detail about topics like *Multiplexing*[369] and Connection Management in *About the Cardano Network*[370] and the Network protocol design overview[371] in the Cardano Docs or Go to *Ouroboros Network* in the GitHub repo.

Cardano Entropy (Randomness)

It shouldn't be possible to anticipate or influence future blockchain states if the system is genuinely decentralized. All future on-chain events must be fully random. Cardano makes this possible by including an extra entropy mechanism that may be applied to assure the system's randomness. Any complicated cryptographic system relies on true randomness. A source of pure, unexpected randomness must exist for a cryptographic environment, like the Cardano blockchain, to operate and be accepted by the community as truly decentralized and fair. This assures that the chain's future path cannot be altered by anybody with knowledge of the past.

The entropy parameter specifies Cardano's randomization source. Outside of the Cardano ecosystem, this signifies something unexpected, ensuring that no one can 'hijack' the blockchain's randomness. This parameter's value was computed based on occurrences that could not have been predicted in advance or about which anybody might have had insider knowledge.

Entropy addition mechanism

To appreciate the entropy addition mechanism, one must first comprehend completely decentralized block generation and how the transition nonce[372] will impact this process.

---

[369] In telecoms and computer networks, **multiplexing** (aka muxing) is a method by which multiple analog or digital signals are combined into one signal over a shared medium. The aim is to share an expensive resource. For example, in telecoms, several telephone calls may be carried using one wire. Multiplexing originated in the 1870s and is now widely applied in communications.

[370] About the network, docs.cardano.org/explore-cardano/cardano-network/about-the-cardano-network#gatsby-focus-wrapper

[371] Network protocol overview, docs.cardano.org/explore-cardano/cardano-network/networking-protocol#gatsby-focus-wrapper

[372] A **nonce** is an arbitrary number that can be used just once in a cryptographic communication. It is similar in spirit to a nonce word, hence the name. It is often a random or pseudo-random number issued in an authentication protocol to ensure that old communications cannot be reused in replay attacks.

The Ouroboros protocol uses an evolving sequence of leadership nonces to decide which pools are chosen as block producers (cryptographic seeds used to generate a sequence of values using a repeatable random number generation algorithm). These nonces determine the block production schedule. This timetable is determined by each leader nonce for a whole 5-day epoch, during which the nonce controls the stake pools used to guide the development of each block. To achieve the basic ledger features needed, the leadership nonces and stake distributions develop in lockstep.

Nonce Value

IOG added a transition nonce to the running leadership nonce just after March 31, 2022. When the stake distribution for the April 10 epoch was decided, the transition nonce then had to depend on random values (which are introduced by on-chain transactions) that can't be anticipated. This emphasizes transactions that emerge on the blockchain between the 12-hour mark — when the stake distribution is settled — and the 42-hour mark, when the hash value is removed.

The transition nonce is a reflection of entropy generated by a multitude of external, uncontrollable elements. All transactions posted to the blockchain before Wednesday, April 7 at 15:44:51 UTC play a significant role in Cardano's history: the transactions' accumulated hash value (reflected in the 'previous-block hash' from the first block created on-chain on or after this time) will determine the transition nonce, and thus contribute directly to Ouroboros' perpetual cycle of randomness generation.

A user gives a nonce for a transaction when using the Cardano command line interface (cardano-CLI), however the nonce retrieved when viewing the details of the transaction is different. You can review more details and the relevant command line options in Cardano docs here.[373]

February 2, 2021… How can you explain verifiable randomness to a layman? CH:

> *That's easy so imagine your gambling against the server, you know, like for example you're playing Blackjack. So, when you play Blackjack in human life, you have the dealer and the dealer playing against you and he's giving you cards, you want to believe that the deck is randomly shuffled but it doesn't have to be. What if the dealer had pre-set the cards up so he always gets good cards, and you get bad cards? So, what does a dealer do to give you some faith in the process? He shuffles the cards in front of you. If you believe that shuffling is a randomization process then you will be satisfied that you're playing a fair game, but the problem is what happens if you can't see them shuffle the cards?*
>
> *This is the problem when you gamble with central servers, so you're playing blackjack against blackjackstarz.com or whatever the hell these sites are. Well, how do you know that that's a fair deck? Well, they have a random number*

---

[373] Explanation of the nonce value, docs.cardano.org/explore-cardano/explain-nonce

generator, but how do you know it's not biased so that they win more than you win? Well, you trust that maybe a regulator stepped in and did that. What if you had a cryptographic protocol, you could verify the person's running and you trust the protocol to produce true randomness, then that protocol would guarantee that they're shuffling correctly.

That has to be done for a proof-of-stake system. Why? Because we are replacing traditional proof of work, where it's a meritocratic thing where your computer is chipping away at computations, with a synthetic lottery proportional to your amount of stake you have in the system. So, if you have 25% of the total stake in the system, you should win on average 25% of the time. But what if randomness is biased? Then what can happen is even though you have 25% (of the stake), maybe you only win 8% of the time, because I biased the numbers in a way to reduce your chance of winning. So, you have to have faith that the randomness in the system is secure, it's true.

Fees on Cardano

Cardano has a transaction fee scheme that covers the cost of transaction processing and long-term storage.

Fees are not paid directly to the block maker in the Cardano ecosystem, which makes it unique. They are instead pooled and given to all pools that produced blocks during an epoch. There are no costs for the memory cost of keeping track of the accumulated chain state, specifically UTXO.

Halting economic attacks

The Shelley hard fork changed the Cardano blockchain from federated to entirely decentralized, thus increasing the incentive for bad actors to carry out economic attacks.

When the expenses paid by the operators of a system are not compensated by fees imposed on the system's users, an economic attack could occur. These conditions enable users to impose charges on operators without incurring the whole cost themselves, possibly resulting in a significant decline in operator involvement and, eventually, the system's collapse.

To avoid a scenario like this, it's critical to handle both the current unaccounted operator costs as well as the additional expenses.

Cardano's fee structure is straightforward.

The structure of fees is based on two constants (a and b).

- *a* and *b* are protocol parameters, and the method for determining minimum fees for a transaction (tx) is a * size(tx) + b
- size(tx) is the size of the transaction in bytes.

Protocol parameters

Cardano's update system may adjust protocol settings to respond and adapt to changes in transaction volume, hardware pricing, and ada valuation. Changing these settings is considered a hard fork since it affects which transactions the system accepts.

Parameter a

The transaction cost is dependent on the transaction size, as indicated by parameter a. Larger transactions require more resources to store and complete a transaction.

Parameter b

Regardless of the magnitude of the transaction, the value of b is the fee that must be paid. The purpose of this option is to avoid Distributed Denial-of-Service (DDoS) attacks. b makes such attacks extremely costly and removes the chance of an attacker flooding the system with millions of small transactions.

From Twitter Space, April 18, 2022, 'Sunday Chat with Charles' **Re: Rewards going down, compensated by Transaction fees.** [374]

> *Well, there's a formal curve in the specification, so if you look at the inflation, it's over a 140-year period, I think, so it goes down. But it's bounded and there's precise formulas for how that works. It's unlike Bitcoin, which has a step function which reduces every four years by half. This is a continuous emission decline, so it's a nice gradual monotonically decreasing curve that's quite smooth.*
>
> *Now Cardano is unique, unlike Bitcoin, where sidechains are going to really change things. So what people don't seem to understand is that when a sidechain comes out, the sidechain is going to do its quorum sampling from stake pool operators. And when you mine that sidechain, you have to pay a block reward to get those stake pool operators interested in it, but then that gets paid to the operators and to the delegators, just like ada rewards are.*
>
> *So as a sidechain ecosystem starts building up, and we have dozens and eventually hundreds of sidechains, that means when you hold ada, in addition to getting ada rewards, you'll also get tokens from all the sidechains that are supported. So that plus transaction fees is really going to change the calculus. The other thing is that ada is a very volatile asset. So yeah, block rewards are worth something, but you know, ada was $3 less than seven months ago. It could be $5 in seven months. It could be $0.05 in seven months. So, percentages certainly matter, but the real value does as well. And there's some elasticity there. So, I think the introduction of sidechains increases the transaction volume, and then also the volatility of the price of the underlying asset is going*

[374] Twitter Space 'Sunday Chat with Charles', twitter.com/IOHK_Charles/status/1515872352395055109?s=20&t=ivZvNmtLVKrKk_ZEg-1e_A

to really be a game changer for the return for holding in that respect, and this is what makes it fun.

You know, the other thing is multi-resource consensus is going to come at some point. It's one of our proposals for the long-term road map, and there, you'll have different ways of creating resources for consensus, and those could either be directly monetized with ada or they could be monetized with a different asset. So, there's a lot there. That said, ada is a deflationary asset. Bitcoin Maxis (maximalists) seem to hate us, but we actually have the same monetary policy in that respect.

Fixed supply 45 billion, we're gradually earning our way up to it and it's monotonically decreasing inflation. So it's a deflationary asset, at its core, and that's one of the reasons why a lot of people like ada. But there's going to be a whole ecosystem of tokens, a constellation of them, and lots of utility and things to do. DeFi also changes the equation as well, because you can use your ada and DeFi at the same time, so you can also augment your yields to offset the decline in yields. So, it just basically comes down to what your risk profile is from that respect.

The 3 different sides of full Decentralization

Decentralization is the transfer of power from a central authority to smaller entities. However, in the context of cryptocurrencies and blockchain, this definition merely scratches the surface. Cardano's technological road to complete decentralization gradually unfolded, with stake pool operators (SPOs) producing varying degrees of blocks, peer-to-peer (P2P) network discovery, and 'gossip' with peers trading information among themselves. It entails the implementation of sophisticated community-led governance and decision-making mechanisms, with completely decentralized software and protocol changes as a result.

Pushing power to the edges

The balance of power has moved from the people to businesses like Facebook and Google, resulting in a virtual information monopoly. Centralized authority has data hegemony over their customers due to their unassailable market positions.

Decentralization is the antidote to power concentration and the dangers it entails. Decentralization allows individuals to make choices and decisions, restores personal information ownership to the individual, pushes authority to the margins, and gives every network member (or ada holder) a stake. Cardano's decentralization is built on three principles: block production, networking, and governance. These are inextricably intertwined and work together to produce a cohesive result: complete decentralization, which lies at their intersection.

1. Decentralized block production

To develop and prosper, every blockchain depends on the creation of new blocks. Core nodes – maintained by IOG, Emurgo, and the Cardano Foundation – were solely responsible for building blocks and maintaining the network throughout the Byron era deployment. Shelley and the Incentivized Testnet, which launched in 2019, served as a testbed for decentralized block production. The Incentivized Testnet experiment demonstrated that Cardano could be supported by a network of community-run stake pools.

The number of stake pools continues to grow and grow, with a good number of them forming blocks and rewarding delegates. Exchanges control some, while single-pool community operators handle others. Everyone contributes to the network's worth. The former because of their capacity to attract new ada holders into the ecosystem, and the latter because of their contribution to decentralization and grassroots involvement. IOG is dedicated to promoting decentralization, and while they tweaked parameters in the past, the reigns will be handed over to the community gradually in 2023 with the *Age of Voltaire*.

2. Decentralized Network

The introduction of peer-to-peer (P2P) networking is the second pillar of Cardano's decentralization. The goal is to connect geographically dispersed pools to create a safe and reliable blockchain platform.

This feature will leverage a collection of mini protocols[375] and a categorization of cold, warm, and hot peers on mainnet to allow a node to make the best connection choice possible. In terms of networking, there was a hybrid era where SPOs had to use manual methods to maintain network connections. As SPOs took over block production at $d=0$, all core nodes were decommissioned. IOG continued to maintain relays, but the SPO network are gradually taking over this duty. To learn more about this, watch March 2021 Cardano360 episode,[376] in which IOG's principal architect Duncan Coutts outlined the P2P future.

3. Decentralized Governance

Cardano has already got transaction metadata and native tokens thanks to the Goguen rollout. Since the Shelley launch, this has perhaps been the most visible evidence of Cardano's development and success.

At the same time, something even more powerful has emerged with Project Catalyst: an active community of builders, innovators, and entrepreneurs. The Catalyst community has a worldwide membership of entrepreneurs, professionals, and specialists from a variety of fields that make up this pool of decentralized talent, which offers a broad

---

[375] Marcin Szamotulski, 'Cardano's Path to Decentralization', iohk.io/en/blog/posts/2020/07/09/cardanos-path-to-decentralization-by-marcin-szamotulski/

[376] Decentralization unpacked with Colin Edwards, Duncan Coutts, Lars Brunjes & Shawn McMurdo , youtu.be/mXYIQDUitYI

reservoir of innovation to guarantee the greatest and brightest ideas receive the financing they deserve.

Cardano's ultimate goal is to create a blockchain where a community of stakeholders make practical choices regarding the chain's protocol and growth, which is supported by a layer of robust governance. Catalyst was the forerunner of Voltaire, the development era that will usher in the third and ultimate degree of decentralization by integrating governance and on-chain decision-making/voting. Chapter 9 is all about the *Age of Voltaire* and how the governance mechanisms will be rolled out.

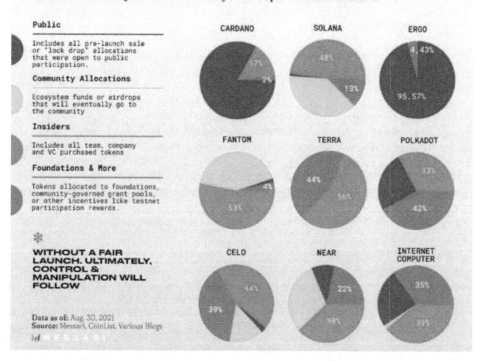

Figure 15: Messari Initial Token Allocation Chart

September 8, 2021. Re: Catalyst. CH:[377]

> *The cryptocurrency space, as a whole, is not aware of this yet, they're still thinking that it's just all centralized and top down, and there's a few people*

---

[377] Charles Hoskinson Explains Cardano's Secret Weapon (Project Catalyst), youtube.com/watch?v=vQOvX-HAQDQ

floating around who make all these calls. They don't really understand that we've silently built one of the world's largest decentralized organizations and decentralized decision-making machines, and it's in its infancy.

We have constructed this meta brain, that runs this meta machine in the sky, and all these people whether in the south of France, or an island, or right here in Colorado with a lobster on the mic... we somehow just come together, with different values, different languages, different perceptions of reality and we converge to a point where we actually can vote on, and move forward, and make change and get funding behind people... more and more of the community is going to be involved in deciding the direction and governance of Cardano in general.

What's so cool about this is it's completely bottom up. There's not a lot of top down here, the top down stuff is just ensuring that there's best practices and good infrastructure ...and asking questions about what tools we need to construct and how do we improve things? ...but the solutions are coming bottom up, and it's growing rapidly, and more and more people come in every time we do a fund, it just massively increases [..]...we don't even have the mobile interfaces in yet, or the Daedalus integration in yet.

Half a million, million people are going to be in this club next year, if not more. So, this is a great opportunity for us to kind of explain where this is going, and why this is the heart of Cardano and what's going to make Cardano frankly not only here to stay, but the dominant protocol of all the protocols.

Edinburgh Decentralization Index

'Decentralized' has become a meaningless buzzword for many crypto projects. How does one judge claims with so much misinformation, willful ignorance, FUD (fear uncertainty and doubt) and good old-fashioned greed and corruption prevalent? The politest description of many claims is that they are subjective and warrant scrutiny. Blockchain and crypto are complex and nuanced for most casual investors, who have little time in their busy lives to do any deep research into projects.

With a regulatory vacuum and no requirement for transparency, it's not hard to make a digital asset look superficially attractive. With no agreed definition of what decentralization is, who is to say something is not decentralized? Who decides on the criteria of what we are all supposed to be measuring? Who has any remit in a permissionless and open industry? With many blockchains categorized based on high-level criteria, they are often very different once you look closer.

Consider just some of the findings from a well-researched article[378] by the *Cardanians (cardanians.io)* published in October 2022:

---

[378] Comparing the decentralization of Cardano and Ethereum, cexplorer.io/article/comparing-the-decentralization-of-cardano-and-ethereum

- Cardano has one entity (Binance) with more than 10% share in the network. Ethereum has numerous such entities with largest having 30%+ share
- Cardano's minimum attack vector (MAV)[379] is approx 24, Ethereum and Bitcoinn both have a MAV of 3.
- Anyone can stake their ada on Cardano, with no need to entrust your ada to a third party. You can spend or withdraw your ada anytime. Liquid staking means your funds are never locked. With Ethereum, there is no protocol-level stake delegation. If you have less than 32 ETH, you are obliged to trust a validator with your coins and signing keys.
- It is easy and inexpensive to run a Cardano stake pool. On Ethereum, you are required to lock 32 ETH to run a validator (stake pool equivalent).

While the above study is compelling and the numbers speak for themselves, such a study is complex and nuanced as configurations change all the time. Definitions of the different terms vary based on who you ask. Clearly, a more permanent and objective formal analysis is required. An academic institute may be the best candidate to host such a research agenda. Enter the *Edinburgh Decentralization Index (EDI)*, a project launched by Dr. Daniel Woods and Prof Aggelos Kiayias at ScotFest[380] The goal is to propose a structured approach to quantifying decentralization in blockchain systems.

The EDI will be a bellwether for the industry, a north star for retail investors, regulatory bodies, and governments. The research at Edinburgh will be a collaborative, interdisciplinary initiative spearheaded by one of IOG's oldest academic partners, the UoE's Blockchain Technology Laboratory (BLT).

The EDI will be based on a unified framework for assessing different aspects of decentralization. The researchers will start with Bitcoin and eventually include other chains. The index measures the following criteria:

- Hardware
- Software
- Network
- Consensus mechanism
- Tokenomics
- API
- Governance
- Validators' geographic distribution

To dig deeper into the EDI, study the research paper[381] which outlines the framework.

Related work

---

[379] The **minimum attack vector** (MAV) is the minimum number of participants required to hijack control in order to attack, or manipulate, the network.

[380] The first of its kind, introducing the Edinburgh Decentralization Index, youtube.com/watch?v=8GJQDsH854Q

[381] Karakostas, Kiayias, Ovezik (2022), 'SoK: A Stratified Approach to Blockchain Decentralization', arxiv.org/abs/2211.01291

Dr Laura Reder and Sooraj Saju co-wrote a useful companion piece to the EDI. Their book, *Assessment Framework for Layer 1 Blockchains,*[382] scrutinises all the top proof-of-stake cryptocurrencies based on how they tackle the blockchain trilemma. Ethereum's staking model, CH[383]

> *Ethereum spent 7 years to give their community a staking model that is vastly inferior to ours. It's custodial, it's not liquid, it's really just a mess ...and maybe one day you get your money back, but right now Ethereum is the Hotel California of the cryptocurrency space ...and 7 years of effort with 10 times the resources we have, meanwhile we figured it all out in 2020, and brought it to Market ...and now we're talking about how do we take it to an exponential level, where basically the system scales with the network speed forever.*

---

[382] A 3-Step Metrics-Based Assessment Framework for Layer1 Blockchains, t.co/qW9RRE43v7

[383] Let's Talk Basho, youtu.be/fhVo-2QUjLM?t=1869

Chapter 5: Goguen (Smart Contracts)

*'The most damaging phrase in the language is...
it's always been done this way'*

— Grace Hopper

Erik Voorhees ✔
@ErikVoorhees

Noise: Bitcoin doesn't have smart contracts

Noise: Bitcoin does have smart contracts

Signal: Bitcoin has some smart contract ability, but it's far more limited than other protocols such as Ethereum.

Signal: Ethereum has greater complexity & attack surface due to this.

Charles Hoskinson ✔
@IOHK_Charles

Signal: Cardano's EUTXO and Plutus have the expressiveness of Ethereum with the attack surface of Bitcoin.

Extended UTXO

Blockchain networks are complicated data structures. Transactions traverse the chain on a regular basis, leaving digital fingerprints[384] that must be carefully tracked and managed to maintain the underlying ledger's integrity and trustworthiness. In the blockchain world, there are two main types of accounting ledgers: UTXO-based blockchains (like Bitcoin) and Account/Balance chains (Ethereum, and others).

The accounting models of these two models vary in many ways. The Unspent Transaction Output (UTXO) model is used by Bitcoin, Cardano, Zcash, Ergo, Avalanche and others while the Account/Balance model is used by Ethereum, Polkdot, Algorand, etc.

---

[384] **Digital footprint** or digital shadow refers to one's unique set of traceable digital activities, actions, contributions and communications manifested on the Internet or on digital devices. On the World Wide Web, the internet footprint; also known as cyber shadow, electronic footprint, or digital shadow, is the information left behind as a result of a user's web-browsing and stored as cookies.

Cardano aimed to create an Extended UTXO (EUTXO) accounting model by combining Bitcoin's UTXO model with Ethereum's capacity to handle smart contracts. The adoption of EUTXO makes it easier to integrate smart contracts into the Cardano network.

How does the accounting model work?

The analogy of a balance sheet is often used to explain the account model. A balance sheet is required by any commercial entity to maintain an accurate record of profit, loss, cash flow, and other factors. Companies can visualize their financial situation at any moment in time by keeping meticulous records of all this information. Another benefit of a company's accounting ledger is the ability to track the origins and ownership of funds. Blockchain networks also need an accounting model to establish who owns what currencies, monitor where those coins move, which ones are used up, and which ones are still accessible for spending.

Account/Balance model vs. UTXO model

Accountants used to maintain records of the transfer of funds in physical ledger books with handwritten entries. Electronic versions of the same thing are being used by businesses. To monitor provenance and ownership, blockchains employ transactions as records (much like entries in a ledger book). These transactions include a lot of information (where the coins came from, where they're going, and how much change is left over).

UTXO

An unspent transaction output (UTXO) is the term for the amount of digital currency that remains after a cryptocurrency transaction. The flow of assets is documented in a UTXO model as a directed acyclic graph[385] with nodes representing transactions and edges representing transaction outputs, with each successive transaction consuming some UTXOs and adding new ones. Users' wallets determine the users' balance by keeping track of a list of unspent outputs connected with all addresses held by the user.

In many respects, UTXO is identical to currency. 'Cash in cash out' is the commonly used analogy. Let's say you have to pay a restaurant bill of €15. You forgot your credit card so pay in cash. You pay with a €20 note (input) and want to leave a €2 tip. The waitress puts €15 in the till (output 1) and gives you back a €2 coin (output 2) and a €1 coin (output 3). She puts the €2 tip (output 4) in the tip jar. Regardless, if you decide to leave a tip or not, or give exact change, the inputs and outputs must match.

The same is true for UTXOs. Any balance you have in your blockchain wallet may be built up using a variety of UTXO combinations depending on prior transactions, but the total value stays the same. In other words, a wallet address's balance is the total of all unspent UTXOs from prior transactions.

---

[385] A **directed acyclic graph** is a directed graph with no directed cycles. That is, it consists of vertices and edges, with each edge directed from one vertex to another, such that following those directions will never form a closed loop.

Concept of 'change' in UTXO models

UTXOs introduce 'change,' much like currency transactions at a shop. You can't cut a €50 note into smaller pieces to pay for anything that costs €15, for example, when you take it out of your pocket. You must hand over the whole €50 money and the clerk will give you your change. The same is true for UTXOs. A UTXO cannot be 'split' into smaller pieces. UTXOs are used in their entirety, with the remainder being returned to your wallet's address in the form of a smaller UTXO.

UTXO advantages

One can derive reliable information regarding the blockchain's use and financial activities by examining and tracking the size, age, and number of UTXOs being moved around.

Other benefits of UTXO models may be found like better scalability, especially for state channels and sharding solutions. On privacy, UTXO makes it difficult for a malicious actor to link transactions. A user can constantly change their receiving address, with new addresses having no previous owner. Also, since each UTXO may only be consumed once and in its whole, the transaction logic is streamlined, making transaction verification considerably easier.

To summarize UTXO:

- A UTXO is the result of a prior transaction that may be spent in the future
- There are no accounts in UTXO chains. Instead, coins are kept as a list of UTXOs, and transactions are made by consuming existing UTXOs and creating new ones in their place
- Balance is the total number of UTXOs possessed by a certain address (UTXOs are used whole).

The Account/Balance model is a method for keeping track of, and balancing, your finances. An account (which may be managed by a private key or a smart contract) is used to keep a coin balance in blockchain models that employ an Account/Balance accounting model, as the name implies. Assets are represented as balances inside users' accounts in this architecture, and the balances are saved as a global state of accounts maintained by each node and updated with each transaction.

Account/Balance chains (such as Ethereum) function similarly to regular bank accounts in many ways. When coins are deposited, the wallet's balance rises, and when coins are moved elsewhere, the wallet's balance falls. The key distinction is that, unlike UTXOs, you may only utilize a portion of your balance. So, if you have 50 ETH in your account, you may transmit a piece of it to someone else (for example, 15 ETH). As a consequence, your account balance will be 35 ETH, and the address to which you delivered the coins will be increased by 15 ETH. In Account/Balance accounting models, the idea of change does not apply as it does in UTXO accounting models.

Transaction sizes are generally smaller with the account model, compared to UTXO, as only basic data regarding sender, receiver, amount and signatures are captured. Onboarding new nodes is therefore easier as there is less data to sync.

To summarize the Account/Balance concept:

- This accounting approach works similarly to how a bank does
- Users have accounts that keep their coin balances
- Partial balances may be spent
- The idea of change is irrelevant
- Account models are suited for Layer 2 deployments as transaction size/metadata is light.

Transactions Outputs and Inputs

The word 'transaction' frequently conjures up images of money. While this definition applies to Bitcoin (since the Bitcoin is used to transfer payments between peers), many other blockchains (like Cardano) are more flexible. The word 'transaction' is significantly more complicated in these circumstances. Transactions may be thought of as value transfers.

Each transaction in a blockchain system may have one or more inputs and one or more outputs. If one wishes to grasp how a transaction works and how it connects to UTXO, one must first comprehend the notion of inputs and outputs. Consider a transaction to be the operation that unlocks past outputs while also creating new ones.

Transaction output

An address (which you might view as a lock) and a value are included in the transaction output.[386] In line with this analogy, the address's signature is the key that unlocks the output. An output may be used as an input after it has been unlocked. New transactions use previous transactions' outputs while also producing new outputs that may be consumed by subsequent transactions. Each UTXO may only be used once, and it must be consumed in its entirety. Only one input may spend each output.

Transaction input

The output of a preceding transaction is referred to as a transaction input. A pointer and a cryptographic signature that serves as the unlocking key are included in transaction inputs. The key unlocks a prior transaction output, and the pointer refers back to it. The blockchain labels an unlocked output as 'spent' when it is unlocked by an input. New inputs may then refer to new outputs produced by a given transaction, and the chain continues. The UTXOs are the new outputs (which have not yet been unlocked, i.e., spent). Unspent outputs are just that: outputs that haven't been used yet.

---

[386] **Transaction output:** Outputs produced by transactions. They are consumed when they are spent by another transaction. Typically, some kind of evidence is required to be able to spend a UTXO, such as a signature from a public key, or (in the Extended UTXO Model) satisfying a script.

How UTXO works

Transactions consume unspent outputs from earlier transactions and create fresh outputs that may be used as inputs for future transactions under a UTXO accounting model.

These UTXOs are managed by the users' wallets, which also start transactions using the user's UTXOs. At all times, every blockchain node keeps track of a subset of all UTXOs. This is called the UTXO set. In technical jargon, this is the chainstate, which is kept in each node's data directory. The chainstate is changed whenever a new block is added to the chain. The list of recent transactions is included in this new block (including of course a record of spent UTXOs, and new ones created since the chainstate was last updated). Every node keeps a duplicate of the chainstate.

Why Cardano chose EUTXO

Cardano's UTXO accounting mechanism is not the same as Bitcoin's, since Cardano is meant to do more than only manage payments. The necessity for increased programming expressiveness in the Alonzo era's smart contracts feature required a unique ('Extended') approach.

The 'basic' UTXO concept has a restricted programmability expressiveness. With the establishment of an account-based ledger and related contract accounts, Ethereum's Account/Balance accounting model addresses this particular challenge. However, the contract code's semantics grew significantly more sophisticated as a result, which had the unintended consequence of compelling contract writers to fully comprehend the semantics to prevent the insertion of potentially extremely expensive flaws in the code.

An 'extended' UTXO solution would need two features that the current UTXO model lacks:

1. To be able to keep the contract in its current state.
2. To be able to ensure that the same contract code is used throughout the transaction sequence. This is what is referred to as continuity.

The EUTXO model has the advantage of being able to forecast the fees necessary for a successful transaction before it is processed. This is a characteristic that account-based models do not have.

Why is it called EUTXO?

UTXO is 'extended' by allowing for extra 'locks' and 'keys' controlling under which conditions an output may be unlocked for consumption by a transaction (in addition to value), and by allowing for custom data to be added to outputs. In other words, rather than having public keys (hashes) for locks and accompanying signatures serve as 'keys,' EUTXO allows arbitrary logic to be implemented using scripts. This arbitrary logic examines the transaction and data to determine whether or not the transaction may use an input.

What's so great about EUTXO?

Cardano's ledger architecture extends on the UTXO model to accommodate multi-assets and smart contracts while maintaining the UTXO model's benefits. Groundbreaking research allows Cardano to do functions that no other UTXO ledger can, making it a unique contender in the blockchain space.

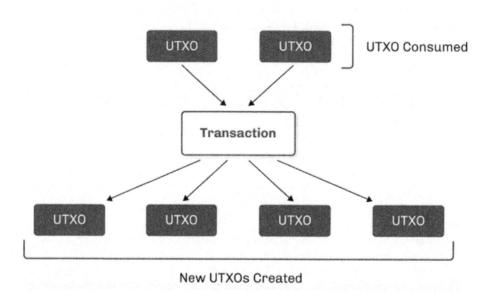

Figure 16: UTXO model

The extended UTXO model

The UTXO model is extended in two ways by the EUTXO model:

1. The lock-and-key analogy is used to extend the idea of an 'address.' Addresses in the EUTXO model may include arbitrary logic in the form of scripts instead of confining locks to public keys and keys to signatures. When a node verifies a transaction, for example, it evaluates whether the transaction may utilize a certain output as an input. If the output can be used as an input, the transaction will look up the script supplied by the output's address and run it.

2. The second distinction between UTXO and EUTXO is that, in addition to an address and a value, outputs may contain (virtually) any data. By enabling scripts to carry state, they become considerably more powerful.

Furthermore, EUTXO expands on the UTXO concept by enabling output addresses to include complicated logic to determine which transactions are allowed to unlock them, as well as by allowing custom data to be added to all outputs. When verifying an address,[387] the script will look at the data carried by the output,[388] the transaction being checked, and some extra data known as redeemers[389] that the transaction supplies for each input. The script[390] provides enough context to deliver a 'yes' or 'no' response, in what may be very complicated circumstances, by uncovering all of this information.[391]

EUTXO allows for arbitrary logic to be expressed in the form of scripts. This arbitrary logic examines the transaction and data to determine whether or not the transaction may use an input.

The graph structure of the UTXO paradigm differs significantly from the account-based model employed by several current smart-contract enabled blockchains. As a consequence, design paradigms for DApps on account-based blockchains do not easily adapt to Cardano. Because the underlying representation of the data is different, new design patterns are required.

The per-branches architecture of the UTXO (Bitcoin) model is carried over to EUTXO, where one branch is defined as a series of transactions requiring a succession of validations. Building DApps and other solutions with numerous UTXOs is vital for splitting the functionality over various branches and enforcing additional parallelism.[392] This has scalability advantages, just as creating Bitcoin services necessitates breaking one wallet into sub wallets.

EUTXO Advantages

Compared to other accounting models, the EUTXO model has several distinct benefits. The transaction's success or failure is solely determined by the transaction and its inputs, not by anything else on the blockchain. As a result, before a transaction is posted to the blockchain, the legitimacy of the transaction may be confirmed off-chain. A transaction may still fail if another transaction consumes an input that the transaction is expecting at the same time, but if all inputs are still available, the transaction will succeed.

---

[387] The **address of a UTXO** says where the output is 'going'. The address stipulates the conditions for unlocking the output. This can be a public key hash, or (in the Extended UTXO model) a script hash.

[388] A **script output**: A UTXO locked by a script.

[389] **Redeemer**: The argument to the validator script which is provided by the transaction which spends a script output.

[390] A **validator script** is the script attached to a script output in the Extended UTXO model. Must be run and return positively in order for the output to be spent. It determines the address of the output.

[391] **Validation context**: A data structure containing a summary of the transaction being validated, and the current input whose validator is being run.

[392] The term **Parallelism** refers to techniques to make programs faster by performing several computations at the same time.

This contrasts with an account-based approach (such as Ethereum), which allows a transaction to fail in the middle of its execution. In EUTXO,[393] this will never happen. Also, transaction execution costs may be calculated off-chain before transmission, which is something that Ethereum does not allow.

Cardano's EUTXO paradigm provides a safe and flexible environment for processing many operations without causing system issues. This architecture provides superior scalability and privacy, as well as more straightforward transaction logic, since each UTXO can only be used once and in its entirety, making transaction verification considerably easier.

The EUTXO model has the advantage of being able to forecast the fees necessary for a successful transaction before it is posted. This is a feature that account-based models do not have. Account-based blockchains, such as Ethereum, are indeterministic, meaning the impact of a transaction on the chain cannot be guaranteed. This ambiguity raises the danger of financial loss, unexpectedly expensive costs, and a broader attack vector for hackers to exploit.

A deep technical analysis of EUTXO ledger's architecture is beyond the scope of this book, however, you can get 'into the weeds' by reviewing IOG's blog 'Architecting DApps on the EUTXO Ledger'[394] where they provide a sample architecture. SundaeSwap[395] and Axo (previously Maladex) also blogged about their solution while ERGOdex[396] talked about their philosophy on *Cardano with Paul*[397] YouTube channel. There are also some code samples from IOG on avoiding concurrency using multi signatures in the Lobster Challenge.[398] IOG analyze a sample order book pattern[399] architecture in their blog. For a deeper dive into EUTXO, read the handbook.[400]

[393] Fernando Sanchez, 'Cardano's extended UTXO accounting model', iohk.io/en/blog/posts/2021/03/12/cardanos-extended-utxo-accounting-model-part-2/

[394] Jean-Frédéric Etienne, 'Architecting DApps on the EUTXO ledger', iohk.io/en/blog/posts/2021/11/16/architecting-dapps-on-the-eutxo-ledger/

[395] SundaeSwap blog, sundaeswap-finance.medium.com/sundaeswap-labs-presents-the-scooper-model-678d6054318d

[396] What is ERGO + ERGOdex Concurrency Solution For Cardano, youtube.com/watch?v=xlDlNmIFrFM

[397] Cardano with Paul, youtube.com/watch?v=xlDlNmIFrFM

[398] IOHK Lobster challenge, github.com/input-output-hk/lobster-challenge/tree/concurrency-multisig

[399] Order book pattern, plutus-apps.readthedocs.io/en/latest/plutus/explanations/order-book-pattern.html#what-is-the-order-book-pattern

[400] EUTXO handbook, ucarecdn.com/3da33f2f-73ac-4c9b-844b-f215dcce0628/EUTXOhandbook_for_EC.pdf

'Neither smart nor a contract'

While Vitalik Buterin and others[401] have opined that smart contracts are neither smart nor a contract, let's not be pedantic for the sake of brevity. A smart contract is a code-based automatic digital agreement that records, validates, and executes the contract's binding transactions between numerous participants. When preset criteria are satisfied, the smart contract code automatically executes the contract's transactions. A smart contract is just a brief program whose inputs and outputs are blockchain transactions.

vitalik.eth ✓
@VitalikButerin

Replying to @CleanApp @cryptoecongames and 4 others

To be clear, at this point I quite regret adopting the term "smart contracts". I should have called them something more boring and technical, perhaps something like "persistent scripts".

6:21 PM · Oct 13, 2018 · Twitter Web Client

Smart contracts are self-executing and dependable, requiring no third-party intervention or presence. The smart contract code is kept on a decentralized blockchain network and spread throughout it, making it transparent and irrevocable.

Smart contracts are immutable because they cannot be modified, they are distributable and tamper-proof, they are quick and cost efficient because there is no middleman, saving money and time, and they are secure because they are encrypted.

Why smart contracts?

Intermediaries are engaged in many commercial procedures that include the exchange of value (such as money, property, or shares) to ensure that the conditions of the agreements are comprehensive, clear, and met before the exchange may take place. The cost of a transaction is increased by these middlemen. Smart contracts have evolved as a technique of decreasing the time, third-party participation, and expense of reliably executing an agreement.

Smart contracts are software programs that are stored on the blockchain in an immutable format. They're run on virtual computers, and their data is stored in the same immutable architecture. Businesses aiming to improve their operations might profit greatly from smart contracts. Many sectors, including automotive, supply chain, real estate, and

---

[401] Neither Smart Nor Contracts: Smart Contracts Need a Rebrand, netguru.com/blog/smart-contracts

healthcare, are investing in research to see how this technology might help them compete more effectively.

Metadata on Cardano

The need for metadata

Remember, money is a social construct. It is only valuable if people acknowledge and believe in it. Most transactions have a context that needs to be captured in metadata. Bitcoin and its contemporaries have abandoned the requirement for reliable identities, information, and reputation in commercial transactions in their quest to anonymize and disintermediate central players. Adopting centralized methods to add this data loses the auditability, global availability, and immutability that is the whole idea of using a blockchain.

Transactional information is abundant in legacy financial systems such as those based on SWIFT. Regulation often involves attribution of individuals engaged, compliance information, reporting suspicious behavior, and other records and activities in addition to knowing how much value transferred between accounts. The metadata might be more essential than the transaction in certain instances. The metadata is the story of the transaction.

As a result, it appears logical to conclude that tampering with metadata may be just as dangerous as counterfeiting money or changing transaction history. Making no allowances for actors who want to freely participate in these domains seems to be detrimental to mainstream acceptance and consumer protection.

Adding metadata to transactions was the first step in preparing Cardano for DeFi. Cardano evolved into a smart contract platform with the launch of Goguen. This began by including metadata — information about the data being processed – in transactions, which was introduced to the blockchain. Cardano has evolved from a transaction-focused platform to a utility platform available to partnerships, businesses, and commercial applications that may be used for the complex processes that will characterize the decentralized financial future (DeFi).

With the growing number of cryptocurrency transactions, having access to immutable data that cannot be changed is critical, particularly for applications like wealth management. The Cardano blockchain keeps permanent records of completed transactions, guaranteeing a transparent and auditable history of financial activity. However, to give financial operations greater responsibility and visibility, context must be given to these transactions. Facts such as sender and recipient information, processing circumstances, and processing time are examples of additional information. This is accomplished by including transaction metadata.

Data about data

The term 'metadata' refers to information about information. It defines the context, content, and structure of records, in other words. Metadata promotes confidence through permanent data attestation, since blockchain technology offers a transparent ledger for preserving information immutably and securely.

Whether it's a purchase for a product or service or a money transfer to a family member, all transactions have a definite purpose. When making an online purchase, for example, there is a lot of information that can be gathered about the transaction. Metadata may help convey the tale of a product purchase by revealing information about the customer and seller, the date of the transaction, the product maker, and the supply circumstances.

March 31, 2019. On metadata. CH:[402]

> *An example of this…. let's say that Bob goes to an ATM and withdraws $300 of value out of an ATM …now that's a transaction …now let's say Bob did that next in an Italian restaurant on his birthday and all of his friends happen to be there …you would say 'oh it looks like Bob's pulling money out to pay the check' ….or in some way is connected to this event, he's at a celebration, there's people there…. it's expensive and let's say it's at 12 o'clock …it's lunchtime… Bob can then go take 300 dollars from an ATM, so the same type of transaction but now I've changed the metadata….*
>
> *Let's say it's 2:00 a.m. right next to a known brothel ….so basically the exact same type of transaction …the same type of value, the same actor involved… this is his account and his money, but because you've changed the metadata it has vastly different implications…. So, what if you could swap these metadata and then suddenly you can now make the Italian restaurant look like a brothel? ….whoever controls that story has a lot of power.*

With the advent of Bitcoin, developers began using blockchain technology to add small amounts of new data to the chain, knowing that the data would be accessible for the rest of time. In 2015, the University of Nicosia[403] became the first university to issue academic certificates whose authenticity could be verified through the Bitcoin blockchain. Adding information to the chain became the norm over time.

Transaction metadata

Metadata is a useful tool for certifying and validating information. It lets cryptocurrency assets save information about their previous owners, transfers, and values. This is especially useful when dealing with non-fungible assets that reflect value, such as property or intellectual property. A public key may also be used to sign and certify a variety of documents, proving the document's authenticity.

One of the most well-known applications of metadata is in the supply chain. Factories, customers, suppliers, and delivery services are all part of the supply chain. Participants must give proof of interconnected services that are available to everyone for verification

---

[402] Surprise AMA 03/31/2019, youtu.be/sc4D2KrvaNA?t=2315

[403] Blockchain Certificates (Academic & Others), unic.ac.cy/iff/blockchain-certificates/

in order to allow effective data tracking. In this situation, metadata may give a full view of supply chain activities by combining fixed data on the blockchain ledger with metadata. For all parties, this ensures openness, immutability, and confidence.

Atala

IOG's Atala product suite, which includes Atala PRISM, Atala Trace, and Atala Scan solutions, saw early commercialization of metadata deployment on Cardano. The IOG team is developing metadata support while connecting with the Cardano ledger to improve the entire product functionality in terms of data feasibility, accountability, and traceability.

Atala PRISM[404] is a decentralized identification system that allows individuals to control their personal data and communicate with organizations in a seamless, private, and safe manner. On Cardano, the Atala PRISM team is using metadata to certify and store DIDs and DID documents. It will also be able to cancel credentials such as university certificates, in addition to creating them.

Atala Trace and Atala Scan are being developed to help brand owners get a better understanding of supply chain operations while also establishing product provenance and auditability. Metadata integration will be employed in these circumstances to store tamper-proof supply-chain information.

Both organizations and the developer community have varied approaches to dealing with metadata. Using the metadata service established by IOG's Professional Services Group is one such method. IOG have been working on integrations with a number of partners and have a lot more planned. Transaction metadata was an early component of Goguen utility and smart contract capability, which were expanded and developed by a variety of additional features.

Cardano's metadata strategy

Metadata has a wide range of applications. With this in mind, IOG has been trying to make it as simple as possible for developers to include metadata into their applications. IOG also want to ensure that ada holders have a simple means to see information about their transactions.

Differentiators

Metadata conveys a transaction's narrative, and there are several methods to engage with it. Ada users may search for particular information in the Cardano Explorer, and developers can make use of metadata by embedding details directly into a transaction. The data may be directly contributed, or a Merkle tree[405] of the data can be created and

---

[404] Atala PRISM, atalaprism.io/

[405] A hash tree or **Merkle tree** is a tree in which every leaf node is labeled with the hash of a data block, and every non-leaf node is labeled with the cryptographic hash of the labels of its child nodes. Hash trees allow

the root hash of the Merkle tree placed on the blockchain for larger data sets. Once this is completed, it can be shown that the data exists at a certain moment in time and that it is permanently stored on the chain for future use.

It's also worth noting that transaction information is recorded on the blockchain and sent with every transaction. The fact that it is kept on-chain rather than in the ledger state is advantageous since it has no impact on transaction validation and does not degrade ledger performance.

Metadata service

Business consultancy and technology services are provided by IOG's Professional Services Group (PSG). The PSG offers services to assist businesses in designing and implementing blockchain solutions by connecting their systems with distributed ledger technology in a simple and easy manner. The metadata service was created with a range of uses in mind, but particularly for commercial purposes.

This interface manages wallet interactions, sends low balance alerts to users, and wraps everything up in a Docker container. This removes the complication of manually providing information in the wallet's backend API. Before a transaction is declared complete, the metadata service just needs the requested information and the number of blocks in which it should be stored.

One may add the following in the metadata request:

- The actual metadata, which includes the sender and receiver's identities, as well as comments and tags.
- The depth: the number of blocks in which the metadata-containing transaction should be kept before being declared complete.
- The wallet to be utilized is indicated by the client identification.
- Transaction identity: in the event of failures or restarts, this functionality is helpful.

It enables clients to re-examine metadata that has already been supplied. The metadata service stores a transaction on the blockchain after incorporating all of the details, allowing transaction information to be accessed via Cardano Explorer. All that is required is the specification of a transaction identification.

PSG metadata service may also be supplied via language-neutral protocol buffers. Client generators support a wide range of programming languages, including Python, Java, and Scala, which enhances the number of possible applications. The process of integrating with the Cardano blockchain is made easier by these expanded options.

---

efficient and secure verification of the contents of large data structures. Hash trees are a generalization of hash lists and hash chains.

To read more about the 'Self Serve UI' and API features, visit the PSG docs.[406] On GitHub, you can learn more about the PSG Cardano wallet API[407] and how it lets clients execute tasks like transaction submission and listing, wallet management, and node monitoring.

Wallets and the Cardano-CLI

Submitting metadata straight from a wallet or the Cardano command-line interface (CLI) is option. These procedures need some coding skills as well as familiarity with the Cardano node and CLI. Because developers may verify important data in their own way, direct interaction with metadata unlocks enormous opportunities for creating decentralized apps on Cardano.

The format of the metadata is established in the Cardano wallet and CLI via a mapping from keys to values (key-value pairs) that integrate info for many uses into a single transaction.

- Metadata keys serve as a schema identifier for the metadata value they represent

- Metadata values are simple terms, consisting of integers, text strings, byte strings, lists, and maps; keys are unsigned integers with a maximum size of 64 bits; Values need to be structured so that they can be viewed and controlled more easily, especially by scripts.

The sole additional cost is that metadata increases the transaction's size in bytes, and the processing price is depending on transaction size. The Concise Binary Object Representation (CBOR)[408] and Concise Data Definition Language (CDDL)[409] notations may be used to create metadata. Check the Cardano wallet's transaction metadata and how to use transaction metadata schemes in Cardano CLI.[410]

Token Locking on Cardano

Cardano's growth has been envisioned as a journey encompassing five overlapping development eras, each of which is supported by the Ouroboros consensus system. As Cardano developed, the protocol adapted as well, as new features and functionality were added to the platform. Upgrades need progressive modifications to the network protocol.

---

[406] PSG services docs, psg-services.readthedocs.io/en/latest/

[407] PSG Cardano Wallet API, github.com/input-output-hk/psg-cardano-wallet-api

[408] **CBOR (Concise Binary Object Representation)** is a binary data serialization format loosely based on JSON. Like JSON it allows the transmission of data objects that contain name–value pairs, but in a more concise manner. This increases processing and transfer speeds at the cost of human-readability.

[409] **Concise data definition language** (CDDL) expresses Concise Binary Object Representation (CBOR) data structures. Its main goal is to provide an easy and unambiguous way to express structures for protocol messages and data formats that use CBOR or JSON (JavaScript Object Notation).

[410] Transaction Metadata, github.com/input-output-hk/cardano-node/blob/master/doc/reference/tx-metadata.md

The introduction of token locking

Token locking was the main feature of the second Goguen protocol upgrade. *Allegra* was the name for this development stage. This was the next major update for Goguen, after the network integration of metadata.[411]

This was a minor technical adjustment to the consensus process that had little effect on the ledger. It was crucial, though, since it prepared the platform for smart contracts and the production of Cardano-based assets (in addition to ada). It also supports voting, an essential piece of Voltaire (governance) functionality.

Token locking is a method of locking the usage of a single token for a defined purpose (such as voting or running a smart contract). The assets that are tallied by the blockchain ledger are referred to as tokens. There was just ada before this, but many more custom tokens were able to utilize the Cardano platform since. In this scenario, locking means 'reserving' a particular quantity of tokens for a certain length of time so they can't be sold for a profit.

Token locking enable smart contracts

Token locking is required to implement sophisticated smart contracts and certain circumstances, such as when completing a purchase. When someone gets into a contractual arrangement to sell a painting to an art gallery, the seller promises that the painting will not be sold to anyone else. In this scenario, the token might represent the painting, while the 'promise' represents the real token locking. If the painting is sold to a third party, the contract's guarantee will be breached, and any penalties will apply. With the introduction of token locking and the use of ada coins as tokens, contract providers will have access to this exact capability.

Those ada holders who participated in the Catalyst Fund2 voting process had to 'freeze' ada. This indicated their voting privileges, based on how much ada they had locked. It proved each person had a certain amount of votes and avoided the chance of votes being tallied twice. Individuals were unable to assign more votes than they had, vote on opposing proposals, or duplicate vote.

Unseen work

Token locking was implemented in a behind-the-scenes manner. It had no impact on ada holders' experience since Daedalus and Yoroi wallets were automatically updated.

Following the implementation of token locking on the mainnet Cardano ledger, future hard forks included multi-asset and other smart contract features. These features leverage token locking as well, giving Cardano users a plethora of additional options. This paved the way for non-fungible (unique) tokens to be created on the Cardano blockchain.

---

[411] Alan McSherry, 'Getting to grips with metadata on Cardano', iohk.io/en/blog/posts/2020/11/03/getting-to-grips-with-metadata-on-cardano/

Cardano has a safe, seamless route to frequent protocol changes, each of which adds new value and usefulness to the network while reducing interruption and risk, thanks to IOG's hard fork combinator.

Native Tokens

Tokens on Bitcoin

Protocols were built early in Bitcoin's existence to enable users to issue assets that piggybacked on Bitcoin's accounting system to monitor numerous currencies at the same time. The Bitcoin protocol does not support these protocols natively, but they were created through hacks. Light clients are forced to depend on trustworthy servers in the case of Bitcoin overlays like Colored Coins and Mastercoin (now Omni). Transaction fees must still be paid in bitcoins. These characteristics, together with the fact that transactions are approved via a single pipeline, render Bitcoin unsuitable for multi-asset accounting.

Tokens on Ethereum

In July of 2015, Ethereum was launched. Even though Bitcoin had been in existence for six years at the time, the cryptocurrency world was a nascent industry. When Ethereum first appeared on the scene, its schtick was smart contracts. This meant that third-party developers could create their own apps and run them on the Ethereum blockchain in a decentralized way. Ethereum outperformed Bitcoin in terms of marketability and adaptability.

On the Ethereum blockchain, smart contracts allowed for the creation of user-defined tokens. The ERC20[412] standard allowed for the creation of fungible Ethereum tokens, whereas the ERC721[413] framework allowed for the creation of unique, non-fungible tokens. However, since the Ethereum chain did not enable native token support, user defined Ethereum tokens (both fungible and non-fungible) had an inherent inefficiency: they required the construction and execution of custom code.

What is Tokenization?

Tokenization is the process of converting physical objects into digital assets. Tokenization replaces a non-sensitive data element for a sensitive data element. This non-sensitive equivalent is known as a token, and it has no intrinsic or exploitable value or meaning.

---

[412] **Ethereum ERC20 Contract** is a standard for building tokens on the Ethereum Blockchain. Before ERC20 tokens, Cryptocurrency exchanges had to build custom bridges between platforms to support the exchange of any token. For this reason, six rules were created by an Ethereum developer named Fabian Vogelsteller and placed under the name ERC20, which means 'ethereum request for comment.'

[413] **ERC721** is a free, open standard that describes how to build non-fungible or unique tokens on the Ethereum Blockchain.

Reduced transaction costs, transparency, higher liquidity, decentralization, and increased efficiency are just a few of the benefits of this. Tokenization is a very adaptable feature that may be used to achieve a variety of goals. Tokens[414] are programmable; thus they may be made unique, which adds to their usefulness.

Tokens may, for example, be designed to provide holders access to unique material, personalized items, or even a voting right. It makes no difference what the aim of the voting process is. Finally, tokenizing the capacity to vote provides individuals the sense of being a part of something bigger than themselves, and that their opinions may be heard.

Financial goods and economic models may be created via tokenization. Collectibles, alternative investments, gift cards, sports betting, in-game assets, commodities, video clips of your favorite NBA star[415] and a variety of other areas are all possible examples. This has the ability to link physical products, services, and activities to the virtual world.

Tokenization on Cardano

Goguen added a technique that handles tokenization natively. Rather than depending on smart contracts, the logic is based on the Cardano ledger. IOG created an efficient tokenization technique that is superior to the Ethereum blockchain's ERC20 and ERC721 standards by following this approach.

On the Ethereum blockchain, user-defined tokens (both fungible ERC20 and non-fungible ERC721 tokens) are non-native, meaning that the underlying ledger does not directly support them. ERC20 and ERC721 tokens are fundamentally distinct from Ether, Ethereum's native coin.

The Cardano approach to tokenization allows for the representation of custom assets on the blockchain without the use of smart contracts, as well as for those assets to behave similarly to the primary currency, ada, with the exception that:

- native tokens, unlike ada, can be minted and destroyed; and
- Ada is the only currency that can be used to pay fees, rewards, and deposits at present. This may change with the introduction of *Babel Fees* and tokens specific to different new sidechains. More about this later.

Native tokens parlance

In the crypto industry, the phrases 'coin' and 'token' are often interchangeable, and sometimes they aren't. And, in other cases, the word 'token' is used to refer to all digital

---

[414] **Token:** A cryptographic token that reflects the value as defined by the community, market state, or self-governed entity. A fungible or non-fungible token may be used as a payment unit, a reward, a trade asset, or a data holder.

[415] What's all the fuss about NBA top shot?, si.com/nba/2021/03/17/nba-top-shot-crypto-daily-cover

assets. Cardano's tokenization strategy is as unique as the blockchain itself, therefore here's a glossary to help you grasp the native tokens architecture.

- A token is defined as a representation of an asset kept on the Cardano blockchain
- An asset is defined as anything that can be quantified
- A token bundle is a representation of numerous tokens in Cardano
- Token logic that runs on the Cardano ledger rather than smart contracts is referred to as *native*.

Native tokens on Cardano vs Ethereum

Token code for both standards (ERC20 and ERC721) is copied and modified, rather than being part of the system itself, therefore Ethereum needs custom code for user-defined tokens to be supported on the chain. This adds a layer of complexity, expense (*gas[416]* is required to pay for the execution of the code), and inefficiency. This is an inherent flaw in the Ethereum blockchain since it allows for human error. If coding best practices are not followed, dodgy custom code might bring problems that can result in significant financial loss. Software vulnerabilities contributed to the loss of $300m worth of ether in one especially memorable[417] occurrence. Solana[418] has been restarted several times and suffered an expensive Wormhole hack. Cardano seeks to avoid such debacles.

The native tokens framework in Cardano enables user-defined tokens natively, that is, without the requirement for special programming. Native tokens are a kind of accounting system that is inherently provided by the ledger. This eliminates the complicated, unpredictable and expensive aspects of tokenization on Ethereum.

Cardano is a kind of decentralized ledger. Typically, a distributed ledger can only track a single asset type when it is created (usually its own cryptocurrency). However, as the ledger gets more decentralized, the requirement and capability of monitoring different kinds of assets on the same infrastructure emerges, which is why blockchains need to handle numerous assets such as stablecoins, utility tokens,[419] credential tokens, and security tokens. Native tokens, unlike ERC20, do not need extra event-handling logic or specific transfer costs to monitor transactions.

---

[416] **Gas (Ethereum)** refers to the fee, or pricing value, required to successfully conduct a transaction or execute a smart contract on the Ethereum blockchain platform. Priced in small fractions of the cryptocurrency ether, commonly referred to as gwei or sometimes nanoeth, the gas is used to allocate resources of the Ethereum Virtual Machine (EVM) so that decentralized applications such as smart contracts can self-execute is a secured fashion. The maximum amount of gas that you're willing to spend on a particular transaction is known as the gas limit.

[417] '$300m in cryptocurrency' accidentally lost forever due to bug, theguardian.com/technology/2017/nov/08/cryptocurrency-300m-dollars-stolen-bug-ether

[418] 3 Reasons Solana Isn't Really Decentralized, makeuseof.com/reasons-solana-isnt-really-decentralized/

[419] **Utility token:** a digital token that represents a certain project or environment and has specific capabilities. These tokens may be used as payment units, prizes, or as a means of gaining entry to a particular network.

The accounting infrastructure established in the ledger model, initially intended for processing ada-only transactions, was extended to support transactions that employ many kinds of assets at the same time. Native tokens have the advantage of not requiring smart contracts to transmit their value and may be traded alongside other kinds of tokens.

Security is another benefit of native coins over ERC20. ERC20 tokens have been shown to be subject to a variety of security problems that are well documented.[420] This is because creating ERC20 tokens requires manual changes of the contract standard, which might lead to mistakes and flaws. Because the ledger manages the token logic, creating and transacting tokens natively eliminates this risk. Additionally, native tokens do not suffer the same overflow and underflow vulnerabilities as ERC20 tokens since Cardano's scripting language does not employ fixed-size integers and the ledger itself (as opposed to the ERC20 user code) monitors token movement.

Four Differentiators of Native Tokens on Cardano

Lightweight Architecture

The native token architecture is constructed around token bundles and is based on a multi-asset ledger structure. A token bundle might include a mixture of ada and other tokens. Instead of ada, these token-containing structures are recorded as outputs on the ledger. The asset ID of each kind of token contains a hash reference to the token's minting policy. The minting policy is only verified during the minting or burning process, and it is not maintained on the ledger, making this method very light.

The asset ID also captures the fungibility connection in a lightweight way: tokens with the same asset ID are fungible with one other, but not with tokens with different asset IDs. The asset ID of unique tokens is coupled with a quantity of precisely one.

Within a single token bundle and throughout the whole ledger, the asset ID identifies each kind of token. It also indicates the token's position inside the token bundle's internal two-level map structure. This underlying data structure makes it possible to express fungible and non-fungible tokens in the same way. It also allows the system a lot of flexibility in terms of the types of asset use cases that can be tokenized. It's simple to represent, say, a collection of one-of-a-kind works of art covered by a single minting policy set by the artist.

When we examine how Ethereum's ERC20 handles asset transfers between two contracts, the inherent simplicity of native tokens is underlined even more. Smart contract code is necessary in this scenario, which adds complexity, as well as possibility for mistake and expense. Because several kinds of tokens may be traded in a single transaction, the structure of token bundles allows for a more lightweight approach to asset transfer.

Inexpensive

---

[420] Blockchain Vulnerabilities: Vulnerable ERC20 Tokens and How to Avoid Writing Vulnerable Code, apriorit.com/dev-blog/555-erc20-token-vulnerability

Transferring any amount of tokens between two peers in an ERC20 token ecosystem necessitates the execution of a smart contract, which comes with an execution charge (gas). The transfer of assets (tokens, ada, custom currencies, and so on) in Cardano's native multi-asset ecosystem does not need a smart contract and does not incur an execution cost.

More Security, less custom code

Native tokens have a lighter and less expensive design than Ethereum's ERC20 and ERC721 protocols. These two elements, however, would be useless without a strong security layer to ensure the system's integrity.

System integrity with native tokens is based on the ledger attribute of value preservation (that is, that the sum of all the inputs is equal to the sum of the outputs). Unlike user-defined smart contracts, all native token transfer logic is embedded in the ledger. This guarantees that the system behaves predictably and consistently, and it eliminates the need for users to master smart contracts, which can often be vulnerable to exploitation by hackers.

While the ledger ensures accounting accuracy, the minting and burning of tokens is governed by their user-defined minting policies. A minting policy is hash-linked to the tokens it covers indefinitely, and there is no way to modify it. This ensures that an issuer's policy cannot be amended to enable the minting or burning of a token that was not permitted under the initial policy. The policy for each kind of token being minted is verified and must be met whenever a minting transaction is put to the ledger. Except for ada (Cardano has limited supply of 45m ada), every token in circulation must have a minting policy and must have been minted pursuant to that policy.

As a result, the policy is the only custom code necessary to alter tokens in Cardano. Because the policy hash is linked to the asset identification, there is no need for a global asset registry, making asset creation cheap and simple. The technology is still basic, light, and simple to operate.

Simplicity

Now that Goguen's native tokens are implemented, the ledger treats all tokens in the same manner. To avoid ambiguity and any errors or flaws, a token may only be minted in one method. This streamlining of development via the use of a uniform methodology resulted in speedier development and a better overall development experience.

IOG has provided more detail on GitHub under native tokens and how they compare to ada and ERC20.[421] There is also a native tokens explainer video.[422] Momentum built steadily after the *Mary* and *Alonzo* upgrades, with developers realizing the benefits of

---

[421] What is a native token and how does it compare to ada and ERC20?, github.com/input-output-hk/cardano-ledger-specs/blob/master/doc/explanations/features.rst

[422] Welcome to native tokens on Cardano!, youtube.com/watch?v=PVqsCXh-V5Y

deploying native tokens and NFTs on Cardano. Cardano blockchain insights[423] report almost 3.3 million wallets, over 4.5 million native tokens, 5,000+ NFTs, and more than 1,100+ projects deploying to Cardano as of January 2023.[424]

Multi-Asset Support (MAS)

Single asset ledgers

Single-asset ledgers are cryptocurrency ledgers that track just one kind of asset.

Multi-Asset support

When a blockchain, ledger, or cryptocurrency enables recording the transfer and ownership of several kinds of assets on its ledger, it is said to have multi-asset (MA) support. The native tokens feature in the Cardano ecosystem provides this capability.

This feature extends the accounting infrastructure specified in the ledger model, which was intended to handle ada-only transactions, to transactions that employ a variety of assets at the same time. Ada and a range of user-defined custom token types are among these assets.

Native versus non-native

Some cryptocurrency ledgers have features that allow you to monitor the ownership and transfer of many types of assets. Native MA (multi-asset) support is the name given to this sort of MA support. The MA functionality of Cardano is built-in or 'native'.

It is possible to monitor assets for which there is no ledger accounting support if a cryptocurrency platform has sufficiently sophisticated smart contract capabilities. This is accomplished utilizing a Layer 2 solution based on smart contracts. This is a non-native form of MA support.

Assets

On the blockchain, an asset is an item that represents value. A digital asset like ada, a position, a certificate, or a number of products are all examples of these items.

The word asset might refer to one of two things:

- the identifier of a class of objects, such as ada or 'johnCoin'; or
- an exact amount of a certain thing, eg. '10 lovelace', '33 johnCoin', 'this book' or 'these jars of marmalade'

---

[423] Blockchain Insights, datastudio.google.com/u/0/reporting/3136c55b-635e-4f46-8e4b-b8ab54f2d460/page/p_wxcw6g0irc

[424] Statistics to date (updated weekly), essentialcardano.io/development-update

An asset ID is a combination of the policy ID and the asset name that uniquely identifies it. It's worth noting that, although ada may be used as an asset, it doesn't have an explicit policy ID.

Tokens with the same asset ID are fungible with each other, however they are not fungible with tokens with different asset IDs. An asset ID is a fungible token collection's unique identifier.

PolicyID - The unique ID linked with a minting policy. The ID is a sequence of letters and numbers that is generated by applying a hash function on the policy itself.

Asset name - an asset's (immutable) property that is used to differentiate amongst assets within the same policy. The asset name, unlike the policyID, does not correspond to any code or set of rules and may be any common term, such as 'tickets' or 'VIPTickets.' Valid asset names may, however, be limited by the policy that defines how an asset is scoped.

For distinct tokens, various policies might use the same asset names.

Tokens

A token is a short word for 'asset token,' which is an asset's on-chain representation and accounting unit. One ada, one home, or a ton of tea, for example, may be represented by a token.

Currencies

Currency is a term used to describe a monetary unit that serves as a means of exchange for goods and services. Cardano accepts ada and native tokens, both of which function equally on the network.

However, at this moment, ada is the only currency used to pay fees and make deposits, and it is also the only currency in which rewards are issued. The architecture of the underlying consensus protocol is responsible for this attribute of ada (and no other sort of asset).

Native tokens are a kind of accounting unit that may be used for payments and transactions, as well as being transmitted to an exchange address. Because the Cardano accounting ledger has built-in functionality for tracking ownership and transfer of several types of assets, these tokens are supported by the ledger without the need for extra smart contracts. While both ada and native tokens have value and may be used to pay and transact, only ada is utilized for fees and rewards, and only native tokens can be customized.

Conditions when using ada

Cardano's main currency is ada (₳). Because each address must have a minimum ada value, having ada (along with other currencies) is required to transfer multi-asset tokens between addresses (min-ada-value, currently set at 1 ada).

As a result of its design, the following conditions apply:

1. Creating outputs that exclusively include custom tokens is not possible.

2. The quantity of each kind of token in an output has no effect on the output's min-ada-value, but the number of types of tokens raises the min-ada-value. (This is because the names and policy IDs of each of the different sorts of tokens take up extra space in the output.)

3. When sending custom tokens to an address, the min-ada-value of ada is always sent together with the custom tokens (by including the ada in the same output). The ada supplied with the tokens no longer belongs to the sender if the address is not spendable by the person sending the tokens.

Users may opt to employ off-chain dialogue to discuss who gives the ada to cover the min-ada-value in the output created by the transferring transaction before transferring custom tokens.

4. To retrieve the ada placed along with custom tokens in an output O, the user must either:

> • Spend the output O and burn the custom tokens that it contains

> • Spend an output O and an output O', then combine the tokens in those outputs with the same set of custom tokens stored in another output (spent within the same transaction).

5. Because some ada must be provided in each output, splitting custom tokens into more outputs than they were before the transaction was run needs more total ada to cover the min-ada-value.

What are Token bundles?

A token bundle is a collection of tokens that is heterogeneous ('mixed'). Tokens of any kind may be packaged together. On the Cardano blockchain, token bundles are the standard way to represent and store assets. Token bundles group tokens into a certain data structure, ensuring which tokens are fungible with other tokens is clearly defined.

Ada amounts were stated in transaction and UTXO outputs in prior versions of the Cardano ledger. These amounts have been expanded with token bundles, which may define an ada amount with quantities of other assets in a single output, thanks to the addition of multi-asset functionality.

Token bundles are stored in transaction outputs and mint fields, as well as the UTXO set outputs, which are monitored by the ledger. Certain elements of a transaction, such as the fee field, must still explicitly state ada amounts.

Token bundle storage

Token bundles can be found:

- As a transaction's mint field, indicating that the transaction is producing the bundle's tokens
- In a transaction's output or an output in the current UTXO recorded by the ledger, alongside the address of the output, e.g. `Multi { MyAddress, value: TB_Example }`

Splitting and combining token bundles

Token bundles may be split and combined arbitrarily by transactions.

Minting policy

A minting policy is a collection of rules that control the minting and burning of assets that are within the policy's control. A minting policy specifies the circumstances under which tokens are minted (or burned). The rules might, for example, describe who has authority over the asset supply through minting and burning.

Users that wish to produce a new asset establish the minting policies. For example, a user may choose to limit themselves to just minting a certain kind of token. This is something that would be outlined in the policy.

The following are the rules for minting:

As a very simple set of rules, it consists of the following (ANDs and ORs):

- A list of the signatures required to enable the mint to operate (e.g., a multisig specification, where no code is needed)
- With a Plutus Core script, a specification of when the script may be spent (e.g., after slot 10 and before slot 30).

When a transaction is executed, the node checks for compliance with minting regulations by executing the code or validating the appropriate signatures. All minting policies for all assets that the transaction is seeking to mint must be followed.

Minting: Terms & Conditions

- A minting policy is required for all assets. Ada's minting policy, for example, states that 'new ada can never be minted'

- A token has just one minting policy connected with it

- A single policy describes the requirements for both minting and burning tokens that fall within its ambit. Its compliance is monitored both during minting and during burning

- An asset's related minting policy cannot be changed at any time, it's irreversible. Current tokens cannot be linked to a new policy. With a new minting policy, users may purchase back and burn all current tokens while still minting new ones. This is by design, it's not a fault in the system

- An existent asset on the ledger that is scoped under a certain policy is guaranteed to have been minted in accordance with that policy

- The actual policy is unimportant until tokens of that policy are generated in a transaction. Its only purpose is to serve as a unique ID for the asset

- Assets related with various minting policies are never interchangeable. They can be exchanged in the same manner as USD can be used to acquire Euros: the quantity of Euros you can buy with a specific amount of USD is determined by the exchange rate.

Relationship between an asset and its minting policy

For security reasons, the link between an asset and its minting policy is permanent. This feature protects users and the system against falsely minted tokens.

When a token's minting policy changes, it's no longer the same token, and its value can't be compared to the original token's. In order to define high-assurance policies, this permanent asset-policy association method is essential. Cardano's MA (Multi Asset) technique becomes vulnerable to a variety of attacks if this identification is loosened. It's best to ensure that every token was minted in line with its minting policy, not any other policy it may have previously been linked with, by having a permanent link between them.

Minting policy Types

There are several more sorts of minting policies to consider.

Single-issuer policy

A single-issuer minting policy states that only the entity with a certain set of keys may mint tokens for a specific asset group. For example, the minting transaction must have been signed by the set of keys provided in the minting policy.

Tokens representing Panini football cards are an example of an asset category that would adopt a single-issuer policy. The firm that makes authentic collectors' cards would provide the keys needed to mint fresh football cards, as required by the minting script. This means that no new football card tokens may be produced without the approval of the firm. There is no need to use Plutus smart contracts when creating this form of policy.

Figure 17: Panini soccer cards

Time-locked minting policy

AKA token-locking. This policy may be used to limit the number of tokens that can be spent from a certain address.

- only during or after a defined time slot
- only before a defined time slot

Typically, this form of policy isn't employed on its own. It is often used in combination with a multisignature or single issuer policy, for example. Only a transaction signed by key 'k' may spend this output after slot 's'. This form of policy may be created without the need for Plutus smart contracts.

One-time minting policy

In a one-time mint policy, a single transaction mints the whole set of tokens for a specified asset category. This indicates that there will never be any more tokens in that asset category. This sort of policy necessitates the use of Plutus smart contracts.

For example, a one-time mint policy may be used to create ticket tokens for the Super Bowl. Because the venue's capacity is known ahead of time, there will be no need to issue more tickets.

Minting transactions

Each transaction has a mint field that may be used to add fresh amounts of new tokens to the ledger (minting) or to remove existent tokens (burning). Minting transactions are transactions in which the mint field is not empty. The usage of this field must be strictly regulated to guarantee that tokens are minted and burned in accordance with the token's minting policy.

Minting transactions must include the minting rules for the tokens they are minting, in addition to the mint field, so that these tokens may be inspected during validation.

The ledger will record the assets contained in the mint field, which is included in the transaction's balancing: if the field is positive, then the transaction's outputs must have more assets than the inputs supply; if it is negative, then they must contain fewer.

It's worth noting that a single transaction might result in the creation of tokens with numerous minting rules. For instance, (Policy1, SomeTokens) or (Policy2, SomeOtherTokens). A transaction might also mint and burn tokens at the same time.

The metadata registry

Metadata is a description of native assets that anyone may read in Cardano. These assets are held on-chain using non-human-readable IDs. The readable version of this data is held in public token registries, not on the blockchain. These registries, which will first be controlled by the IOG, will eventually be owned and configured by the community, allowing Cardano to achieve another degree of decentralization. IOG guarantees that the community can completely trust the datasets by allowing the community to own and configure these registries. Because the users are the owners of the data, it is in their best interest to behave honestly.

There is a draft *CIP 26 - Cardano Off-Chain Metadata* which proposes a standard for off-chain metadata that maps on-chain identifiers to human readable metadata.

Creating native tokens on Cardano

Users can select between simple and sophisticated tools to bring their assets to life on Cardano. Tokens are becoming more popular for financial transactions. They reduce fees while boosting transparency, increasing liquidity, and, of course, remaining independent of centralized entities like the banks. Tokenization is the process of converting actual assets (such as fiat currencies, equities, precious metals, and real estate) into digital tokens that may be used to build commercial financial instruments.

Many tokenization options[425] are available in Cardano. The ledger's accounting architecture handles not just ada transactions, but also transactions that hold several asset types at the same time.

Utility

---

[425] Tim Harrison, 'Native Tokens on Cardano', iohk.io/en/blog/posts/2020/12/08/native-tokens-on-cardano/

To fulfill commercial or business goals, developers, enterprises, and apps may build general purpose (fungible[426]) or specialized (non-fungible) tokens. Custom payment tokens or rewards for DApps, stablecoins tied to other currencies, and unique assets, like eBooks, that represent intellectual property are just a few examples. All of these assets may then be traded, swapped, or used to purchase goods and services.

Users will be able to transmit, receive, and burn their tokens without paying transaction fees or installing event-handling logic to monitor transactions since native tokens do not need smart contracts to transfer their value. Users are able to produce, distribute, trade, and store tokens in one of four ways, depending on their preferences and technical expertise:

1. Cardano CLI

Developers may create (mint) assets and submit test transactions to various addresses using the native tokens testing environment.

Because of the nature of working with the CLI, it is assumed that you are comfortable with setting up and administering a Cardano node, as well as dealing with transactions and managing addresses and values. To generate native tokens using Cardano CLI, follow the steps outlined in the documentation.[427] At a high level, the steps are as follows:

- Create and start a Cardano node
- Generate verfication and signing keys
- Generate a payment address, fund and check the balance
- Start the minting process, create a policy and mint a new asset
- Lastly, build the raw transactions, submit and sign transactions to send the tokens to the target address.

On the Cardano docs site[428] IOG provides native token tutorials and exercises to enable developers create tokens, implement monetary rules, and understand how to conduct multi-asset transactions.

2. Token builder GUI

The CLI requires a certain amount of programming expertise. As a result, IOG established other methods for less technical users to generate tokens. After the mainnet CLI launch, IOG deployed a token builder to do this.

The token builder is a graphical user interface that simplifies the process of creating tokens. The token builder may assist you in building tokens for your decentralized

---

[426] In economics, **fungibility** is the property of a good or a commodity whose individual units are essentially interchangeable, and each of its parts is indistinguishable from another part.

[427] Getting started with native tokens, docs.cardano.org/native-tokens/getting-started

[428] Learn about native tokens, docs.cardano.org/native-tokens/

application, tokenizing your property, making NFT collection cards represented as specialized assets, or establishing a stablecoin tied to the value of other currencies.

To make a token, just fill in the following fields:

- The token's name (for example, CardanoForTheMasses)
- the token's symbol (for example, CFTM)
- the token's icon (generated automatically)
- Amount to be made (eg, 10m)
- Cardano wallet location (your address to host newly created tokens).

The monetary policy is generated automatically by the token constructor, so you won't have to describe it yourself. This accelerates and simplifies the token generating process for non-technical users.

After tokens have been minted, the 'Mint more' option will allow you to mint more. This may be done using the same policy to produce additional tokens of the same kind or using a new policy to create tokens that represent various values. You might, for example, make *CardanoForTheMasses* tokens for each edition of this eBook. Initially only minting for the 'Vasil Edition'. When the next HFC event occurs, no more 'Vasil edition' tokens are minted. New tokens are now minted for the new edition with new cover art and an updated eBook. Each edition will have a different minting policy.

The token builder seeks to simplify token production while simultaneously emphasizing the improvement and visual display of functional procedures. As a result, users want to be able to see all of the tokens that have been produced, their values, amount, and the addresses to which they are being transferred — all in one spot.

There are various 3rd party token building tools also, such as *cardano-native-token.com*

3. Tokens on Daedalus

Users that do not want to generate their own tokens but want to use current ones for payments, purchases, or exchange can use Daedalus, Yoroi, Flint,…most wallets now support this functionality.

The Policy ID and the Asset Name are two hexadecimal integers recorded on-chain that uniquely identify native tokens. IOG generated fingerprints to make it simpler for users to identify native tokens since these numbers aren't 'human-friendly.' Fingerprints are 44-character alphanumeric strings with the prefix 'token' at the start.

The Cardano token registry, which was controlled initially by the Cardano Foundation, includes additional token data presented in the wallet UI (name, description, and acronym). adaHandle ($handle, adahandle.com) was one of the first projects to launch after Goguen as '*An NFT-powered naming solution for your Cardano wallet address, secured entirely on-chain via the Handle Standard*'.

4. **Third party platforms.**

For example, Dripdropz (dripdropz.io), the 'Cardano Token Distribution System' has added great value to the ecosystem.

The lifecycle of native tokens on Cardano

The native token lifecycle will be complete after all of the required components have been deployed. It is divided into five stages:

- Minting
- Issuing
- Using
- Redeeming
- Burning.

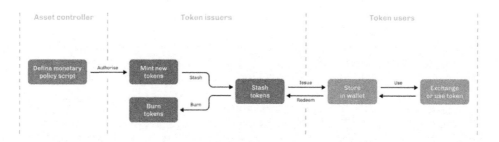

Figure 18: Lifecycle of native tokens on Cardano

Each of these logical processes includes Cardano blockchain transactions, which may result in ada fees. The following are the primary actors:

- Asset controllers, who determine the asset class's policy and authorize token issuers to mint and burn tokens. They might also retain co-signing rights for any tokens that are minted or burned

- Token issuers, who create new tokens, keep a reserve of them in circulation, distribute them to token holders, and destroy them when they're no longer useful

- Token holders, who keep tokens, send them to other users, use them for payment, and then redeem them with the issuers when they're no longer needed. Normal 'Joe Soap' users, exchanges, and other entities may be token users.

The lifespan of multi-asset tokens begins with their creation – minting, which is the process by which one or more token issuers generate new tokens in line with the monetary policy script provided by the asset controller. In most cases, new tokens will be issued to serve a particular function. Tokens that are fungible or non-fungible (unique)

172

may be developed for particular payment, buying, or exchange requirements, for example. When a new token is created, the overall token supply for that token grows, but the ada supply remains the same. Minting coins and transferring them to new addresses may need the payment of ada, which might be proportional to the quantity of distinct tokens possessed.

Token holders will store tokens in their wallets and will be able to transfer them on to other users, swap them for objects of value (including non-native tokens), and so on, just like they would with ada. When a user's token has been used up, they may opt to redeem it. Meaning tokens are returned to their original issuer (perhaps in return for a product, service, or some other currency, for instance). Tokens may then be re-issued to other users as required after they were redeemed. To pay for transaction fees, token holders will need to keep some ada in their wallets.

If required, tokens may be burnt when they become redundant, in line with the underlying monetary policy script. The act of burning these tokens eliminates them (removing them from circulation), reducing the overall token supply. At this time, any deposits will be refunded. Fungible and non-fungible tokens are both burned in the same way.

The multi-asset token lifecycle may enable tokens to be acquired and reissued by other parties, such as token holders acting as reissuers. This may be done to facilitate trading across different asset classes, maintain liquidity in one or more tokens (by serving as a broker), or reduce the effort/cost of token minting, issuance, or metadata server maintenance, for example. As a result, such a transaction benefits both reissuers and issuers by reducing costs and effort, preserving separation and integrity, and infusing value into the asset class.

Min-ada-value requirement

On the ledger, UTXOs may contain a mixed bag of tokens, including ada. The maximum total size taken up by UTXO entries on the ledger at any one moment is limited by requiring some amount of ada to be included in every UTXO (where that amount is dependent on the size of the UTXO, in bytes).

By adjusting the min-ada-value setting, the maximum permissible UTXO size (the total of the sizes of all UTXO entries) is implicitly modified. The limitation prevents the Cardano ledger from going above a specific size in this manner. A ledger without size restrictions is prone to becoming overburdened with data to the point that users will be unable to process it (or operate a node) on devices that satisfy the required node criteria.

There is more detail in Cardano Docs on the 'ada-only' case, 'min-ada-value' calculation and with worked examples.

As a result of this strategy,

- You cannot create outputs only containing custom tokens

- The number of each kind of token in an output can have a slight bearing on the output's min-ada-value. There is some affect as the minimum UTXO value takes memory overhead into account when storing it on a computer. The memory overhead isn't affected greatly by an increase in ada but adding multi-assets does have an impact. This is because the names and policy IDs of each kind of token take up extra space in the output

- When sending custom tokens to an address, the min-ada-value of ada is always sent together with the custom tokens (by including the ada in the same output). The ada supplied with the tokens no longer belongs to the sender, if the address is not spendable by the person sending the tokens

- Before the transfer of custom tokens takes place, users may utilize off-chain communication to determine who provides the ada to cover the min-ada-value in the output created by the transferring transaction

- To recover the ada stored alongside custom tokens in an output O, the user must either:

  a) spend the output O and burn the custom tokens therein; or
  b) spend an output O and an output O' and consolidate the tokens therein with the same collection of types of custom tokens stored in another output O. (spent within the same transaction)

  For example, in a new output created by the consolidating transaction, (CryptoBisonPolicy, AmericanBison, 2) in O may be consolidated with (CryptoBisonPolicy, AmericanBison, 4) in O', for a total of (CryptoBisonPolicy, AmericanBison, 6)

- Splitting custom tokens into more outputs than they were before the transaction was executed necessitates using more ada in total to meet the min-ada-value, since ada is required in the extra outputs.

Native Token FAQ

What does 'multi-asset (MA)' support mean and does Cardano have it?
Multi-asset (MA) support refers to a collection of features that a ledger (blockchain / wallet / cryptocurrency / banking platform) may provide that enables it to account for and interact with several types of assets.

Native Tokens is Cardano's MA support feature. Users may transact with ada and an infinite number of user-defined tokens using MA. This is native support, meaning tokens may be transacted with using the accounting system established as part of the cryptocurrency's ledger capabilities, without the need of any smart contracts.

What is the difference between a native asset and a NFT?
Technically, NFTs are the same as native assets. There are characteristics which make a native asset an NFT. A) It must be non-fungible meaning you need to have unique

identifiers or attributes attached to a token to make it unique from others. Usually, NFT's live on the blockchain forever, therefore there needs to be a mechanism to ensure an NFT stays unique and cannot be duplicated.

What is the definition of (asset) tokenization?
Tokenizing an asset entails generating a digital version of it on the blockchain.

What does it mean to 'mint' a token?
'Minting' refers to the process of creating or destroying new tokens. That is, the overall quantity in circulation of the token type being minted changes (i.e. when all addresses on the ledger are put together). Token creation is when a positive number of tokens is minted, whereas token burning occurs when a negative number is minted.

What does it mean to 'burn' a token?
The term 'burning' refers to the process of destroying tokens. It's the same as 'negative minting.'

What does token redeeming entail?
Token redemption entails returning tokens to the issuer to be burnt. This is often done when the tokens being redeemed no longer serve a function on the ledger and the user or contract in possession of them is unable to burn the tokens (according to the minting policy). Although the token issuer/minting policy may not give any reward for redeeming the tokens, the user may opt to do it nevertheless to avoid having useless tokens in their wallet.

What is a minting transaction?
Minting transactions are those in which this piece of transaction data (called the mint field) is not empty. These transactions must additionally include the minting policies for the tokens they're minting, so they can be verified during validation.

The assets contained in the (mint) minting field of the transaction will now be added to the ledger as a consequence of performing a minting transaction. If the quantity of a given asset in the mint field is negative, the total quantity of that asset on the ledger will be lowered by the amount indicated in the mint field when the transaction is processed.

Note that a single transaction may mint tokens associated with many different minting policies. It's also worth noting that a transaction may mint and burn tokens at the same time.

What is a minting policy?
A minting policy is a collection of rules that govern the minting of assets linked to it. For example, who controls the currency's supply (and under what circumstances), as well as its minting and burning. These rules apply to the content of the transaction data for the transaction that the mint is attempting. For example, a minting policy may specify that the minting transaction be signed by a certain set of keys.

The user who desires to mint a new asset defines this set of rules. For example, a user could want to limit themself to just minting this kind of token. This would be specified in the policy. When a transaction is executed, the node checks for conformity to minting regulations by executing the code or validating the appropriate signatures. All minting policies of all assets the transaction is seeking to mint must be satisfied by transaction data.

What is a token builder and what is its functionality?

A token builder is software that enables a user to specify the tokens that will be created and include them in a minting transaction. It also guarantees that the transaction has the necessary extra data to verify that the transaction is authorized to execute the mint.

What is 'multisig' and what does it have to do with minting policies?

The multisig scripting language sets a minimum number of signatures necessary for a transaction to complete a certain operation, typically spending a UTXO entry.

Multisig scripts may also be used to define the most fundamental minting rules, such as those that need a specified set of keys to sign the minting transaction. A multisig script, for example, may be used to specify a single issuer minting policy.

What is the relationship between Plutus smart contracts and native tokens?

The Plutus smart contract language may be used to write minting policies. This enables users to specify a far broader variety of policies than the single issuer policy that multisig may convey. Plutus, for example, may specify a one-time minting policy (but not just as multisig).

What is the definition of a single issuer minting policy?

A single issuer minting policy states that only the entity with a certain set of keys is permitted to mint tokens under that policy. For example, the minting transaction must have been signed by the set of keys provided in the minting policy. Multisig may be used to provide this sort of policy.

Tokens resembling an artist's paintings are an example of a single-issuer policy use case. This would rule out the production of new painting tokens without the artist's signature. The insurance, on the other hand, establishes that all of the existing paintings covered by the policy were properly produced by the artist and nobody else. Tokhun[429] is just one NFT marketplace where artists can sell their paintings as artist Jonathan Dickson[430] explained in this video.[431]

What is a one-time minting policy?

A one-time minting policy mints the whole set of tokens covered by it in a single transaction. This means that under that policy, no further tokens will ever be minted. Smart contracts are required for this form of policy, which cannot be represented via multisig. Minting ticket tokens for the Superbowl is an example of a one-time minting policy in action. Because the venue's capacity is known ahead of time, there will be no need to issue more tickets.

---

[429] Tokhun, tokhun.io/jonathandickson

[430] Twitter Jonathan Dickson, twitter.com/JonathanDickson

[431] Jonathan Dickson Elements NFTs on Cardano, youtube.com/watch?v=F1DR-39RN28

What is the difference between fungible and non-fungible?

Fungibility is the relationship that exists between two assets or tokens. When two tokens are interchangeable, they are said to be fungible. A €10 note, for example, is interchangeable with all other €10 notes (as well as all ten €1 coins and all pairs of €5 notes). Non-fungible assets can't be swapped for one another. Two precious jewels, for example, or two on-chain tokens that represent two real-world jewels. If a token is not fungible with other assets, such as a token representing a painting, it is considered unique (non-fungible).

What is a token bundle, and how does it work?

A mixed set of tokens that are subject to one or more minting policies. Tokens of any kind may be bundled together.

What is the appearance of native tokens in a user's wallet?

A user's wallet stores both outputs with addresses that belong to the user and the quantities of ada that these addresses have prior to the introduction of MA (multi asset) functionality into the Cardano system. (Users address1, someAdaAmount) is an example.

The user's wallet can now include many kinds of assets in a single output with multi asset (MA) support, i.e., the wallet will be able to contain a token bundle. This means that wallets may include the following items:

- Assets covered by many policies in a single UTXO (including ada)
- Assets covered by a single policy and dispersed over several UTXOs

Do native tokens contain IDs and other information that can be read by humans?

Instead of lengthy Policy ID strings and asset names, human-readable names for assets may be registered on a metadata server. When a user looks at their assets in a wallet that is connected to a metadata server, they will be able to see the human-readable names. Users will be able to upload the names of their tokens, as well as any other token-specific information, to a metadata server. Users will have to pick which server(s) to upload or download their metadata from if more than one metadata server is active at the same time. Users may also enter names and other details directly into the transaction's metadata field. Transaction costs will rise in proportion to the amount of metadata added.

What are the fees for generating native tokens and exchanging them?

There are two types of costs associated with multiple assets:

- Fees: Sending and minting tokens has an impact on the fees that the transaction's author must pay. Fees are determined depending on the entire amount of the transaction, just as in an ada-only ledger. There may be extra costs for verifying minting policies, however only multisig policies are currently available, which do not incur additional fees on top of the transaction size-based ones
- Minimum ada-value: Every transaction's output must contain a minimum amount of ada, which is computed depending on the output's size (the number of different token types in it, and the length of their names).

Min-ada-value:
Keep in mind that outputs may include a mixed bag of tokens, including ada, which is a scarce resource. The inclusion of some amount of ada in every output on the ledger (where that amount is dependent on the size of the output in bytes) prevents the Cardano ledger from getting too large.

What kinds of assets can I leverage to pay the expenses of native tokens?
At this time, only ada may be used to pay fees or make deposits.

How does bespoke native token coin selection work?
It works similarly to ada coin selection in that the user chooses the tokens and amounts they want to spend, and the wallet selects suitable inputs and pays fees.

Is it possible to send tokens to an address?
Yes, sending native tokens to an address is accomplished in the same manner as sending ada is accomplished, namely by submitting a transaction with outputs containing the token bundles the transaction author desires to send, as well as the addresses to which they are delivered. See *eutxo.org* for live visuals of real world transactions on Cardano

What level of control over custom token assets does the user have?
Multi asset tokens may be spent, sent, traded, and received in the same manner as ada tokens. Users may mint and burn native tokens, unlike ada.

Users may spend tokens in their wallets or tokens in outputs that are locked by scripts that let this user spend the output. Sending tokens to other users: Users may send (spend) tokens in their wallet to any address.

Minting tokens: Users may mint custom tokens in accordance with the asset's policy. These tokens may be sent to the user's or anybody else's address during the minting transaction. The policy may limit the specific output address for the tokens if required.

Note that, depending on the policy rules, even if a user has specified a policy, that user may not be allowed to mint or burn assets covered by that policy. Regardless of the identity of the user who developed the policy, a minting policy governs the minting of any assets covered by it.

Burning tokens: The policy linked with the asset also controls the burning of tokens. The user must be able to spend the tokens they are trying to burn in addition to being able to burn them (always in compliance with the minting policy).

Even if the minting policy clearly allows it, users cannot burn tokens over which they have no control, such as tokens in someone else's wallet.

How do Cardano native tokens compare to Ethereum custom tokens ERC721 and ERC20?
Cardano's approach to custom token creation varies from non-native implementations of custom tokens, such as ERC721 or ERC20, which use smart contract capabilities to

mimic the transfer of custom assets (i.e., a ledger accounting system). Because the ledger architecture permits accounting on non-ada native assets, Cardano's technique for creating custom tokens does not need smart contracts. Another significant distinction is that, unlike ERC721 or ERC20, the Cardano multi-asset ledger allows both fungible and non-fungible tokens without the need of specialized contracts and is flexible enough to incorporate a mix of fungible and non-fungible tokens in a single output.

Multi-assets on Exchanges

Native assets are defined by their *minting policies*, which are set by users when creating (minting) new asset(s). These policies specify the maximum and lower bounds of what a token may do, as well as who can do it and when it can be done throughout the transaction lifecycle.

The network protocol and ledger-defined rules bind a minting policy. The minimum UTXO value is one such guideline (the minimum amount of ada that must be sent in a single transaction). Because the value is presently fixed to one ada, a minimum of one ada must be included and accounted for in each native asset transaction on the Cardano network.

cardano-graphql or cardano-rosetta may be used to validate and locate these unique native asset transactions.

Multi-Asset Management

Exchanges that list ada are likely to face one of two scenarios:

Scenario 1: Spending a UTXO with a multi-asset attached

This situation is only relevant for exchanges that control their own UTXOs.

How do I discover UTXOs with a native asset attached? Local block explorers (cardano-graphql or cardano-rosetta, for example) are often used by exchanges and third-party wallets that maintain their own UTXOs.

cardano-graphql is a query language and runtime component for the Cardano API that allows you to satisfy queries using data from the cardano-db-sync PostgreSQL[432] database. It offers customers the ability to request the information they need by giving them a clear and comprehensible description of the data. As a result, both the growth of client APIs and the deployment of developer tools are simplified.

Getting started

---

[432] **PostgreSQL**, also known as Postgres, is a free and open-source relational database management system emphasizing extensibility and SQL compliance. *See Appendix: Cardano Architecture.*

After you've seen how a native asset transaction works, you may wish to produce or burn some native assets or tokens on the testnet. To begin minting native assets, check out these requirements[433] and follow the steps below:

- Connect `cardano-node` to testnet
- Build `cardano-node` and connect to testnet
- Download `cardano-cli` prebuilt binary or use build from source
- Follow the steps in docs

How do I spend a UTXO with native assets attached?

It's critical to account for two factors when using cardano-cli to generate a transaction using native assets, as described in this section:

1. The value of the ada you want to send
2. The number of tokens

Any exchange or third-party that wishes to spend, refund, or store any multi-asset must follow the same rules. Getting a multi-asset transaction is, by definition, the same as receiving any other Cardano transaction. The only distinction is that the transaction may include additional data, such as multi-asset.

It's best practice for all exchanges and third-party wallets to check and process any multi-asset transactions in the block. It is up to the user to decide how these sorts of transactions are handled.

What about unwanted tokens? The function of any multi-asset may be anything you want it to be, but it's crucial to remember that, like ada, it's part of the transaction and must be managed and balanced accordingly.

Multi-assets will not present any problem, whether they are in the wallet of the issuer or the wallet of the exchange. Until it is redeemed, utilized, or burnt, it will be 'live'.

The exchange or third-party wallet is ultimately responsible for deciding what to do with a multi-asset.

To handle and maintain UTXOs, cardano-wallet employs a UTXO algorithm. On the blockchain, a multi-asset managed via cardano-wallet might easily go undetected.

Choosing a UTXO means taking into account the asset associated with that UTXO. An out-of-balance error will result if this additional input is not handled appropriately.

You have complete control over the native asset. You have two options: return it to the sender if you know the address or transfer the native asset to an address in your wallet while complying with network conditions and the minimum UTXO value.

---

[433] Getting started with native tokens, docs.cardano.org/native-tokens/getting-started

For more information on establishing and balancing a transaction with a native asset attached, see the *native tokens* section of Cardano Docs.

Scenario 2 – Surprise receipt of multi-asset in `cardano-wallet`.

Note: This scenario only applies to exchanges that use `cardano-wallet`.
Confirm you have received a multi-asset

1. Check the wallet information to confirm
2. To confirm the wallet information, use the curl command below:

Shelley

```
curl http://localhost:8090/v2/wallets
```

3. Confirm in the assets section:

```
"assets": {
     "total": [
          {
               "asset_name": "2e7444437f696e",
               "quantity": 10,
               "policy_id":
"f325fdd8f936d76d3d9944358380cff64d0db66e545f99a3cc01ab97"
          }
     ],
     "available": [
          {
               "asset_name": "6e7466636f696e",
               "quantity": 10,
               "policy_id":
"f125fdd8e336d56d3d9943117380cff64d0db66e545f99a3cc01ab97"
          }
     ]
}
```

What about token redemption or getting rid of unwanted multi-assets from cardano-wallet? Tokens generated using a minting policy adhere to a set of guidelines. For example, the minting policy might enable token holders to burn or produce new tokens. If you obtain undesirable tokens, you must usually return them to the issuer or sender, or store them someplace else for protection. For further information on minting policies, see minting policies docs section.[434]

---

[434] Minting policies and the multi asset ledger, cardano-ledger.readthedocs.io/en/latest/explanations/policies.html

Note that transmitting any quantity of native asset costs one ada plus the transaction fee as a minimum. For more details on the minimum UTXO requirements, see the minimum ada value requirement section in the docs.[435]

Option 1: Return tokens to the sender or issuer:

1. Confirm the sender's / issuer's address.
2. In cardano-wallet, create a JSON transaction with a minimum UTXO of one ada and include the native asset.

Sample transaction for sending a multi-asset:

```
curl -XPOST
http://localhost:8090/v2/wallets/{wallet_id}/transactions \
H "Content-Type: application/json \; charset=utf-8"
d "{
    "payments": [
        {
            "address":"{destination_address}",
            "amount":{
                "quantity":5000000,
                "unit":"lovelace"
            },
            "assets": [
                {
                    "policy_id":"asset_policy_id",
                    "asset_name": "6e7436436f646e",
                    "quantity": 5
                }
            ]
        }
    ],
    "passphrase":"mylittlepony"
}'
```

Confirm that the multi-asset transaction is complete, and that the assets have left the wallet.

Shelley

```
curl http://localhost:8090/v2/wallets
```

4. You should see the following result:

```
"assets": {
```

---

[435] minimum-ada-value requirement, cardano-ledger.readthedocs.io/en/latest/explanations/min-utxo-mary.html?highlight=minimum%20ada%20value%20requirement

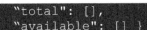

```
"total": [],
"available": [] }
```

Option 2: Move tokens to an address inside the existing wallet:

1. Confirm you have native tokens in the wallet.
2. Specify an address from the wallet to send the tokens.
3. Follow the steps in Option 1 to send the tokens to an address.
4. Keep track of the address containing native assets.

Listing native assets on an exchange

Many native assets are now functioning on Cardano, and new ones are being added on a regular basis. Some of these native assets have performed well in the market, where community members and financial institutions have shown interest and invested. There is a non-exhaustive list of native assets that are on *CardanoAssets.com*.

Going public with native assets

Token creators have two options for making their tokens available to the public:

1. Sell the native asset privately in a token sale, or
2. List the native asset on an exchange while adhering to the exchange's policies and guidelines.
3. Third party platforms like Dripdropz, the 'Cardano Token Distribution System'

Private token sale

Native asset producers who want to sell their tokens privately should do their due diligence and research first before deciding on the best way to do it.

Listing on an exchange's marketplace

Native asset developers may choose to list and sell their tokens on an exchange. When it comes to token listing, each exchange has its own set of regulations, standards, and laws.

From a technical standpoint, IOG can assist with any queries. IOG can help with things like token generation, minting, and burning, but any inquiries about the listing process should be handled to the appropriate exchange. Listing processes vary by exchange, eg. Kraken,[436] Coinbase or Binance.[437] If you are planning to list a native asset on an exchange, it's best to speak with the exchange directly first.

Technical support: When it comes to technical assistance for exchanges, the Cardano Foundation is the initial point of contact. If you have any technical problems or

---

[436] Kraken listing process, support.kraken.com/hc/en-us/articles/360001388206-New-coin-listing-requests

[437] Binance listing process, binance.com/en/support/faq/053e4bdc48364343b863d1833618d8ba

difficulties, contact them through the standard support channels, or submit a support request.

Smart Contracts Rollout

Alonzo built on Cardano's token improvements to provide developers with the tools they needed to create commercial DApps. IOG laid the groundwork for Cardano to become the premier smart contract platform by introducing transaction metadata,[438] token-locking[439] with *Allegra* in December 2020, and native token issuance.[440] Shortly after came *Mary*, a multi-asset protocol update in March 2021 that enabled users to create native tokens for Cardano transactions.

These features were built into Alonzo, the following protocol update in September 2021. Alonzo contributed functionality for smart contracts (digital agreements) to Cardano leveraging IOG's hard fork combinator technology. By facilitating the construction of smart contracts and decentralized apps (DApps) for decentralized finance (DeFi), it offered up new possibilities for developers.

Cardano's progress as a global distributed ledger continued with smart contracts. When it comes to regular commerce, a blockchain must ensure that people can transfer their money and pay for goods in a safe manner.

Smart contracts may be used to settle complicated transactions, keep the funds in escrow, and secure funds transfer under predetermined criteria. DApps may interface with Cardano's ledger to keep track of their actions and execute smart contracts. These digital agreements tell the tale of a transaction, specifying where money should go and under what circumstances they should be transferred, and only finalizing a deal if all the requirements have been satisfied. Cardano can handle such applications thanks to *Alonzo*.

Alonzo presented a flexible framework for constructing smart contracts, while multi-asset support lets users design unique currencies that fulfill business demands. Collectibles, crowdsourcing, and auctions, for example, are now possible.

Deployment of escrow-based decentralized cryptocurrency exchanges (DEX) or the development of sophisticated apps supporting centralized stablecoins might be explored. Users may utilize token-locking to create utility tokens with vesting periods, which means that tokens can be locked, or frozen for a certain duration of time, before being released.

Validating with signatures and scripts

---

[438] Alan McSherry, 'Bringing new value and utility to the Cardano blockchain', iohk.io/en/blog/posts/2020/10/29/bringing-new-value-and-utility-to-the-cardano-blockchain/

[439] Kevin Hammond, 'Goguen brings token locking to Cardano', iohk.io/en/blog/posts/2020/12/02/goguen-brings-token-locking-to-cardano/

[440] Tim Harrison, 'Building native tokens on Cardano for pleasure and profit', iohk.io/en/blog/posts/2021/02/18/building-native-tokens-on-cardano-for-pleasure-and-profit/

Validating the actions that are being taken is a vital part of executing a transaction. When data in the particular field to that action is provided in a transaction, it is deemed to be taking action. When a transaction has a reference to 'U' in its input field, it is spending UTXO 'U', and when its mint field contains 'X', it is minting a token 'X'.

When a node processes a transaction, it checks to see whether it can do the action. For this, the transaction's creator must give necessary data, such as scripts, redeemers, or signatures. Spending a UTXO locked with a public key is a typical example of an operation that needs validation. To accomplish this step, the transaction must give a signature from the associated private key.

Cardano validates actions via scripts. The code in these scripts implement Pure functions with True or False outputs. The process of calling the script interpreter to execute a given script with given parameters is known as script validation.

Plutus Scripting

IOG developed the essential tools and infrastructure with *Alonzo* to enable Plutus Platform application development. Alonzo enhanced Cardano Shelley's basic multi-signature scripting language (multisig) with a rigorous methodology based on formal methods and verification. For more sophisticated and secure scripting capabilities, Multisig was updated to the Plutus Core language. The Alonzo ledger uses Plutus Core to enable advanced scripting leveraging the extended unspent transaction output (EUTXO) accounting model.

The foundation for smart contracts must be both safe and dependable. As a result, Haskell was selected as the programming language for Plutus Core smart contracts. Haskell is a high-level programming language that is used by developers to code, which is then compiled into Plutus Core.[441]

Haskell has been around since 1987, and it stands out among computer languages because of its high degree of trustworthiness. Smart contracts written in Haskell, and Plutus, are designed to accomplish precisely what is expected of them and can be checked for correctness before being implemented. This ensures that smart contracts written on Cardano will be simple and secure, which is critical for applications that manage automated trading or large-scale money transfers.

Tools and APIs

On Cardano, developers can test and adapt transaction validation using functional tools. The Plutus Core code is deployed and run-on Cardano while communicating with wallets and the ledger, coupled with an extension of the API library.[442]

---

[441] Michael Peyton Jones, 'Plutus Tx: compiling Haskell into Plutus Core', iohk.io/en/blog/posts/2021/02/02/plutus-tx-compiling-haskell-into-plutus-core/

[442] API library, github.com/input-output-hk/cardano-node/tree/master/cardano-api

What smart contracts technology is currently available?

Of the 18,000[443] cryptocurrencies around today, with only 70 having smart contracts according to CryptoSlate.[444] PolkaDot, Solana and Ethereum are among the participants on the market that support smart contracts. Technology is changing to suit the market needs for systems that are quick, secure, accurate, and dependable. Many firms have attempted to install large-scale apps on these platforms and have run across 'issues'. For example, the DAO hack,[445] the Parity bug and the shambolic Solana Wormhole hack[446] where $320m went missing. Despite recurring hacks and rug pulls,[447] the most critical problems in smart contracts continue to surface.[448] There is plenty of space for innovation here, and IOG is working hard to establish itself as a leader in the space.

The concurrency non-issue

What is concurrency?

Concurrency may enhance or harm a system's performance, throughput, and responsiveness. The max number of simultaneous operations that may be executed is limited by the level of concurrency. Processors or other agents in a UTXO-based blockchain should be able to do several activities at the same time to achieve real performance benefits. The max achievable parallelism rises as the amount of concurrency increases. As a result of this strategy, performance and throughput increases. It also has a number of benefits over account-based systems such as Ethereum.

FUD

Shortly after smart contracts were introduced with the Alonzo hard fork, there was a spate of memes and false accusations that Cardano was only able to process one transaction at a time due to concurrency issues.[449] An objective analysis can only

---

[443] Adam Hayes, '10 Important Cryptocurrencies Other Than Bitcoin', investopedia.com/tech/most-important-cryptocurrencies-other-than-bitcoin/

[444] CryptoSlate Smart Contract Coins, cryptoslate.com/cryptos/smart-contracts/

[445] The DAO Hack Explained: Unfortunate Take-off of Smart Contracts, ogucluturk.medium.com/the-dao-hack-explained-unfortunate-take-off-of-smart-contracts-2bd8c8db3562

[446] More than $320 million stolen in latest apparent crypto hack, cnbc.com/2022/02/02/320-million-stolen-from-wormhole-bridge-linking-solana-and-ethereum.html

[447] A rug pull is a crypto scam in which fraudsters lie to the public to attract funding and quickly run off with investors' funds and/or digital tokens.

[448] Nikolic, Kolluri, Sergey, Saxena, Hobor (2018), Finding The Greedy, Prodigal, and Suicidal Contracts at Scale, arxiv.org/pdf/1802.06038.pdf

conclude this was FUD (fear, uncertainty and doubt) spread mostly by Cardano competitors.

Addressing the concurrency FUD, Charles Hoskinson used the analogy of single core processor vs multi-core processor:[450]

> *The analogy I like to use here is when we went from single core processors to multi-core processors. You'd see the marketing dual core, quad-core, 8 core, 16 core, that meant software under the hood actually had to be written a little differently to take advantage of parallelism. If you didn't do it you could have 16 cores, 32 cores ..but only one would actually be engaged, one thread would be engaged in that application, unless the application was rewritten for it. It's a bit disingenuous then to say, 'oh well intel's a scam ...ARM is a scam and AMD is a scam... they lied to us they said 16 cores, but I only use one core'. Well, that's a software contingent thing, those are there, you can access them, there are design patterns to do that. We've gotten a lot better today than we were when the dual core world came out, but you still need to introduce parallelism into your code in order to do that.*

One or more inputs may be used in a blockchain transaction, as well as one or more outputs. If one wishes to grasp how a transaction works and how it pertains to the Unspent Transaction Output (UTXO) accounting model, one must first comprehend the idea of inputs and outputs. Consider a transaction to be the operation that unlocks past outputs while also creating new ones.

Transaction output

An address (which you might regard as a lock) and a value are included in the transaction output. In line with this analogy, the address's signature is the key that unlocks the output. An output may be used as an input after it has been unlocked. New transactions use previous transactions' outputs while also producing new outputs that may be consumed by subsequent transactions. Each UTXO may only be used once, and it must be digested in its entirety. Only one input may spend each output.

Transaction input

The output of a preceding transaction is referred to as a transaction input. A pointer and a cryptographic signature that serve as the unlocking key are included in transaction inputs. The key unlocks a prior transaction output, and the pointer refers back to it. The blockchain labels an unlocked output as 'spent' when it is unlocked by an input. New inputs may then refer to new outputs produced by a given transaction, and the chain continues. The UTXOs are the new outputs (which have not yet been unlocked / spent). As the name implies, unspent outputs are outputs that haven't been spent yet.

---

[449] Cardano Founder Deals With Concurrency FUD, a Second Japanese Exchange Lists $ADA, cryptoglobe.com/latest/2021/09/cardano-founder-deals-with-concurrency-fud-a-second-japanese-exchange-lists-ada/

[450] More on Concurrency, youtu.be/OVh-eiACtzY?t=325

Multiple transactions

There are some pointers to keep in mind when submitting multiple transactions. When the mempool fills up, users that need to submit several transactions one after another may have issues. This is referred to as 'high throughput.' Some transactions may not be approved if the user continues to submit transactions after the mempool is full. The system has never guaranteed a transaction can be submitted reliably. In a distributed system like Cardano, such a guarantee is difficult to offer. Resubmission logic must be handled appropriately by submitting agents.

The cardano-submit-api is the proper endpoint to utilize. The thread is halted when the mempool is full. As a result, the API user may queue several transactions, which will be handled as soon as mempool capacity is available. However, the application must account for the fact that the number of in-flight transactions is restricted by the operating system's maximum number of open files. If this limit is reached, cardano-submit-api simply quits, and no more requests are processed. Using *ulimit*[451] to raise the number of open files permitted by the operating system will increase the number of in-flight transactions available, reducing UTXO congestion.[452]

To avoid the requirement for complex queue management, you may use the cardano-submit-api serially or with extremely low concurrency.[453]

It is a general rule that simplicity promotes resilience; if your use case allows, just submit one transaction at a time and wait for it to be verified before moving on to the next.

How EUTXO handles concurrency on Cardano

The EUTXO paradigm in Cardano offers a safe and adaptable environment for processing many operations without experiencing system problems. Cardano is a UTXO-based blockchain that uses a different programming model than existing account-based blockchains like Ethereum for decentralized applications (DApps). Cardano employs the Extended Unspent Transaction Output (EUTXO) paradigm, which was implemented with the *Alonzo* update. As a consequence, EUTXO provides a distinct solution to parallelization, allowing for increased security and cost predictability (without nasty shocks) in smart contract execution.

The per-branch architecture of the UTXO (Bitcoin) model is carried over to EUTXO, where one branch is defined as a series of transactions requiring a succession of validations. Building DApps and other solutions with numerous UTXOs is vital for splitting the functionality over various branches and enforcing additional parallelism.

---

[451] **ulimit** is a built-in Linux shell command that allows viewing or limiting system resource amounts that individual users consume. Limiting resource usage is valuable in environments with multiple users and system performance issues.

[452] **UTXO congestion**: The effect of multiple transactions attempting to spend the same transaction output.

[453] **Concurrency,** the property of program, algorithm, or problem decomposition into order-independent or partially-ordered units.

This has scalability advantages, much as creating Bitcoin services necessitates breaking one wallet into sub wallets.

Cardano DApps aren't restricted to only one transaction per block. In actuality, the block budget (the max number of transactions it can carry) permits hundreds of simple transactions and numerous complicated scripts to be executed simultaneously. The EUTXO approach, on the other hand, only permits a transaction output to be spent once. Because users may experience contention while attempting to access the same UTXO, it is critical to employ a range of UTXOs. This is significant unless the architecture would gain from a rigorous ordering of clients. Design patterns that involve semaphores[454] may be implemented using sets of UTXOs.

Furthermore, several users may interact with a single smart contract without causing a concurrency problem. This is because a smart contract can manage a variety of UTXOs that make up its present state, as well as off-chain metadata that enables those UTXOs to be interpreted.

Parallelism

Blockchains provide transaction processing immutability and transparency. To address the ever-increasing requirement for safe but efficient operation processing, every blockchain system should have the following properties:

- Throughput: the number of processes a system can complete in a given amount of time. This refers to the number of transactions or smart contracts completed in a second, for example

- System performance: how quickly the system operates. The execution time of a transaction or smart contract is measured by performance.

- Scalability: the system's capacity to handle many processes without overburdening the network or affecting performance.

The system's throughput can be raised while maintaining the speed of individual operations by boosting parallelism, but this kind of scalability will always be restricted by some degree of contention.

Concurrency, parallelism, and contention are all system considerations when it comes to scalability. Concurrency is required in order for several actors to work on a job without disturbing each other. Parallelism enables such development to be made simultaneously without interfering with each other. Contention happens when different actors work concurrently, or in parallel, and interfere with one another.

Launching DApps on a UTXO ledger

---

[454] A **semaphore** is a variable, or abstract data type, used to control access to a common resource by multiple threads and avoid critical section problems in a concurrent system such as a multitasking operating system. Semaphores are a type of synchronization primitives. A trivial semaphore is a plain variable that is changed depending on programmer-defined conditions.

Cardano's approach to DApp deployment is unique, with a steep learning curve requiring a new approach. Choosing from multiple programming languages is a similar analogy: there is usually a single end goal to implement something, but there is a plethora of languages you could use to get to this goal.

Concurrency optimization is a competence that must be mastered. Developers must code in such a manner that contention is limited (e.g., avoiding shared states and watch for accidental dependencies). This concurrency must then be turned into parallelism by the system. Several developers (such as SundaeSwap[455]) have previously found approaches to this problem, while others are currently working on them. In April 2022, WingRiders (wingriders.com) innovative DEX was successfully launched.[456] It is not possible to simply apply the same skills learnt on another blockchain directly to Plutus smart contracts. The learning curve is steep, but the benefits outweigh the effort.

In any case, it's vital to remember that a developer can't simply use an adapted Ethereum contract to build a scalable DApp on Cardano. Cardano uses the UTXO model rather than the account-based one. As a result, a single on-chain state will not satisfy the concurrency property on Cardano. DApps should instead distribute their on-chain state across several UTXOs. As a result, their application's concurrency will grow, enabling greater throughput.

UTXO alliance

IOG collaborates with other UTXO-based blockchains to develop novel solutions that will improve interoperability, programmability, and scalability. IOG announced a partnership with Ergo (ergoplatform.org), Nervos (nervos.org), and Topl (topl.co) to form the UTXO alliance during the 2021 Cardano Summit.[457] They then invited Komodo (komodoplatform.com), Alephium (alephium.org) and DigiByte (digibyte.org) into the alliance as well.

The UTXO alliance will help cross-ecosystem activities to expand UTXO's smart contract capability. The joint goal of collaborating with other blockchain sector initiatives is to stimulate and support further research, development, and education throughout the whole area.

The UTXO alliance's purpose is to keep the UTXO model evolving in terms of interoperability, scalability (sharding,[458] state channels, etc), and smart contract solutions. Improving these solutions and leading major projects to develop bridges across

---

[455] SundaeSwap blog on concurrency, sundaeswap.finance/posts/concurrency-state-cardano

[456] Cardano-based DEX WingRiders Hits $44 Million TVL Within 24 hours of Launch, thecryptobasic.com/2022/04/13/cardano-based-dex-wingriders-hits-44-million-tvl-within-24-hours-of-launch/

[457] UTXO alliance announcement, summit.cardano.org/sessions/taking-outputs-as-inputs

[458] **Sharding** splits a blockchain company's entire network into smaller partitions, known as 'shards.' Each shard consists of its own data, making it distinctive and independent when compared to other shards.

blockchains enables everyone to have access to fair and accessible global finance. This also provides a collaborative effort to promote UTXO-based ledgers in the industry. Bitcoin is obviously the most well-known UTXO blockchain but spin-offs like Bitcoin Cash, Litecoin, and Zcash are among the other projects that use this approach.

Building bridges

Instead of depending on expensive middlemen, blockchain technology tackles the difficulties of centralization by allowing trustworthy peer-to-peer transactions based on cryptographic verification. To create a safe and decentralized environment for financial transactions, several blockchain solutions have developed. While these initiatives differ in terms of consensus protocols, accounting models, and smart contract approaches, they all concentrate on similar use cases.

DeFi Growth[459] has been consistent and shows no signs of slowing. However, fragmented ecosystems, differing governance standards, technology versions, and feature support slow the development of the blockchain environment. Nasdaq's forecast on DeFi Growth is shared by Romain Pellerin, IOG technology chief:

> *Mainstream blockchain adoption will pass only through the interconnection of networks, similar to how the Internet was built by the interconnection of intranets and extranets.*

With this in mind, it's critical to guarantee that the whole sector is working toward interoperability. Users should be able to interact with one another without being bound by a single ledger, smart contracts should work in a variety of contexts, and decentralized apps (DApps) should be cross-platform compatible. Only in this manner will the blockchain sector be able to realize its full potential, resulting in increased adoption.

No one-size-fits-all

The UTXO alliance is also interested in blockchain programmability enabling the development of DApps and smart contracts. In reality, new languages must be created to adapt to the UTXO model's particular transaction and data storage management (for example, Ergo's[460] and Cardano's EUTXO). Antara, CKB-VM, ErgoScript, and Plutus are the smart contract languages created by the alliance's founding members. To quickly extend the number of use cases that may be executed on UTXO-based blockchains, alliance members are pooling expertise and cooperating in the development of such technologies.

Furthermore, such languages are constructed as domain-specific languages (DSLs) on top of widely used programming languages such as Scala, Haskell, C, JavaScript, Go, Rust,

---

[459] Why Privacy and Interoperability Will Fuel Exponential Growth in DeFi, nasdaq.com/articles/why-privacy-and-interoperability-will-fuel-exponential-growth-in-defi-2021-03-04

[460] Learning Ergo 101 : eUTXO explained for human beings, dav009.medium.com/learning-ergo-101-blockchain-paradigm-eutxo-c90b0274cf5e

and others. Those mainstream languages, however, may not always provide the security or convenience of use that smart contract developers seek.

IOG selected Haskell as the programming language for Plutus smart contracts to guarantee increased security and code verifiability. For application development, it is the most extensively used functional programming language. Haskell is a secure and formally verified programming language. In terms of acceptance, it is appropriate for a broad variety of financial use cases, providing for quick transfers of payments, accurate outcomes, and scalability. In terms of state distribution and parallelization for increased scalability, this programming approach works well inside the UTXO model.

The UTXO alliance will investigate the best-case scenarios for creating a uniform smart contract landscape where a range of programming languages may be built and utilized on various blockchain platforms, taking into account various development initiatives. This will be critical in enabling more blockchain interoperability.

True Scalability

It's also vital to consider a network's scalability potential in terms of transaction processing and throughput as it expands. Because the UTXO model is based on the local state, it differs from the account-based model and hence necessitates a distinct programming paradigm.

These two models have diverse features and provide different trade-offs, different benefits and drawbacks. The account model promotes the creation of use cases that depend on the global state, but the UTXO model assures determinism, predictability, and scalability by managing local states, meaning small sections of the overall graph of transactions. This slows things down as the whole graph of transactions needs to be processed before validation.

As a result, the UTXO architecture has the advantage of ensuring the execution of transactions and contracts prior to their submission to the blockchain, with no fees or validation surprises. Also, since it is easier to shard a graph of transactions by breaking it into a collection of sub-graphs, the UTXO paradigm will enable higher scalability.

It's also simpler to detach a specific transaction or collection of transactions (that transfer data, scripts, and assets) and continue work off-chain before returning to the mainchain with a result, ensuring scalability by off-loading operations off the mainchain. IOG, for example, has created Hydra state channel solutions that boost system performance while allowing several tasks to occur in parallel without sacrificing scalability. To learn more, read about concurrency[461] on Cardano. Hydra[462] and other scalability solutions are covered in Chapter 8.

---

[461] Olga Hryniuk, 'Concurrency and all that: Cardano smart contracts and the EUTXO model', iohk.io/en/blog/posts/2021/09/10/concurrency-and-all-that-cardano-smart-contracts-and-the-eutxo-model/

[462] Sebastian Nagel, 'Hydra – Cardano's solution for ultimate Layer 2 scalability', iohk.io/en/blog/posts/2021/09/17/hydra-cardano-s-solution-for-ultimate-scalability/

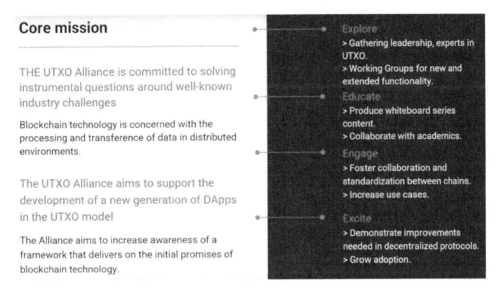

Figure 19: Slide from James Aman's talk 'UTXO Alliance' at ScotFest

Together is better

The UTXO alliance works together to improve the UTXO model and establish a common UTXO standard. Its goal is to provide a variety of options to ada holders, cryptocurrency users, businesses, and the development community that are not tied to a particular standard. For this, the alliance will perform academic research and publish a number of papers that support the creation of safe and scalable smart contracts using the UTXO architecture.

While interoperability is important, blockchain solutions are also necessary for better financial security, transaction processing scalability, and, of course, smart contract capabilities. To allow the use of diverse functionalities in a blockchain-agnostic manner, the alliance is dedicated to tackling such critical concerns as:

- How to transmit data across multiple blockchains in a smooth manner

- What is the appropriate data size for transactions?

- What should the data processing speed be?

- What should the transaction fees be?

As a result, the alliance is concentrating on developing a system that allows for smooth and safe transactions across multiple blockchains in order to encourage more widespread use of blockchain technology. This will also encourage the creation of reliable DApps and DeFi solutions. This is only the start, as Cardano is looking at partnering with other ecosystems to enhance the UTXO model and contribute to open-source research.

Chapter 6: Plutus

'There is no honest man! not one, that can resist the attraction of gold!'

— Aristophanes

This chapter is just an overview of Plutus. To become an expert, you only need to know this one page: *Plutus Resources*[463] connects you to everything going on in the Plutus ecosystem. The documentation is a little scattered and constantly changing, exactly how it should be for a burgeoning programming language. IOG categorizes smart contracts and financial transactions into two scenarios:

In one scenario, you want to communicate a sense of value transfer from one actor to another. Financial contract(s) must represent that value, as well as the rules and circumstances that control it, as well as a trigger event. Financial contracts are best implemented with a domain-specific language.

In other scenarios, you'd like to write programs, possibly with a view to disrupting an industry, replacing a major corporation, or solving a smaller problem.

These applications normally comprise three things:

- The client which is the part of the program running on your computer
- The server is a computer (or node) that operates on another user's computer (or it can be multiple servers)
- The smart contract is the code that enables a decentralized system to function.

The two main programming languages for Cardano are:

- Plutus - the primary platform to code DApps which interact with the Cardano blockchain
- Marlowe - a domain-specific language for building financial contracts, discussed in the next chapter.

What is Plutus?

Plutus is a platform that offers a native smart contract language as well as the supporting infrastructure and tools to implement smart contracts on Cardano.

The Plutus Platform enables developers to create *DApps* that interact with a *distributed ledger* featuring *scripting* capabilities. This is why it's an entire platform, not just a language. It doesn't just provide a few tools to make the bare minimum possible, it supports DApp development in its entirety, end-to-end from writing scripts, to testing, runtime support, and verification.

To master Plutus, one must grasp three concepts:

- The Extended Unspent Transaction Output (EUTXO) model
- On-chain code, Plutus Core, which runs on the blockchain and is compiled by the Plutus compiler

---

[463] Plutus Resources docs.cardano.org/plutus/plutus-resources

- Off-chain code which runs on the user's device. The Plutus Application Framework (PAF) may be used to write off-chain code, which is subsequently compiled by the GHC (Glasgow Haskell Compiler)

Plutus smart contracts are essentially Turing-complete Haskell programs, with both on-chain and off-chain code written in Haskell. You can be sure that your smart contracts will be executed correctly if you follow best practice with Plutus. Haskell is the foremost purely functional programming language and builds on recent language research to create a secure, full-stack development environment.

To assist you with getting started, the Plutus Playground[464] includes 'how to' guides and tutorials. To understand more about the Plutus language, you should read the Plutus explanations.[465] If you want assistance when using Plutus, create an issue in the Plutus repository[466] including as much information as possible.

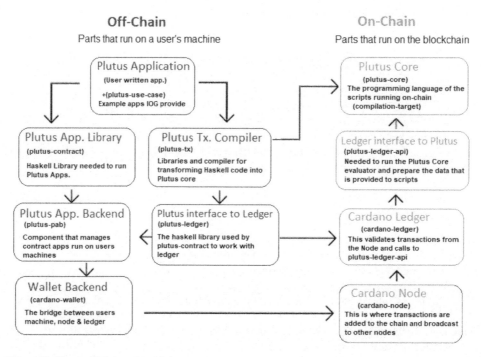

Figure 20: Plutus off-chain and on-chain

Plutus uses extended UTXO (EUTXO)

[464] Plutus Playground, playground.plutus.iohkdev.io/

[465] Plutus explanations, plutus-apps.readthedocs.io/en/latest/plutus/explanations/index.html

[466] Plutus github repo, github.com/input-output-hk/plutus

196

Cardano employs the extended UTXO accounting model (EUTXO), which extends the UTXO model's unspent (U) transaction (TX) output (O) accounting model (used by Bitcoin). A transaction in the UTXO paradigm contains inputs and outputs, with the inputs being unspent outputs from prior transactions. When an output is used as an input in a transaction, it is considered spent and cannot be reused. An address (a public key or public key hash) and a value are used to specify the output (consisting of an ada amount and optional, additional native token amounts).

EUTXO improves the UTXO architecture by enabling output addresses to include complicated logic that determines which transactions are allowed to unlock them, as well as by adding custom data to all outputs. Compared to other accounting models, this one has certain distinct benefits. The transaction's success or failure is solely determined by the transaction and its inputs, not by anything else on the blockchain. As a result, before a transaction is transmitted to the blockchain, it may be validated for legitimacy off-chain. The transaction, on the other hand, is guaranteed to succeed if all inputs are still present.

The workings of a Plutus transaction

A transaction is a piece of data that has both inputs and outputs, and they may incorporate Plutus scripts. The unspent outputs from prior transactions (UTXO) are referred to as inputs. A UTXO gets spent as soon as it is used as an input in a transaction and cannot be used again. An address (a public key or public key hash) and a value are used to specify the output (consisting of an ada amount and optional additional native token amounts). This flow diagram provides a better understanding of the technical components of a transaction:

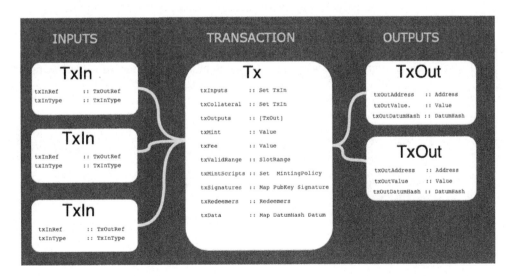

Figure 21: Transaction inputs and outputs

In a nutshell, inputs are references to UTXOs introduced by earlier transactions, and outputs are the new UTXOs produced by this transaction. Since new data may be stored in the generated outputs, this enables the status of a smart contract to be modified.

Plutus Tx refers to parts of a Haskell program that are used to compile a contract application's on-chain component into Plutus Core (this compiled code is then used for validating a transaction, hence the 'Tx'). The Plutus Core expression that results may be included in transaction data or saved in the ledger. Plutus script refers to certain chunks of code that need specific processing on the blockchain. You can manage the flow of execution of a Plutus script by utilizing transactions. As a result, a transaction can be thought of as a series of messages sent to the smart contract.

While assessing the off-chain code, the wallet should initiate a transaction. Once the transaction is submitted, it will be verified, and a validator node will analyze the Plutus code. The transaction will be deemed legitimate if the script evaluates correctly. The transaction will be denied otherwise.

The PAF may be used to write off-chain code, which is then compiled by the GHC (Glasgow Haskell Compiler), while the Plutus compiler compiles on-chain code (written in Plutus Core). It's critical to grasp the link between these Plutus principles and native tokens functionality to realize how the latter becomes a more powerful feature as a result of their interaction.

Plutus Core

Cardano's programming language, Plutus Core, is utilized to build the EUTXO paradigm. Plutus Core scripts may be written in a concise, functional language comparable to Haskell, and a significant portion of Haskell can be leveraged. You don't write Plutus Core as a smart contract programmer; In practice, you'll create validator scripts in Haskell, which will be automatically compiled into Plutus Core using a GHC (Glasgow Haskell Compiler) plug-in called Plutus Tx.[467] These scripts will be run 'live' on the chain by nodes during transaction validation. They will either use validator scripts[468] to unlock UTXOs, or minting policies to regulate the minting and burning of native tokens.

In a sign of a maturing ecosystem, there are now many third-party alternatives to Plutus Tx. Just some on a growing list are:

- **plu-ts**[469] is a library to enable Cardano-related software to be written entirely in TypeScript
- **Aiken**[470] is not intended as a general purpose language. It is bespoke to Cardano, delivering high-quality developer tools.

---

[467] **Plutus Tx**: The libraries and compiler for compiling Haskell into Plutus Core to form the on-chain part of a contract application.

[468] Validator scripts, docs.cardano.org/plutus/Plutus-validator-scripts

[469] plu-ts, github.com/HarmonicLabs/plu-ts

[470] Aiken, github.com/txpipe/aiken/

- **Helios**[471] is a non-Haskell alternative to Plutus. It is a Domain Specific Language (DSL) that compiles to Plutus-Core. All you need is the Helios library, written in Javascript, to compile Helios scripts and build Cardano transactions.
- **Pluto**[472] is essentially Untyped Plutus Core (UPLC)[473] with a little bit of syntactic sugar
- **Imperator**[474] is a proof of concept imperative language that transforms a lightweight imperative language into Pluto
- **Plutarch**[475] is a typed eDSL (embedded domain specific language) in Haskell for writing efficient Plutus Core validators.
- **eopsin**[476] is an implementation of Cardano smart contracts written in a strict subset of valid Python.
- **Cardano Multiplatform lib**[477] is a library form dcSpark, written in Rust, that can be deployed to multiple platforms (Rust crate, JS, Typescript, WASM, etc)

dcSpark was founded by former Emurgo and IOG developers and have already, in a short space of time, made significant contributions such as the *Flint* wallet and the *Milkomeda* sidechain. dcSpark are trailblazers for Cardano, attracting developers to enter the space and ensure there is diversity in the ecosystem, and not an over-reliance on IOG. Twitter space host and educator, Bullish Dumpling, observed:[478]

> *I think it's going to make such a difficult and fun quiz question to ask people 'Please name all products that dcSpark has developed, and is developing...', there's just so many they're working on, so many things*

Plutus Application Framework (PAF)

Validator scripts' on-chain status can only be changed by transactions that spend and create script output. When designing a Plutus application, both the on-chain (the Plutus Core scripts) and the off-chain (the transaction building and submission) components must be taken into account.

Unlike Ethereum, where the on-chain code is written in Solidity while the off-chain code is written in JavaScript, the Cardano off-chain code is written in Haskell, exactly like the

---

[471] Helios, github.com/hyperion-bt/helios

[472] Pluto, github.com/Plutonomicon/pluto

[473] Plutus Tx: compiling Haskell into Plutus Core, iohk.io/en/blog/posts/2021/02/02/plutus-tx-compiling-haskell-into-plutus-core/

[474] Imperator, github.com/ImperatorLang/imperator

[475] Plutarch, github.com/Plutonomicon/plutarch

[476] Cardano smart contracts in Python, github.com/ImperatorLang/eopsin

[477] Cardano Multiplatform lib (CML), github.com/dcSpark/cardano-multiplatform-lib

[478] Dec 28 2022: Recap for Cardano projects 2022, youtu.be/hx5TNM5U958?t=673

on-chain code. The business logic[479] will only have to be written once this way. The validator script and the code that creates the transactions that execute the validator script may then employ this reasoning.

Many applications need to monitor the UTXO set[480] for changes to certain addresses, so if the contract is written as a state machine,[481] you need to keep track of the unspent output, which reflects the machine's current state, and update your local state if the on-chain state changes. Many applications need communication with the wallet backend to access the crypto funds they are using for transactions. The Plutus Application Framework (PAF) makes it simple to access services that are often used by Plutus apps.

Plutus Application Backend (PAB)

The Plutus application backend, which offers runtime support for access to the blockchain as well as additional concerns like persistence, logging, and monitoring, may be used to execute applications built using the framework's libraries. Applications built on top of the PAF provide an HTTP and WebSocket[482] interface that allows users to interact with the app from a web browser.

The Plutus off-chain component is executed by the PAB, which is constantly iterated upon with each release. It handles wallet backend and node application requests, saves application state, and provides an HTTP API for managing application instances.

Native tokens and Plutus

With the Mary hard fork in February 2021, native tokens became accessible on Cardano. Tokens, like ada, may be created by anybody, and they can be transferred and received freely.

Each native token has its own minting policy,[483] which specifies the circumstances under which tokens may be minted and burned. Users create minting policies in Haskell and

---

[479] **Business logic** or domain logic is the part of the program that encodes the real-world business rules that determine how data can be created, stored, and changed. It is contrasted with the remainder of the software that might be concerned with lower-level details.

[480] The **UTXO set** is the comprehensive set of all UTXOs existing at a given point in time. The sum of the amounts of each UTXO in this set is the total supply of existing currency at that point of time. Anyone can verify the total supply at any time in a trustless manner.

[481] A finite-state machine (FSM) or simply a **state machine**, is a mathematical model of computation. It is an abstract machine that can be in exactly one of a finite number of states at any given time. The FSM can change from one state to another in response to some external inputs and/or a condition is satisfied; the change from one state to another is called a transition. An FSM is defined by a list of its states, its initial state, and the conditions for each transition.

[482] **WebSocket** is a communications protocol, providing full-duplex communication channels over a single TCP connection. The Transmission Control Protocol (TCP) is one of the main protocols of the Internet protocol suite. It originated in the initial network implementation in which it complemented the Internet Protocol (IP). Therefore, the entire suite is commonly referred to as TCP/IP.

compile them to Plutus Core after Plutus was deployed. During the minting or burning process, the Plutus Core policy script will be run in the context of the transaction, and it will have to approve or reject the action. This feature has boosted Cardano Non-Fungible Tokens (CNFTs) adoption by allowing for the use of considerably more complicated minting policies and trustless NFT issuance.

Minting policies are made up of a series of basic rules that define signatures and timelocks. For example, a policy may declare that transactions can only mint or burn tokens if they are signed by two of the five potential signatures. A different policy can allow minting only before or after a certain time.

Strengths of Plutus

Plutus offers significant security benefits. It provides a simpler, more reliable method of demonstrating that your smart contracts are accurate and will not experience the issues that have plagued prior smart contract language designs.

Plutus allows for a new integrated approach to smart contract and distributed application development that is easier and more secure than prior options. The same language is used for both on-chain and off-chain programming. You employ a common code base, which the Plutus toolchain[484] divides into on-chain and off-chain code and packages for deployment. Plutus also enables user-defined tokens (both fungible and non-fungible) natively, which needs much less code than Ethereum.

A key differentiator of EUTXO, and Plutus, is its predictability, often referred to as determinism. At ScotFest,[485] James Aman (CTO of Topl) coined the phrase:

> *'Not your output, not your outcome' because if you want a thing to happen in the world, you need the output, the actual thing that goes into state, to reflect your desire… because those outputs then help you achieve your desired outcomes*

Plutus Scripts

Cardano validates operations via scripts. Pure functions with True or False outputs are implemented in these scripts. The process of invoking the script interpreter to run a script with relevant arguments is known as script validation. A script is code that determines if the transaction spending the output is approved. This kind of script is known as a validator script since it checks if the transaction is permitted. A simple validator script would verify whether the spending transaction was signed by a certain key, just as basic pay-to-pubkey outputs do. Scripts may be used to express meaningful logic on the chain. Metadata and scripts are bundled together in a single transaction for greater throughput.

---

[483] Minting policy, github.com/input-output-hk/cardano-documentation/blob/staging/content/07-native-tokens/01-learn.mdx#minting-policy

[484] A **toolchain** is a set of programming tools that is used to perform a complex software development task or to create a software product, which is typically another computer program or a set of related programs.

[485] The UTXO Alliance, youtube.com/watch?v=j-Mil0RcKhQ

The EUTXO paradigm operates by passing three parameters to validator scripts:

- Datum: This is a piece of data that is linked with the output and is locked by the script (just the hash is present). This is usually used to carry state.

- Redeemer: a piece of info associated with the spending input. This is usually used to provide the spender's input to the script

- Context: this is the metadata concerning a spending transaction. This is used to make assertions about how the output is sent (for example, 'John signed this one'). The context can be made up of inputs (outputs from previous transactions to be spent), reference inputs (just for ref, not to be spent), new outputs, fees, minted values, certificates, reward withdrawals, date ranges, transaction signatures, redeemers, map of datum hashes, transaction IDs).

Simple example

A customer 'John' wants to buy 'Cardano for the MАsses' which costs ₳10. There must be confirmation they have enough ₳ in their wallet before they can buy it.

```
if EnoughADA(book=CardanoForTheMasses, customer=john):
    buyBook()

def EnoughADA (book,customer):
    return customer["balance"] >= book["bookPrice"]

def buyBook():
    print ("You have enough ADA to buy the book")

CardanoForTheMasses = {"bookPrice":₳10}
john = {"balance":₳11}
```

In the above example:

- The datum is the information about this transaction: *john.balance*
- The context is the state of the world, at that point meaning: *CardanoForTheMasses.bookPrice*
- The redeemer, is the action to perform: *buyBook()*

The validator script is the function that uses all that information, in this example, *EnoughADA*

IOG's GitHub contains examples of validator scripts on every smart contract:

- Plutus transaction tutorial[486]

- Plutus Hello World[487]
- Plutus pioneers English Auction[488]

Cost model parameters

A number of parameters in the cost model for Plutus Core scripts are also included in the Cardano protocol parameters. Individual settings may be tweaked by developers.

See the following for more details:

- A list of cost model parameters and their brief description[489]
- Sources to find out more about the meaning of parameters[490]

Plutus Versions

Cardano, like any other blockchain, is a decentralized ledger or database that keeps track of all transactions and blocks made on the network. This database distributes records with all participants and synchronizes with blockchain activity on a regular basis to deliver transparent and up-to-date data to anybody. In layman's terms, a ledger is just a system that tracks who owns what.

Cardano DB Sync[491] retrieves such blockchain information and lets users run CLI commands to access transaction and block details. You can use the Cardano Explorer – a graphical user interface that exposes information in a straightforward manner – for more easy and user-friendly data analysis.

Before a transaction is submitted to a block,[492] it is validated by a block producer. To avoid double-spending, the sender must have adequate funds, and all nodes across the ledger must establish consensus. Let's look at how this worked in the Shelley ledger, and how Plutus scripts changed it to enable multi-asset transactions and smart contracts.

---

[486] Plutus transactions model, github.com/input-output-hk/Alonzo-testnet/blob/main/Alonzo-tutorials/Plutus_transactions_tutorial.md#transaction-to-lock-funds

[487] Plutus HelloWorld, github.com/input-output-hk/Alonzo-testnet/blob/e27563ec0c0c3723376f4d12881cd003a7a7157f/resources/plutus-sources/plutus-helloworld/src/Cardano/PlutusExample/HelloWorld.hs#L47

[488] EnglishAuction.hs, github.com/input-output-hk/plutus-pioneer-program/blob/024ebd367bf6c4003b482bfb4c6db7d745ec85aa/code/week01/src/Week01/EnglishAuction.hs#L103

[489] Cost model parameters, plutus.readthedocs.io/en/latest/reference/cost-model-parameters.html

[490] Plutus bibliography, plutus.readthedocs.io/en/latest/reference/bibliography.html#id13

[491] The purpose of **DB Sync** is to follow the Cardano chain and take information from the chain and an internally maintained copy of ledger state. Data is then extracted from the chain and inserted into a PostgreSQL database. SQL queries can then be written directly against the database schema.

[492] Cardano Nodes, docs.cardano.org/new-to-cardano/cardano-nodes

Transaction validation before Goguen

When an output is used as an input in a transaction, it is considered spent and cannot be reused. The following are the parameters for the output:

- an address which holds a payment credential and an optional stake credential, which may be either a public/verification key hash or a script hash. The stake credential might alternatively be a link to the registration certificate.
- a value: this is the amount of ada that may be spent.

The owner of the private key (also known as the signature key), which corresponds to the payment credential supplied in the address, must sign a transaction. Only ada transactions were supported by Cardano Shelley. The Shelley formal specification introduced the idea of multi-signature (multisig) scripts,[493] which are captured wholly by ledger rules. If a predetermined combination of signatures is given, this multisig approach allows an unspent transaction output to be used as an input to a new transaction.

For example, if two people must sign the transaction at the same time, two out of three keys must be given, and so on. Multisig is a very simple language that enables you to interact with RequireSignature, RequireAllOf, RequireAnyOf, and RequireMOf, among other constructors. Scripts should be designed to allow more phrases for expressing a variety of different conditions as the ledger's functionality grows.

Alonzo (Plutus V1)

With the introduction of multi-asset support and smart contracts on Cardano, upgrading the fundamental multisig scripting language with more complex options was required. As part of the Alonzo upgrade, IOG implemented the required tools and infrastructure, as well as support for a new programming language called Plutus Core.

The Alonzo ledger employs the extended unspent transaction output (EUTXO) paradigm to upgrade multisig to Plutus Core to give strong scripting features.

Alonzo made the following adjustments to the ledger data:

1. Plutus scripts can lock UTXOs.
2. Script state-like functionality was enabled via a new component added to the contents of the output pieces of UTXOs. A UTXO locked by Plutus scripts includes a datum in addition to assets and an address. A datum is a piece of information that represents an interpretation of the script state.
3. A number of new protocol parameters were added to enforce extra transaction validation requirements. These include upper restrictions on how much processing power scripts may use.

Transactions were updated to support Plutus scripts as follows:

---

[493] MultiSig scripts, github.com/input-output-hk/cardano-node/blob/master/doc/reference/simple-scripts.md#multi-signature-scripts

1. The transaction now has a redeemer, which is a user-specified parameter for each of its activities. A redeemer may fulfill a variety of functions depending on the script. It may, for example, serve as the user's decision to 'hit' or 'stand' in a game of blackjack or a 'like' or 'share' in some utopian decentralized social media DApp.
2. The transaction defines each script's computational execution budgets.
3. Alonzo leverages collateral to verify that a transaction can pay its execution cost
4. Transactions include an integrity hash, which is used to confirm that it hasn't been tampered with, hasn't expired, and so on.

The node runs Alonzo-specific tests to guarantee that the transaction is built successfully. It must not, for example, exceed the maximum execution resource budget. It also runs the scripts by using Plutus script interpreter.

Ethereum's non-deterministic 'gas' model has the potential to charge consumers extortionately high fees. This form of indeterminism is addressed in Cardano scripts by requiring that both the resource budget and the fee necessary to cover it be included in the transaction. When designing a transaction in Alonzo, a user may forecast both locally. Script execution will always return one of two values: True or False, and it will not loop endlessly. This is because every action a script does requires a non-zero amount of resources, which the interpreter keeps track of. If the transaction's budget is exceeded, the script is terminated and False is returned.

The following critical features help to forecast the results of script and transaction validation:

- When applied with the same parameters, the script interpreter will always terminate and deliver the same validation result
- During validation, a transaction should correct all variables provided to the script interpreter
- A transaction enumerates all of the operations it performs that need script validation
- a transaction's mandatory signatures guarantee that it can't be tampered with by an attacker in a manner that causes scripts to fail.

In the EUTXO ledger paradigm, implementing a transaction is deterministic.

Vasil (Plutus V2)

There were three Cardano Improvement Proposals implemented with the Vasil hard fork to enhance the way Plutus operates, to make things easier for developers. All three dovetail together and complement each other.

Sebastien Guillemot
@SebastienGllmt

...

Pretty cool: 50% of the Cardano ledger changes for the upcoming Vasil upgrade were CIPs (Cardano Improvement Proposals)

CIP31[494] defined **reference inputs,** a major step forward for how developers interact with UTXOs. A reference input is a transaction input associated with a specific transaction output, however, rather than spending the output, it just references it.

A datum can be thought of as the data for your script, bits of data attached to outputs, where you might store data like a user handle, or avatar etc. Before Vasil, if you wanted to read your handle, or score of a soccer match etc., in your DApp, you had to consume the UTXO and then recreate it after you had read the datum.

Reference inputs allow you to read the datum, or the data that's stored at a UTXO, without consuming it and recreating it. This means that multiple DApps can read from the same datum simultaneously. This boosts concurrency and throughput dramatically.

Ergo, pioneers in the UTXO space, already introduced a similar concept called 'data inputs'[495] in 2020.

CIP 32 defined **inline datums**. Before Vasil, this high score, or other data from the datum wasn't stored on-chain. The hash (fingerprint) of it was stored on-chain and it was up to the developer to include it when they were interacting with the script. Since Vasil, the data can be stored on-chain, eliminating the need for hashes and moving closer to a truly decentralized architecture.

CIP 33 is about **reference scripts**. Plutus script references can be linked to transaction outputs, allowing them to be stored on-chain and reused later. It means you are no longer required to provide a copy of the script with each transaction, thereby reducing developer friction. Using the same script in several transactions decreases transaction sizes, boosts throughput and lowers script execution costs.

Before Vasil, developers had to share the scripts offline so that they could be included in transactions. However, it was harder to share those scripts with different people so that they could interact with their DApp.

Reference scripts allow developers to put Plutus scripts on-chain and then, rather than include them in a transaction, they can instead include a pointer in the transaction that

---

[494] CIP (Cardano improvement proposals), cips.cardano.org/

[495] Ergo data inputs, docs.ergoplatform.com/dev/scs/data-inputs/

just references that script on the existing chain. That means that a user doesn't need to have a copy of this script to interact with it. You just need to let people know the address it's at, and then users anywhere can use the same script and point to it.

This enables a use case where a developer can put reference scripts on-chain and allow others to use them as a library. There could be several libraries considered to be core to Plutus, and IOG will put them where anyone can use them and then publish the address. This allows anyone in the ecosystem to take libraries and make them available to the wider public, a powerful enhancement.

Looking at all three CIPs holistically, these enhancements pushed Plutus forward and make developers' lives easier. IOG is putting more on-chain, freeing developers from the need to monitor scripts and share scripts and datums and increases concurrency by allowing users to interact with UTXOs.

CIP 49: ECDSA and Schnorr signatures in Plutus Core[496]

Known internally as the 'SEC P' update, CIP 49 was implemented as an Intra-era hard fork[497] in February 2023.

Cryptographic primitives are like the Lego blocks used to create secure transactions and develop algorithms when building DApps. They can be random number generators, entropy (randomness) sources, basic memory or math operations that are required by the cryptographic algorithms.

Before we go any further, let's unscramble some of the terminology:

Elliptic Curve Digital Signature Algorithm or *ECDSA* is a cryptographic scheme for producing signatures using public and private keys. It uses a variant of Schnorr signature based on twisted Edwards curves. So what is a Schnorr signature?

A *Schnorr signature* is a digital signature produced by the Schnorr signature algorithm that was described by Claus Schnorr. It is known for its simplicity, efficiency and for generating short signatures.

Secp256k1 is the name of the elliptic curve used by Bitcoin, Ethereum and others to implement its public key cryptography. Whereas Cardano, Monero, Ripple and others employ *edwards25519* elliptic curve as a basis for their key pair generation. The curve comes from the *Ed25519* signature scheme.

Initially, the Vasil hard fork was to add built-in support for *secp256k1* on Cardano, enabling developers to interact with signatures from those other blockchains. However, after extensive testing, it was decided to omit this enhancement from Vasil. As this upgrade impacted the Plutus interpreter, it needed to be implemented as a hard fork. After Vasil, it was decided that future updates would only be scheduled if certain critical mass

---

[496] CIP 49: ECDSA and Schnorr signatures in Plutus Core, github.com/mlabs-haskell/CIPs/blob/c5bdd66fe49c19c341499f86cebaa2eef9e90b74/CIP-0049/README.md

[497] Intra-era hard fork is a small and focused semantic change to the ledger requiring a hard fork.

indicators were met. A set percentage of SPOs would need to be running the new node. Exchanges would need to be consulted. Impact to other Cardano components would need to be assessed. *Cexplorer.io/versions* is a good page to track for 'hard fork readiness'.

As Nigel Hemsley (IOG Chief of Delivery) explained in a Cardano350 episode,[498] this time the community was more involved in the release cycle. The primitives went through extensive testing on a devnet, preview and pre-prod environments before it was pushed to mainnet as a hard fork combinator event.

The changes, outlined in CIP 49, enable DApp developers to effectively build cross-chain applications with bridges, sidechains and wrapped assets. The new functionality is crucial for bridges to sidechains, and other interoperability solutions like *Wanchain*.[499] These primitives are supported as built-in functions native to Cardano, implemented and audited by security experts. This gives Plutus developer more options. For example, Schnorr-based designs are well established and adopted by the wider DApp community.

As is often the case with Cardano, an analogy helps understanding. Emmanuel (@thepizzaknight_)[500] provided this New Year's Day gift:

> *For the purposes of this thread, regard Crypto Primitives as real-world language families, let's use the Indo-European language family. Cardano uses Curve25519, think Germanic (English, Deutsche, etc) Ethereum, Bitcoin, etc. use SECP256k1, think Romance (French, Spanish, etc).   As you can imagine, it can be tough to do business as an English speaker with a Spanish-speaking person. You have to hire translators and go through a lot just to get work done. This is what it's like now for dApp (and Bridge) builders on Cardano trying to go cross-chain. Thankfully the next Chain Upgrade Event fixes this by adding support for SECP256k1 as a Built-in function on Cardano (think of it as adding a new DNA strand). This will allow Cardano (English) to naturally understand other chains (Spanish). What does this mean for you as a user or a builder? New cross-chain opportunities with better bridges and access to new tokens and dApps from other chains. With the Sidechain strategy, Cardano needs this improvement for its Interoperability vision to be feasible and real.*

Backwards compatibility

The Cardano Ledger tags scripts with a language (V1 for Alonzo, V2 was Vasil). This dictates how the ledger treats the script. Plutus V1 must remain the same forever, or else anyone could manipulate existing scripts, potentially making outputs un-spendable and

---

[498] Nigel Hemsley (Cardano 360 October 2022), youtube.com/watch?v=hZRwLWKNNfQ&t=257s

[499] Wanchain, the Wide Area Network chain, is an interoperability solution with a mission to drive blockchain adoption through crosschain interoperability by building fully decentralized bridges that connect siloed blockchain networks

[500] thepizzaknight_ primitives' analogy, twitter.com/thepizzaknight_/status/1609373418759012353?s=20&t=2BonGRIWcKofrMSWJe4qYg

breaking users' assumptions. For this reason, if Plutus needs significant updating, a 'new' language in the ledger is required.

Generally, each hard fork will produce a new 'Plutus language version' with additional functionality. From the ledger's perspective, they are completely unrelated and there is no requirement that they be similar in any way. Your old scripts are still valid and will function as before. You are not obligated to use the new language version, which is a superset of the prior version. You obviously need to tag your script with the correct version to avail of new features, see 'language versions' in the docs for more details.

To understand what kinds of changes require a new language version, see CIP 35–Plutus Core Evolution.[501]

Typical Plutus Use Cases

Plutus is often used for the following high-level use cases, among others:

- Oracles — fully operational oracles that interact with and feed smart contracts by bringing off-chain data onto the chain. Oracles also provide Plutus applications with a centralized and trusted off-chain data feed (for example, price feeds from various centralized exchanges)

- DEX token swaps — building a decentralized exchange system that lets users swap supported tokens. Users may form liquidity pools (or contribute funds to existing ones), which will provide coins for trading. They may earn fees for any transactions that utilize their funds in exchange for this. Users may also donate to liquidity pools for any supported token and earn commissions in the form of exchange fees in return for their efforts. When a user provides liquidity to a pool, the user is given a liquidity token that represents the deposit. Fees should be calculated by the contract and then distributed to liquidity providers based on each provider's portion in the liquidity pool

- Lending and borrowing - developing a lending protocol that allows users to lend and borrow cryptocurrencies in a safe and secure manner, with variable and stable interest rates. Users may take part as either depositors or borrowers. Lenders must deposit funds into liquidity pools in order to transact, and borrowers must borrow from these liquidity pools. Depositors are rewarded with interest-bearing tokens. To protect against volatility, each pool has a reserve pool

- NFTs — developing core functionality for minting, sending, and receiving NFTs into a wallet, as well as additional use cases

---

[501] CIP 35–Plutus Core Evolution, cips.cardano.org/cips/cip35/

- Decentralized finance (DeFi) tools — building multifunctional dashboards (web-based or mobile) that interface with smart contracts to provide value to native token traders. These solutions may have numerous functional dashboards that display token and liquidity pool balances, among other things. They may also combine many services into a single transaction, such as swaps and providing liquidity, making DeFi adoption simpler

- Crypto-backed stable coins — leveraging Cardano's Atala PRISM decentralized ID system to create a new stable coin implementation based on-chain collateral. Transfer restrictions, asset freezes, and other measures may be implemented.

- Over-collateralized stable coins — the COTI team worked closely with IOG's Plutus team when implementing the Djed stablecoin.

Plutus Tools

Developers can leverage a variety of tools to assess and implement smart contracts on Cardano.

Plutus Playground

The Plutus Playground is a place where smart contracts may be written and tested before being put on the Cardano blockchain. It's a web-based platform for Plutus development with modest resource consumption. The Plutus Playground offers a web-based simulator for building and executing smart contracts, as well as access to popular smart contracts that have already been developed.

There is no need to install anything to use the Plutus Playground, which can be accessed from a web browser. The user interface is divided into three parts:

- editor
- simulator
- transactions

The simulator displays how a contract will function on Cardano. One of the key parts of this is that it can be used as a teaching tool for beginners. The wallets that interact with a contract, as well as the actions that affect the result, may be defined and updated by users. The outcomes may then be analyzed to determine what occurs on the blockchain and how transactions take place. Visit the Plutus github repository or watch the Plutus application compiling and testing tutorial[502] for further details.

Plutus Application Backend

---

[502] Plutus Playground - Video Tutorial: Compiling and testing a Plutus App, youtube.com/watch?v=DhRS-JvoCw8

The Plutus Application Framework (PAF) includes the Plutus Application Backend (PAB), which is the off-chain infrastructure in the UTXO paradigm that produces the transactions that power the DApps. Because it has to look at the ledger state, take some information from the ledger, and put it all together to produce a transaction with the proper bits of data in the right location, this off-chain architecture is somewhat complex. The PAB is a Haskell library that simplifies the development of both off-chain infrastructure and on-chain scripts.

The PAB assists in the construction of UTXO transactions in two ways:

- The read path entails retrieving data from the blockchain and responding to events that occur there
- The write path - This is where the transactions that execute the Plutus scripts are built.

Plutus Application Backend (PAB) offers the components and environment that allow developers to interface with smart contracts and design and test DApps before deploying them to a live production environment. It's a sandbox environment, similar to the Plutus Playground and the Marlowe Playground,[503] where developers may test DApp features before committing to a full Cardano deployment.

The PAB eliminates the need for developers to build their own infrastructure from the ground up (including chain indexes,[504] etc.), cutting down on development time. It enables developers to model how an application would operate on-chain for testing and error reduction before launch, ensuring a smooth transition.

It's an off-chain backend service that manages and handles the application instance's demands throughout its lifespan. This involves interacting with third-party clients (such as wallet frontends) and serving as a link between Plutus apps, the node, the wallet backend, and end users. PAB commands and dummy components enable easy simulations and integration of DApps.

It assists in the construction of UTXO transactions for both the read and write routes by obtaining information from the chain, responding to events, and generating the transactions that execute the Plutus scripts.

The PAB's main goal is to:

- provide a standard environment for Plutus apps to run in
- offer disciplined state management
- provide external clients with discoverable interfaces
- keep track of on-chain data for smart contract applications
- make it possible for developers to operate in either an emulated or non-emulated environment

---

[503] Marlowe Playground, alpha.marlowe.iohkdev.io/#/

[504] A **Chain index** is a database of information obtained from Cardano transactions.

- handle requests like starting contract instances, passing user input to these instances, and informing these instances of ledger state changes.

The PAB can effortlessly transition between emulated and non-emulated (real network) contexts. This makes writing various types of tests — unit tests, integration tests, property-based tests, and so on – much simpler. Because the PAB's backend can receive and send messages, DApps can easily interface with it. As a result, the DApp may make standard requests to endpoints provided by the PAB, which correspond to actions and operations that each smart contract can handle.

The PAB, which offers runtime support for access to the blockchain to further conduct smart contract activities triggering transactions based on the EUTXO paradigm, can run applications built using the framework's libraries. PAB also includes capabilities such as persistence, logging, and monitoring.

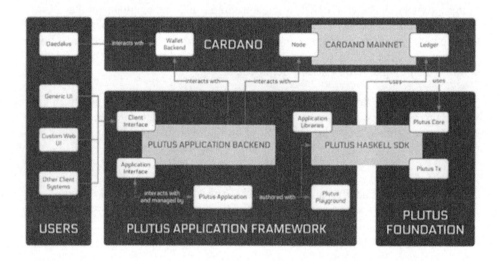

Figure 22: A high-level architecture of the Plutus Platform, with an emphasis on applications. From CardanoDocs.com

In this diagram, the Platform breaks down based on which part of the system we're interested in:

- Plutus Foundation[505] is there to support writing the trusted kernel of code, and executing it on the chain
- The Plutus Application Framework is for writing Plutus DApps

The following components must be present in addition to the PAB:

---

[505] Plutus Foundation, plutus.readthedocs.io/en/latest/explanations/plutus-foundation.html#what-is-plutus-foundation

- Chain index: a database of information obtained from Cardano transactions. It must be co-located with a Cardano node and utilizes the Cardano node's chain sync protocol. The PAB's chain index is a read-only component. As a result, a single instance of the chain index may be shared by several instances of the PAB. A HTTP API is used to serve all chain index requests
- Cardano node: the PAB leverages a socket protocol to subscribe to ledger changes from the node.

While not mandatory for DApp creation or implementation, the PAB is a useful Cardano tool that makes developing DApps easier, safer, and more cost-effective. It relieves developers of mundane duties by offering information from relevant sources in an accessible style. As the ecosystem matures, the community are developing their own tooling and API-based alternatives.[506]

Innovative new platforms like Genius Yield (geniusyield.co) are trailblazers for Plutus, creating custom PAB alternatives that are open source, available to other builders. Dr Lars Brünjes, Chief Technology Officer (IOG Education Director and Genius Yield CTO) talked about open-source ethos in a *Learn Cardano* interview:[507]

> *It's one of my pet hates, I can't understand how you can possibly not make it open source. I mean, the whole point of smart contracts…when I explain to somebody what a smart contract is….you always say 'with normal human contracts, there's always ambiguity, and legal issues and you replace that with mathematics and code, and so it's crystal clear what's what'   …but this whole point is mute if you don't make your smart contracts public, because then nobody can check the actual logic. I mean then you can just as well forget about blockchain and do it centralized. So in my opinion, you have to at least make the smart contracts public… and this PAB replacement that we mentioned a couple of times now, we definitely also want to make it open source, so that everybody can profit from it, and not every project has to reinvent that over and over again.*

Plutus fee estimator

IOG performance specialists created the Plutus fee calculator as an in-house tool for pricing benchmarking and comparison. It predicts the fees that will be charged for a transaction using data from real-world Plutus transactions. The estimator may be used to estimate costs for individual script transactions or whole DApps before or during development, as well as to compute fees for existing transactions (e.g., to assess the fees that will be charged if network parameters change).

The Cardano ledger's design principles enable great performance while maintaining stringent security standards. The Extended Unspent Transaction Output (EUTXO) accounting model allows for Cardano transactions and scripts to be checked locally (off-chain), enabling users to see whether a transaction is legitimate before executing it on-

---

[506] API alternatives, youtu.be/W2R3zl91U24?t=357

[507] Learn Cardano Interview w/ Genius Yield, youtube.com/watch?v=7KBhfe6GVAA&t=1763s

chain and incurring fees. Furthermore, transaction fees are fixed with no surprises. For comparison, the cost of executing a smart contract on Ethereum varies based on network traffic, ranging from $5 to hundreds[508] of dollars. Even unsuccessful Ethereum transactions may incur fees, adding to the price unpredictability.

Users on Cardano, on the other hand, may assess the prospective transaction processing fees in advance. There is no need to pay for a transaction that may fail since the user knows whether the transaction is legitimate or not in advance. This prevents money from being wasted and eliminates on-chain failures. Cardano's ada execution fee is always consistent because it is based on predetermined network protocol parameters rather than, for example, varying network congestion variables.

Cardano's pricing strategy is based mostly on market demand rather than real supply. With Cardano's smart contract functionality, many types of demand are now vying for the same supply. As a result, both relative and absolute price[509] must be considered. One means of doing this is by examining the implications of smart contract pricing, non-fungible token (NFT) activities, and other factors with regard to a common value — in this example, the use of Cardano's processing power.

Smart contract pricing in Cardano is based on a fixed cost, which is determined by the price of used resources (UTXO size or computation/memory consumed while executing). Stake pool operators' (SPO) labor and resources that verify network transactions must be adequately compensated with fees. Furthermore, ensuring that any method of adopting Cardano is not significantly less expensive than another helps to prevent a wide range of adversarial attacks (e.g., a DDoS attack).

Flexibility is also a significant characteristic of the Cardano protocol, since it allows users to adjust their settings and respond to price swings. If the value of ada rises dramatically, protocol settings may be modified if necessary to avoid the user from overspending for smart contract execution.

IOG created the Plutus fee estimator tool for pricing benchmarking and comparison. The estimator may be used to estimate costs for individual script transactions or whole DApps before or during development, as well as to predict fees for existing transactions. It might also be used to see how script updates or optimizations affect costs.

The fee calculation formula used by the estimator is the same as that used by the Cardano node. It can provide an accurate estimate of the required fee if the inputs are sufficiently correct. A user may simply forecast how much a DApp will cost by summing the charges from many transactions. The estimator contains a number of real-world examples that have been cross-checked against actual fees.

---

[508] Ethereum Gas Fees Continue to Rise, analyticsinsight.net/ethereum-gas-fees-continue-to-rise-while-bitgert-zero-gas-fee-blockchain-is-booming/

[509] **Absolute vs. Relative Price**: Absolute price is the number of dollars that can be exchanged for a specified quantity of a given good. Relative price is the quantity of some other good that can be exchanged for a specified quantity of a given good. Suppose we have two goods A and B. The absolute price of good A is the number of dollars necessary to purchase a unit of good A. The relative price of good A in terms of B is the amount of good B necessary to purchase a unit of good A.

Three pieces of information are needed to calculate fees:

- The size of on-chain transactions in bytes: a basic transaction is roughly 300 bytes, a transaction containing metadata is around 650 bytes, and Plutus scripts are generally 4,000-8,000 bytes (ongoing optimizations will improve these)

- The number of computational (CPU) steps used by the script: each step on a benchmark system equals 1 picosecond of execution time. Scripts should use less than 1,000,000,000 CPU units (1 millisecond) on average

- The number of memory units used by the script: this is the number of bytes allocated by the script. Scripts should use fewer than 1,000,000 memory units in most cases (1MB of memory allocation).

A user just has to enter in relative information to utilize an estimator, which may be retrieved from the Plutus compiler after generating a script in it. There is also no need to run a node for this, which makes the procedure much easier for non-techies.

Test Drive the Plutus fee estimator[510] and see how easy it is to estimate the processing fee without saying goodbye to your funds if a transaction fails.

Cooked Validators

With the *cooked-validators* library, you can write off-chain code and obtain property-based testing for free. As a Haskell developer using formal methods, you should be devoted to using tools and procedures to ensure the safety and soundness of decentralized applications (DApps). Writing and deploying a DApp is inadequate; all on-chain code and Plutus scripts should be carefully tested against a variety of bad actors.

With this in mind, *Tweag* introduced *cooked-validators,*[511] a collection of ready-to-use tools for working with Plutus validator scripts. This library aids in the implementation of the innermost layer of off-chain code, which is responsible for transaction generation and submission. You receive property-based testing at the transaction level for free by using this library.

You may verify various safety and correctness aspects of your on-chain code by utilizing cooked-validators to create your off-chain code, which can considerably boost your trust in the code's correctness. During an audit, this may save time and money. The first step in a Tweag audit is to leverage cooked-validators to write transaction-generating code, allowing them to interact with their client's infrastructure.

---

[510] Plutus Fee Estimator, docs.cardano.org/cardano-testnet/tools/plutus-fee-estimator

[511] Cooked validators, github.com/tweag/plutus-libs/tree/main/cooked-validators

Writing Plutus transactions

Writing a Plutus transaction is accomplished in the following order:

1. Write your Plutus on-chain code.
2. Convert your Plutus code to text envelope format (this is the format expected by the cardano-cli .ie. command line interface).
3. Using the Plutus script(s) available, create your transaction.
4. Execute Plutus script by submitting the transaction.

Myth busting

It's important to note that Plutus Tx is a high-level language for scripting the validation logic of the smart contract. This logic determines whether a transaction is allowed to spend a UTXO. Plutus Tx is a subset of Haskell, and it is then compiled into Plutus Core, a low-level language based on lambda calculus. Plutus Core is the code that runs on-chain, and often referred to as a Plutus script or Plutus validator.

To implement a smart contract, you would also require off-chain code for building and submitting transactions, deploying smart contracts, querying for available UTXOs on-chain, etc. You will likely also need a front-end UI to make it easy for users.

After a bumpy start, which is to be expected with a brand new language, the developers and user experience improved throughout 2022 and will continuously evolve with greater tooling. At the *Overcoming challenges and the road to mass adoption* talk at the 2022 Summit, the most experienced Cardano developers talked about the progress since the early days. They all agreed that most of the code required is off-chain, and can be written in whatever language that you prefer.

Andrew Westberg, NEWM CTO[512]

> *It's an entire myth that you have to be a Haskell developer to work on Cardano, most of the Cardano developers I know spend more of their time in other languages. There's a lot of Rust, there's a lot of Kotlin, there's a lot of JavaScript... everybody's doing their own language, and you can actually bring your own language that you're used to, and comfortable for you to Cardano.*

Ignore the 'concurrency' FUD

Concurrency may increase or hurt a system's performance, throughput, and responsiveness. The number of simultaneous operations that may be executed is limited by the degree of concurrency.[513]

---

[512] Building on Cardano: overcoming challenges and the road to mass adoption, youtu.be/bASyKD2dnys?t=715

[513] **Concurrency,** the property of program, algorithm, or problem decomposition into order-independent or partially ordered units.

Processors in a UTXO-based blockchain should be able to do many actions at the same time to achieve real efficiency. The maximum parallelism possible increases as the amount of concurrency increases. As a result of this strategy, performance and throughput increase. It also has several benefits over account-based systems (like Ethereum).

Determinism, parallelism, and concurrency

These features are differentiators for Plutus. There's a structure called a directed acyclic graph mentioned previously, which can be thought of sometimes like a spider web of little nodes, little circles and they have lines to the next one and lines to the next one as a web grows, especially if it goes in one way.

The Cardano ledger forms a graph of transactions, and graphs are great for parallel processing. Cardano enables, by definition, parallel processing with the way UTXOs work. This means that because Plutus core is deterministic, and because scripts only have access to local information, it's possible to parallel process many things during both validation of the Plutus script and validation of the ledger.

When you're building on Cardano, better concurrency can be achieved by using multiple UTXOs and exploiting the parallelism and you can build with this style a scaling architecture that's massively parallel and allows you to service all of your users at the same time.

Deploying DApps on UTXO ledgers is different

To recap from earlier, remember Cardano's approach to DApp deployment is different. It requires scaling a steep learning curve and employing a careful strategy.

Concurrency optimization is a discipline that must be studied: developers must create code in such a manner that contention is limited (e.g., by avoiding shared states and accidental dependencies). This concurrency must then be translated into parallelism by the system. Several developers have previously found successful approaches, while others are currently working on them. It is not possible to simply transfer skills learnt on one blockchain to another; although there is a learning curve, the benefits outweigh the effort.

In any case, it's vital to remember that a developer can't simply utilize an adapted Ethereum contract to build a scalable DApp on Cardano. Cardano is built on the UTXO paradigm rather than the account-based approach; hence a single on-chain state will not satisfy Cardano's concurrency condition. DApps should instead distribute their on-chain state across several UTXOs. As a result, their application's concurrency will increase, allowing for faster throughput. Read how to design a scalable Plutus application[514] to learn more about scalability, and the order book pattern[515] to learn more about how to organize DApps on Cardano using patterns.

---

[514] Writing a scalable app, plutus.readthedocs.io/en/latest/plutus/howtos/writing-a-scalable-app.html

The Cardano ledger was built with high certainty, security, and formal verification in mind. In line with this philosophy, it's also critical to make sure transaction processing is deterministic, which means a user can anticipate the effect and result of a transaction before it happens.

With the addition of smart contract capabilities, the ability to guarantee the cost of transaction execution and how the transaction acts on the ledger before it is submitted becomes even more important. The deterministic design of Cardano and Plutus scripts[516] ensures this possibility.

Datums and Redeemers

Datums and redeemers are two crucial features in Plutus; it's important to know what they are and how to use them when submitting transactions. The datum is a piece of data that may relate to a UTXO and is used to hold script state information like the script's owner or timing metadata (which can define when the UTXO can be spent). It's typically used in conjunction with a redeemer, which is arbitrary data provided in a transaction that's used as a script input.

Transaction validation over two phases

The unspent outputs from prior transactions are referred to as inputs. The datum hash and a value (consisting of an ada amount and optional, extra native tokens) are kept in a UTXO at an address (public key or public key hash). The script decides whether to 'unlock' the funds when a UTXO at a script address is an input to a valid transaction. This may be implemented if the script's requirements are met (an arbitrary combination of factors including datum, redeemer, and script context). A transaction must be signed by the holder of the private key associated with the address during the first validation step.

From the perspective of a redeemer transaction, it's critical to grasp the following concepts:

1. Script address: the Cardano address that stores funds guarded by a Plutus script that can be further unlocked. It is a hash of the Plutus script.
2. Datum hash: the datum hash must be linked to a UTXO at a script address in Cardano. This is done to save memory and allow for quick access when verifying transactions.
3. Plutus script is a ledger-based executable application that performs further (phase two) transaction validation.
4. Datum value: you need to supply the datum value that matches the datum hash supplied in the locking transaction when sending a transaction to redeem funds.

---

[515] What is the order book pattern? playground.plutus.iohkdev.io/doc/plutus/explanations/order-book-pattern.html

[516] Plutus validator scripts, docs.cardano.org/plutus/Plutus-validator-scripts

5. Redeemer value: the same arbitrary data format as datum is used. The redeemer value is utilized by the script to verify the transaction and is tied to the input transaction to release funds from the script.
6. Script context: a synopsis of the transaction that is also required by the Plutus script in order to verify it.

The process of working with datums and redeemers is beyond the scope of this book, but you can study worked examples in the Plutus Pioneer Program[517] and Cardano Docs.[518]

March 12, 2019. How is a simple transaction different from running a smart contract? CH:[519]

So, the goal of Plutus is to actually turn all transactions into a smart contract in some way. So basically, if you look at the difference between what Ethereum does and what a UTXO system like Cardano does… they're different data structures. So one is kind of a mutable ledger and you send messages to it to wake it up, and then you're going to have all the state management that you have to contend with …and it's really difficult especially as the system grows and especially as you want to shard the system to keep track of everything …so you have to add a lot of complexity into your model.

When you look at UTXO system it's what's called a data flow graph …and basically it's just saying alright you have all these threads… and you have outputs and all you have to do to wake one of them up is just claim that you have the right to spend it …and then if you have the proof that it validates, it spends…

… so what we've done is we've taken that model and we've extended it to include some state information and include the value and include some data …and we call this the Extended UTXO model… so you keep the same semantics of Redeemer validator[520] (btc scripts) that Bitcoin introduced over 10 years ago… but now you've added a capability of having enough information in it, that you actually can have code running, this is what Plutus is basically all about…

Now the advantage of this type of a system is that now all transactions can be either as simple as push value from Alice to Bob ..or they can be as complicated as a smart contract that you would see like creating a currency or something like that… so there's a whole spectrum of complexity there …and you can chain these things together.. and you can also more easily interact with that on-chain transaction with off-chain code …because when you actually look at these smart

---

[517] Plutus Pioneers Welcome & Intro., youtube.com/watch?v=X80uNXenWF4&list=PLK8ah7DzglhgK0bEyELK8EzbW0mn6xavC

[518] Datums and redeemers, github.com/input-output-hk/cardano-documentation/blob/staging/content/10-plutus/07-datums-redeemers.mdx

[519] Surprise AMA 03/12/2019, youtu.be/f-rqaTLwWgs?t=1575

[520] Redeemer validators, bitcoinmagazine.com/articles/thinking-transactions-1401650873

contracts generally what they are they're wrapped in complexity from things living outside of the system… so you'll have some JavaScript code and some web3 action going on and that's running on a server or a client …and then that's talking to something living on-chain …that's the Ethereum model

…with Cardano it'll just be Plutus… template Haskell… Haskell and then that runs and it runs as a single unit …and you can write all the code together and it's very easy to validate that the off-chain and on-chain code is actually working correctly together

[..] So, we have a nice framework there and you can do a lot of property-based testing and a lot of cool validations… and say things are working correctly …because it's running this data flow model that's immutable …what's really nice about it is that it is much easier to shard these types of transactions… So basically the answer to your question, succinctly, is that all transactions are technically smart contracts in this Redeemer validator model… it's just their complexity is up to the user and how they run these types of things

Collateral mechanism

The collateral mechanism is a crucial component that guarantees smart contracts are run successfully.

Cardano uses a two-phase validation mechanism, relying on the assurances offered by the ledger's deterministic architecture. The primary goal of implementing two-phase validation is to reduce the amount of uncompensated validation effort performed by nodes. Each phase has a specific role to play in reaching this goal:

- The first phase verifies that the transaction has been accurately structured and that the processing fee can be paid
- The transaction's scripts are executed in the second phase.

Phase-2 scripts are executed if the transaction is phase-1 compliant. If phase 1 fails, no scripts are executed, and the transaction is rejected right away. If phase-2 verification fails, collateral is utilized to ensure that nodes are rewarded for their efforts. As a result, collateral is when a user gives a monetary guarantee that the contract has been properly constructed and rigorously tested. The amount of collateral input is set and included when the transaction is created. The transaction's collateral amount is the entire balance in the UTXOs corresponding to these specifically tagged inputs. The collateral is secured if the user meets the guarantee's requirements, and a contract is implemented.

The problem

If a smart contract fails without collateral, the user is not penalized. However, by the time the transaction fails, the network has already paid for the transaction to be initiated and validated. A hostile adversary might spam the network with dummy transactions, thus depriving other users of service for very little expense.

How collateral solves this

When a user starts a transaction, they commit enough ada to satisfy the transaction's cost of execution. Transactions that employ non-native smart contracts (also known as phase-2 contracts) need adequate collateral to cover the expenses of any transaction failures. This sum may seem insignificant, but it is enough to make a denial of service (DoS) attack prohibitive. Only if a transaction fails validation are collateral costs collected. The transaction costs are paid if the contract passes validation, but the collateral is not. The collateral of an honest user is never in danger of being lost.

Transaction costs on the Cardano blockchain are predictable since they are solely influenced by local values and state. A user may predict the transaction's execution cost (in ada) before initiating it. Other blockchains, like as Ethereum, whose design lets other network activities impact the gas cost. The amount of collateral needed is solely determined by the execution cost.

The Cardano testnet[521] offers a secure environment with free test ada (tAda), allowing DApp developers to extensively stress test their smart contracts before publishing them to the mainnet. If transactions go well on the testnet, the developer may be certain that all of the scripts will run smoothly as well.

If the on-chain circumstances have changed after the transaction was created, the transaction will be completely rejected with no fees collected. No collateral would be charged if a signature was absent, for example.

In practice

The total ada included in the UTXOs referenced by collateral inputs is referred to as collateral. If a phase-2 script fails, a transaction uses collateral inputs to pay its fees.

The idea of 'multi-signature' scripts was introduced by the Shelley formal specification. The ledger rules completely capture Phase-1 scripts like these. Execution costs may therefore be readily estimated prior to the implementation's running, and any fees can be determined directly inside the ledger rule implementation depending on the size of the transaction that contains the script.

Phase-2 scripts, on the other hand, may do any Turing-complete computation, in theory. We want a budget in terms of a number of abstract *ExUnits* for transactions that leverage phase-2 scripts. This budget establishes a quantitative limit on resource consumption in terms of a variety of measures, such as memory utilization or abstract execution steps. The budget is then utilized to calculate the transaction fee.

From the Plutus Technical Report,[522]

---

[521] Cardano testnet, testnets.cardano.org/en/testnets/cardano/overview/

[522] Peyton Jones, Kireev, 'The Plutus Platform', hydra.iohk.io/build/12983030/download/1/plutus.pdf

*Resources are tracked in terms of two abstract units: abstract time, and abstract (peak) memory. Together we refer to these as **exunits**. Why are the units here 'abstract'? They must be, because we need to be able to keep things deterministic, and so we cannot use real time or memory usage. Rather we have to define some abstract measures which we try to align with real resource usage.*

For more info, read the Cardano ledger specification for Plutus Core.[523]

CIP 40 - Explicit Collateral Output further improved the user experience. Some dodgy code in certain wallets meant too much collateral was committed in error. In such a scenario, nothing too catastrophic would happen, but ultimately the collateral got taken, so users lost collateral. It was similar to overcharging a fee.

IOG wanted to improve the user experience, so they found a way where a transaction could be submitted, but the collateral included is just enough to cover. If you include an extra '0' by an accidental fat finger or whatever, like a million ada, you get back everything that's not required. A welcome correction. This was all part of a journey in getting Plutus to be a great user experience. If people make innocent mistakes, like typos, they don't get harshly penalized.

Learning Plutus

As Plutus is based on Haskell, a good starting point is the popular book *Learn You a Haskell for Great Good* by Miran Lipovača (learnyouahaskell.com) which has been many peoples' first foray into Haskell.

You can study the original Plutus Tutorial[524] from the documentation. The IOG education team wrote an introductory Plutus ebook, available on Amazon[525] and LeanPub. *Plutus: Writing reliable smart contracts* is aimed at beginner-level Haskell developers focusing on the fundamentals with real-world examples. They also recently released a 'zero to everything' Haskell Course on GitHub.[526]

Plutus Pioneers Program

IOG created the Plutus Pioneer Program in anticipation of the Alonzo hard fork. The program is not for beginners, so it's perhaps best to first study the online course Haskell

---

[523] A Formal Specification of the Cardano Ledger integrating Plutus Core, hydra.iohk.io/build/7172824/download/1/alonzo-changes.pdf

[524] Plutus Tutorial, plutus.readthedocs.io/en/latest/plutus/tutorials/index.html

[525] Plutus: Writing reliable smart contracts, amazon.com/Plutus-Writing-reliable-smart-contracts-ebook/dp/B07V46LWTW/ref=sr_1_1, leanpub.com/plutus-smart-contracts

[526] Haskell course, github.com/input-output-hk/haskell-course

and Crypto Mongolia Sept 2020[527] available on YouTube, delivered by Andres Löh, co-founder of the Well-Typed consultancy and Dr. Lars Brünjes, Education Director at IOHK.

There is plenty of help from the community also. Plutus and Atala Prism Pioneer Oussama Benmahmoud wrote *How to prepare for the Plutus Pioneer Program.*[528] Chris Moreton (@PoolChess[529]) has transcribed the Plutus Pioneer Program lecture notes. Visit his 'readthedocs' site[530] where you can also download a pdf or epub version.

You should now be ready to apply[531] for the next cohort. You can also engage the community directly about Plutus on the Cardano Forum[532] or on the IOG Technical Discord.[533]

Developer Adoption

IOG established a new Developer Experience department (DevX), directed by Moritz Angermann,[534] to ensure that developers at IOG aren't hampered by the tools they use on a daily basis. The department works closely with all engineering teams and is in charge of maximizing team synergies and simplifying development processes. As a logical extension of the 'tools' team that is now part of DevX, another priority of DevX is developing Haskell tooling.

The DevX team is working on developing technology that will allow for continual ledger updates and improvements. This toolset caters to the demands of developers and provides for more efficient use of diverse building libraries. The following are some of the things that can be done to make the Haskell development experience more efficient:

- Significant enhancements to cross-compilation capabilities
- Improved plugin support
- Interoperability with the Rust programming language and other languages.

These enhancements allow developers to not only use Haskell libraries written in other languages, but also to leverage Haskell libraries written in other languages. In addition,

---

[527] Haskell and Crypto Mongolia, youtube.com/watch?v=ctfZ6DwFiPg&list=PLJ3w5xyG4JWmBVIigNBytJhvSSfZZzfTm&index=4

[528] How to prepare for the Plutus Pioneer Program, essentialcardano.io/article/how-to-prepare-for-the-plutus-pioneer-program

[529] PoolChess on Twitter, twitter.com/PoolChess

[530] PoolChess PP Lecture notes, plutus-pioneer-program.readthedocs.io/en/latest/plutus_pioneer_program.html

[531] Register for the Plutus Pioneer Program, testnets.cardano.org/en/plutus-pioneer-program/

[532] Plutus on the Cardano Forum, forum.cardano.org/c/developers/cardano-plutus/148

[533] IOG Tech Discord, discord.com/invite/w6TwW9bGA6

[534] Moritz Angermann, iohk.io/team/moritz-angermann/

the department focuses on improving the workflow associated with the use of Nix,[535] the Glasgow Haskell Compiler (GHC), and GHCJS (Haskell to Javascript compiler).

IOG anticipate that when Cardano evolves into a completely open infrastructure model in 2023, these enhancements will empower the larger developer community with improved capabilities for working on various projects and deploying them on Cardano. Third party tooling is more prevalent as well as IOG's *Plutus tools in development.*[536]

Charles Hoskinson has outlined[537] his wish for Cardano to mirror other OSS (open source systems) such as Linux.[538] In June 2022, The Cardano Foundation joined *The Linux Foundation* as a Gold member, becoming the only non-profit active at this level. More about the on-chain governance overhaul announced at ScotFest in Chapter 9.

Cardano Stack Exchange

IOG encourages developers to join in one location — Cardano Stack Exchange[539] – to exchange ideas, ask and answer questions regarding all aspects of Cardano development and operations, and pool resources. This site, which is run by Cardano community members, is one of the tools for learning how to create DApps and smart contracts, or if you just want to know 'What is Layer 0?'[540]

Cardano Stack Exchange originated from Stack Overflow.[541] It's a community-moderated Q&A site where all Cardano developers, including Plutus pioneers, may obtain answers to a wide range of questions, from installation questions to configuration and implementation specifics. Stack Overflow's community-driven, decentralized mentality meshes especially well with Cardano's open-source, decentralized philosophy.

April 10, 2020. Do you regret going with Haskell? CH:[542]

---

[535] **Nix** is a cross-platform package manager that utilizes a purely functional deployment model. Software is installed into unique directories generated through cryptographic hashes. It is also the name of the tool's programming language, specifically for software configuration and deployment.

[536] Plutus tools in development, plutus-apps.readthedocs.io/en/latest/plutus/explanations/plutus-tools-component-descriptions.html#

[537] Cardano's 2022 vision: Hoskinson may finally have a release date for 'Mamba', ambcrypto.com/cardanos-2022-vision-hoskinson-may-finally-have-a-release-date-for-mamba/

[538] Cardano Founder Charles Hoskinson Lays Out 2022 Plans, coindesk.com/tech/2021/12/27/cardano-founder-charles-hoskinson-lays-out-2022-plans/

[539] Cardano Stack Exchange, cardano.stackexchange.com/

[540] 'What is Layer 0?', cardano.stackexchange.com/questions/8244/what-is-layer-0

[541] **Stack Overflow** is a question-and-answer site for professional and enthusiast programmers. It is a privately held website, the flagship site of the Stack Exchange Network, created in 2008 by Jeff Atwood and Joel Spolsky.

[542] LIVE with Cardano's Charles Hoskinson, youtu.be/x6TZSBmDWMw?t=5107

We probably could have gotten away with F# or Scala over Haskell and gotten a lot of the Haskell benefit. I didn't realize that Haskell was going to require as much as it did ...and I wasn't prepared for it, we didn't set up the organizational structure that we needed at the beginning for that and had I been better prepared in the beginning, we probably could have avoided some of our growing pains that we had. On the other hand, we were able to attract some of the brightest minds in the world and work with those minds to solve problems in completely original creative ways and so Cardano was ultimately a better product for it but our time to market suffered. Whether that was the right decision or not... Who knows?!

Because we have to look at the project in 2022 and 2023 and if we're the size, scope and scale of Ethereum and we have a resilient robust ecosystem then it was the right decision ... if we're not there, it was the wrong decision... but we just won't know. We did actually look aggressively at Scala; in fact we wrote a product in Scala... and we wrote Mantis[543] which is an Ethereum Classic client in Scala. It was a great experience, I loved it... I had so much fun we had no delays, it was easy to get out, it was like paint-by-numbers... so I like Scala a lot, it's one of my favorite languages and I think there's a huge amount of advantages in that ecosystem. The sharp edges have been mostly muted.

That said, because of work we did with Haskell and the improvements we've made especially with GHCJS[544] and the improvements[545] we've made on Windows and the library level improvements we've made... if somebody chose Haskell today for a project, with the things that we've done, and the ecosystem has done, I think it would be a lot easier to build a product in Haskell. We've left a template to do that and future projects won't have the growing pains that we had.

At one point, I actually considered writing Cardano in JavaScript... I really thought about it, I said we have formal semantics through the JSCert program, out of Imperial College London,[546] and there are some functional things we can do... and we could do formal verification of some of the JavaScript code ...so here's a crazy thought ...why don't we actually get some Haskell hard core programmers and then force them to actually write JavaScript? ...and build a whole ecosystem around it, write up a whole bunch of beautiful JavaScript

[543] Niamh Ahern, 'The new Mantis: Bringing security and stability to the Ethereum Classic ecosystem', iohk.io/en/blog/posts/2020/12/09/the-new-mantis-bringing-security-and-stability-to-the-ethereum-classic-ecosystem-1/

[544] Luite Stegeman, 'Looking to the future of Haskell and JavaScript for Plutus', iohk.io/en/blog/posts/2020/06/04/looking-to-the-future-of-haskell-and-javascript-for-plutus/

[545] Sylvain Henry, 'Improving Haskell's big numbers support', iohk.io/en/blog/posts/2020/07/28/improving-haskells-big-numbers-support/

[546] JSCert: Formalization of the JavaScript programming language, wp.doc.ic.ac.uk/fswp/project/jscert-formalization-of-the-javascript-programming-language/

tooling for QuickCheck[547] and for all this other stuff and actually create a TLA[548] port ...so we can do TLA+ and connect it with JavaScript code.

---

[547] Quickcheck, hackage.haskell.org/package/QuickCheck

[548] **TLA⁺** is a formal specification language developed by Leslie Lamport. It is used for designing, modeling, documentation, and verification of programs, especially concurrent systems and distributed systems

Chapter 7: Marlowe

'Hell is just a frame of mind'

— Christopher Marlowe, Dr. Faustus

What is Marlowe?

Marlowe is a simple programming language for writing financial smart contracts for Cardano. It is named after the Elizabethan poet, dramatist and spy, Christopher Marlowe. Marlowe is limited to financial applications and is not Turing-complete. It is for people who are experts in finance rather than having programming knowledge.

Marlowe is based on peer-reviewed research carried out by a team led by Prof Simon Thompson, first at the University of Kent with the help of an IOG research grant, and then as an internal IOG team in collaboration with the University of Wyoming Advanced Blockchain R&D Laboratory. The research has resulted in several published papers.[549]

Context for Marlowe

'Machine code' was used to program the first computers. Each system had its own code, which was low-level and inexpressive: programs were long sequences of extremely simple instructions that were incomprehensible to anybody who hadn't created them. Higher-level languages such as C, Java, and Haskell may now be used to program systems. The structure of the programs mirrors what they perform, and the same languages may be used on a variety of devices. Languages like Plutus, Solidity, and Simplicity are blockchain counterparts. These higher-level languages are general-purpose in that they may be used to address a wide range of problems; yet the solutions they represent are still programs, and using them successfully demands programming expertise.

Marlowe, on the other hand, provides blockchain financial contracts that anybody can write. It's a domain-specific language (DSL) for creating and executing financial contracts that lets users utilize their domain knowledge to quickly create and manage contracts without the steep learning curve that comes with software development, blockchain, and smart contracts.

Marlowe is a user-friendly programming language that may be used to mimic financial products. It's a decentralized finance (DeFi) platform that allows for direct peer-to-peer lending, contracts for difference (CFDs),[550] and other related products. Marlowe contracts are tailored for financial transactions, development platforms, and a fast track for financial service providers to establish competence in smart contracts and blockchain technology.

Marlowe contracts are simpler to read, write, and comprehend because they are written in a special-purpose language. It's also safer: certain faults are impossible to create, and IOG can fully analyze contract behavior without running a contract. Marlowe has several

---

[549] Marlowe papers, play.marlowe-finance.io/doc/marlowe/tutorials/introducing-marlowe.html#research-based

[550] In finance, a **contract for difference (CFD)** is a contract between two parties, typically described as 'buyer' and 'seller', stipulating that the seller will pay to the buyer the difference between the current value of an asset and its value at contract time (if the difference is negative, then the buyer pays instead to the seller).

advantages over a Turing-complete language. It's more secure, predictable and addresses the halting problem[551] by guaranteeing termination.

Marlowe's design features:

- No recursion[552] or loops as contracts are finite
- There are timeouts on all actions, guaranteeing termination
- Commitments and timeouts are central to how Marlowe works in a blockchain context
- All contracts have a defined lifetime
- No assets are retained on close
- Value is conserved.

Who is Marlowe's target audience?

Because Marlowe enables you to write contracts graphically as well as in more conventional code, it may be used by someone who is an expert in the subject of financial contracts or business but lacks programming abilities and expertise. It may be used by financial institutions to create and deploy unique instruments for their customers and clients.

The Marlowe language is embedded in both JavaScript and Haskell, giving you a variety of editors to choose from, depending on your preferences and skill level. You can write contracts in these languages and then convert ('compile') them to Marlowe in the Marlowe Playground. Haskell is a functional programming language with its own established ecosystem and robust testing environment, but JavaScript provides flexibility and speed of usage with a vibrant community.

Marlowe may interact with real-world data, such as oracles, and contract participants can choose what occurs on and off-chain, such as in a wallet, by making decisions inside the contract flow. Marlowe is blockchain-agnostic, allowing smart contacts to be expressed on top of account-based models like Ethereum as well as Cardano's extended unspent transaction output (EUTXO) model. Marlowe is an industry-scale solution that incorporates examples from the ACTUS[553] (actusfrf.org) taxonomy and financial contract standard.

Marlowe language structure

---

[551] In computability theory, the **halting problem** is the problem of determining, from a description of an arbitrary computer program and an input, whether the program will finish running, or continue to run forever.

[552] **Recursion** occurs when something is defined in terms of itself or of its type. Recursion is used in a variety of disciplines ranging from linguistics to logic. The most common application of recursion is in mathematics and computer science, where a function being defined is applied within its own definition. While this apparently defines an infinite number of instances (function values), it is often done in such a way that no infinite loop can occur.

[553] **ACTUS** (Algorithmic Contract Types Unified Standards) Contract Types are defined based on the underlying contractual algorithm patterns that respectively cover different classes of financial products that each Contract Type pattern is able to express.

Marlowe is based on special-purpose financial contract languages adopted by academics and companies like LexiFi (lexifi.com), which produces financial contract software. IOG customized these languages to function on blockchain while creating Marlowe. Marlowe is a simple language with a few distinct structures that define behavior with a fixed, limited number of roles for each contract. These responsibilities are carried out by the contract parties.

Contracts may be constructed by combining a limited number of these constructs, which can be used to describe and represent a wide range of financial contracts. A running contract that can make a payment to a role or a public key, a contract that can wait for an action by one of the roles, such as a currency deposit, or a decision from a set of options are just a few examples. Importantly, a contract cannot wait forever for an action to be taken: if no action is taken by a certain period (the timeout), the contract will proceed on a different path, such as taking a corrective action such as refunding any funds in the contract.

A contract may choose between two different future courses of action, each of which is a contract, depending on its present condition. The contract will terminate when no more activities are necessary, and any leftover money in the contract will be reimbursed. When a contract is executed, the duties it entails are completed by participants (blockchain identities). Each position on the blockchain is represented by a token, and roles may be exchanged during contract execution, thereby allowing them to be traded.

Marlowe as a domain-specific language for DeFi

There are many benefits to being domain-specific rather than general-purpose. Contracts are written in a finance-oriented language rather than a blockchain-specific language. As a result, certain types of mistakes are impossible to write, and some types of improper contracts are eliminated. Every Marlowe contract, for example, will have a fixed lifespan after which it will stop performing acts and any monies attached to the contract will be returned to the participants, meaning funds in a contract can never be locked up eternally.

Without needing to execute a contract, it is possible to analyze how it will react in all scenarios automatically. For example, you can assess whether a contract may fail to make a payment in certain circumstances or if it is guaranteed to make full payments in all circumstances.

Contract behavior may be replicated in a browser, allowing users to test out various scenarios before committing cash and executing the contract for real. Users may construct DeFi contracts in a variety of methods, including writing them in text or using visual programming to create smart contracts by connecting blocks that represent the various components. Users may also choose and select from a variety of templates, which they can then customize as required.

Marlowe differentiators

The way Marlowe ensures that the contract is followed is where it distinguishes from non-blockchain alternatives. This assumes not just that the contract's directions are followed, but also that the participants commit and do not leave money locked up in the contract indefinitely. Timeouts are used to accomplish this.

A contract can request a person to make a deposit of a certain amount, but it cannot compel that person to do so. Instead, the contract can wait for them to commit to the contract for a set amount of time, after which it will proceed to follow some alternate instructions. This prohibits a party from canceling a contract by refusing to participate, ensuring that there's not a stalemate.

Timeouts safeguard all of Marlowe's constructs that need user input, such as user deposits and user selections. As a result, it's straightforward to observe that an user's commitment to a contract is finite: Marlowe can foresee when the contract will be completed - when it may be closed. Any unspent assets in the contract are repaid to participants at this time, and the contract comes to an end. As a result, any assets deposited into the contract by a participant cannot be locked up indefinitely: the commitment essentially terminates at this moment.

Furthermore, it is simple for us to read from the contract when it will end, which Marlowe refers to as the contract's lifespan: all parties will be able to determine this lifetime prior to entering into any contract.

A running contract in Marlowe cannot demand a deposit or a choice; it may only seek a deposit or a selection from a user. It can't 'push' these actions, but it may 'pull' them. However, it may make payments automatically, thus some features of a Marlowe contract might 'push' for certain events to occur, such as guaranteeing that a payment is sent to a participant by generating an appropriate transaction output.

Because Marlowe is a DSL, it can predict how Marlowe contracts will function without having to execute them: meaning you can leverage static analysis[554] to deliver important diagnostics to users before they sign a contract. Marlowe can also leverage logic tools to explicitly establish Marlowe contract properties, providing users with the maximum level of certainty that their contracts will perform as intended.

Marlowe roadmap

IOG will complete the implementation of Marlowe on Cardano as part of the Goguen deployment, allowing individuals and organizations to execute DeFi contracts that they have written themselves or received from a contract repository, transferring crypto assets according to the contract conditions. Marlowe will operate on the Cardano blockchain initially, but it is ultimately blockchain-agnostic and might work on other blockchains in the future.

Through oracles, Cardano smart contracts will be able to retrieve external data values like the exchange rate between ada and Bitcoin. In some respects, an oracle is similar to a participant who makes a decision, and as part of the implementation, IOG wants to

---

[554] **Static analysis**, static projection, or static scoring is a simplified analysis wherein the effect of an immediate change to a system is calculated without regard to the longer-term response of the system to that change.

provide oracle values, enabling contracts to obtain values straight from a stock market 'ticker' or a data feed like CoinMarketCap.

Depending on their programming ability, finance professionals and developers may now start writing financial smart contracts directly in Haskell or pure Marlowe, or graphically using the Marlowe Playground. Later into the Goguen era, you can simulate and analyze the contracts you build in the Playground to ensure that they perform correctly and are ready to be released into the world of decentralized money. As IOG prepares to finish Marlowe's implementation on Cardano and introduce financial smart contracts to the blockchain itself, the IOG Marlowe team will continue to implement examples from the Actus standard.

Marlowe Language Structure

Haskell types

The different components of the contract, such as accounts, values, observations, and actions, are represented using Haskell types. These Marlowe components are used to manage how a running contract evolves by supplying external information and inputs. Basic portions of Marlowe are modelled using a mix of Haskell data types, which develop new types, and type synonyms, which give an existing type a new name.

You can use one of the following visual programming environments in addition to developing contracts in the textual version of Marlowe:

Using Blockly[555]
Using JavaScript[556]
Using Haskell[557]

Marlowe contracts

In Marlowe, a contract is made up of a small set of building blocks that may be used to express a variety of financial transactions, such as making a payment, making an observation, waiting until a specific condition becomes true, and so on. After that, the contract is executed on a blockchain, such as Cardano, and it interacts with the outside world.

Marlowe is written in Haskell, and it is represented as a set of algebraic data types, with contracts specified by the Contract type:

```
data Contract = Close
              | Pay Party Payee Token Value Contract
```

---

[555] Writing Marlowe with Blockly, docs.cardano.org/marlowe/writing-marlowe-with-blockly

[556] Marlowe: Using JS Editor, docs.cardano.org/marlowe/using-javascript-editor

[557] Using the Haskell editor, docs.cardano.org/marlowe/using-the-haskell-editor

```
| If Observation Contract Contract
| When [Case] Timeout Contract
| Let ValueId Value Contract
| Assert Observation Contract
```

Marlowe offers six different means of constructing contracts. Five of these methods – Pay, Let, If, When, and Assert – combine smaller contracts to create a more complicated contract, while the sixth method, Close, is a basic contract. Effects – payments – and warnings may be created at each phase of execution, in addition to producing a new state and continuation contract.

Pay

A contract of payment **Pay a p t v cont** will transfer the value **v** of the token **t** from account **a** to payee **p**, which will be one of the contract participants or another account in the contract. If the value **v** is not positive, or if the account balance is insufficient to cover the payment in full, a warning will be produced (even if there are positive balances of other tokens in the account). A partial payment (of all available funds) is made in the latter situation. The continuation contract, **cont,** is given in the contract.

Close

The contract **Close** denotes the closure (or termination) of a contract. Its only function is to provide refunds to account owners who have positive balances. This is done one account at a time, however all accounts get refunded at the same time.

We must first define values, observations, and actions before going on to additional contract types:

- Values - consist of quantities that vary over time, such as 'the current slot interval,' 'the current balance of some token in an account,' and any previous decisions. These are 'volatile values'. Values may also be conditional on an observation and merged using addition, subtraction, and negation

- Observations - are Boolean values that may be joined using typical Boolean operators and are obtained by comparing values. It's also possible to see whether any decisions have been taken (for a particular identified choice). Observations will be useful at every stage of execution

- Actions - occur at certain moments throughout execution, such as:
  - depositing funds
  - selecting from a variety of options, including an oracle value
  - alerting the contract of an observation that turned out to be true

- Oracles - Oracles such as Carli3 (charli3.io) and Ergo Pools are being built for the Cardano blockchain and will be usable in Marlowe on Cardano. Until that time comes, there is an oracle prototype in the Marlowe Playground. Oracles are represented as decisions made by a participant with the dedicated Oracle role.

If

The predicate `if obs cont1 cont2` will result in `cont1` or `cont2`, based on observation `obs`'s Boolean value each time this construct is executed.

When

With the form `When cases timeout cont`, this is the most complicated contract constructor. It's a contract that's triggered by events that may or may not occur at any specific slot: the contract's cases define what occurs when certain events occur.

In the contract `When cases timeout cont`, the list `cases` holds a collection of cases. Each case has the form `Case ac co` where `ac` is an action and `co` a continuation (another contract). When a certain action occurs, for example, `ac`, the state is updated and the contract will resume as the corresponding continuation `co`.

In order to ensure the contract ultimately completes, the contract `When cases timeout cont` will continue as `cont` once the `timeout`, a slot number, is reached.

Let

A let contract `Let id val cont` allows a contract to record a value, in a specific point in time, and name it using an identifier. In this example, the expression `val` is evaluated, and stored with the name `id`. The contract then resumes as `cont`.

This approach not only allows us to leverage abbreviations, but it also allows us to capture and preserve volatile data that may change over time, such as the current price of gas or the current slot number, at a specific moment in the contract execution, to be used later in the contract execution.

Assert

An assert contract `Assert obs cont` does not impact the state of the contract, it resumes straight away as `cont`, but it gives a warning when the Observation `obs` returns false. It can be used to guarantee that a property holds at any stage of the contract, since static analysis[558] will fail if any execution forces an `Assert` to result as false.

There is a Sample Escrow contract[559] in Cardano Docs.

Escrow in Marlowe

Extra constructs are included in Marlowe contracts to guarantee that they progress appropriately. When we observe a **When**, we must also supply two extra details:

• A timeout value after which the contract will continue
• The continuation contract to which it advances

---

[558] **Static analysis is** a simplified analysis wherein the effect of an immediate change to a system is calculated without regard to the longer-term response of the system to that change. If the short-term effect is then extrapolated to the long term, such extrapolation is inappropriate.

[559] Sample escrow contract, github.com/cardano-foundation/docs-cardano-org/blob/main/marlowe/marlowe-lang-guide.md

Marlowe accounts and token usage

A Marlowe Account may store a variety of currencies as well as fungible and non-fungible tokens. A set amount is indexed by a **Token**, which is a pair of **CurrencySymbol** and **TokenName**. Consider an Account to be a Map Token Integer, where:

```
data Token = Token CurrencySymbol TokenName
```

Cardano's ada token is denoted as **Token adaSymbol adaToken**

Marlowe Playground

Users would ideally like to understand how contracts will perform once deployed to the blockchain, but without the risk of actually deploying. Marlowe can help here as it replicates the contracts behavior off-chain in the Marlowe Playground.

The Marlowe Playground is an online sandbox environment where you may build, model, simulate and test the process of developing smart contracts, without having to install anything. Its goal is to empower all sorts of developers to create financial products on Cardano, even if they have no previous Haskell or JavaScript knowledge. There are a number of tutorials[560] available that detail sample contracts as well as general information about Marlowe and how contracts should be modeled.

The Marlowe Playground is a platform for creating end-to-end financial smart contracts. Developers may use it to not only build smart contract code, but also to undertake early iterative design using simulations, formally validate smart contracts, and test them. These characteristics, together with a dedicated DSL (domain specific language) for finance, guarantee that contracts are simple to create, secure, verifiable, and well tested.

Marlowe written in the Playground may be saved as a GitHub gist.[561] At a later time, projects can be reloaded or cloned. The project is stored across sessions even if you don't use GitHub, however, be careful as clearing your browser cache may delete your work.

Getting started

When utilizing the Marlowe Playground, you have three choices to select from. You may write in Marlowe text directly, but you can also utilize the visual. Blockly is a visual programming tool that allows you to design contracts by connecting blocks that represent the various components.

---

[560] Marlowe tutorials, alpha.marlowe.iohkdev.io/doc/marlowe/tutorials/index.html

[561] **GitHub Gist** allows developers to instantly share code, notes, and snippets. Every gist is a Git repository, which means that it can be forked and cloned.

You may also use the inbuilt Haskell or JavaScript editors to help you write more readable and concise Marlowe contracts. Once a contract is created, you may examine its behavior, such as determining if any of the contract's payments might possibly fail. You may also simulate the activities of the parties to see how a contract would function.

Figure 23: Marlowe getting started

Using Blockly with Marlowe

You can use the Blockly visual interface to link together the pieces of the contract or write Marlowe code directly as Marlowe text. This is a great tool for people who are not comfortable with programming editors and prefer to write contracts graphically. Blockly is used by hundreds of other projects such as MIT App Inventor[562] which I used myself, many moons ago, to create these exam primer apps.[563] It was a seamless user experience to make these with Blockly.

With just a few clicks, it was easy to create a contract in Blockly using a 'Zero Coupon Bond' demo file. The contract 'Loan to buy John's book' took about 10 mins to create. I just needed to update a few placeholders before I could then view the contract as blocks

---

[562] MIT AppInventor, appinventor.mit.edu/

[563] Greenelight Apps, androidblip.com/dev/greenelight___a55fdd36512db0ebd6faad85f5a7e76687f8b28592819d76d5f18ec86f3b1cde.html

or as Marlowe code. The Blockly editor also gives you access to the metadata editor and static analysis.

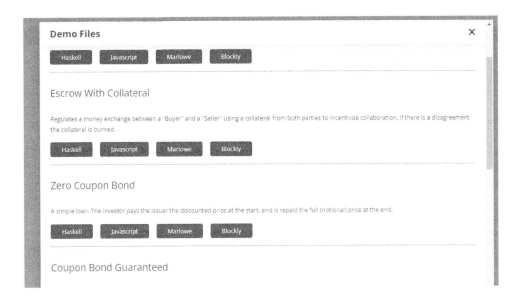

Figure 24: Blockly Demo Files

Contracts are built by dragging and dropping components to the holes in the blocks. Blocks are selected by just clicking on them, the current active block you are using will have a yellow outline.

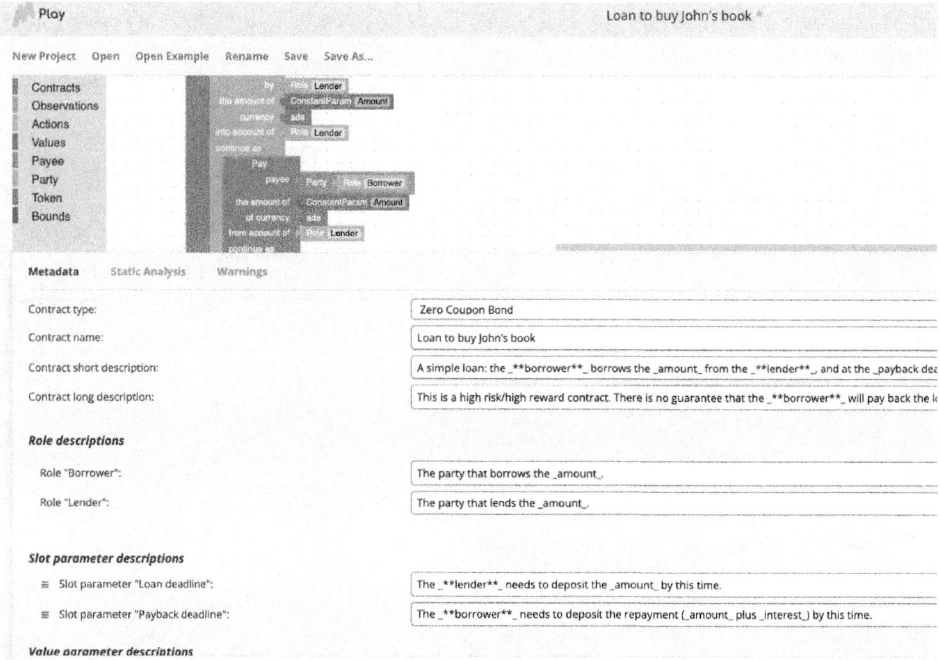

Figure 25:. Blockly Tabs

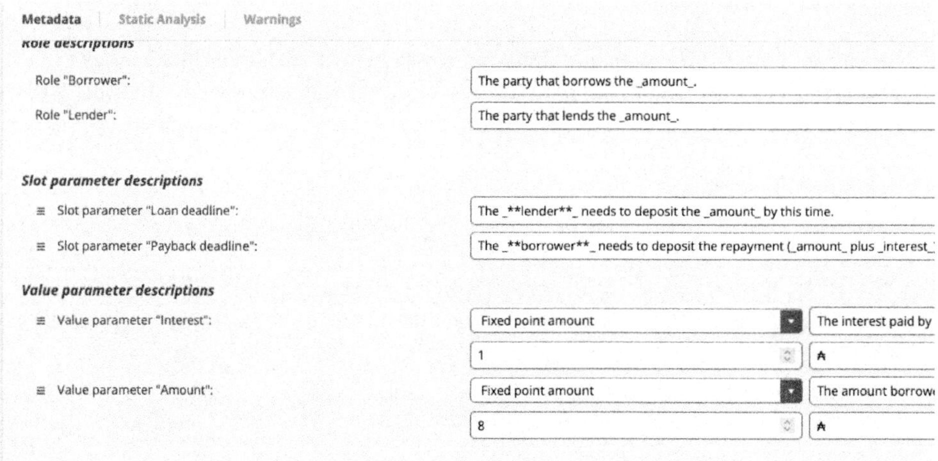

Figure 26: Blockly Metadata

Figure 27: Blockly warning

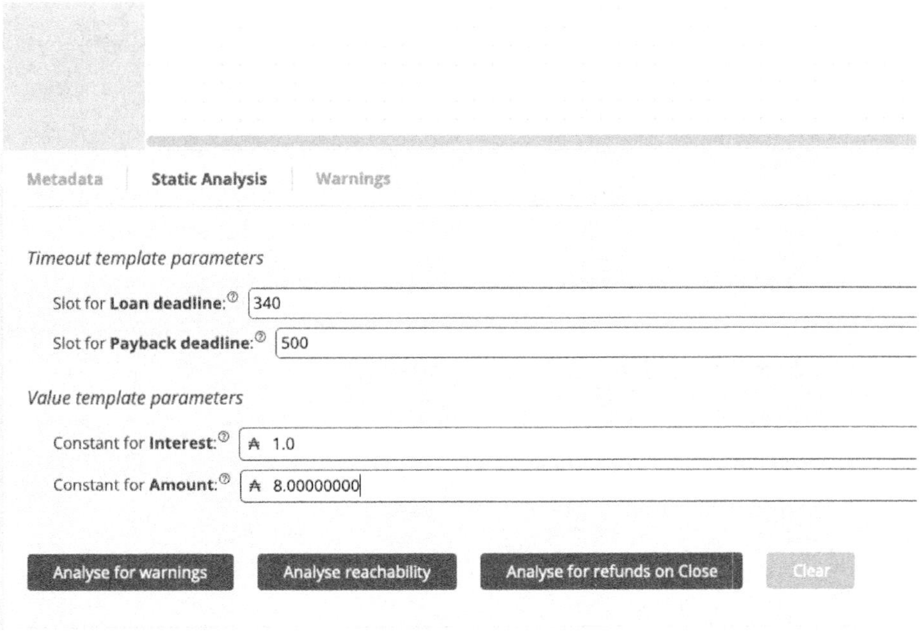

Figure 28: Blockly static analysis

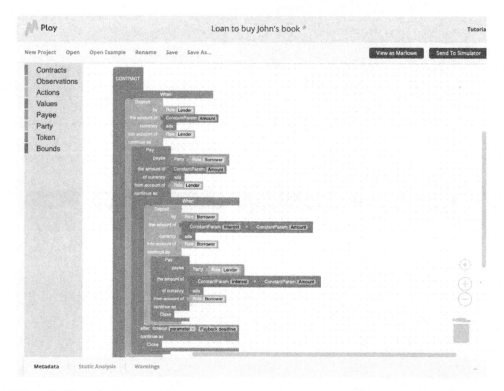

Figure 29: Block example

Figure 30: Marlowe Haskell

Using the Editor for Haskell or JavaScript

You can use the Haskell editor to produce Marlowe code if you're a seasoned Haskell developer. Because Marlowe is built as a Haskell data type, creating Marlowe smart contracts using Haskell is easy. Just select 'Haskell' in the sample 'Demo files'. You can use Haskell to make contract definitions more readable by using Haskell definitions for sub-components, abbreviations, and simple template functions. The editor will assist you with auto-complete, error checking during editing, and binding tips on mouse over..

Zero Coupon Bond

A simple loan. The investor pays the issuer the discounted price at the start, and is repaid the full (notional) price at the end.

Haskell	Javascript	Marlowe	Blockly

Figure 31: Zero Coupon Bond

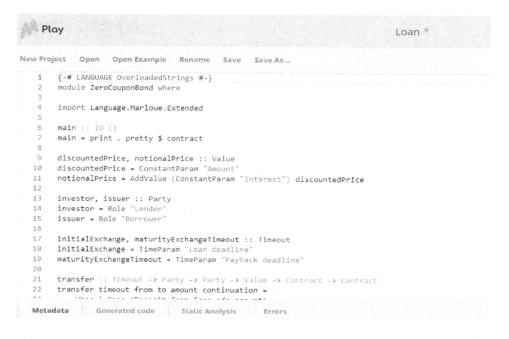

```
         Play                                                                    Loan *

New Project    Open    Open Example    Rename    Save    Save As...

    1    {-# LANGUAGE OverloadedStrings #-}
    2    module ZeroCouponBond where
    3
    4    import Language.Marlowe.Extended
    5
    6    main :: IO ()
    7    main = print . pretty $ contract
    8
    9    discountedPrice, notionalPrice :: Value
   10    discountedPrice = ConstantParam "Amount"
   11    notionalPrice = AddValue (ConstantParam "Interest") discountedPrice
   12
   13    investor, issuer :: Party
   14    investor = Role "Lender"
   15    issuer = Role "Borrower"
   16
   17    initialExchange, maturityExchangeTimeout :: Timeout
   18    initialExchange = TimeParam "Loan deadline"
   19    maturityExchangeTimeout = TimeParam "Payback deadline"
   20
   21    transfer :: Timeout -> Party -> Party -> Value -> Contract -> Contract
   22    transfer timeout from to amount continuation =

Metadata    Generated code    Static Analysis    Errors
```

Figure 32: Marlowe JavaScript

Once you get a successful compilation, you can send the result to the simulator or to Blockly. Just click on the 'Send to Simulator' and 'Send to Blockly' buttons in the top right-hand corner.

Because Marlowe is coded as a Haskell data type, describing Marlowe smart contracts in Haskell is simple. However, because Marlowe contracts are just data, you can express them in other languages like TypeScript (a superset of JavaScript), as outlined in the documentation.[564]

Marlowe code may be written using the integrated JavaScript editor. You can code JavaScript to make contract definitions more readable by using JS definitions for sub-components, abbreviations, and simple template functions. The editor is user-friendly with auto-complete, error checking during editing, and mouse over tips on bindings. The Compile option in the top right will execute the code in the editor, and the JSON object returned by the function is parsed into a real Marlowe contract; you can then hit 'Send to simulator' to commence contract simulation. If the compilation was successful, the generated code may be viewed by choosing 'Generated code' in the page's footer; it can also be minimized.

---

[564] Marlowe embedded in Javascript, play.marlowe-finance.io/doc/marlowe/tutorials/javascript-embedding.html

Figure 33: Marlowe code editor

You can expand the footer section and review the different tabs where you can examine and edit the contract Metadata and review the results of Static analysis, etc.

Figure 34: Marlowe Play

Marlowe Run

Marlowe Run[565] is an end-user client for downloading and running Marlowe contracts on the Cardano blockchain. In only a few minutes, you can have your smart contracts up and running. For you to conduct financial agreements with your friends, coworkers, or customers on the blockchain, Marlowe Run offers an easy, clear, and smooth interface. It provides you with access to carefully prepared, secure smart contract templates for every sort of agreement.

Marlowe Run is a simple and quick method to utilize and run Cardano contracts. You'll uncover a variety of financial contract templates to help you choose the best smart contract for your needs. After you've chosen a template, all you have to do now is fill up the roles and conditions, and then run your contract.

UTXO and Marlowe Run

The UTXOs, which are secured cryptographically by a private key controlled by the owner, are the source of value on the blockchain. These keys can be used to redeem the output and therefore as inputs to subsequent transactions, thereby spending the value in the inputs. In a cryptographically secure wallet, users keep track of their private keys and the values associated with them.

Users will need to leverage the Marlowe Run client application to engage with a blockchain contract. Since deposits are made from users' wallets and payments are received by them, Marlowe Run interacts with the wallets to validate transactions that spend crypto-assets. Note that these are off-chain activities that must be initiated by code running off-chain, which is usually found in the Marlowe Run application: they cannot be kicked off by the contract running on-chain.

Note: The following screenshots are from a demo version of Marlowe Run which uses dummy funds and test contracts.

Marlowe Run Demo
To access and view the dashboard, follow these steps:

1.   Go to Marlowe website[566] and click **Marlowe Run** on the main menu.
2.   Click **Try demo**.
3.   The Marlowe Run demo launches:

---

[565] Marlowe Run, run.marlowe-finance.io/

[566] Marlowe Website, marlowe-finance.io/

Run
Demo

To being using the Marlowe Run demo,
generate a new demo wallet.

Generate demo wallet

Why do I need to do this?

Or select an existing demo wallet from the
list or paste in a demo wallet key.

Choose wallet or paste key

‹ Back to home page   **Docs**

Figure 35: Marlowe Run

For this demo version, you generate a test wallet so that you can try it out. You can use
any wallet on Marlowe Run using the 'demo wallet ID'. This will become the integration
point with a real wallet in the full release version of Marlowe Run.

4. Click **Generate demo wallet** to use a demo wallet.
5. Enter a nickname such as 'testwallet'.

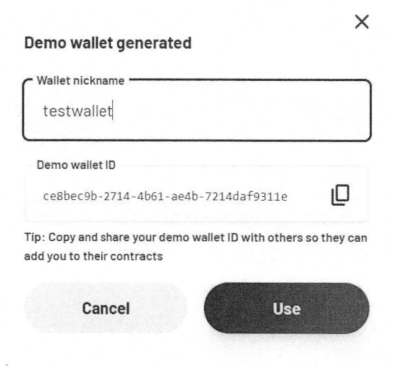

Figure 36: Marlowe demo wallet

6.   Click **Use**.

After you have selected your wallet, the following screen is displayed:

Figure 37: Marlowe template

7. Click **Choose a template** to create your contract.

The Contract templates selection card is displayed with three options:

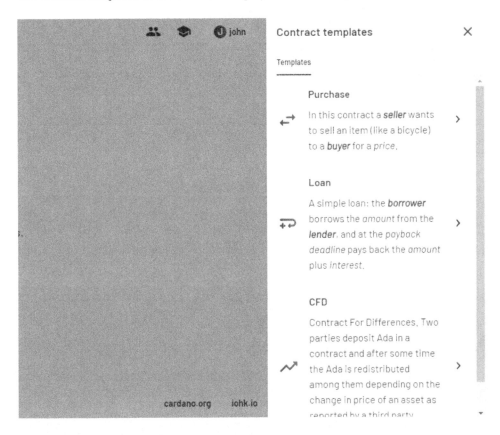

Figure 38: Marlowe contract templates

8. Click the contract template you want to use, for this example, Loan.

An dialogue wizard guides you through the self-explanatory steps, as follows:

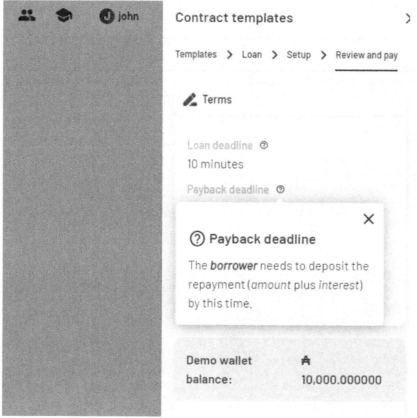

Figure 39: Marlowe UI

248

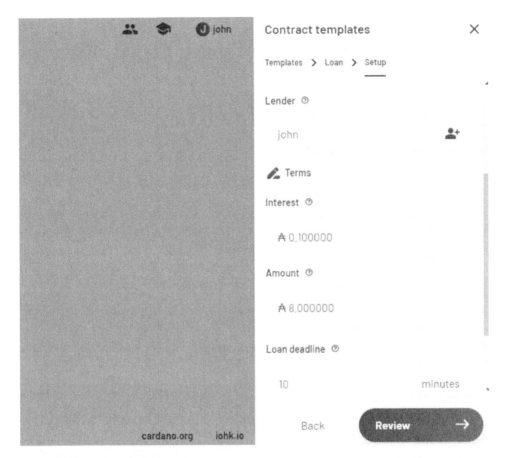

Figure 40: Marlowe Contract template dialogue box.

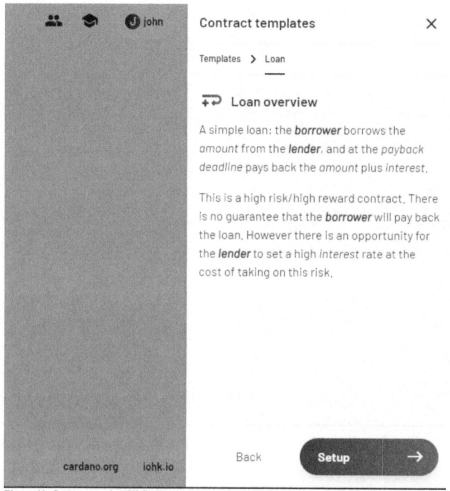

Figure 41: Contract template UI flow

Figure 42: Marlowe CardanoBookLoan

Simulation

The Marlowe Playground supports an *omniscient* contract simulation, where the user can perform any action for any role, and thereby review the execution from the perspective of all the users simultaneously.

Marlowe Run differs in that each participant can only review the contract from their own point of view. Participants are only able to interact with a running contract which is awaiting their input. If that's not the case, then they will see that the contract execution is waiting for someone else's input.

Actus Smart Contracts

As the world moves into the era of decentralized finance, it's worth reviewing the nuances of the language and the many methods of building Marlowe smart contracts. The Algorithmic Contract Types Unified Standard (Actus) for financial contracts was implemented by IOG in Marlowe with their approach to oracles, which import 'real world' information into a running contract.

IOG purposefully kept the language as minimal as possible so that it would be easy to implement. Marlowe specifies the movement of cryptocurrency between participants, and to do so on the Cardano blockchain, code must be performed both on-chain and off-chain; however, just one Marlowe contract covers both sections.

The on-chain section accepts and verifies transactions that meet the smart contract's requirements: this part is built as a single Plutus script for all Marlowe contracts, with each Marlowe contract having a datum that is provided via the transactions. Off-chain, the Marlowe contract will be accessible via the user interface and wallet, allowing users to make deposits and decisions, as well as receive bitcoin payouts.

A contract's behavior can be mimicked in the Playground, allowing prospective users to walk through various contract scenarios based on different activities done by the parties. Users have an omniscient point of view in the primary simulation, and may execute activities by any participant, with the possibility to reverse the acts performed at any moment and subsequently choose an alternative course.

This simplicity also allows you to represent Marlowe contracts in an SMT solver,[567] a logic engine that checks the characteristics of systems automatically. IOG can examine whether or not a contract will fail to fulfill a payment using this model, which they call static analysis, and if it will, they can collect proof of how it will fail, allowing the author to alter the contract if they desire.

IOG can use a proof assistant to create a formal model of their implementation, from which they can generate machine-checked proofs of how the language works. While the SMT solver works on individual contracts, the proof assistant may prove characteristics of contract templates and the system as a whole: for example, IOG can demonstrate that the accounts referenced in any running contract can never be in debit. Simulation, static analysis, and proof are three layers of assurance for a contract to which users would commit assets to guarantee that it acts as it should.

Oracles

One of the most common questions with Marlowe is about financial oracles, or how to get a contract to account for external data values like the exchange rate between ada and bitcoin. Because an oracle is essentially the same as a participant who makes a decision, Marlowe's semantics can already deal with external values. However, as part of the implementation, the aim is to provide oracle values, which would allow contracts to obtain values directly from a stock market ticker, or a data feed like Coinbase or Binance. Simultaneously, the Plutus team is investigating the best method to deal with oracles in general, and there will be support for it in the future.

Why Actus?

The blockchain guarantees that the contract is fulfilled, therefore Marlowe has the potential to let individuals establish financial promises and exchanges without the need for a third party to facilitate them. IOG is developing a Marlowe implementation of disintermediated contracts for end users who wish to conduct peer-to-peer financial transactions without the involvement of a third party. Financial contracts are classified by

---

[567] **Satisfiability modulo theories (SMT)** is the problem of determining whether a mathematical formula is satisfiable. It generalizes the Boolean satisfiability problem (SAT) to more complex formulas involving real numbers, integers, and/or various data structures such as lists, arrays, bit vectors, and strings. The name is derived from the fact that these expressions are interpreted within ('modulo') a certain formal theory in first-order logic with equality (often disallowing quantifiers). **SMT solvers** are tools which aim to solve the SMT problem for a practical subset of inputs.

the Actus Financial Research Foundation using a taxonomy[568] that is outlined in a technical specification.[569]

Financial contracts are legal agreements between two (or more) counterparties on the exchange of future cash flows, according to Actus. Such legal agreements have always been expressed in natural language, resulting in ambiguity. As a result, Actus uses a set of contractual words and deterministic functions to translate these terms to future payment obligations to construct contracts. As a result, most financial instruments may be described using 31 contract types or modular templates.

What does Actus look like in Marlowe?

Products in the Actus taxonomy, such as the principal at maturity contract, may be presented in Marlowe in a variety of ways, depending on how willing they are to accept modifications in their terms throughout the course of the contract's existence.

In the most basic scenario, all cash flows are established, or frozen, at contract start, ensuring that the contract's operation is completely predictable, given that all participants continue to participate with it throughout its existence. Actus-F contracts are such a contract (F for fixed or frozen).

Dynamism, or change during a contract's development, may take two forms. Participants may make unplanned payments, which will necessitate a recalculation of the remaining cash flows, as well as modify the cash flows by factoring in external risk variables. Actus-M models the whole range of contracts that accomplish both (M for Marlowe).

Intermediate stages are also available: Actus-FS (fixed schedules) contracts have set schedules, enabling risk factors to be considered but no unexpected payments; Actus-FR contracts, on the other hand, enable payments to be made at any time but do not take into account risk factors.

Finally, Actus-H (H for Haskell) models contracts directly as Plutus or Haskell programs, with Marlowe used to validate each transaction over the contract lifespan by producing Plutus code from the Marlowe description of the contract logic.

Why are there so many distinct Actus contract models?

The reason for this is because there's a trade-off between the dynamic nature of contracts and the certainty IOG can provide customers about how they'll function before they're executed.

- Actus-F (fixed or frozen) contracts have a completely established payment schedule that can be reviewed directly by the parties, making it easy to

---

[568] ACTUS taxonomy, actusfrf.org/taxonomy

[569] ACTUS technical spec, actusfrf.org/techspecs

determine, for example, that all payments from such a contract will be successful

- Contracts in the Actus-FS and -FR series have greater dynamism, yet they are readable and simple to examine. Furthermore, they are subject to static analysis to ensure that all payments, for example, will be successful
- Because Actus-M (M for Marlowe) contracts are written in Marlowe, they can be analyzed. However, due to the unpredictability of the activities that the contract will take at any given moment in time, analysis takes much longer. It's worth noting that assurance may be provided for scaled-down contracts that have the same computational content but grow over a shorter period of time, resulting in fewer interactions
- Because Actus-H (H for Haskell) contracts are written in a blend of Plutus and Marlowe, they are not as easy to static check as the others. This platform, on the other hand, provides complete extension and customization of the Actus standard implementation for corporate customers.

Users may build Actus-F (fixed or frozen) and -FS contracts from the terms of the contract using a visual presentation of the data necessary in IOG's implementation of Actus, which was accessible as a pre-release version under the Labs tab of the Playground.

Marlowe is a DSL (domain specific language) that solely defines financial contracts, not smart contracts in general. It varies from general-purpose blockchain languages like Solidity and Bitcoin Script[570] because of this.

Marlowe is a large-scale project. IOG created Marlowe contracts using examples from the Algorithmic Contract Types Unified Standards (Actus) framework, which is one of the most popular projects for financial smart contracts. These and more examples are available in the Marlowe Playground.

Marlowe for P2P Finance

If you ever tried to sell your Bitcoin or ada and withdraw funds from Binance in a hurry, you could very well be blocked from doing so. Binance often suspends withdrawals due to a backlog[571] or you may be forced to withdraw via an expensive option instead of a relatively cheap bank transfer.[572] Are centralized exchange fees[573] any less extortionate than legacy banking fees? Most people would have thought that in the crypto space, they

---

[570] **Bitcoin Script** is a simple, stack-based programming language that enables the processing of transactions on the Bitcoin blockchain

[571] Binance hit by crypto withdrawal suspension, fnlondon.com/articles/binance-hit-by-crypto-withdrawal-suspension-20211101

[572] Binance suspends SEPA transfers for irish investors, businesspost.ie/investing/binance-suspends-sepa-transfers-for-irish-investors-1ac95e7c

[573] Cryptocurrency Exchange Fees Are A Mess. Will They Ever Improve?, forbes.com/sites/kenrapoza/2021/10/17/cryptocurrency-exchange-fees-are-a-mess-when-will-they-ever-improve/?sh=477a74be2f4c

would always be able to access their assets, make trades and withdraw without third parties blocking you or charging hefty 'processing fees'.

Is it ever true that you can have complete control over our finances? Most people have no choice but to entrust the management of their money to a third party, leaving it up to them to determine if and when those monies may be accessed, utilized, or even seen. The primary point of control is something that all of these third-party banks and brokers have in common. An external self-interested actor may influence, attack, or manipulate the primary point of control, making it the opposite of democratized finance.

Adrian Weckler
@adrianweckler

Bank Of Ireland, 2022

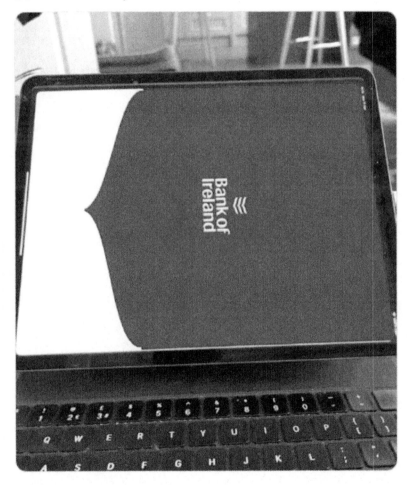

Figure 43: Online Banking in 2022

This is the driving force behind decentralized finance, often known as DeFi. Lending, escrows, derivatives, swaps, and securities are among the financial instruments provided by DeFi, which are comparable to those supplied by Wall Street. DeFi platforms distinguish themselves by being able to provide various financial products without the need of central market makers, banks, or brokers. Each financial arrangement is recorded on the blockchain as a smart contract that is settled algorithmically. Because of their decentralized character, they are significantly more resistant to market manipulation and centralized system failure.

IOG is working on a set of Marlowe products to help democratize money and make financial agreements more accessible. This includes Marlowe Run, a tool that will allow users to securely and independently execute off-the-shelf financial agreements with friends or businesses. This peer-to-peer system will be cost-effective and, more significantly, democratizing, with increased automation capabilities and no need for third-parties.

Marlowe suite

IOG wants to democratize finance with Marlowe by allowing peer-to-peer agreements to operate on a blockchain. They aim to provide individuals the ability to build their own financial instruments and make agreements with whomever they choose to deal with. Marlowe will provide a number of distinct products, each of which will cater to a particular set of consumers and functions. Marlowe's product strategy is divided into three categories: Marlowe for developers, Marlowe for end users, and Marlowe for enterprise.

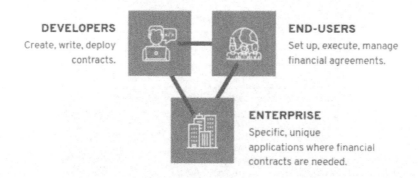

Figure 44: Marlowe user groups

Developers

Developers may use Marlowe Build and Marlowe Play (also known as the Marlowe Playground), and also the input to the Marlowe Library. The combination of Marlowe Build and Marlowe Play allows for end-to-end financial smart contract creation.

Marlowe Build allows developers to write smart contract code. They may then use simulations to undertake basic iterative design and formally verify and test smart contracts on Marlowe Play. These characteristics, when combined with a finance-specific domain-specific language (DSL), guarantee that contracts are simple to create, as well as secure, verifiable, and well tested. Developers may donate their smart contract templates to the Marlowe Library, an open-source smart contract template library, after they've been developed and tested.

End users

Marlowe for end users will provide a simple, intuitive, and seamless interface for users to sign financial agreements on the blockchain with their friends, colleagues, or customers. This contains Marlowe Run and offers you access to the Marlowe Library's financial instrument templates. These products were designed with the user in mind by IOG. The user does not need to be a blockchain expert or know how to develop smart contracts to form financial agreements on the Marlowe Run.

Every step of the contract is explained in layman's terms, and each action is carried out only with the user's express permission. IOG has designed a set of carefully tested and confirmed financial mechanisms like escrows, debt securities, and swaps that may be utilized on the Marlowe Run. The Marlowe Library makes these, and many more validated open-source contracts, accessible.

Enterprise

Marlowe for Enterprise seeks to take DeFi beyond individual users, allowing businesses to reap the advantages of smart contracts in a practical way. This will feature a customized, configurable set of capabilities and financial agreements geared to a specific business use case, as well as smart contract templates based on the Algorithmic Contract Types Unified Standards (Actus) for financial contracts.

Marlowe on Cardano

IOG released the Marlowe Playground Alpha[574] in 2020. This allowed contracts to be written in JavaScript in addition to Haskell or directly in Marlowe. Proof-of-concept oracles were also added, with the ability to retrieve external data such as price straight from a stock market 'ticker' or, in the future, data feeds like Kraken.[575] IOG created guides to help developers with the rollout, then expanded on this effort by improving the user experience and developing, testing, and verifying a growing bank of smart contract templates.

IOG is finishing the implementation of Marlowe on Cardano as part of the Goguen era deployment, allowing individuals and organizations to execute DeFi contracts that they have authored themselves or obtained from a contract repository. Marlowe will initially

---

[574] Marlowe Playground Alpha, alpha.marlowe.iohkdev.io/#/

[575] Kraken feed, api.cryptowat.ch/markets/kraken

operate on the Cardano blockchain, but it is blockchain agnostic and might run on other blockchains in the future to reach a wider audience.

Marlowe will be made available to end users in phases. The first was the Marlowe Run prototype, which allows users to showcase and test their own financial agreements. Users could modify a set of financial smart contract templates to meet their specific requirements. This prototype enabled users to experiment with forming decentralized financial agreements in a peer-to-peer setting without the need for a value-extracting third party. Users didn't need actual tokens to use the Marlowe Run prototype, so they could check it out before committing.

IOG's developers created a set of template financial instruments for this deployment. On Marlowe Run, these templates can be used to run test agreements. IOG shared several demos of Marlowe Run such as this one[576] on their 'IOHK' YouTube channel. Check out marlowe-finance.io/ for details on webinars, events, etc.

Marlowe Playground evolves

You can make your own templates out of Marlowe contracts and utilize unique metadata to provide user suggestions. The sandbox setting of the Marlowe Playground is where you may experiment drafting financial contracts. This playground lets you work directly in a variety of languages, including Marlowe, JavaScript, Haskell,[577] or Blockly, depending on your preferences. New tools for creating and modifying templates and customizing information, as well as a new JSON download option for the contracts themselves, were introduced to the Marlowe Playground.

Template support

With the release of Marlowe Run, IOG expanded the Marlowe Playground to include template support. An enhanced version of Marlowe (aka Extended Marlowe, available in the Marlowe Playground) is used to create these templates. Users will be able to easily reuse and repurpose contracts using these new templates for a variety of scenarios and contexts.

Extended Marlowe is more versatile than ordinary Marlowe (or Core Marlowe). Contracts are quite specific, and timeouts are specified in absolute values, first through slot numbers, and subsequently using standardized POSIX[578] timestamps.

Marlowe Values are usually hardcoded in Marlowe, with the exception of those supplied as Inputs. For example, you may use a **Choice** in a **When** construct to create a loan for

---

[576] Demo: Cardano's Marlowe Run, youtube.com/watch?v=sfLLoIEhSGU

[577] Marlowe embedded in Haskell, play.marlowe-finance.io/doc/marlowe/tutorials/embedded-marlowe.html

[578] The **Portable Operating System Interface (POSIX)** is a family of standards specified by the IEEE Computer Society for maintaining compatibility between operating systems. POSIX defines the application programming interface (API), along with command line shells and utility interfaces, for software compatibility with variants of Unix and other operating systems.

₳100 or one that asks the user how much to lend, but before you couldn't have a reusable Marlowe contract that could be deployed at any moment and with any provided parameters. The ability to incorporate contract parameters in Extended Marlowe resolves these constraints. Currently, extended Marlowe is almost the same to plain Marlowe, with the exception of two additional constructors that represent template parameters:

- `SlotParam` — In a **When** construct, it may be used instead of a timeout.
- `ConstantParam` — a type of **Value** construct
- Both constructors accept a single parameter, which is a string that acts as a parameter identifier, such as:
- `SlotParam "Payment deadline"`
- `ConstantParam "Price"`

Even if they exist in separate locations, two parameters of the same type (**SlotParam** or **ConstantParam**) and with the same identifier are considered the same parameter. If a contract has parameters (if it is a template), the user will be prompted to provide values for those parameters before beginning a simulation or deploying the contract in Marlowe Run.

It's worth noting that the value template parameter input field isn't merely an integer field. Rather, it expects a decimal number with a currency sign on the label to indicate that the predicted value reflects an amount of ada. Also, quantities of ada do not have to be represented by choices, they may be used to indicate anything, such as a ratio. Each parameter has its own set of clues, which may be accessed by clicking the purple question mark beside each box. The suggestions text ('tool tip') is unique to the contract template.

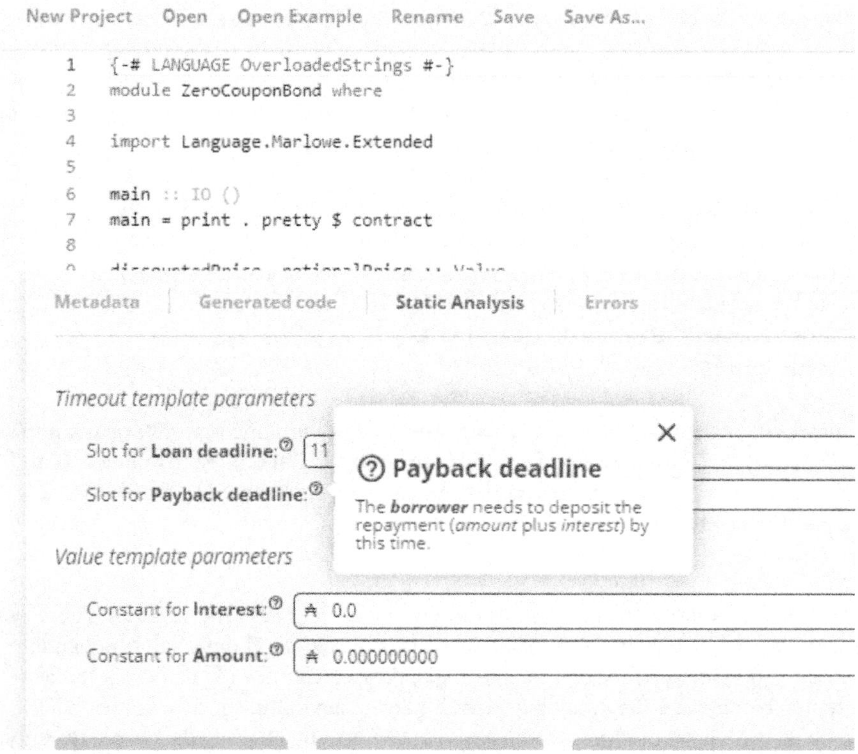

Figure 45: Marlowe static analysis

Metadata customization

Metadata may be used to alter elements in user-defined contracts. Each of the editors in the Marlowe Playground has a Metadata tab at the bottom. Users may change the metadata to suit their needs. Every contract is required to provide some fundamental metadata, such as contract type, contract name and descriptions. The metadata tab also allows you to format the choices and value parameters.

In the Metadata tab, each new role, choice, slot, or value parameter added to a contract will be highlighted in red. It may be required to compile the code successfully first in the case of the Haskell and JavaScript editors.

By pressing the red '+' button, a new metadata entry for the selected object will be created. Similarly, if a role, choice, slot, or value parameter is no longer used in the contract, the existing metadata will be highlighted in red and the user must remove the metadata item from the contract by using the '-' button.

Ordering of metadata

The sequence in which the parameters are set is critical. The end user can choose from a number of slot parameters so it would make sense to present those parameters in order of their occurrence. The user can now drag items into the appropriate order to organize metadata, for example:

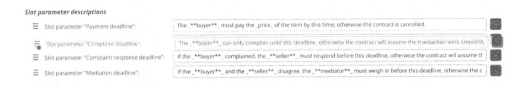

Figure 46: Marlowe drag and drop

The order of the parameters in the metadata will be utilized to generate the form that will be shown at the start of the simulation or contract execution.

In April 2022, IOG introduced the Marlowe CLI (command line interface) tool.[579] For users who wish to manage contracts from the command line, this new tool provides a simple approach. It allows you to concentrate on the Marlowe contract while the tool handles the specifics of the contract's input and state. It also automates several parts of Plutus, as well as interactions with the Cardano node itself, to relieve users of some of the heavy lifting.

This new CLI tool will be beneficial for teaching users how to get up to speed with Marlowe. It was used heavily in the inaugural Marlowe Pioneer Program. Late 2022 saw the launch of *Marlowe Runtime,[580]* an application backend for Marlowe contract handling. Developers can use Marlowe Runtime's APIs and backend to build and deploy Marlowe Web3 DApps. This saves them the hassle of needing to manually orchestrate the backend workflow. To help you get started, there is a Marlowe Runtime client for AWS Lamba[581] on the GitHub repo with several demo videos from Brian Bush.[582]

Marlowe FAQs

Q: Where can I learn more about Marlowe?
A: This chapter was just an overview of Marlowe. To learn more, subscribe to Prof Simon Thompson's YouTube channel[583] and review his videos. In May 2022, Niamh Ahern (IOG Education Manager) announced the inaugural Marlowe Pioneer program.[584]

---

[579] Marlowe CLI Tool, github.com/input-output-hk/marlowe-cardano/blob/cli-blog-april2022/marlowe-cli/ReadMe.md

[580] Marlowe Runtime, github.com/input-output-hk/marlowe-cardano/tree/main/marlowe-runtime

[581] Marlowe Runtime client for AWS Lambda, github.com/input-output-hk/marlowe-lambda

[582] Brian Bush, iohk.io/en/team/brian-bush

[583] Prof Simon Thompson on YouTube, youtube.com/user/simonjohnthompson/videos

The first cohort graduated in July 2022, all the lectures are available on the 'IOGAcademy' YouTube channel.[585] Read the docs[586] and register to be in the next cohort at *pioneers.marlowe-finance.io*

Q: Are there any new additional smart contracts on Marlowe Run?
A: You have the option of utilizing Marlowe Build to create your own contract. IOG are generating new contract templates for users to test, which will be uploaded to the contract catalogue soon.

Q: Can I edit a contract after it's created?
A: You may make modifications to your contract before it starts operating. You may simply modify the Roles and Terms fields. All conditions are established once it begins to run, exactly as they are with a typical legal contract.

Q: Are you using real funds with Marlowe Run?
A: No, when you utilize Marlowe Run, you are running and executing your contracts using test funds.

Q: Is there a hard limit to the number of contracts I can run in parallel?
A: IOG are not putting any hard user-specific limitations on the prototype but may do so in Marlowe Run. Keep in mind that IOG servers have a limit on the number of contracts and transactions they can process at any one moment, although this is not user-specific at this time.

Q: Can I create a contract with a user from a different blockchain, ie. not Cardano?
A: Because all financial agreements initially were established between Cardano wallet addresses, all agreements should be made with someone who possesses a Cardano wallet. IOG may allow agreements on other chains in future editions, since Marlowe is fundamentally blockchain-agnostic.

Q: Can I create new smart contracts on Marlowe Run?
A: You may create financial agreements right now utilizing a variety of templates from Marlowe Marketplace, a smart contract template library. You may even create your own financial contracts on the Marlowe Playground if you wish to. After that, you can submit them to Marlowe Market and run them via Marlowe Run.

Q: Where does Marlowe Run begin and Marlowe Playground end?
A: Marlowe Run is a product aimed towards a bigger audience of non-developer end users. The Marlowe Playground is designed for technical developers, and contracts may be created there and then utilized on Marlowe Run.

---

[584] Niamh Aherne, 'Learn how to create low-code, low-cost financial smart contracts in the Marlowe Pioneer Program', iohk.io/en/blog/posts/2022/05/11/learn-how-to-create-low-code-low-cost-financial-smart-contracts-in-the-marlowe-pioneers-program/

[585] Marlowe Pioneers 1st Cohort, youtube.com/channel/UCX9j__vYOJu00iqBrCzecVw/playlists?view=50&sort=dd&shelf_id=2

[586] Marlowe docs, play.marlowe-finance.io/doc/marlowe/tutorials/introducing-marlowe.html

Q: Where can I get help with Marlowe Run?

A: If you have any problems, use the 'Submit Feedback' email form on the Marlowe website's Feedback page, Sign up for the Marlowe Pioneer Program to collaborate with IOG and help IOG stress test Marlowe even further.

Q: What are Marlowe's use cases?

A: Marlowe contracts may be leveraged in a variety of ways, such as automating the functioning of a financial contract that transacts cryptocurrency on a blockchain using Marlowe software. It might also be used for auditing reasons to track user compliance with a contract that is being implemented in the real world.

Marlowe is simply one example of a DSL operating on a blockchain. It serves as an example of how new DSLs may be constructed to cover supply-chain management, law, insurance, accounting, and other areas.

Q: When should I not use Marlowe?

A: Although Marlowe is a financial DSL, what if you need to build other types of contracts? Cardano uses Plutus, a blockchain-based general-purpose language, to create them. Plutus contracts can manage a wide range of crypto assets and lack the limitations of Marlowe contracts, such as the length of time they can be active and the number of individuals they may include. Every Marlowe contract is managed by the Marlowe interpreter, a single Plutus application.

Q: This all sounds too easy, is it really just a matter of dragging and dropping blocks around?

A: No, you should study the content and become a Marlowe Pioneer before developing DApps that use other peoples' funds. Start by reviewing the best practices, 'bad smells' and 'Potential problems with contracts' in the docs.[587]

---

[587] Potential problems with contracts, play.marlowe-finance.io/doc/marlowe/tutorials/potential-problems-with-contracts.html

Chapter 8: Basho (Scalability)

'The journey itself is my home'

— Matsuo Basho

There are two eras left on the Cardano roadmap, and we'll see over the next two chapters just how interconnected they are. They are being worked on in parallel.

Scalability Defined

Cardano's roadmap initially focused on establishing a decentralized, secure network. The innovative proof-of-stake model needed time to bed down and mature. There are now over 3,000+ stake pools confirming transactions, agreeing on the network state. This brings with it challenges in scaling a distributed system with no central, trusted nodes. The system must reach consensus to transfer assets, record of state and cryptographic proofs globally with constraints like network speed, differing hardware setups, etc.

Scalability is a blockchain's **ability to handle usage or adoption**. Measuring scalability is not simply measuring the TPS (transactions per second) in any random scenario. Scalability is more nuanced than that.

'Yes, but can it do a million TPS?' is a familiar refrain often used without any context on crypto twitter. TPS (transactions per second) is perhaps the crudest measure to use as a comparison out of all those available. Transactions occur in a variety of sizes and formats. While this is true for Cardano, it is much more important when comparing two systems that are so significantly different. More pertinent questions are… can it handle demand today? Does it have a realistic roadmap to handle billions of users in future?

Scaling a blockchain means improving the blockchain design using the various techniques and features outlined in this chapter. Many of them are complementary and interdepend on each other. The overall goal is to increase throughput. Digging deeper, this means improving performance based on these metrics:

- Throughput: the quantity of data that a system can process in a given length of time. Measured in Bytes per second (kilobytes per sec, kB/s)
- CPU seconds (milliseconds) ms/s per wall clock for **script execution time,** ie. how long was the CPU busy for.
- Finality: the amount of time it takes for an action's consequence to become immutable and true for everyone in the system
- Concurrency: the amount of work that various actors can do without interfering with one another.
- Size of transaction(s)

As of November 2022, blocks on the Cardano mainnet are created approximately every 20 seconds, at a max block size of 88kB. Therefore, the data throughput is ~ 4.4kB/s.

Any blockchain can appear fast and sexy using tiny transaction sizes and no scripts. Some high profile blockchains have centralized characteristics such as a minority of validators controlling disproportionate amounts of stake. It's easy for a blockchain to compromise on decentralization then boast astronomical TPS figures, but if it needs to be stopped and restarted regularly, it should be a clue that it's not really what it seems.

TPS on Cardano is yet more nuanced due to its native asset standard. EUTXO allows hundreds, even thousands, of native assets to be transferred in a single transaction. A more accurate metric[588] is TPT (transactions per transaction). eUTtxO.org is a blockchain explorer created by Peter Oravec. It is an excellent learning tool to understand and visualize how transactions work on Cardano.

Figure 47: @oravecpeter tweets about eUTtxO.org '*There are 923 outputs of these two transactions, each output can be different recipient so 923 TX... this is superpower of UTxO... everyone will use this because it's super cheap to do all this stuff in single TX...*'

---

[588] Performance engineering: Lies, damned lies and (TPS) benchmarks, youtube.com/watch?v=gpSnyCn2s9U

Unlike many blockchains who adopt a 'move fast and break things' approach, Cardano has always stuck to a deliberate, careful and methodical strategy. Despite this relative conservatism, Cardano was the most developed crypto project on GitHub in 2021[589] and again in 2022.[590]

IOG outlined their Basho strategy in a 2022 blog post.[591]

There is no 'magic bullet' for scaling blockchains, it's done by tweaking parameters and combining different solutions that generally fall into two categories:

- Layer 1 solutions: upgrades applied to the mainchain protocol, cardano-node, etc.
- Layer 2 solutions: offloading workloads, extending functionality and integrating other blockchains with sidechains, ZK rollups and state channels like Hydra.

So far Cardano has scaled to meet demand, given its ambitious goal and numerous constraints. Changes since the Vasil hard fork are already bearing fruit however DeFi and RealFi will begin in earnest in 2023. There are several stablecoins launching, Oracles like Charli3 will mature, over 1,000 projects are ready to join the existing ~100 projects.

IOG will continue implementing their research throughout 2023. **On-chain solutions** encompass block size increases, pipelining, input endorsers, parameter adjustments, Plutus script enhancements, node enhancements and on-disk storage improvements. **Off-chain solutions** include sidechains, Hydra, off-chain computing and Mithril.

Ongoing enhancements

As part of the Basho development phase, IOG will continue updating parameters. A flexible infrastructure that can bend, but not break, is key as conditions change. Some of the considerations are:

- **Increased block size:** enabling more transactions to be fitted in a block. During times of network saturation, there will be reduced waiting time for transactions to be accepted by a block, which is a positive. There is, however, a cost. It takes longer for larger blocks to propagate throughout the network. Nodes will also need additional time to validate transactions as a result of this. Although increasing the block size might improve network speed, such adjustments should be done with care. IOG progressively alter settings and monitor the outcomes during high saturation times to guarantee that the increase does not impact block

---

[589] Cardano became the most developed crypto project on GitHub in 2021, cointelegraph.com/news/cardano-became-the-most-developed-crypto-on-github-in-2021-santiment

[590] Cardano Surpasses Ethereum In GitHub Daily Development Activity, investing.com/news/cryptocurrency-news/cardano-surpasses-ethereum-in-github-daily-development-activity-2956870

[591] Tim Harrison, 'How we are scaling Cardano in 2022', iohk.io/en/blog/posts/2022/01/14/how-we-re-scaling-cardano-in-2022/

adoption time.

- **Block level limit**: increasing the amount of memory units (abstract memory units) available to each script in the block. Scripts express various kinds of logic in order to spend UTXOs.

- **Mempool size**: The size of the mempool is continually tweaked. When adding transactions to a block, the mempool acts as a network buffer and may cause a little delay. However, increasing the size of the mempool will not boost network throughput since transaction queues would remain the same. The mempool enables for a fair adoption of new transactions that arrive at random

- **Plutus requires resources,** both computational (CPU) units and memory units, in order to do useful things with a Plutus script. Plutus memory limitations were extended, allowing them to create more complex Plutus scripts or allowing current scripts to handle more data items, enhance concurrency, or otherwise extend their capabilities.

- Since the d (decentralization) parameter had been '0' for over a year, it was completely removed from the protocol as part of the Vasil hard fork.

Timeliness consideration when increasing throughput:

- Timeliness: the time it takes to adopt a block. The entire 'budget' for block adoption is set at 5 seconds for a block to spread through 95% of the network, with Plutus scripts having a budget in the milliseconds. This is done to avoid monopolization by allowing the block to contain both scripts and simple transactions.

- Throughput: Users will experience longer block adoption times if the number of blocks is raised dramatically all at once. That's because throughput and timeliness are at odds: boosting throughput means greater network performance, but it might come at the expense of delays when the system is overburdened.

Congestion is minimized by efficient systems. Cardano's network utilizes '**backpressure**' to control overall system stress. While certain individual users may report higher transaction wait times during a big NFT drop, this does not indicate that the network is 'struggling.' It really signifies that the network is working properly, in what's known as graceful degradation.

Ouroboros (**Praos**) has precise criteria that must be fulfilled to achieve its **security objectives**, with block propagation time being a priority. Block propagation time refers to how long it takes for a newly minted block to be propagated through 95% of the staked ada nodes on the network. For Praos to remain secure, new blocks must be propagated every 5 seconds.

This 5s limit is seen by IOG as a 'budget' that they may use to increase the block size, for example. Increased block size would automatically lengthen the time it takes to propagate blocks; thus, they must carefully monitor any modifications they make to improve speed without jeopardizing the network's security. This budget will be expanded in future Ouroboros iterations. Meanwhile, IOG will concentrate on preserving security while extending the network to meet increased demand.

Node (cardano-node) enhancements

The node is central to everything in Cardano. It stores a full copy of the blockchain, processes ledger rule and plutus scripts, creates transactions and certificates, distributes (diffuses) transactions and blocks across the network. It calculates and distributes staking rewards to the delegators directly as well as to the stake pools. The node ensures decentralization as 3,000+ stake pool operators run the node. When you use your wallet, you are using the node. So, a lot going on under the hood to make the chain work. It makes sense, then, to improve the node's performance where possible.

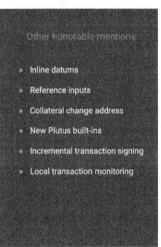

Figure 48: Key node enhancements, from Kevin Hammond's talk at ScotFest.

Some of the significant changes and improvements from 2022 were:

- Ability to generate transactions that comply with the Concise Data Definition Language (CDDL) using the node's native tools CLI, rather than relying on third-party tools.

  The way computers store data when they're executing is not necessarily a great way to store data when you're trying to send it across the network. When data is taken out of the computer's memory and passed on to another peer to propagate a block, it's important that a representation is taken out of the computer's memory and put through a process which is known as serialization. Serialization[592] takes the data object and represents it in a way that is efficient for transport.

---

[592] In the context of data storage, **serialization** is the process of translating data structures or object state into a format that can be stored (for example, in a file or memory buffer) or transmitted (for example, across a

- IOG uses Concise Binary Object Representation (CBOR) for serialization. It's based on JSON,[593] used extensively in web development. The change IOG made was to CDDL. CDDL (Concise Data Definition Language) is like a schema for CBOR. IOG tried to enhance this schema for their underlying serialization representation. As a result, sending data across the network was now done more efficiently.

- Support for transactions with multiple signatures in incremental stages. While it was already possible to have a Cardano transaction signed by many entities using their private keys (equivalent to a joint bank account), this update allowed for incremental signing of a transaction. Instead of needing to sign the transaction simultaneously, one party could now sign it first, and then send it to the other

- SPOs could now check the leadership schedule using a new CLI tool. This tool allowed SPOs to inspect the slots where the SPO delivering the command will mint a block for the following epoch. Some were concerned that this capability raised security concerns, however the tool is structured such that each SPO may only examine their own impending schedule. They are unable to verify the schedules of any other SPOs

- A CLI tool for inspecting local mempools. This is a developer tool that allows you to view the local mempool, which is where transactions are stored before being included in a block. This feature enabled developers to track the status of a transaction before it is put to a block

- A command-line tool for estimating script costs. Node users could now estimate the cost of executing a Plutus script with more accuracy. This is helpful since it allows developers to see what resources (memory / CPU limits, etc.) they're using when building smart contracts or validation scripts, which is especially valuable for creating Plutus transactions. Developers could now see how much resources their scripts would need while running on-chain.

- Dynamic peer to peer for nodes: gradually rolled out mechanisms to enable a self-organized network based on connection speed, and on the quality of connections between the different nodes in the system.

Improvements allow for a more uniform distribution of stake and reward calculations over epochs, allowing for larger block sizes. Memory use is also more efficient overall. Memory compression minimizes RSS[594] footprint, while memory sharing reduces the amount of data that needs to be instantiated.

---

network) and reconstructed later (possibly on a different computer). When the resulting series of bits is reread according to the serialization format, it can be used to create a semantically identical clone of the original object.

[593] **JavaScript Object Notation (JSON)** is an open-standard file format that uses human-readable text to transmit data objects consisting of attribute value pairs and array data types (or any other serializable value).

The Node team attended the workshops around the Voltaire upgrades outlined in CIP 1694 (the proposal on how Voltaire should be implemented). There will be gradual, iterative upgrades to the Node to accommodate the changes to the on-chain governance structure. The node will facilitate on-chain voting, including the guardrail mechanisms outlined in the constitution. The constitution itself will be recorded as a hash on-chain. Much of the detail for CIP 1694 still needs to be thrashed out but the cardano-node will naturally be central to everything.

As updates are ongoing, it's best to check the release notes[595] for the very latest.

Plutus V2 enhancements

At ScotFest in Edinburgh, Andrew Sutherland (Plutus Compiler Team Lead), reviewed the year since PlutusV1 was launched and subsequently enhanced with V2 in September 2022. Over the year his team ran, on average, half a million Plutus scripts per month on a nightly regression testing[596] system. Such a focus on quality bore fruit with Plutus compiler optimizations and a 30% increase in script efficiency. The various enhancements made with the Vasil hard fork led to faster core interpreter, faster untyped Plutus Core execution and lower transaction fees. Sutherland credited the CIP process as the steering force behind the progress.

MuesliSwap (muesliswap.com), the first native DEX on Cardano, took part in a benchmarking case study for Plutus V2 scripts. The results were a 90% reduction in transaction size and a 50% saving on transaction fees.

The CIP 49 'SEC P' update (intra-era hard fork) in February 2023 opened up a new world of interoperability options. These are crucial building blocks for bridge security, among other use cases. As they were tested by the community since November 2022, we should see them applied in DApps very soon.

---

[594] **Resident set size (RSS)** is the portion of memory occupied by a process that is held in main memory (RAM).

[595] Cardano node release notes, github.com/input-output-hk/cardano-node/releases

[596] Regression testing is re-running tests to ensure that previously developed and tested software is performing as expected after a change.

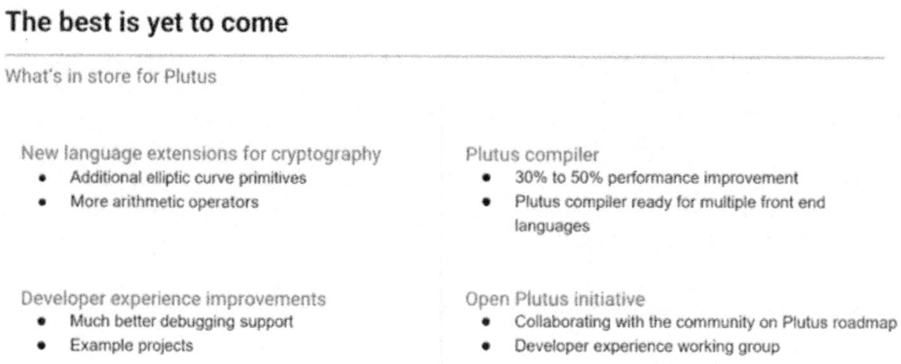

The best is yet to come

What's in store for Plutus

New language extensions for cryptography
- Additional elliptic curve primitives
- More arithmetic operators

Plutus compiler
- 30% to 50% performance improvement
- Plutus compiler ready for multiple front end languages

Developer experience improvements
- Much better debugging support
- Example projects

Open Plutus initiative
- Collaborating with the community on Plutus roadmap
- Developer experience working group

Figure 49: from Andrew Sutherland's ScotFest talk 'Scaling Cardano with Plutus V2'

Pipelining

Before Pipelining was introduced, a block was minted by an SPO, that's a new block in the blockchain that had to be validated and sent onto a peer. The problem was that peers also had to validate it and then send it onto their peer and that's how the blocks diffused across the network.

By combining validation with propagation, the time it takes for a block to propagate is reduced. By minimizing the 'dead time' between blocks, the objective is for blocks to be propagated to at least 95% of peers within 5 seconds (block propagation overhead). This allows flexibility to make other scaling adjustments, such as raising block size, or other Plutus parameter limits.

Pipelining is a natural progression of Cardano's 'plumbing'. It's an important part of the scaling strategy, and one of a series of stages outlining IOG's logical approach to ramping up Cardano's capacity as the ecosystem expands. IOG carefully monitors and reviews each update for at least one epoch (5 days) before proceeding with subsequent changes. A decentralized network architecture must be scaled depending on real-world usage, notwithstanding the substantial research and technical effort that has gone into creating and installing the system.

Diffusion pipelining

Pipelining, or more specifically, diffusion pipelining, is a consensus layer innovation that allows for speedier block propagation. It allows for more headroom, allowing Cardano's performance and competitiveness to improve even more. It's important to understand the system behavior of how blocks propagate, to see how this strategy accomplishes its purpose.

As it passes around the chain, a block goes through 6 stages:

1. Block header[597] transmission
2. Block header validation
3. Block body request and transmission
4. Block body validation and local chain extension
5. Block header transmission to downstream nodes
6. Block body transmission to downstream nodes

The path of a block is highly sequential. At each node, all steps occur in the same order every time. Block transmission takes a long time due to the large number of nodes and the ever-increasing quantity of blocks. Diffusion pipelining layers some of the above stages on top of one another, allowing them to happen simultaneously. This takes less time and boosts throughput.

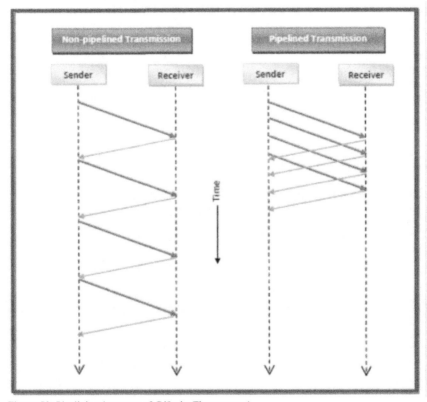

Figure 50: Pipelining (courtesy of @jJosjuaThreatt tweet)

The time savings provided by this technique will allow Cardano to expand even further, including adjustments to:

---

[597] **Block header**: The portion of a block that contains information about the block itself (block metadata), typically including a timestamp, a hash representation of the block data, the hash of the previous block's header, and a cryptographic nonce (if needed).

273

- Block size – the larger the block, the more transactions, and scripts it can accommodate
- Plutus memory limitations - the maximum amount of memory that a Plutus script may use
- Plutus CPU limits - a script may be given extra computing resources to execute more effectively.

Pipelining makes sure that the block header referencing the hash of a previous block is propagated correctly. Metadata included in the next block contains the body of the previous block. This is a safeguard to prevent DDoS (distributed denial of service) attacks even without full block confirmation.

From theory to practice

Diffusion pipelining was created with the goal of achieving quicker block propagation while avoiding 'destructive' alterations to the chain. Because nodes depend on these current approaches, IOG did not want to eliminate any of the protocols, primitives, or interactions currently in use in Cardano. Instead of modifying how things operate now, they're establishing a new mini protocol whose purpose is to pre-notify subscribing entities when a new desired block is detected, prior to full validation. Implementing Pipelining didn't require a hard fork and can be rolled out with a standard node release. It was introduced without fanfare the same time as the Vasil hard fork.

The ability to pre-notify peers and provide them a block before it is verified, allowing the downstream peer to pre-fetch the new block body, is the most significant feature brought by pipelining. This saves a lot of time since the time it takes to verify a block over several hops is reduced significantly. The network was stress tested post-Vasil and the initial results were very positive. The node is now running faster, with more throughput.

Rick McCracken DIGI
@RichardMcCrackn

Hey @IOHK_Charles we are trying our hardest over here to break #Cardano but we have failed. We cannot break it. Your did it! ⭐ #Cardano #Vasil

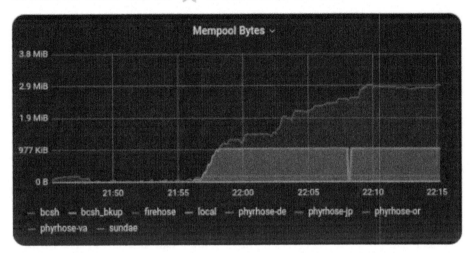

Figure 51: Tweet from Rick McCracken post-Vasil… *'We are hitting the chain as absolutely hard as possible from DripDropz…. The graph shows the mempool in red on the phyrhose way above the Cardano chain capacity and the chain is running perfectly fine.'*

On-disk storage

IOG are acutely aware that the Cardano node needs RAM[598] when it's running. They want to start moving things out of RAM, out of that expensive volatile memory into on-disk storage. This is a common practice in computer science. On-disk storage will improve the user experience for developers on Cardano.

By storing elements of the protocol state on disk, nodes will use less memory, allowing RAM-starved systems to operate nodes as long as they have enough storage, and memory will no longer be a scaling restriction. The blockchain state will be able to increase significantly as a result of this.

There is a 'UtxO HD' project ongoing to move Cardano's ledger state from being completely in-memory to being stored more on-disk. This is required to be able to scale

---

[598] **RAM (random-access memory)** is a form of computer memory that can be read and changed in any order, typically used to store working data and machine code. A random-access memory device allows data items to be read or written in almost the same amount of time irrespective of the physical location of data inside the memory.

to larger ledger states. It will also naturally ease RAM requirements for nodes. This feature will enable other roadmap items, such as parts of Ouroboros *Leios*.

There is a living document[599] on GitHub which goes into more technical details.

Off-chain computing

Offloading part of the computing, such as via Asynchronous Contract Execution[600] (ACE), may improve the efficiency of the core network. Transactions take place outside of the blockchain, yet a trust model allows for quick and inexpensive transactions. This concept is still in research mode and will likely be implemented in a future update.

Mithril

Mithril allows users to get the current state of a blockchain without recovering its entire history. Light, fast, efficient, and secure …Mithril is named after the fictional metal found in J. R. R. Tolkien's Middle-earth writings. It is lightweight but *'wrought of pure silver to the power and strength of triple steel'*.

At the Cardano Summit 2021,[601] IOG researchers Pyrros Chaidos and Roman Oliynykov presented Mithril – a new protocol and network based on the research paper[602] by Chaidos and Prof Aggelos Kiayias. Mithril utilizes a stake-based threshold multi-signature (STM) scheme to solve chain synchronization, state bootstrapping, and trust issues in DApps. Mithril has evolved into an open-source project with an aggressive biweekly release cadence. The release process[603] is constantly refined for a smooth developer experience.

The original paper, and related blog[604] by Olga Hryniuk, are quite technical and outline the long-term vision for the protocol. Like all agile, open-source projects, the final implementation might vary. What is clear is the burning need for a solution like this to enable faster syncing to the blockchain.

Piggybacking on the security of Cardano's staking system, Mithril enables stakeholders to vouch for some fact, with a weighting proportional to their stake. Mithril's initial proof of concept is to bootstrap a full Cardano node, however, it is flexible to apply to other

---

[599] draft UTxO HD design document for review, github.com/input-output-hk/ouroboros-network/commit/f4f9be4f73a4f4cc31e98ec6a0511d9c7e9a4601

[600] Wust, et al, (2019), 'ACE: Asynchronous and Concurrent Execution of Complex Smart Contracts', eprint.iacr.org/2019/835.pdf

[601] Cardano Summit 2021, youtube.com/watch?v=rmknjCvRH-Y

[602] Chaidos, Kiayias (2021), 'Mithril: Stake-based Threshold Multisignatures', eprint.iacr.org/2021/916.pdf

[603] Mithril Release Process, mithril.network/doc/dev-blog/2022/12/05/release-process

[604] Mithril: a stronger and lighter blockchain for better efficiency, iohk.io/en/blog/posts/2021/10/29/mithril-a-stronger-and-lighter-blockchain-for-better-efficiency/

protocols. For example, it's main feature of validating the state snapshot can be applied to data exchange between sidechains, roll-ups, on-chain voting... any many-to-one scenario is a potential use case.

Mithril is an overlay sitting on top of Cardano's Layer 1 mainchain, allowing users to create proof certificates. The certificates produced by Mithril have the same security properties that Ouroboros has. This has profound benefits. For example, millions of votes could take place off-chain, and then be aggregated together as a threshold signature. It would ultimately only be a single transaction on-chain. A full node like Daedalus can synch much quicker and a light wallet like *Lace* now has full node security, even though it's a light client.

How it works

The STM scheme described in the original research paper is now available as a stand-alone core library on GitHub. It contains the full set of primitives of the Mithril protocol and is stand-alone in that it's blockchain agnostic, it can potentially run on any PoS blockchain.

The Mithril Network sits on top of the Mithril Core library. There are three node types in the current proof of concept setup.

- **The Mithril Signer** run by (SPO) stake pool operator, side by side with the Cardano node. It signs the ledger state, ie. creates individual signatures.
- **The Mithril Aggregator** collects the Signers' signatures and creates multi-signatures, then embeds them in certificates. The aggregator also creates and stores the ledger state snapshot archive. These can be large, in the tens of GBs, and will grow as a blockchain grows.
- **The Mithril Client** restores (bootstraps) a full Cardano node by taking a snapshot and its certificate chain from the Aggregator node and verifying their validity with Mithril cryptographic primitives.

Lottery Analogy

IOG Architect Arnaud Bailly speaking on Cardano360 May 2022[605]

> One analogy that you can use to think about it is the lottery. So depending on the amount of stake, you draw tickets from a lottery, and depending on the amount of stakes you draw, depending on the amount of tickets you bought, your chances of having a winning ticket are higher. And so this is the same for Mithril ...you can potentially have several winning tickets. Once enough winning tickets have been drawn, over all the stake pool owners, then a certificate can be issued which provides a certified signature of the current state of the chain from a share, some share of the stake pool owners, from some predefined share... and this is what we call a snapshot.

---

[605] Cardano360 May 2022, youtu.be/Ar_8Lo0nV1s?t=228

Now the snapshot is made available to clients, and the clients can verify it, they can verify these snapshots by checking the aggregate signatures from all the lottery winners, so to speak, and so from all the signers....and check that they are actually legit and this check also rests on checking that the stake distribution is legit, and this is done through checking the chain certificate down to some general certificate ...and once they have verified the validity of certificate, now they can just download the snapshot itself, bootstrap the node, without having to go through the hassle of verifying everything.

Progress to date

The Mithril Network was tested as a centralized version initially (IOG-operated Mithril Aggregator). This paved the way for a *decentralized* version on the Cardano testnet where SPOs run the Mithril Aggregators. At ScotFest,[606] Jean-Philippe Raynaud's demo showed how a Daedalus wallet synched 15 times faster with Mithril, compared to classical bootstrapping. Mithril is crucial for trustless light wallets like *Lace* as they would otherwise need a third party to sync blockchain history. Mithril will enable fast synch times but also benefit from the mainchain's security properties. The coming on-chain voting planned for the *Age of Voltaire* is dependent on Mithril also.

Mithril will be deployed to mainnet in 2023.

Community driven

Follow mithril.network for the latest updates and contribute to the Mithril repository on GitHub[607]

The best way to contribute is to setup and test Mithril in different proof-of-stake contexts. The Mithril docs provide step by step tutorials to bootstrap a Cardano node, run a signer node or run a private Mithril network.

Lace

At Consensus 2022, which took place in Austin, Texas, IOG announced their new light wallet *Lace* (lace.io) was in development. Charles Hoskinson ran through a demo[608] explaining that *Lace* will not just be a wallet but a platform enabling users to tie together identity, voting and DApp Store experience. Lace will clearly be pivotal for Cardano adoption.

IOG's full node implementation is the *Daedalus* wallet, which is a desktop client that is fully synchronized with the blockchain history. Full node wallets are an excellent alternative for more advanced users, but because they carry a full copy of the blockchain,

---

[606] Light, fast, efficient, and secure - Mithril, youtube.com/watch?v=VyxsqwNWZt4

[607] Mithril on GitHub, github.com/input-output-hk/mithril

[608] Lace: a lightwallet platform, youtube.com/watch?v=Q4Z83TSdEfg

they use a lot of resources and take a long time to sync. As a result, a full-node wallet may not be suitable for users that want immediate access to their funds. As Cardano expands into more mainstream countries, particularly in emerging nations, a viable alternative is necessary. Lace will focus on driving adoption by offering a great user experience.

It will initially support the basics: storing your ada, sending/receiving ada, storing NFTs and delegating your ada. Long term it will integrate with Atala Prism (IOG's Decentralized Identity solution) and the DApp Store, enable Catalyst voting and be interoperable with other blockchains.

In an interview[609] with Eleanor Terrett for FoxBusiness, Charles Hoskinson talked more about *Lace*:

> *So, what we wanted to do was build a very consumer-friendly platform that evolves very quickly. So, every 6 to 9 weeks, new features and functionality come out. It gives you kind of a Swiss army knife of cryptography, so you can do some very complicated things over time like multisig transactions, partial delegation, and proxy keys[610]... but ultimately you go multi-chain, multi-asset. It's a place to store your digital life in that respect. So, it's a place where you can interact with people, a place where you can share identity, multiple identities which you can share. Identity for GameFi, one for compliance, one for friends, one for NFTs... all these types of things.*
>
> *[..] So it's really nice to have a platform where, not only can we make technological innovations, and integrate innovations and kind of bring everyone together and unify... but also user interface innovations to ultimately make using cryptocurrencies easier for people... because if you want to go from 10 million to a billion people, that delta is usability, not functionality. Usually, your functionality is great at 10 million but it's the 'best kept secret'. The billion is only when you have great usability in that respect.*

Hydra

Hydra introduces isomorphic[611] state channels to increase throughput, decrease latency, save money with reduced transaction fees and storage needs. IOG developed Hydra as a solution for Cardano and related networks using a principled, evidence-based methodology. Hydra is the result of substantial research and a critical step toward allowing decentralized networks to grow securely to meet global demands. Hydra makes it easier to perform transactions off-chain while still utilizing the main-chain ledger for secure settlement.

---

[609] Interview with Charles Hoskinson, twitter.com/i/broadcasts/1eaKbNQkpBqKX

[610] Re: Proxy Keys. Surprise AMA 11/21/2021, youtu.be/NJcVEJ1a6eg?t=2114

[611] **Isomorphism:** corresponding or similar in form and relations.

Hydra can sound very complicated and is sometimes confused with similar solutions. Let's begin by clarifying what 'isomorphic state channels' are. 'Iso' is a prefix meaning equal, for example, isometric means equal measurements. 'morphic' means relating to shape or form. So isomorphic means having the same structure and properties.

'State channels' extend the notion of payment channels to also support smart-contracts over off-chain channels. Participants in the channel can now, in addition to traditional transactional payments, execute scripts to handle complex logic, off-chain, before committing the result back to the layer 1 later.

Participants lock funds into a smart contract. They can then transact with others in the state channel, off-chain, in whatever fashion meets their use case. Afterwards, the outcome is settled on-chain, without requiring the full transaction history of what occurred off-chain in the meantime.

Developers can leverage Cardano's proven infrastructure to develop wallets and DApps that communicate with the layer 2 system, drastically reducing the learning curve for Hydra. A Hydra Head may also be formed without the need for any initial funds from the receiving party, ensuring a seamless user experience.

Hydra protocols

Hydra is a distributed ledger scaling solution that meets all three of the aforementioned scalability challenges: high transaction throughput, low latency, and minimum storage per node. While Hydra is being developed in collaboration with the Ouroboros protocol and the Cardano ledger, it may also be used with other systems that have the same properties as Cardano.

Hydra's overall aim is to provide a cutting-edge layer 2 scaling solution for Cardano. Hydra will save expenses while boosting throughput and ensuring security. Hydra replicates the main chain's functionality while minimizing friction for users, but still allows the flexibility of having a different fee structure and timing constraints on the layer 2.

Hydra is a system made up of many subprotocols that work together to solve a single problem: scalability. Cardano's ecosystem is diverse, with numerous organizations with varied technological capabilities: the system needs to support stake pools, light wallets, DEXs, and other end-users with a variety of computing performance and availability characteristics. It's unreasonable to expect a single-protocol, one-size-fits-all method to provide overall scalability for such a diverse group of network actors.

In an early blog,[612] the Hydra architecture was broken down into four components: the head protocol, the tail protocol, the cross-head-and-tail communication protocol, as well as a set of supporting protocols for routing, reconfiguration, and virtualization. Although

---

[612] Prof Aggelos Kiayias, 'Enter the Hydra: scaling distributed ledgers, the evidence-based way,' iohk.io/en/blog/posts/2020/03/26/enter-the-hydra-scaling-distributed-ledgers-the-evidence-based-way/

it was originally developed as part of the Ouroboros research agenda, it has taken its own route and is now an agile open-source project with a release cadence of weeks.

Hydra Head

The Hydra 'head' protocol was the first part of the Hydra architecture to be released. The Head protocol began to take shape in 2020, especially during this early implementation and proof of concept[613] stage. IOG's understanding has evolved since then, and 2022 saw the formalization and implementation of a variation on the 'Head' protocol in the original paper.

Hydra acts as DApp-embedded software for developers seeking to scalability. It is implemented in two parts:

- On-chain scripts that execute the Hydra Head protocol
- Hydra node, a software stack which provides a high-level interface using standard web technologies like WebSocket and JSON.

To operate a Hydra Head, a working Cardano node is a pre-requisite. You then run a Hydra node, connected to other Hydra nodes and a Cardano node. Each Hydra Head can be comprised of several Hydra nodes. The Hydra team state in the docs that their current goal is anything up to 100 nodes per head. On-chain code will be the same between Cardano and a hydra head. This is one of the major selling points of the hydra design.

The potential Hydra Head topologies and use cases are listed in detail on the aptly named website https://hydra.family. The community is actively encouraged to give feedback on the roadmap.[614]

Hydra Head 'Poker game' analogy

The Hydra Head protocol is best used where participants, well-known to each other, agree to form a network but don't trust each other with the funds. A Hydra Head enables them to do so with ways to secure their assets, backed by the ability to settle disputes on the layer 1.

There are several use cases explained on the Hydra site, but the poker game is perhaps the most intuitive analogy to explain Hydra Heads. Consider Heads as a 'private poker table' where players bring their own chips to play with. The game may be played for as long as the participants like. If no one participates, the game will not advance. Participants are, however, able to leave with their chips. The game will terminate with the existing pot distributed if they do so.

A channel is a communication link between two or more peers. To be a part of a Head, you must be one of the peers. Channels establish isolated networks that may develop

---

[613] Sebastian Nagel, 'Hydra – Cardano's solution for ultimate Layer 2 scalability', iohk.io/en/blog/posts/2021/09/17/hydra-cardano-s-solution-for-ultimate-scalability/

[614] Hydra Head roadmap, github.com/orgs/input-output-hk/projects/21/views/7

independently of the main network. Participants on these alternate networks use a different, simpler consensus algorithm: everyone must agree on all transactions that pass through. As a participant, I am unable to lose money that I have not specifically decided to lose. Why? Because every binding transaction needs my express permission.

Participants may make financial commitments to a Head while creating it. This entails transferring funds off-chain to a script address that binds them to a set of rules. The script ensures that the protocol is executed safely on-chain, and that participants cannot defraud one another. Any participant, however, may choose to leave the Head at any moment by closing it. In this situation, everyone gets the most recent state they consented to off-chain, on their parallel network.

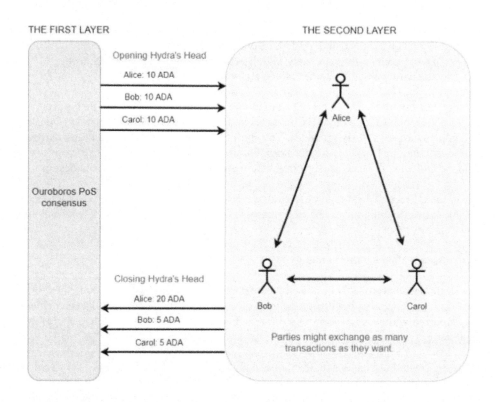

Figure 52: Courtesy of Cardanians's medium post 'Hydra: Cardano Scalability Solution'[615]

The on-chain script's dealer at the table guarantees that everyone follows the rules and doesn't cheat. In conclusion, there are the same number of chips out as there were before the game began, although they may have been rearranged throughout the game. While the ultimate outcome is known outside of the table, the players are the only ones who know the history of all bets taken throughout the game. The funds, or existing table pot, are unlocked based on the most recent agreed upon snapshot.

---

[615] Cardanians Hydra blog, cardanians-io.medium.com/hydra-cardano-scalability-solution-36b05ddc91cf

Payments

- Tipping
- Pay-per-use APIs
- In-app purchases
- E-commerce integrations
- Machine-to-machine
- Royalties
- Prepaid
- Loyalty points

Smart Contracts

- Auctions
- NFT drops
- Voting
- DEX protocols (swaps, OBM)
- Decentralized oracle feeds

Figure 53: Hydra Head use cases, from ScotFest talk by Hydra Product Manager, Nebojša Vojvodić

Evaluating the Hydra head protocol

Hydra Heads are known for their ability to achieve near-instant finality inside a Head. Setting up and closing a Head might take a few blocks. Simulations have shown that a single Hydra head can reach up to 1,000 TPS (Transactions per second), so if 1,000 heads are run in parallel, so it should be able to get a million TPS. That's impressive, and it puts Cardano far ahead of the competition, but it can be pushed further. What if each of the current 3,000+ stake pools ran a head? That's 3m TPS. Furthermore, different implementation enhancements may increase the 1,000 TPS single head measurement, boosting the protocol's possible performance even further.

So, is Hydra able to call whatever TPS number it wants? In principle, the answer is yes, which highlights a flaw in the prevalent[616] use of TPS as a system comparison measure. While it's easy to simplify the complexity of evaluating protocol performance to a single number, a lofty TPS claim is almost worthless without further information.

Clearly, a higher standard is required. Is the Hydra head protocol a good one to use? Will it hit the network's actual constraints, not just a TPS figure? To guarantee that the data IOG present is credible, they adopted the following technique:

- IOG explicitly describes all of the variables that affect the simulation: transaction size, time to verify a single transaction, time required for cryptographic procedures, allotted bandwidth per node, cluster size and geographical distribution, and transaction parallelism limitations. It would be difficult to replicate these numbers without this controlled setting

---

[616] TPS on crypto twitter, twitter.com/bitcoinissaving/status/1437240100807749633

- IOG evaluated the protocol's performance on baselines that define the underlying network and hardware infrastructure's exact and absolute bounds. How effectively IOG approaches such boundaries indicates how much space for progress there is.

The research paper[617] (Section 7: Simulations) has further information and graphics. The Hydra team regularly post testing results on the site[618] and welcome more real-world test scenarios. Hydra is starting to bear fruits. Obsidian Systems and IOG announced *Hydra for Payments*[619] which is exciting prospect for micropayments on Cardano. At the Rare Bloom community event in Denver, SundaeSwap demoed how their protocol could work as a Hydra Head.[620]

Hydra clarifications

- There has been some discussion promoting Hydra as the 'ultimate' be-all and end-all Cardano scalability strategy. Hydra Heads provide a solid basis on which to develop Cardano's scalability layer. They are a critical building piece that allows more complicated solutions to be built on top of the Extended Unspent Transaction Output (EUTXO) architecture. They are an important part of the scaling journey, but they are not the end goal.

  Mithril's development is closely tied to that of Hydra, with overlapping teams. Some of Mithril's components can connect and work fine with Hydra. Their websites, mithril.network and hydra.family, share a similar format with excellent quick start guides, glossary, etc. As they are both open-source projects, anyone can contribute to these pages on GitHub.

- A Hydra Head is usually a relatively small-scale network created by a small number of people. Because these groups will be autonomous at first, looking at the total of their separate metrics is deceptive. Although Hydra Head protocol's initial iteration will enable small groups of participants to scale up their traffic at a reasonable cost, it will not provide a solution for worldwide consumer-to-consumer (micro) payments or NFT sales right away.

  Why? Because the consensus inside a Head necessitates each participant's response to each transaction, everyone needs to agree on each transaction. While this offers security assurances to participants in a Hydra Head, it limits the total number of participants in practice. IOG, and the growing number of contributors to the project, continue to research ways to expand the Hydra Head protocol's capabilities. In 2021, there was a paper released from Tokyo Institute of

[617] MMT Chakravarty, S Coretti, M Fitzi, P Gazi, P Kant, A Kiayias, and A Russell (2020) 'Hydra: fast isomorphic state channels'(Section 7 – Simulations), eprint.iacr.org/2020/299.pdf

[618] Hydra Head benchmarking, hydra.family/head-protocol/benchmarks

[619] Hydra for Payments, /en/blog/posts/2022/11/10/hydra-for-payments-introducing-developer-tooling-to-unlock-micropayments-on-cardano/

[620] SundaeSwap Labs Hydra demo, twitter.com/sundaeswap/status/1580969361892085762?lang=en

Technology titled *Interhead Hydra: Two Heads are Better than One*.[621] It is an iteration on top of Hydra Head proposing a mechanism for linking two Hydra Heads together, allowing the formation of a network of linked Hydra Heads in the long term.

- There is a **risk for non-participants** as your funds are in the hands of the participants operating the Hydra Head.

- A Hydra Head protocol is **not a sidechain**. There are no blocks created in a Hydra Head, nor is there any transaction history available outside the Head. New participants cannot join an existing Head. They need to be there from the start as an operating Head is an isolated, private channel.

Hydra's future

Hydra's team lead, Sebastian Nagel, presented at the 2022 Cardano Summit in Lausanne.[622] Afterwards the team sat down to finalize strategy for the coming year. The goal now is for Hydra to be the number one DApp on Cardano, regardless of how this is measured.

Those familiar with Cardano's weekly dev updates will already know 2022 was about building out Hydra Heads's functionality and stabilizing performance so early pioneers could test. 2023 will be all about adoption and exploring new use cases. For example, TxPipe are working on *Hydra Head as a service* through their platform Demeter (demeter.run)

Hydra Head is due to for V1 release early 2023 but is only the first part of a larger group of protocols as described in Chakravarty and co *Hydra: Fast Isomorphic State-Channels*. As Hydra matures and adoption grows, several topologies will be implemented. It's best to check hydra.network for the latest roadmap. Current plans include a 'Delegated Node', a 'Managed Hydra Head' (aka Hydra as a Service) and a 'Star-shaped Network'.

IOG collaborated with Mlabs (mlabs.city) to produce the *Implementing auction projects using Hydra*[623] paper. The study explores various ways to implement digital asset auctions using the Hydra Head protocol. This is central to how DEXs and NFTs will function on Cardano. The paper addresses current project needs and considerations in detail. Discussions are ongoing on Discord and GitHub.

Sep 21, 2022. Re: Hydra: CH[624]

---

[621] Jourenko, Larangeira, TanakaInterhead Hydra Two Heads are Better than One, eprint.iacr.org/2021/1188

[622] Sebastian Nagel Hydra talk, summit.cardano.org/agenda-day-2/cardano-ballot-speaker-winner-presentation-6/

[623] Implementing auction projects using Hydra, iohk.io/en/blog/posts/2023/01/20/implementing-auction-projects-using-hydra/

[624] Charles Hoskinson Interview: Your Cardano Questions Answered, youtu.be/PV_C17noXlA?t=3276

When you look at things like Mithril, Hydra… these are extensions of known concepts, like Mithril is a threshold signature idea, and they construct these proof certificates, and then when you do transactions, they're paired with proof certificates, and it gives you the inclusive accountability …it's not a new idea, it's like 10 years of talking about this stuff. We just implemented it. It's a lot of hard cryptography to implement, but once it's done it's done, and it's more about how do you distribute the certificate and build them?

Hydra is everything Lightning[625] wanted to be when it grows up. The problem with Lightning is that it's not a hard protocol… payment channels and state channels. The hard part is the fact that Bitcoin is not programmable. So, 95% of your effort is trying to figure out how do you get a model, that's not designed for this, to work with this.

It's almost like when they were upgrading the Hubble telescope in space, you know, after you've launched the telescope into space, it's not upgradable anymore, but yet NASA is like 'well we need to fix it'. So, they sent astronauts out there, and they put this giant contact lens on it, and they had to figure out how to open shit that you really can only open on Earth, in space. So, you have this guy like basically wearing an oven mitt, with a very tiny screwdriver floating in space, trying to unscrew a panel and gradually upgrade old circuitry, and make it better without getting himself killed. So that's Bitcoin in a nutshell, when you try to apply Lightning.
Well with Cardano, we're on Earth, okay, it's programmable meaning that we can always go and pull a module out, put a new module in, and do these things. So, with extended UTXO and Plutus, there's enough there that you can build rich isomorphic state channels. So basically, you can take state and assets, and you can batch and bundle them together, and put them into a layer 2 solution…and then you can use it for microtransactions, you can use it for smart contracts, but then you can build modules on top of it to do specific applications like DEXs, voting… these types of things. In particular, one area I'm very interested to use Hydra in 2023, is to reuse that technology to do all the stuff we're doing right now with Catalyst and voting.

Oct 3, 2022. Re: Hydra, Let's Talk Basho. CH[626]

So the way that we designed Plutus is that you have an on-chain component, and that's your Plutus script… and then you have this idea of off-chain infrastructure that coordinates with the DApp to run things… and this is very common in the

---

[625] The **Lightning Network** is a Layer 2 payment protocol that operates on top of a blockchain. It theoretically enables fast transactions between participating nodes and has been touted as a solution to the bitcoin scalability problem.

[626] Let's Talk Basho, youtu.be/fhVo-2QUjLM?t=460

Ethereum model as well and they have all these things to combine these two, and then off-chain infrastructure sometimes is centralized, sometimes it's not centralized, it depends on the specific DApp. The idea of Hydra is that it would be part of that off-chain kit, so it would be embedded in DApps that require a lot of scale, and basically it would do something similar to what's occurring with Mithril, where you go many-to-one or some

Sidechains

A sidechain is a blockchain that is linked to a main blockchain (the mainchain, or parent chain) through a two-way mechanism (a 'bridge') that allows tokens and other digital assets from one chain to be utilized in another and the results to be shared back and forth. Multiple interoperable sidechains may be joined to a single parent chain, each of which can function in a different fashion.

A sidechain is the exact same concept as a blockchain. The difference is philosophical, not technical. The sidechain usually aligns with the mainchain, but a sidechain can have its own business logic, cryptocurrency, monetary policy, consensus rules, programming language, application domain, subset of users, smart-contract capabilities, stablecoins, use cases like NFTs, loyalty points, etc. Side chains are the same technically as a standalone blockchain, in that blocks are produced by validators.

Unlike state-channels such as Hydra, they offer data-availability and participation for new users. In a state-channel, typically only participants of the channel can see what is going on in the channel, and they must be decided up front. Joining a sidechain is typically done by burning or locking assets on the mainchain, in return for an equal amount on the sidechain.

Cardano's eUTXO model means the state is pre-sharded on the mainchain, so it's easier to move state to a sidechain. Sidechains are ideal for medium to low-risk protocols. They are ideal for new, or growing ecosystems because the sidechain can avail of an established mainchain's security, liquidity, wallets, and user participation. Sidechains lighten the load off layer 1 mainnet, all the while enjoying the veracity that's provided by its parent chain.

While there will be large transaction volumes running in parallel on sidechains, these transactions don't reconcile on the mainchain so resources on the Layer 1 mainchain aren't consumed by sidechains.

A lot of deep thought and academic rigor went into Cardano's architecture. It's evident in how rewards incentivize sidechain partnerships. Ada holders traditionally get staking rewards in ada. The same SPOs that power the mainchain, will also provide staking liquidity for sidechains. So now, if the SPO you delegate to is also part of the sidechain SPO subset, you get rewards in that sidechain's native asset in addition to your usual ada rewards.

Re: Sidechains, Let's Talk Basho. CH:

> *It's basically like super-Hydra. Hydra is DApp-specific, sidechains are*
> *ecosystem-specific*

There are often trade-offs to running a sidechain. Increased throughput can mean less security. Bridge security is challenging in practice and there have been many hacks in 2022.[627] However, Cardano offers a very secure layer 1 mainchain. Funds in a bridge contract are well protected and assets are securely transferred between sidechains based on the formal definition outlined in IOG's 2019 *Proof-of-Stake Sidechains* paper.[628]

The research describes how a new 'firewall' security property protects a mainchain from its sidechains. Potential failures on the sidechain won't impact the parent chain. Project Catalyst, for example, is run as a sidechain of Cardano. Even if its safety is compromised, no funds are lost on Cardano. The paper also outlines a blueprint describing merged staking, cross-chain certification, and multi-signature for proof-of-stake sidechains.

Based on this research, IOG has developed the Cardano EVM (Ethereum Virtual Machine) sidechain, Mamba, following a deliberate and iterative approach. It is an open-source sidechain protocol with a client written in Scala. Mamba is compatible with Ethereum's tools and libraries enabling developers to write Solidity smart contracts, DApps, and ERC20 tokens on Cardano. Ethereum smart contracts can run unchanged on Mamba, with much lower *gas* fees.

The consensus protocol used on Mamba is Ourorobos BFT. The was an earlier iteration of Ouroboros used on the Cardano mainnet. It is a simple, deterministic protocol for ledger consensus that tolerates Byzantine faults.[629] There are different versions of proof-of-stake (PoS), which are suited to different use cases on sidechains and mainchains. Sebastien Guillemot gives an excellent breakdown of the trade-offs in his video *Cardano & Algorand: Leader Selection Explained.*

On a Carano360[630] episode, Kathryn Stacy, Product Manager for Sidechains, explained how IOG plans to enable more programmability by making it easy for developers to contribute. IOG is granting access to the EVM source code so developers can use the code as a framework to create their own EVM sidechains. This vision is to create an 'ecosystem of ecosystems'.

---

[627] Hackers have stolen $1.4 billion this year using crypto bridges, cnbc.com/2022/08/10/hackers-have-stolen-1point4-billion-this-year-using-crypto-bridges.html

[628] Gazi, Kiayias, Zindors (2019), 'Proof-of-Stake Sidechains', iohk.io/en/research/library/papers/proof-of-stake-sidechains/

[629] A Byzantine fault is any fault presenting different symptoms to different observers. A Byzantine failure is the loss of a system service due to a Byzantine fault in systems that require consensus among distributed nodes.

[630] June 2022 Cardano360 Sidechains clip, youtu.be/ShBFTaD8nss?t=381

Sidechains Toolkit components

Main chain scripts

- Allow main chain expansion without modifications to Cardano
- Enable secure cross-chain transactions

Chain follower

- Tracks data on main chain

Sidechain module

- Interprets main chain data and implements the necessary ledger adaptations

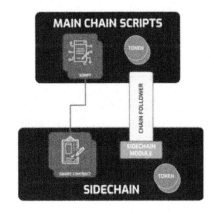

Figure 54: slide from Dominik Zajkowski's talk at ScotFest

Dominik Zajkowski, IOG Technical Architect, expanded on this vision at ScotFest. He explained the Plutus scripts for maintaining the EVM Mamba sidechain would be made available as a toolkit to be used as a reference template, a kind of SDK for future sidechains with Cardano being the core root of trust. Zajkowski explained the toolkit is intentionally incomplete and invited community feedback on features they wanted to see. All these areas will be worked on with the community as we go. The documentation[631] is now live and includes the technical spec.

As use cases are scoped out and placeholders are filled, perhaps a sexy flagship sidechain might jumpstart activity, and that's where *Midnight* comes in…

Midnight in the Garden of Good and Evil

At ScotFest, Charles Hoskinson revealed his team had been working on another cryptocurrency for the past four years. It is called *Midnight* and will be a Cardano sidechain with a native token called *dust*. As mentioned before, the way sidechains work on Cardano is as a partnership. Midnight gains decentralization, security, infrastructure, liquidity and a thriving ecosystem from Cardano. In return, Midnight pays rent in the form of *dust* rewards to the SPOs and delegators.

IOG reviewed existing privacy solutions like Monero and Zcash and felt they could do better. Research on the privacy requirements for smart contracts has been ongoing for

---

[631] Sidechain SDK docs, docs.cardano.org/cardano-sidechains/sidechain-toolkit/introduction

some time. *Kachina-Foundations of Private Smart Contracts*[632] is a paper Charles Hoskinson ranks as 'one of our most forward-thinking publications'.[633]

IOGs brains thrust (the likes of zero knowledge expert Dr Markulf Kohlweiss) went to work and reviewed other solutions like Zexe[634] and concluded that three 'must have' properties were absent in the blockchain space today. Abbreviated to 'ACE', they are: freedom of **A**ssociation, freedom of **C**ommerce and freedom of **E**xpression.

These basic human rights are not always present in some jurisdictions for various reasons. Midnight will offer confidentiality and privacy with the ability to freely associate with people and engage in legitimate commercial transactions.

There is also the regulatory side. It is not illegal to seek confidentiality and privacy in most circumstances. As many people believe crypto is cloaked in secrecy and only used for nefarious activity, new DApps need to protect user rights and wishes, but also enable them to comply with regulatory requirements. DApps on Midnight enable users to protect their own data, to keep their data in their own systems. They don't have to share everything but can share assertions about their personal data based on things like KYC and AML, and the body on the other side of the transaction can trust that those assertions are correct. Selective disclosure is not the same as a 'back door', fake news[635] and FUD has already been called out and corrected on this matter.

Midnight goes beyond just privacy transactions and attempts to support true confidentiality with private smart contracts. To implement this concept of keeping something private to the public, yet still be enabling voluntary or involuntary disclosures. One obvious use case for this is regulation. If you move into an exclusive neighborhood, or upgrade your car to a Ferrari, your friends shouldn't be able to look up your bank balance. Your bank, however, is obliged to enquire where you got your money from, once you go over a certain limit depending on the jurisdiction.

How will this be achieved? Atala Prism will be tightly integrated with Midnight, linking identities and privacy. *Lace* light wallet will provide easy access to innovative features like *dead men switches*[636] for estate planning and multi-party computation[637] features. Monero and Zcash are proven solutions for keeping your transactions and tokens private,

---

[632] Kerber, Kiayias, Kohlweiss (2021) 'Kachina - Foundations of Private Smart Contracts', eprint.iacr.org/2020/543.pdf

[633] Charles Hoskinson Kachina tweet, twitter.com/iohk_charles/status/1261328840023961602?lang=en

[634] Zexe: Enabling Decentralized Private Computation, eprint.iacr.org/2018/962.pdf

[635] Cardano Midnight: Monero Retracts Negative Statements, u.today/cardano-midnight-monero-retracts-negative-statements

[636] A dead man's switch is a switch that is designed to be activated or deactivated if the human operator becomes incapacitated, or dies. Typically, funds may be sent to a preset address after a set time has expired.

[637] MPC (multi-party computation) enables multiple parties – each holding their own private data – to evaluate a computation without ever revealing any of the private data held by each party.

but programmability is required too. The Kachina paper explores how to write private smart contracts, and IOG have been busy bringing the theory to life.

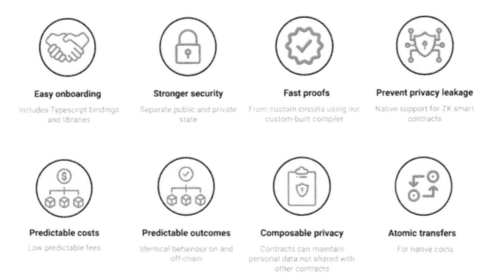

Figure 55: Why *Midnight* stands out, from IOG's Chief Strategy Officer Rob Adams talk at ScotFest

After many years of research and development, they created a virtual machine in Typescript. This is significant in terms of developer adoption. Typescript (~35%), a superset of JavaScript (65%), is one of the most popular programming languages in the world.[638] For perspective, Haskell adoption languishes somewhere between (1-2%). IOG are taking a developer-first approach with Midnight, in contrast to Plutus, which arrived some years after Cardano launched.

With regulation on the industry's doorstep, Midnight looks like an astute strategic move by IOG. Regulators have a daunting task trying to legislate for a nascent industry with emerging technology sometimes not yet in production. Midnight offers a potential middle ground where core principles of crypto can be upheld, but also enable DApps meet compliance requirements in different locales.

Just one example is when a large global enterprise needs to comply with GDPR requirements in Europe, but still have a different US version to comply with requirements in the Bank Secrecy Act. Most companies face large penalties if they fail to keep user data private. There are many other obvious use cases from making medical data accessible, to enabling underground newspapers in volatile societies to operate.

Charles Hoskinson mentioned in his New Year's Eve twitter space[639] sidechains will be rolled out based on the Japanese martial arts concept of *Shuhari* …you learn, you do,

---

[638] The top programming languages, statista.com/statistics/793628/worldwide-developer-survey-most-used-languages/

[639] New Years Eve Hangout with Charles,
twitter.com/IOHK_Charles/status/1609417098396323840?t=42JFCPU8bk_mbwlix8wGlw&s=19

then you teach. IOG 'learned' with the Mamba proof of concept, now they will 'do' with Midnight and 'teach' with various toolkits, blogs and formal papers.

> *What will happen is that you take a subset of the stake pool operators, who currently operate Cardano, they signal that they want to make blocks in this new chain, and then you basically have a selection algorithm that puts them into a BFT protocol, and then they form that quorum for an epoch. Now the advantage of that protocol, with that type of structure is that you get this very optimised high-speed, BFT protocol and your quorum sampling is done from the mainchain ...and so you can roll back the security to the level of participation, and the set of stake pool operators that you have... and how that's going to work generically, will be written down in a research paper, just like we write all these different things. That will be a turnkey model and then the goal is to deploy that algorithm on Cosmos and probably ScoreX and (Hyperledger)Fabric would be the three things that I'd like to see that deployed through. So Fabric 3, ScoreX and Cosmos.*

> *Then you have these sidechain builder kits. Fabric would be a kit, Cosmos and ScoreX would be a kit... and that's a stub, and all the infrastructure is already there, and so you just parameterise the network logic, the ledger rules and the transaction logic in the system... but you wouldn't have to worry so much about how do I make a sidechain? How do I get transactions to move back and forth? ...and how do I get it to work with wallets?.. and all these other things...it's almost like launching an ERC20.*

If you have already read the 2016 'Why cardano?' paper, what was described above might all sound familiar. The original proposal was for a CSL (Cardano Settlement Layer) and a CCL (Cardano Computation Layer). This vision has manifested itself slightly differently in the sidechains model. This multi-computational framework is designed to cater for a broad range of requirements from partner chains. So, in effect, there will be multiple CCLs... Midnight and potentially World Mobile, Hyperledger Fabric and Cosmos are the early candidates to form a library of different templates available for putting various sidechains in place.

Visit *midnight.iohk.io* to sign up for more information

Milkomeda

Not everyone is enamored with Cardano's current architecture. CTO and co-found of dcSpark, Sebastien Guillemot, questioned[640] Cardano's monolithic structure and why it has deviated from the initial vision in 'Why Cardano?'. Having worked on the protocol since the incentivized testnet days, his views should be taken seriously. Having said that, there are trade-offs in any blockchain decisions.

---

[640] Cardano: the problem & the whitepaper to fix it, youtube.com/watch?v=LIEM6qbc-x8

Cardano is an open ecosystem and people are free to launch sidechains using different models. The first Cardano sidechain was launched dcSpark. *Milkomeda* brings EVM compatibility and a bridge for developers to the Ethereum ecosystem. Milkomeda is a portmanteau, named after the *Milky Way* and *Andromeda* galaxies which are due to merge in a few billion years. Milkomeda also brings EVM compatibility to Algorand as well, merging multiple ecosystems. What is interesting is Milkomeda is currently implemented differently on both blockchains. It is a Cardano sidechain with a growing number of DApps, [641] but a Layer 2 solution on Algorand.

Guillemot explained the differences and reasoning at the Rare Bloom event.[642] As discussed previously, a sidechain is a blockchain that aligns technically with a parent chain but differs philosophically on key features. Milkomeda C1, for example, is the Cardano sidechain where they chose to keep the same base asset (ada) but has faster block times (4 secs) with instant finality. It wasn't possible to implement Milkomeda as a Layer 2 solution on Cardano at this time due to some technical obstacles, which will likely be resolved as features like Mithril mature.

With funding from Catalyst,[643] dcSpark will soon add wrapped smart contracts to extend interoperability further. Developers will soon be able to call EVM smart contracts from the Cardano mainnet. The UX will be frictionless, with the end user oblivious to the fact that they're using an EVM underneath. Wrapped smart contracts also enable wrapped Oracles to provide off-chain data. This feature will integrate access to existing EVM-based Oracles to the Cardano mainnet.

Milkomeda A1 is a Layer 2 on Algorand. While a sidechain gives you greater flexibility but less security, a Layer 2 gives you full security with mathematical proofs, but less flexibility as you need to program everything in zero-knowledge (ZK) circuits.

What is a Layer 2 scaling solution?

These are the generally 3 types Layer 2 solutions.

- State Channels (like Hydra, or the Lightning Network on bitcoin)
- ZK Rollups
- Optimistic Rollups

Both ZK and optimistic rollups collect off-chain transactions into a batch, then submit them to the Layer 1 blockchain as one transaction.

A **Zero-knowledge (ZK) rollup** is built on top of the existing Layer 1 blockchain to make the transactions faster, cheaper, scalable, secure, and private by not disclosing everything while transacting with the verifier. The problem with many other Layer 2 solutions is that they are not secure enough. There is a trade-off where they focus more on scalability, which can leave them open to exploits. ZK rollups are so powerful as it's

[641] Milkomeda dApps, milkomeda.com/dapp-store

[642] Sebastien Guillemot Milkomeda Update, youtube.com/watch?v=LlxTmDPw_cs

[643] Milkomeda Oracle, cardano.ideascale.com/c/idea/369192

much faster to prove you know the answer, rather than doing the computing to get the answer.

Optimistic rollups are less secure than ZK Roll-Ups but offer greater flexibility because they don't require everything to be encoded in a ZK circuit. In contrast to ZK rollups where you prove everything is correct, you are just proving dishonesty (with Fraud proofs) as required. As the name suggests, you optimistically presume transactions are valid, or using fraud proofs to prove false transactions within 7 days.

ZK rollups are more scalable as they consume less blockchain resources compared to Optimistic rollups. ZK rollups are **difficult** to implement today, mainly because they take time to compile and can slow down your DApp. This is improving every year, however, and it is hot research space.

Ethereum has a huge focus on ZK roll-ups with many projects trying to dominate. @StakeWithPride[644] pointed out some dubious design fundamentals and values coming out of the Ethereum community. In a video from a core developer, there is an admission that a serious hack is likely with ZK roll-ups on Ethereum. The proposed solution is to leverage Intel SGX trusted enclaves[645] to ensure security.

On Cardano, there was already the unsuccessful Orbis ZK project funded by Catalyst.[646] Dr Markulf Kohlweiss announced the ZK Lab at Edinburgh University and dcSpark have marked ZK research as a priority in 2023.

April 20, 2022, '4/20 Hangout with Charles' Twitter space,[647]

Re: L2 scaling solutions, ZK roll ups… CH:

> *Why do we care about this technology? Why is this useful to me as a consumer? Ok, let's say you go to a bar, and you get carded. When you show your driver's license to the bartender, you reveal more than just your age. You reveal your precise age. Oftentimes, the driver's license has an address on it. If you're an organ donor or not, a picture of you, your gender, you reveal some of them... I think they put Social Security numbers on the driver's license, military ID, and even more, a passport. You get all this stuff that the bartender should not know.*
>
> *The bartender is looking for a threshold condition. Are you above or below the drinking age? That's all they need, it's a Boolean yes or no. Are you over 21?... at or over 21? So, what a zero-knowledge proof can do is, for an identity system with digital ID, you can prove to that bartender that you're over at the age of 21 but reveal nothing else about you. No other metadata, and an abstraction you*

---

[644] *StakeWithPride* re: Ethereum zk roll-ups, twitter.com/StakeWithPride/status/1607511445549514752

[645] The core idea of SGX is the creation of a software 'enclave'. The enclave is basically a separated and encrypted region for code and data.

[646] Orbis: Layer 2 ZK Rollup https://cardano.ideascale.com/c/idea/396617

[647] April 20, 2022, '4/20 Hangout with Charles' Twitter space, twitter.com/i/spaces/1lDGLLABeBkGm

can do that for any challenge response protocol. Are you a US citizen or not? Is the money that I've received taxed or not? Are you fully compliant with laws in the state of Colorado? or not? Yes or no. These types of things. Are you eligible to see this information? Yes or no. You remove that judgment in that respect.

Now the other application is, do you own this money or not? Zero knowledge proofs are perfect for this application, because basically you're proving that the money exists and that you have the right to spend it, but you're not revealing which money it is, and you're not revealing who you are. So that's why they're used in privacy systems.

Other interoperability solutions

There is a growing list of builders on Cardano. For example, Wanchain[648] is a bi-directional decentralized, non-custodial cross-chain bridge linking Cardano to other tier 1 blockchains. As well as being a decentralized interoperability solution, Wanchain is layer 1 proof-of-stake (PoS) blockchain with an Ethereum-like ecosystem that supports industry-standard Ethereum tools, DApps, and protocols. It has certain similarities to Cardano. Wanchain employs the Galaxy Consensus PoS consensus method, which employs several cryptographic approaches, such as distributed secret sharing and threshold signatures, to enhance random number generation and block creation processes. Galaxy Consensus is a continuation of Cardano's own Ouroboros protocol.

To understand more check out *Rollups on Cardano Discussion.*[649] IOG have contributed to this space with their paper on Sonic: Zero Knowledge SNARKS.[650]

Input Endorsers

By separating transactions into pre-constructed blocks, input endorsers increase block propagation speeds and throughput (amount of data transferred). This increases block propagation consistency and enables increased transaction rates.

Input endorsers were described by John Woods (ex IOG, now Algorand CTO) as a 'near end game solution' for Layer 1 scaling that will put Cardano on the top of the pile when it comes to throughput for Layer 1.

The current process is to scoop transactions out of mempool, forge a block, then send it on to peers. With input endorsers, blocks will be created on an ad hoc basis, signed and counter-signed, and will be flying around the network on a near second-by-second basis.

---

[648] Temujin Louie, 'Guest blog: collaborating on Cardano interoperability', iog.io/en/blog/posts/2022/04/27/guest-blog-collaborating-on-cardano-interoperability/

[649] Rollups on Cardano Discussion | Cardano Live #48, youtube.com/watch?v=4DslvkLop04

[650] Maller, Bowe, Kohlweiss, Meiklejohn (2019), 'Sonic: Zero-Knowledge SNARKs from Linear-Size Universal and Updateable Structured Reference Strings', eprint.iacr.org/2019/099.pdf

The existing network Ouroboros Praos, where a block is generated every 20 seconds, is adequately meeting user demands. Input Endorsers will, however, keep Cardano ahead of the curve for the demands coming down the tracks with more and more businesses deploying on Cardano, as Plutus and Marlowe mature.

Currently, blocks are responsible for both consensus and holding transaction data. Input Endorsers divide each block in two. One of the blocks is responsible for consensus, with the other faster block assigned for holding transaction data.

The consensus block will essentially be freed up from its duty of managing transaction data. It will now have a pointer (using 'reference semantics') to the block holding the transaction data. This will reduce bottlenecks and the 20 second wait time, enabling blocks to be streamed constantly.

Input Endorsers were muted as far back as the original Ouroboros paper in 2016. Similar to block producers (BP), input endorsers (IE) are described as a stakeholder entity, in the sense that the amount of stake delegated to them affects their capacity to function.

According to Section 8.1 of the paper:

> *Input-endorsers create a second layer of transaction endorsing prior to block inclusion. [..] Note that input-endorsers are assigned to slots in the same way that slot leaders are, and inputs included in blocks are only acceptable if they are endorsed by an eligible input-endorser.*

also

> *Note that blocks and endorsed inputs are diffused independently with each block containing from 0 up to d endorsed inputs.*

IOG researcher Peter Gaži explained the input endorsers concept[651] at the Cardano Summit 2021. Input endorsers echo some concepts discussed in a paper called *Prism: Scaling Bitcoin by 10,000x*[652] which is complemented by a video presentation[653] on *Prism* (not to be confused with IOG's *Atala Prism* Decentralized Identity solution).

Professor Aggelos Kiayias gave a more detailed explanation in his video[654] whose formulas and math are beyond the scope of this book. It's clear, however, that input endorsers are kind of an anthology of the best of Cardano as they leverage the power of Mithril, the Extended UTXO model, previous research on ledger combiners and the foundations established by Ouroboros.

---

[651] Ouroboros Family (Input Endorsers), youtu.be/PF1SW7e137A?t=1760

[652] Prism: Scaling Bitcoin by 10,000x, arxiv.org/abs/1909.11261

[653] Presentation, Prism: Scaling Bitcoin, youtube.com/watch?v=gTJyDtuWvUQ

[654] Advances in Ouroboros: Scaling for Future Growth, youtube.com/watch?v=xKv94MwSNBw

In the video, Prof Kiayias explained Ouroboros uses a 'longest chain' protocol[655] similar to Bitcoin, except it is based on proof of stake.[656] So it inherits all the decentralization and security benefits of Bitcoin, but with much less energy expenditure. 'Longest chain' protocols have serious performance limitations in terms of throughput. If a pipe represents a consensus protocol, where width is the throughput and length is the settlement time, then we want a nice wide, short pipe.

Based on research[657] IOG published at the *ACM Computer and Communications Security Symposium* in 2021, it's possible to derive the upper bound for the throughput in a longest chain protocol. This works out to be only 8%, leaving 92% of the throughput capacity untapped. Ouroboros *Leios*, and specifically input endorsers, will resolve this critical shortcoming.

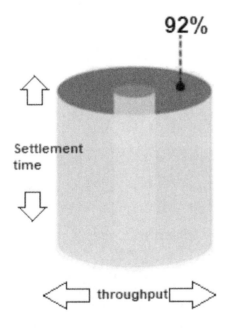

Figure 56: Longest chain protocol represented as a pipe

---

[655] The **longest chain** is what individual nodes accept as the valid version of the blockchain. The rule that nodes adopt the longest chain of blocks allows every node on the network to agree on what the blockchain looks like, and therefore agree on the same transaction history. The Longest Chain Rule ensures that the network will recognise the 'chain with most work' as the main chain. The chain with the most work is typically (not always) the longest of the forks.

[656] Proof-of-Stake Longest Chain Protocols: Security vs Predictability, tselab.stanford.edu/downloads/PoS_LC_SBC2020.pdf

[657] Gaži, Kiayias, Russell (2020), 'Tight Consistency Bounds for Bitcoin', eprint.iacr.org/2020/661.pdf

As mentioned previously, Ouroboros uses a networking strategy of applying *backpressure* to cope with times when there is peak demand for transaction processing. The system processes what blocks it can, while transactions wait in line to be pulled in for processing. Under peak traffic conditions, transactions will still be processed, but they have to wait their turn.

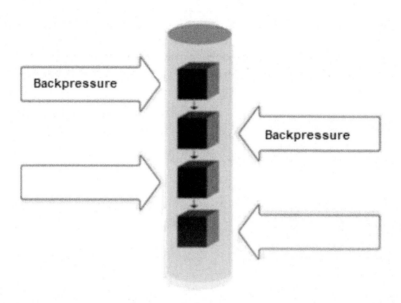

Figure 57: Backpressure networking concept

Input endorsers release segments of mempool (or 'backup mempools with special privileges' as a user on Stack Exchange[658] referred to them) to float around before they're considered for processing in a mainchain block. These floating segments of mempool are called 'input blocks.' This allows block producers to free up space in their mempools so they have more capacity to pull transactions in. Mempool segmentation needs to be concurrent across all block producers.

IOG plans on adopting practices from spread spectrum communications[659] to ensure there is minimal overlap between input blocks. Valid input blocks are checked as with longest chain blocks, but additionally, they are attested via the issuance of Mithril certificates. This means input blocks are transformed into verified transaction batches to be included in the mainchain by reference only. Input blocks' transactions and scripts are processed

---

[658] Input Endorsers on stack exchange, cardano.stackexchange.com/questions/4626/what-are-input-endorsers-and-how-do-they-make-cardano-more-scalable

[659] In telecommunication and radio communication, **spread-spectrum techniques** are methods by which a signal generated with a particular bandwidth is deliberately spread in the frequency domain, resulting in a signal with a wider bandwidth.

externally from the mainchain block validation. Longest chain 'ranking blocks' are used to organize or 'rank' these floating input blocks.

The serialization nature of longest chain protocol resolves 'double-spending' in input blocks. This strategy also leverages the strengths of the Extended UTXO model as script execution and validation occurs away from mainchain validation. The goal of higher throughput is now possible as the idle 92% capacity can now be utilized. The graphic below captures all the moving parts to input endorsers.

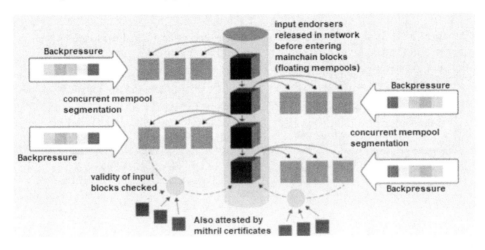

Figure 58: Input Endorsers graphic adapted from Professor Kiayias explainer video

How this groundbreaking academic research will go from theory to a real-life implementation became a little clearer in November 2022. Input endorsers will be the primary component of *Ouroboros Leois* and will be proposed, community-reviewed and finalized via CIP 79. As we are now in the 'age of Voltaire', everything is open source, encouraging feedback and participation. *Leios* will be a 'substantial extension' of the Ouroboros protocol. It is described in greater depth in a longer paper[660] included as part of this CIP.

The paper is also available on GitHub[661] and is surprisingly readable. This is perhaps by design to attract as much discussion and engagement as possible in the initial stages. It was written by IOG chief architect Duncan Coutts, often described as a 'real life wizard' by Charles Hoskinson. You can peer inside his mind and follow the debate with other deep thinkers such as nuclear physicist Michael Lisenfelt here.[662]

---

[660] Coutts, Panagiotakos, Fitzi (2022), 'Ouroboros Leios: design goals and concepts', iohk.io/en/research/library/papers/ouroboros-leios-design-goals-and-concepts/

[661] CIPs/CIP-0079/README.md, github.com/cardano-foundation/CIPs/blob/ouroboros-leios/CIP-0079/README.md

[662] CIP-0079? | Implement Ouroboros Leios to increase Cardano throughput, github.com/cardano-foundation/CIPs/pull/379

The paper details exactly how input endorsers might work. At a high level, the research proposes moving from a sequential blockchain to a parallel blockchain. *Leios* will decouple the consensus from the validation of blocks, meaning blocks will be validated constantly.

With the current Ourorboros Praos protocol, the time during which a block is forged and diffused across the network is only a fraction of the overall average time between blocks. Currently on Cardano mainnet: blocks are produced on average every 20 seconds, but the time to send blocks across the network is within 5 seconds (this is the Δ parameter).

Before the block arrives at a node, that node is idle, and after it has downloaded, validated and forwarded the block then it will return to being idle. *Leois* proposes different ways to make better use of idle resources.

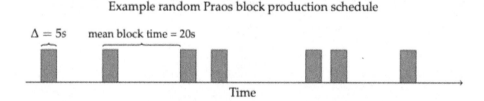

Figure 59: Ouroboros Praos block diffusion time (Δ) is a fraction of time between blocks

A distributed system of nodes is a parallel system, but *Ouroboros Praos* is a sequential algorithm. Any such sequential algorithm running on a parallel system will leave resources unused. The algorithm is sequential because the structure of the blockchain itself is linear.

Ouroboros *Leios* will attempt to deploy a 'concurrent blockchain' to achieve a parallel distributed algorithm for constructing the chain. By controlling the degree of concurrency and parallelism in the algorithm, this will enable larger workloads where currently unused idle resources are put to work. The paper clarifies the terms:

> *We distinguish concurrency and parallelism: concurrency is about data or events that are not sequenced with respect to each other, whereas parallelism is about using more computer hardware to compute more quickly.*

The paper goes into greater detail on how this could be achieved with new types of objects such as input blocks, endorsement blocks, endorsement reports, endorsement certificates, and ranking blocks. The above linked paper and CIP outline the many considerations and risks with such a complex solution and will no doubt evolve and update as further prototyping and simulation eventually arrives at the best design. The first such public simulation was presented by Benjamin Beckmann (IOG Director of Architecture & Infrastructure) at ScotFest.[663]

---

[663] Driving continued technology advancement through Input Endorsers, youtube.com/watch?v=IGu_1bl6UHQ

The exhaustive process will follow the familiar trail of security analysis, peer review, auditing, formalization a precise description of the expected behaviors to clarify the design to engineering, performance testing, prototyping, updates to the ledger…and all this is dependent on progress with other features such as 'On disk storage of ledger state', a successful Ouroboros *Genesis* rollout, increased adoption of light wallets, etc.

Only then will a hard fork to *Leios* be possible. It is an ambitious vision, but IOG and the Cardano community are building on granite, reaping the rewards of doing things the right way from the start. All the features and concepts described in this book are anchored in deep academic research, peer-reviewed by the brightest minds in cryptography and implemented based on formal specifications.

Oct 3, 2022. Re: Input Endorsers, Let's Talk Basho. CH[664]

> So, what happens is that you go from this standard process of a chain of blocks, and there's only one canonical view, to basically, doing a lot of these things asynchronously and in parallel, and they just kind of get batched together, and then asynchronously and in parallel, lots of stuff happens and then they get batched together… So, this concept of input blocks and key blocks, as discussed in our parallel chains paper.[665]

> Now this batching…you think of Mithril certificates where you talk about batching transactions, events together …you also could reuse this technology in the extended UTXO model to patch blocks together. So, it gives you a way of figuring out conflict-free history, and potentially what this means is that you have asynchronous parallel processing of an enormous amount of events. So, the throughput gains, assuming new data structures, and assuming new designs, are gargantuan for this because you basically can be real time, continuously running computations. Right now, in the current design, only 0.25% of your block time budget is for computation.

> So, running execution of scripts… so that's incredibly limiting …0.25%, not 25%, but 0.25% of your block time is for script execution, so it's a very scarce resource. Here it's asynchronous, so it's continuous execution. So, we expect to see not just a 10x, but a very very very significant increase in speed, and a reduction in cost…

---

[664] Let's Talk Basho, youtu.be/fhVo-2QUjLM?t=780

[665] Fitzi, Gaži, Kiayias, Russell (2018), 'Parallel Chains: Improving Throughput and Latency of Blockchain Protocols via Parallel Composition', iohk.io/en/research/library/papers/parallel-chains-improving-throughput-and-latency-of-blockchain-protocols-via-parallel-composition

Chapter 9: Voltaire (Governance)

'No problem can withstand the assault of sustained thinking.'

- Voltaire

Money is social

With a few noteworthy exceptions most cryptocurrencies have made no provision for future upgrades. The capacity to effectively drive a soft or hard fork is critical to a cryptocurrency's long-term viability. As a result, the moneymen are unlikely to invest millions of dollars on protocols whose roadmap and participants are fleeting, petty, or extremist. There must be an efficient procedure for forming agreement on a vision for the underlying protocol's evolution. Fragmentation might split the group apart if this process is difficult.

Cryptocurrencies are an excellent illustration of money's social component. When comparing Bitcoin and Litecoin merely on the basis of technology, there is little difference between the two, and even less between Ethereum and Ethereum Classic. Despite this, both Litecoin and Ethereum Classic have huge market capitalizations, active communities, and their own social agendas.

It might be claimed that a significant portion of a cryptocurrency's worth is generated from its community, how they use their funds, and how involved it is in the currency's progress. Adding to the idea, other currencies, such as Dash[666] or Tezos,[667] have built methods directly into the protocol to allow its users to vote on what should be prioritized for development and funding.

The huge variety of cryptocurrencies also demonstrates their social aspects. Fragmentation and forks result from disagreements over philosophy, monetary policy, or even petty squabbling amongst the core developers. CH at ScotFest:

> *People fall out over values, not facts*

Unlike their digital cousins, however, fiat currencies tend to weather political upheavals and local disputes without a currency crisis. It seems that certain aspects of legacy systems are absent from the crypto sector. IOG believes that protocol users need incentives to understand the social contract that underpins their system and the opportunity to suggest modifications in a constructive manner. This independence applies to every facet of a value exchange system, from market regulation to project funding. However, it cannot be mediated by central actors, nor does it need any credential that may be co-opted by a privileged few.

Funding invariably dries up, regardless of the success of a crowdsale[668] to bootstrap

---

[666] **Dash** is an open source cryptocurrency and is a form of decentralized autonomous organization (DAO) run by a subset of users, called 'masternodes'. It is an altcoin that was forked from the Bitcoin protocol. The currency permits fast transactions that can be untraceable.

[667] **Tezos** (ticker: XTZ) is a decentralized blockchain founded by Arthur Breitman and Kathleen Breitman. The Breitmans also founded Dynamic Ledger Solutions (DLS), a company primarily focused on developing Tezos technology and owns the Tezos Intellectual property. The currency was launched in an initial coin offering (ICO) on July 1, 2017.

[668] **Crowdsales** are a popular use for Ethereum; they let you allocate tokens to network participants in various ways, mostly in exchange for Ether. They come in a variety of shapes and flavors.

development. As a result, Cardano contains a decentralized trust that reduces inflation and transaction fees over time. Through a ballot mechanism, any user should be able to seek funds from the trust, and stakeholders should vote on who becomes a beneficiary. By creating a discussion about who should be financed, the process produces a positive feedback loop like those found in other cryptocurrencies with governance systems, such as Dash. Healthy dialogue ensures that the community is always assessing and arguing its views ahead of crucial decisions.

Long running and, in many instances, unresolved disagreements about the technical and moral direction of the codebase have plagued Bitcoin with its block size debate, Ethereum with the DAO split, and a slew of other cryptocurrencies. Many of these conflicts, as well as the splitting of the community that occurs when action is taken, can be attributed to the absence of any mechanism for implementing change.

Looking to lessons from the past, Bitcoin's adoption of (SegWit) Segregated Witness[669] could have been handled a lot better.[670] Did the DAO attack[671] really have to result in the hard fork on Ethereum? Could it have been managed better so there was not such a dramatic community breakdown?[672]

In the worst-case scenario, moral authority to act might simply devolve to whomever has the developers, infrastructure links, and money, rather than the majority of the community's best interests. It's difficult to gauge if actions are valid if a major segment of the community is unavailable, or disengaged owing to poor incentives.[673]

Some cryptocurrencies like Tezos have a model where the cryptocurrency protocol is handled as a constitution, with three parts (Transaction, Consensus, and Network) and a set of explicit rules and procedures for updating the constitution. However, there is still a lot of work to be done on incentives and how to represent and update a crypto protocol using a formal language.

IOG have been researching governance in crypto for years. They have written papers as far back as 2017 on proposing a treasury for Ethereum Classic.[674] Another paper,

---

[669] **Segregated Witness,** or SegWit, is the name used for an implemented soft fork change in the transaction format of bitcoin.

[670] The Tale Of SegWit: Controversy, Civil War & Adoption, blog.btse.com/segwit/

[671] Understanding the DAO attack, coindesk.com/learn/2016/06/25/understanding-the-dao-attack/

[672] Ethereum fall out, fortune.com/2016/09/04/ethereum-fall-out/

[673] **Incentive**: a method of encouraging members to participate in the network by providing them with a return proportionate to their efforts. By promoting persistent, active, and robust engagement, incentives strive to maintain equality and fairness in a dispersed network of participants. The incentives necessary in Cardano's incentives model are calculated using game theory.

[674] Kaidalov, Kovalchuk, Nastenko, Rodinko, Shevtzov, Oliynykov (2017), 'A proposal for an Ethereum Classic Treasury System', iohk.io/en/research/library/papers/a-proposal-for-an-ethereum-classic-treasury-system/

authored out of Lancaster University,[675] focused on the concept of a treasury system and a viable, democratic method to long-term development financing for Cardano.

Formal methods, machine comprehensible specifications, and combining a treasury with this process for financial incentives are just some of the solutions IOG pursued. Looking back now, it's clear they were putting the chess pieces in place, to create the apparatus necessary for the *Age of Voltaire* vision presented at ScotFest[676] in November 2022. More on this later.

Cardano Improvement Proposals (CIPs)

One of the early governance pieces implemented in November 2020 was CIP 0001,[677] which explains what a CIP is. Anyone who has ideas for enhancing Cardano may present them in the form of CIPs (Cardano improvement proposals). CIPs are a means of formally proposing enhancements in a consensus-based manner. They are an essential component of Cardano governance, even though they are not binding, nor a requirement for treasury or protocol modifications. Before a vote can be taken, someone must submit a proposal for others to consider.

A CIP follows a standard format: the proposal structure is templated to make debate and evaluation easier. This allows other members of the community to weigh in on improvement recommendations, or issues in a proposal. CIPs are kept as text files in a versioned Github repo,[678] and their revision history provides the proposal's historical record. For those who aren't on GitHub, cips.cardano.org is an auto-generated sister site.

There are three different types of CIP:

1. A **Standards Track CIP** is a modification that impacts Cardano implementations. Examples: a network protocol update, or basically any other change that affects the compatibility of Cardano applications. CIPs on the Standards Track have two parts: a design doc and a reference implementation.

2. A **Process CIP** outlines a Cardano-related process or suggests a modification to one. Process CIPs are similar to Standards Track CIPs, however they are used for topics other than the Cardano protocol. They usually need community approval; thus, unlike Informational CIPs, they are more than suggestions that users are not free to disregard.

3. An **Informational CIP** discusses a Cardano design issue or gives broad Cardano community standards or information, but it does not propose anything

---

[675] Zhang, Oliynykov and Balogun (2019), 'A Treasury System for Cryptocurrencies: Enabling Better Collaborative Intelligence', eprint.iacr.org/2018/435.pdf

[676] IO Scotfest: The age of Voltaire, youtube.com/playlist?list=PLnPTB0CuBOBxjkB8DdMhy57MriBCHT1RM

[677] CIP-0001: Cardano Improvement Proposals, github.com/cardano-foundation/CIPs/tree/master/CIP-0001

[678] CIP repo, github.com/cardano-foundation/CIPs

305

new. Users and implementers are entitled to disregard Informational CIPs, or follow their advice because they do not necessarily reflect a Cardano community consensus or suggestion.

Every CIP has the following format: Preamble, Abstract, Motivation, Specification, Rationale, Backwards compatibility, Path to Archive, Copyright.

The concept is developed as a properly written proposal and submitted as a pull request[679] to the CIP repository after initial discussion and feedback. The updated Draft CIP is then publicly processed in the following manner:

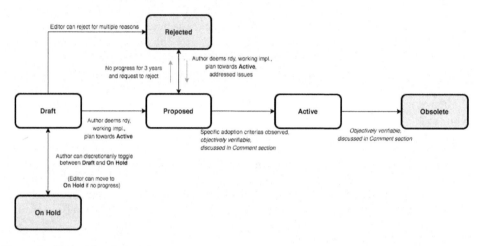

Figure 60: CIP workflow from CIP0001

CIPs are processed in a semi-formal manner: Editors of CIP proposals meet on a regular basis to discuss and assess ideas. Meeting minutes are available to the public,[680] and meetings are held every two weeks. Authors are encouraged to contribute and offer comments, and discussions often take place simultaneously in the Cardano forum CIPs section[681] and/or in the GitHub pull requests.

Consider the CIP repository to be a collection of useful tools - some may play well together, while others will not. You have complete control over which CIPs your implementation adheres to. The community will lean toward some more than others, new ones should be submitted as Cardano grows.

Notable CIPs:

---

[679] **Pull requests** are a feature specific to GitHub. They provide a simple, web-based way to submit your work (often called "patches") to a project. It's called a pull request because you're asking the project to pull changes from your fork.

[680] CIP biweekly meetings, github.com/cardano-foundation/CIPs/tree/master/BiweeklyMeetings

[681] Cardano Forums CIP section, forum.cardano.org/c/english/cips/122

- CIP 1 - CIP process

  'A Cardano improvement proposal (CIP) is a formalized design document for the Cardano community, providing information or describing a new feature for the Cardano network, its processes, or environment in a concise and technically efficient manner.;

- CIP 9 - Protocol Parameters

  'This CIP is an informational CIP that describes the initial protocol parameter settings for the Shelley era of the Cardano blockchain, plus the changes that have been made. It is intended to serve as a historic record, allowing protocol parameter changes to be tracked back to the original settings.'

- CIP 25 - NFT Metadata Standard

  This proposal defines an NFT Metadata Standard for Native Tokens.

- CIP 27 - CNFT Community Royalties Standard

  A community standard for royalties' functionality, that does not require smart contracts to implement.

- CIP 30 - Cardano DApp-Wallet Web Bridge

  This CIP describes the communication bridge allowing DApps to interface with Cardano wallets.

- CIP 31 - Reference Inputs

  'We introduce a new kind of input, a reference input, which allows looking at an output without spending it. This will facilitate access to information stored on the blockchain without the churn associated with spending and recreating UTXOs.'

- CIP 32 - Inline datums

  'We propose to allow datums themselves to be attached to outputs instead of datum hashes. This will allow much simpler communication of datum values between users.'

- CIP 33 - Reference scripts

  'We propose to allow scripts ("reference scripts") to be attached to outputs, and to allow reference scripts to be used to satisfy script requirements during validation, rather than requiring the spending transaction to do so. This will allow transactions using common scripts to be much smaller.'

- CIP 50 - Liesenfelt Shelleys Voltaire Decentralization Update

  Proposed by Dr Michael Liesenfelt, this CIP discusses the justification, methods, metrics, and implementation schedule to increase Cardano's decentralization.

- CIP 79 - Implement Ouroboros Leois to increase Cardano throughput

  This CIP discusses the implementation of *Ouroboros Leios*.

- CIP1694 - A proposal for entering the Voltaire phase

- CIP999 (read as 'CIP minus 1') - Cardano Problem Statements (CPS)

  CPSs complement CIPs. CIP999 explains the need for CPSs, their set structure, statuses and criteria for their success. CPSs were introduced to simplify the process when explaining the problem statement of complex CIPs, replacing the more elaborate '*motivation*' section. They may also exist as standalone 'requests for proposals from ecosystem actors who've identified a problem but are yet to find any suitable solution'.

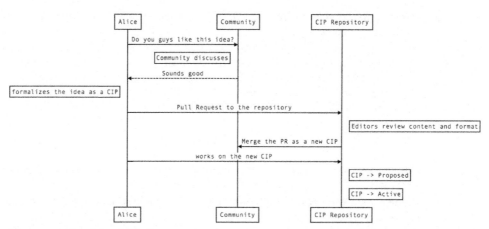

Figure 61: CIP workflow from editors' perspective

Ambassadors program

The Cardano community is not short of committed members who are willing to be part of the Cardano Foundation's Ambassadors Program,[682] established in 2018.

The program's goals are to:

- Boost adoption of Cardano
- Drive awareness

---

[682] Cardano Ambassadors Program, cardano.org/ambassadors/

- Educate the community

To apply to become an ambassador, send the Cardano Foundation an email: community@cardanofoundation.org

What is Project Catalyst?

Another governance piece introduced in 2020 was Project Catalyst. Catalyst is a prototype treasury system that combines proposal and voting processes. Establishing a long-term future for Cardano growth began with a treasury and democratic voting in the Catalyst project. It was previously hosted on IdeaScale[683] but is now moved to its own dedicated site, *projectcatalyst.io*

When creating a proof-of-stake blockchain, it's critical to make sure the system is self-sustaining. It must be able to develop and mature in a decentralized and organic manner. Voltaire[684] is IOG's approach to create this capacity, enabling the Cardano community to maintain the blockchain while also suggesting and implementing system enhancements. This places decision-making authority in the hands of ada holders.

Welcome to the experiment!

- Things may:
  - Break
  - Lack documentation
  - Differ greatly between iterations
  - Disorient, overload and inspire.

Our goal: Provide a safe and lively environment for you to explore the highest potential of human collaboration

Figure 62: The opening screen for each Catalyst Town Hall meeting, (crowdcast.io/iohk)

The foundation of a robust blockchain is a non-trivial, broad area of study and debate. A talk[685] on the necessity of funding for Cardano's development was given during the Shelley conference in July 2021. Project Catalyst, which combines research, social

---

[683] Cardano IdeaScale, cardano.ideascale.com/

[684] Voltaire Roadmap, roadmap.cardano.org/en/voltaire/

[685] Project Catalyst: implementing Cardano's Governance model with Dr Dor Garbash, conferencecast.tv/talk-44699-project-catalyst-implementing-cardanos-governance-model-with-dr-dor-garbash#.talkPage-header

experimentation, and community consent to develop an open, democratic culture within the Cardano community, uses IOG's treasury mechanism capabilities.

Built on democracy

Long-term blockchain sustainability and development need technological advancement and maturity. Growth and system improvements must be supported and funded by someone. Because it allows for collaborative, sustainable choices without depending on a single governing institution, a democratic approach is an important aspect of the blockchain ecosystem. As a result, governance and decision-making must be done collectively. Users should be able to see how improvements are made, who makes decisions, and where the money comes from.

Sustainability

There are various options for raising funds for development. The most frequent methods include donations, venture capital investment, and initial coin offerings (ICOs). While such models may be effective for generating initial cash, they seldom guarantee long-term financing or provide the capital required for development and upkeep. Furthermore, these models suffer from centralized control, making it difficult to reach a consensus that meets everyone's demands and aspirations.

Some cryptocurrency projects use taxes to generate a long-term financing source for blockchain development, collecting a proportion of fees or incentives and depositing them in a separate pool called a treasury. The funds in the Treasury may then be utilized for system development and maintenance. In addition, as the value of cryptocurrencies rises, so does the value of government reserves. This opens up a new potential source of revenue.

When it comes to making judgments on how to guide development, however, finance systems are often in danger of centralization. Only a few people within the organization or firm are authorized to make choices about how to spend available cash in these systems. Because the decentralized nature of blockchain renders centralized management of funds problematic, disagreements among organization members can occur, leading to conflicts.

Cardano's Treasury

To solve the issues, a variety of treasury systems have emerged. These systems might include iterative treasury periods when project funding requests are presented, debated, and voted on. Poor voter privacy and ballot submission security are two typical downsides. Furthermore, if master nodes are coerced, the validity of funding choices may be jeopardized, and a lack of expert input may promote undesired contributions.

Cardano was established as a third-generation cryptocurrency platform to address the issues that previous platforms had. Cardano wants to make the process more democratic by giving everyone influence and guaranteeing that choices are made fairly. It is critical to have transparent voting and financing mechanisms to achieve this. This is where Voltaire enters the picture.

The aforementioned (Lancaster University) paper on treasury systems for cryptocurrencies proposes a community-controlled, decentralized, collaborative decision-making method for long-term blockchain development and maintenance financing. This kind of collaborative intelligence is based on liquid democracy,[686] which is a combination of direct, and representative, democracy that combines the advantages of both.

This method allows the Treasury System to use expert knowledge in the voting process while also guaranteeing that all ada holders are given a chance to vote. As a result, for each project, a voter may vote personally or delegate their voting authority to a community member who is knowledgeable about the subject.

To maintain long-term viability, the community controls the treasury system, which is regularly replenished from sources such as:

- a share of stake pool rewards and transaction costs
- contributions or charities
- newly minted coins held back as financing.

It will be able to finance initiatives and pay for improvement suggestions since ada is always being amassed. As a result, the financing process may be split into 'treasury periods,' each of which is divided into the following phases:

- pre-voting
- voting
- post-voting.

Project ideas may be presented at any time throughout the term, debated by experts and voters, and then voted on to finance the most critical initiatives. Despite the fact that anybody may submit a proposal, only a select few will be funded, based on a community vote.

Decision making process

Scientists (even nuclear physicists [687]), developers, executive types, investors, and the general public are among the ada holders who vote. With such a diverse field of participants, with different agendas and motives, there must be proper mechanisms in place to preserve inclusivity, and ensure fair reviews and voting takes place.

A person's voting power is proportional to the quantity of ada they hold; the more ada they own, the more weight their vote carries. Along with direct yes/no voting, a person might transfer their voting authority to an expert they trust as part of the liquid

---

[686] **Liquid democracy** is a form of delegative democracy where an electorate engages in collective decision-making through direct participation and dynamic representation. This democratic system leverages parts of both direct and representative democracy.

[687] Cardano Network Parameters with Dr. Michael Liesenfelt | Cardano Live #54, youtube.com/watch?v=eAs_L68RO-c

democracy concept. In this instance, the expert will be able to vote directly on the idea that they believe is the most significant.

Following the vote, project ideas may be assessed and ranked depending on the number of yes/no votes; the poorest project proposals will be eliminated. The top-ranked ideas will be financed in turn until the treasury money is depleted, after which the shortlisted proposals will be ranked according to their score. Breaking down the decision-making process into phases ensures each proposal is rigorously and fairly critiqued.

IOG's research team leveraged ZK proofs to safeguard voter privacy. Zero-knowledge (ZK) approaches are mathematical methods for verifying information without exposing any underlying facts. The zero-knowledge proof in this situation indicates that someone may vote without providing any personal information other than their eligibility to vote. Any prospect of voter coercion is eliminated as a result.

Project Catalyst is a treasury system that combines proposals, and voting processes, with the goal of fostering a democratic culture in the Cardano community. Cardano's treasury will initially be replenished by a proportion of stake pool payouts, assuring a long-term treasury supply. Other blockchains have treasury systems, but IOG's combines perfect anonymity thanks to zero-knowledge proofs, liquid democracy thanks to expert engagement and vote delegation, and community participation.

It's also worth noting that this treasury system technique may be used on a number of blockchains other than Cardano. It has previously been suggested that it be implemented for Ethereum Classic[688] and we'll see later how COTI availed of the Catalyst Natives feature. Treasury systems may aid in this process by allowing everyone to see how a network will evolve.

Following a successful limited user group trial, Project Catalyst became accessible to the public. Although Cardano on-chain governance is still in its infancy, all metrics and indicators point to a bright future with the community leading the way.

---

[688] The ETC Cooperative Withdraws Support For The ETC Treasury, medium.com/etccooperative/the-etc-cooperative-withdraws-support-for-the-etc-treasury-c3f8772fff71

Figure 63: Catalyst overview

There are a lot of moving parts to Catalyst. This graphic from IOG's blog post *Project Catalyst - A virtuous cycle of Cardano ecosystem development*[689] is a good summary of the steps involved and end goals.

Catalyst's early funds

In Sept 2020, IOG announced the establishment of Project Catalyst's first public fund, a milestone for Cardano in terms of on-chain governance, treasury, and community innovation.

The public fund was launched after five months of intensive activity across two earlier pilot funds. The first experiment, dubbed 'Fund 0,' was conducted with the help of an IOG focus group. Fund1 was the first time the concept was shared with the Cardano community, enlisting the aid of over 50 people to help IOG construct the platform and procedures. While this voting round did not provide 'real' financing, it was a significant

[689] Tim Richmond, 'Project Catalyst - A virtuous cycle of Cardano ecosystem development', iohk.io/en/blog/posts/2022/05/10/project-catalyst-a-virtuous-cycle-of-cardano-ecosystem-development-investing-in-great-ideas-to-make-positive-real-world-changes/

opportunity for the IOG team and the Cardano community to test and enhance the new process.

There was a long way to go. However, with the help of the community, IOG sustained a steady rate of advancement. If Fund1 was the dress rehearsal, then Fund0 was the technical run through. Fund2, which was announced in September 2020, was the opening night when the community's top performers fought for financing to bring their concept to fruition.

Funding great proposals

IOG's pioneer group of 50 community members assisted them in identifying areas for improvement so that they could build and enhance the process before making it more broadly available. Clarifying the documentation and standards encouraged community members to participate more and submit proposals.

To that end, IOG worked on a guide to assist anybody in creating their best proposal possible for Fund2 and beyond. The community could access up to $250k worth of ada in the first public fund.

IOG started small, asking the community to respond to a challenge statement: 'How can we encourage developers and entrepreneurs to create DApps and businesses on top of Cardano in the next six months?' Funding proposals could address this with a broad range of concepts, including marketing campaigns and infrastructure development, as well as business planning and content production.

The first step was to 'examine the problem,' which included asking members of the community for their input. Then, through a special Telegram chat channel,[690] IOG urged everyone to submit their ideas to the innovation platform, where they could collaborate and debate.

The public votes

IOG put things to a vote after the phases of brainstorming, cooperation, and proposal. Proposals were evaluated on IdeaScale, or via a mobile voting application. When it came time to vote, everyone registered to vote using the voting app. Each participant's 'right' to vote is connected to their ada holdings, and voting will earn them further ada rewards. Voting works similarly to a 'transaction,' enabling all participants to cast a vote to say 'yes' or 'no.'

Up until Fund10, Catalyst was implemented as a mix of on-chain and off-chain components. Proposals lived on IdeaScale, there was a voting center in the Daedalus wallet, the android and iphone voting apps and a dependence on the re-purposed Jormungandr[691] node (previously used for the Incentivized Testnet). As the Voltaire era

---

[690] Catalyst Telegram Channel, t.me/cardanocatalyst

[691] Jormungandr Node, github.com/input-output-hk/jormungandr/blob/master/CHANGELOG.md

unfolds, the voting experience will move into IOG's new light wallet *Lace* (lace.io), complemented by a new website, projectcatalyst.io.

How it works

Voltaire is a critical component of the Cardano ecosystem since it enables every ada holder to participate in choices about the platform's future development and contribute to the ecosystem's growth. Project Catalyst is a critical first step in achieving such capacity.

The inaugural Catalyst-funded entrepreneurship programme, dubbed *BoostCamps*,[692] used the Entreprenerdy (entreprenerdy.com) platform to allow enterprises to participate in sessions aimed at developing their company strategy.

Here's how it works

Innovate together

Got an Idea? Create an impactful proposal and collaborate with the community to develop and refine it.

Vote for your favorite ideas

Use a voting app to choose ideas with impact worth funding. Get rewarded in ada for taking part.

Stay up to date

Receive regular updates on all the funded ideas, so you can follow along and see how things are progressing.

Figure 64: Catalyst 'here's how it works'

In September 2020, Catalyst sprang into action for the first time with Fund2.[693] Thousands of individuals joined together to produce, refine, and prioritize financing for ideas to move Cardano forward. Fund3 went live in January 2021, and with each fund, IOG wanted to grow the Catalyst community by encouraging more individuals to participate.

Every funding round starts with a set of objectives. Each challenge symbolizes the Cardano community's 'intention,' a common objective to accomplish. IOG likes to speak about 'return on intention' as a means of monitoring project success. Each challenge is intended to be wide enough to elicit both technical and general ideas while remaining focused.

Fund2 had a $250,000 ada pool, while Fund3 doubled that, awarding $500,000 in ada to proposers, voters, and community advisors. The breadth, amount of money, and

---

[692] Project Catalyst Fund6 weekly town hall and Q&A #13 November 2021, youtube.com/watch?v=x8134D_Ip9o&t=418s

[693] Dr Dor Garbash, 'Project Catalyst; introducing our first public fund for Cardano community innovation', iohk.io/en/blog/posts/2020/09/16/project-catalyst-introducing-our-first-public-fund-for-cardano-community-innovation/

community participation have all increased with each funding cycle. On the IdeaScale innovation platform in Feb 2021, there were 7,000 members and 1,800 active voters. Adoption was increasing by 10% per week.

Fund4 was the most accessible and ambitious round yet, as well as the first million-dollar round — the ada pot used to finance Cardano development initiatives. The funding was used by proposal teams to create tools, construct DApps, establish developer education and training efforts, and much more.

IOG continued to make the project more available to the Cardano community during 2021 to promote participation. Voter registration increased considerably. Within a redesigned registration center, registration was now completely connected with the Daedalus wallet.

Yoroi lite wallet users could easily register via a browser plugin. After that, voters could finish the process using a specific mobile voting app, which can be downloaded on iOS or Android. Users could also register and vote from their wallets in Daedalus. Project Catalyst had risen to become the world's biggest decentralized autonomous organization (DAO) in less than six months.

Catalyst Circle

As Fund4 came to an end in July 2021, Catalyst had already proven itself as a one-stop hub for teamwork and decentralized innovation. However, this rapid expansion brought with it new obstacles.

Project Catalyst was gaining in contributions from increasingly different functional groups who were helping to bring the collective intelligence forward. Specifically, community advisors, funded-proposers, stake pool operators (SPOs), toolmakers & maintainers, all who contribute to Catalyst's success and expansion, as well as Cardano's success.

Project Catalyst gains from this expanded variety since it allows for the formation of even more ideas and proposals. It also makes communication between all of these groups more difficult. Every cohort wants to be heard, and their thoughts and concerns need to be aired at the project level.

These groups need representation and trustworthy leadership to advocate for them. Project Catalyst's influence would be severely reduced if such representation was inadequate or non-existent. This is why the Catalyst Circle was created.

'Human sensor array'

IOG describes the Catalyst Circle as a 'human sensor array' that serves as a representative body for all the Project Catalyst participants. The Circle keeps track of Catalyst's present state and future intentions for governance. Within the Catalyst ecosystem, it identifies and discusses issues, objections, and possibilities. For example, the Circle might debate the amounts distributed to a fund, tweaks or conditions to incentive parameters, the Catalyst API, and so on.

This activity will give an insight into the hopes, desires, needs, and worries of the community inside Project Catalyst by documenting meetings and collecting activities in a backlog available to everyone.[694] The Circle is also in charge of choosing its own future form and designing the Circle election procedures.

The Circle exists to achieve four main objectives:

- To make it easier for various functional groupings to communicate with one another.
- To give people notice when lines are crossed
- Suggest enhancements to Project Catalyst's plans and procedures
- Define the Circle election process.

Elected members

The Circle, like Project Catalyst, will grow and change over time. Initially, elected members will serve three-month terms, with further elections to improve and iterate the process. These basic tasks and obligations have been specified for elected members. Each member should:

- Represent the people who chose them
- Use their best judgment when it comes to topics that come before the Circle
- Educate other members about their communities' initiatives, activities, goals, dreams, and concerns
- Take advantage of opportunities to incorporate policy recommendations into the Circle's agenda for discussion on a regular basis
- Inform their communities about the Circle's efforts.

Each team member is expected to:

- Attend regular meetings every fortnight
- Keep an agile backlog to keep track of concerns in between sessions
- Review and comment on items on the agenda ahead of time
- Remain informed of their community's interests and concerns
- Distribute the Circle's outputs in a clear and accessible manner
- Study and practice good meeting processes
- Create a protocol paper for the next elections
- Participate in training seminars on inclusive and lean startup leadership
- Provide comments on the Circle's efficacy.

Inaugural election

---

[694] Catalyst Circle meeting minutes, catalyst-swarm.gitbook.io/catalyst-circle/minutes

IOG organized the first election in July 2021 for Catalyst Circle members globally. Members will be able to establish the agenda for each meeting and submit policy recommendations to the Catalyst Circle for consideration on a regular basis. The bootstrapping version is the 'minimal functional group,' which is based on conversations with Catalyst community leaders and Governance Alive (governancealive.com), an expert group in the area of new governance structures.

The Circle may expand and split as best practices are established. In the end, it will be up to members to help IOG achieve their aim of legitimizing decentralized government, opening the road for a viable alternative to the status quo, and breaking new ground in the development of blockchain governance.

In December 2022, Catalyst Circle V3.5 asked DripDropz (dripdropz.io) to run an on-chain vote for five new V4 Circle representatives. Thirty candidates have applied. You can follow the latest news on their blog.[695]

Catalyst Natives

As part of Project Catalyst,[696] the first Catalyst Natives pilot was launched in late 2021. Catalyst Natives allows any project to tap into the collective intelligence of the community to solve business challenges and outsource projects. Catalyst Natives gives decentralized innovation fund management to partners, some external to Cardano, aiming to develop their ecosystem by incentivizing innovators to assist in finding solutions to problems.

COTI, the first Catalyst Native

Catalyst Natives expands access to Project Catalyst to organizations outside of the Cardano ecosystem could now present challenges and give incentives and rewards to individuals who successfully satisfy the challenge with their suggested innovations.

COTI presented the community with a novel technological challenge in this pilot. By adding a plug-in to their site, any small and medium businesses using platforms like Shopify and WooCommerce can take advantage of new and innovative methods to accept ada payments with seamless integration.

Following the pilot, IOG allowed Catalyst Natives to accept more challenges from other entities; however, these challenges are selected by IOG, in the first phase, to ensure they provide value to the Cardano ecosystem. Organizations proposing challenges via Natives will finance those ideas, thus Catalyst Natives will not utilize Cardano Treasury funds to pay for the initiatives that have been successfully voted on. COTI distributed $100k in COTI tokens plus fees in Fund7, which was in addition to the $8m ada fund.

---

[695] Catalyst Circle v4 Voting, news.dripdropz.io/catalyst-circle-v4-voting-c8863e5697d6

[696] Our million-dollar baby: Project Catalyst, iohk.io/en/blog/posts/2021/02/12/our-million-dollar-baby-project-catalyst/

Catalyst Natives is an opportunity for businesses of all sizes to have access to a vault of ideas and the people who can help them come to life. Catalyst Natives is now aiming to assist Cardano ecosystem partners, and native asset token projects, handle particular pain points for which they either do not have the resources, or simply do not have a solution, and outsource them as Catalyst challenges for proposers to solve.

IOG 'OG' and Ergo strategic advisor Dan Friedman[697] announced on an Ergo update[698] that Ergo is planning to be the next Catalyst 'Native'. Anyone interested in Catalyst Natives can apply here.[699]

Later Funds

Every Catalyst fund cycle has provided new, remarkable accomplishments. Fund7 was no different.

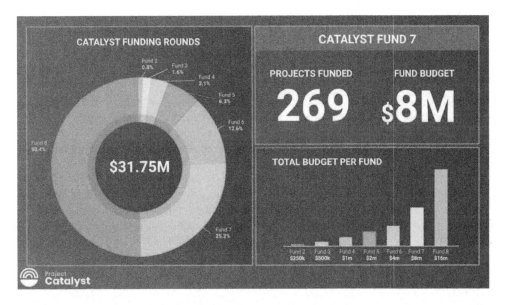

Figure 65: Fund7 stats

After the votes were tabulated and counted in Fund7, 269 additional initiatives[700] were selected to get ada. Given that each of these projects was created in response to 24 real-world problems provided by the Cardano community, as well as one additional task issued by COTI, Cardano's first Catalyst Native pioneer, these were impressive numbers.

---

[697] Daniel Friedman, iohk.io/en/team/daniel-friedman

[698] Weekly Update & AMA - April 22, 2022, youtube.com/watch?v=rPBZwEPk5Q8

[699] Catalyst Natives application, forms.gle/BA8LmtrAWWmHHcY59

[700] Fund 7 initiatives, drive.google.com/file/d/193GZulHuk0zhpTrMiLhcNC4OeEMoRyIa/view

This time around, over 52,500 wallets registered to vote, and community advisers reviewed over 900 proposals to assist voters make informed judgements. The number of ideas financed by the Cardano Treasury had almost quadrupled in a short period of time, reaching 575 projects.

The Cardano Treasury now contained roughly 800m ada in order to maintain and build the ecosystem. Many of the projects that were funded in previous rounds have now been completed and their end products were being showcased.[701]

Fund8

Every three months, a new Project Catalyst innovation fund campaign launches, offering the chance to obtain resources from the Cardano Treasury. Fund8 offered $16m funding in ada.

The Catalyst community established and agreed on each and every task in Fund8. What were the goals? Within Cardano's open-source architecture, to speed up the developer and DApp ecosystem. Cardano Ecosystem Foundations & Development, Community Development, Outreach & Adoption, Identity & Interoperability, and Project Catalyst Improvements were among the 23 challenges.

Proposals included innovative decentralized finance (DeFi) apps aimed at reducing financial inequity and RealFi, which removes frictions from real-world economic operations and provides people with cheaper financial products. For example, the collective manufacturing project (wayacollective.com) run by African entrepreneurs and employees.

Fund8 results[702] confirmed the momentum just keeps growing as voting turnout increased and a diverse range of projects were funded. One of the smallest amounts requested, and funded, was also one of the most significant. Sebastien Guillemot's successful proposal[703] meant he was the first CIP editor to be paid for his time. More editors followed, serving as stewards of the CIP process.

Catalyst also partnered with the Financial Times and Seedstars (seedstars.com) to launch the *FT x Cardano Blockchain Challenge* where selected startups participated in a 3-day Bootcamp and connected to Seedstars' network of mentors. 24 startups were selected to participate in a 3-month Acceleration Program.' More details are on Seedstar's website.[704]

---

[701] Project Catalyst - Funded Projects Reporting (public MVP), docs.google.com/spreadsheets/d/1bfnWFa94Y7Zj0G7dtpo9W1nAYGovJbswipxiHT4UE3g/edit#gid=416498551

[702] Fund 8 results, drive.google.com/file/d/1s3jCE7pmoUujy3ASMia-UhFl2KLi_hnf/view

[703] CIP Editor funded, twitter.com/SebastienGllmt/status/1525139808926191618

[704] 'FT x Cardano Blockchain Challenge', seedstars.com/community/entrepreneurs/programs/ft-cardano-blockchain-challenge/

April 21, 2019… Who pays? Who decides? CH:[705]

> *This is why it's so incredibly important that you have a treasury system …and voting systems because right now here's how the cryptocurrency space works and this is why things get so toxic ….you have a very small group of people who are developers, investors, big people who are actually building stuff in the space, the entrepreneurial class, developer class the infrastructure class… then you have the speculators which are everybody else …and they hold the currency, they're fans of it, maybe even philosophically aligned with it …but they don't have a voice, they can't do anything …they're just sitting there just hoping for things to materialize.*

> *….and then a subset of them maybe move into the other class when they have smart contracts or whatever… but the vast majority of them are there yet they have opinions about where things should go…what they should do …and so the key is to give them tools to organize… tools to vote… tools to discuss the philosophy and direction …to have teeth, not just 'here's my opinion', but also when my opinion is let manifest and gets a democratic consent behind it …then that opinion will turn into money …that then can be used by the other class.*

> *All of a sudden everybody has power and actually has a voice ..and an opinion and you're not just talking about when is this coming out, or what is is it that is coming out …you're actually talking about where do we want to go, and how are we going to get there and the things we need to do to get there… who's the best leader to get there… you can't fork that…. you can fork the code and have another Treasury system…but it's like saying well that big meetup group over there… I'm going to host my own meetup group and I'm going to copy everything… the same banners and the same catering and the same everything… it doesn't mean other people are going to show up*

The Cardano cFund

The cFund, which was first unveiled at the 2020 Shelley summit, is an early-stage investment fund that focuses on creative firms on Cardano. Wave Financial, in collaboration with IOG, manages the cFund, a crypto-native hedge fund. The fund uses an early-stage venture approach to invest in creative technological firms that are building Cardano-based apps, services, and products, as well as other R&D projects that IOG is working on.

The 'c' in *c*Fund

The letter 'c' in the name relates to the mathematics word 'coefficient,' which refers to a variable's multiplier. cFund is positioned to provide a multiplier effect in terms of growth and reach for its portfolio firms by using both IOG's and Wave Financial's subject knowledge and industry relationships.

---

[705] Post Conference recap, thoughts and an AMA 04/21/2019, youtu.be/pBXZVrBQ6U8?t=5003

Services offered

The cFund serves as a funding provider, adviser, and partner to its portfolio firms and the greater Cardano ecosystem. cFund delivers access and direction to its portfolio by using IOG and Wave Financial resources, reputation, knowledge, and network. cFund is a great believer in adding value to its investments and strives to be the first port of call for management teams.

According to IOG's foundational philosophy of 'cascading disruption,[706] most of the structures that make up global financial, governance, and social systems are inherently unstable, and slight disturbances may generate a ripple effect that radically reconfigures the system. The purpose of cFund is to find and fund solutions that bring these disparities together in a fair and transparent way for all participants. While other cryptocurrencies[707] have strong ties to Silicon Valley, Cardano is innovating with Catalyst acting as its own 'built in' VC Fund.

COTI, a decentralized and scalable payments network for the e-commerce sector, was cFund's first investment in this area.

Another example is Occam.Fi, a suite of DeFi solutions optimized for Cardano. Their initial product is a decentralized financing platform. The next generation of DeFi apps will be able to raise funding utilizing the Cardano blockchain thanks to this launchpad.

October 16, 2020. …. There are a lot of different funds so could you explain to us what is DC fund, cFund and the Cardano Foundation fund? CH:[708]

> *So, the DC fund is what we've termed the funds that are coming out of Catalyst… and those are grant models … Cardano doesn't have agency, so we can't own land, it can't have intellectual property… it can't have equity, these types of things …so when it gives out funding… It's like when the National science foundation (NSF) gives out funding, or DARPA[709] gives out funding …where it's funding the development of something because we, as a society, have determined that that is a good idea.*
>
> *So, for example when NSF gives research for theoretical physics …it says we, as a society, would like our brilliant physicist to be well funded so that they can figure out how time works and gravity works and so forth …but there's no*

---

[706] Cardano | The First Domino, youtube.com/watch?v=W7gGO058rtU

[707] Crypto Startup Solana Raises $314 Million to Develop Faster Blockchain, wsj.com/articles/crypto-startup-solana-raises-314-million-to-develop-faster-blockchain-11623240001

[708] Entrevista CEO IOG Charles Hoskinson e Maria Carmo #Cardano #ada Delegue na CARDs ou @cardanistas, youtu.be/rHu6oLTZ7kI?t=3061

[709] **DARPA**: The Defense Advanced Research Projects Agency is a research and development agency of the United States Department of Defense responsible for the development of emerging technologies for use by the military

money that comes out of that …or these things but there's a social benefit, that potentially could be leveraged over time to make the country better… Perhaps we invent anti-gravity at some point …. but it's not the primary goal.

So, we look at DC fund like that …. where we say it's a 'return on intention'. Grants are coming through, and the goal is to make Cardano better…. but it's not to make Bob a millionaire, or something like that…

cFund is a venture capital arm of my company and Waves[710]… we're working together and setting all of that up and basically that's going to be where you run a project and you come to Charles and the others who are involved with that… you say, 'I would like you to invest in my company… and give me the resources I need to get it to the next level…. and then we would look at you like any venture capitalist would look at you…. ask you the same questions Andreessen Horowitz (a16z.com) will ask you, or Kleiner Perkins (kleinerperkins.com) will ask you and so forth …and if we determine it's a good investment, I'll open up the checkbook and cut a check and send your way and we get equity back for that, because that's a private investment.

Then the Cardano Foundation they have something called the CCCI, Commercially Critical Cardano Infrastructure… and that's saying there needs to be some product validation and bootstrapping, that Cardano really is competitive, or capable of doing the things that Ethereum and EOS and Tezos and Algorand do.

So we're going to give out some very specific very targeted grants to help get the ecosystem along …okay the DC Fund, the community is in charge of that … the grants from the (Cardano) Foundation, the Foundation's in charge of that and they're very directed towards catching us up and getting us where we need to go to compete with Ethereum and the rest of the gang …and the cFund is a good old-fashioned investment for things that I think we ought to have on our ecosystem.

dReps

IOG introduced the notion of delegating your voting rights to a Delegate Representatives (dReps), and urged people interested to register during a Fund8 Project Catalyst Town Hall.[711]

This ongoing growth of the Cardano ecosystem is great news but, on the other hand, offers a problem. The community's obligation to examine and vote on ideas grows as the quantity of proposals grows. A new approach is needed to guarantee that all ideas get the attention they deserve, as well as to support further development.

---

[710] Waves, everipedia.org/wiki/lang_en/waves-cryptocurrency

[711] Project Catalyst Fund8 launch - Town Hall #1 February 2022, youtube.com/watch?v=rNZJvzjgduM

Ada holders may give their votes to one or more dReps through delegation. This provides the more passive voter a chance to have their voice heard, but now across a larger number of proposals than they could read and evaluate personally.

These dReps will vote on most Project Catalyst proposals, improving the quality of decision-making within each Fund. dReps will collaborate to develop policy, gather and evaluate data, consult with experts, and ultimately vote on a variety of initiatives and issues proposed by the community. IOG is soliciting interest in joining the first dRep cohort to promote inclusion and diversity. If you'd like to get involved, you can join the dRep pioneers here.[712]

Fund9

Catalyst's relentless, Borg-like momentum continued with Fund9 opening in June 2022. There is typically something new and innovative with the arrival of each fund, and this time Cardashift[713] joined the Catalyst Natives program.[714] Their challenge was based on value creation through positive impact-oriented projects. Cardashift list Cardano's 'green' credentials, it's focus on Africa and its deterministic nature among their reasons for partnering with Catalyst in their medium blog post.[715] As with every quarterly fund, the rewards for successful proposals increased. The Fund9 launch guide[716] outlined how the 16m ada was to be allocated.

Tactical Pause for Catalyst

Although Catalyst has been a huge success in many ways, it's not perfect. There were also questions[717] asked of Fund6 winner Cardax DEX after launching on Milkomeda (dcSpark's Cardano sidechain) instead of Cardano mainchain as initially proposed.

There were rumblings of discontent when one the 205 winners of Fund9 was a controversial proposal called *Daedalus Turbo*. The problem statement of the proposal read:

---

[712] Catalyst dRep applications, bit.ly/3rSyHvP

[713] **Cardashift** is a community-run launchpad that raises funds, builds and accelerates startups that are solving social and environmental issues.

[714] Fernando Sanchez, 'Introducing Catalyst Natives - How any business can leverage the Cardano innovation engine', iohk.io/en/blog/posts/2021/11/10/introducing-catalyst-natives-how-any-business-can-leverage-the-cardano-innovation-engine

[715] The 3 reasons why we choose Cardano to maximize our impact, cardashift.medium.com/the-3-reasons-why-we-choose-cardano-to-maximize-our-impact-28b2e914e894

[716] Fund9 launch guide, drive.google.com/file/d/1kJ8F6doXUIJQRiA5pmSMxXc9feVfF21y/view

[717] @cwpaulm questions CardaxDEX, twitter.com/cwpaulm/status/1597666144059432960?s=20&t=HBr5f_ZkSoMQ4rzv0eIdOA

Daedalus, the decentralized Cardano wallet, is painfully slow, taking a whole day to sync initially and hours to resync when used only occasionally—an unfavorable impression of Cardano for new users.

Rick McCracken DIGI ✓
@RichardMcCrackn

wtf is Deadalus Turbo?

3:49 PM · Sep 27, 2022

Most Cardano users felt aggrieved as the sum rewarded was large, with other projects missing out. Anyone conducting a basic 'gap analyses,' as SPO Rick McCracken tweeted,[718] would probably arrive at same conclusion that the project was not timely as years of research and product development were already devoted to Mithril. For anyone following Cardano, IOG's *Lace* (lace.io) light wallet has been prioritized over Daedalus for some time.

From a user experience perspective, many people felt overwhelmed trying to track over a thousand proposals for a given fund on IdeaScale. Many promising projects have gone unfunded. It was generally welcomed by the community when IOG announced a 'time out' for Catalyst in a November 2022 blog post.[719]

It has not all been negative, for example, dcSpark's rapid release cycle[720] is sponsored by regular funding via numerous Catalyst proposals. Harris Warren outlined Catalyst's achievements since 2020 in his presentation at ScotFest.[721]

- Nearly $48m in innovation grants and rewards
- 60,000+ participants
- 58,000+ registered voters
- 1.7m+ votes cast.
- 4,700 proposals
- 1,200+ funded proposals
- Over 91 different countries reached

A new website projectcatalyst.io and integration with light wallet *lace* (lace.io) will be pivotal in for Catalyst in 2023. However, as we learned in subsequent *ScotFest* presentations, Catalyst is merely a sighter for the *Age of Voltaire*.

---

[718] Daedalus Turbo gap analysis,
twitter.com/RichardMcCrackn/status/1575057817181966337?s=20&t=XXfR1C0qB9jx6InYxgpQEA

[719] Repositioning Project Catalyst ahead of the next funding round,
iohk.io/en/blog/posts/2022/11/01/repositioning-project-catalyst-ahead-of-the-next-funding-round/

[720] dcSpark blog, medium.com/dcspark

[721] Project Catalyst (ScotFest), youtube.com/watch?v=NAfwwj1ukvc

Participating in Catalyst

There are several ways to participate in Project Catalyst. Submit a proposal, vote, review, comment or become a mentor. Registering an account on the collaboration platform is the first step. Another option is to join the Project Catalyst community at TownHall every Wednesday, which is live broadcast on IOG's YouTube Channel.[722] You can track each fund and check in on proposals that were previously approved here.[723]

The Age of Voltaire

CIP 1694[724] was named after Voltaire's year of birth. It is arguably the most important CIP to date as it is a proposal to bootstrap the *Age of Voltaire*. Co-authored by Charles Hoskinson, it is the first CIP he has gotten directly involved with. It's clear a lot of thought went into it, and it's intentionally written as a transitional, living document.

When Cardano was formed, there was a tripartite structure with Emurgo, Cardano Foundation (CF) and IOG with remits for ecosystem growth, governance and engineering respectively. It was always the intention to move to a members-based organization (MBO) that would manage the bureaucracy of protocol governance. It was hoped originally that the Swiss-based CF would be this entity but due to limitations with the stiftung[725] structure, it was not viable.

CIP 1694 is the fruit of years of research. IOG have been working on the idea of a decentralized update system for some time. For example, they wrote a paper *Updateable Blockchains*[726] with the European Union, with a Horizon 2020 grant, to explore ways to implement this vision.

Early in 2022, IOG and the CF held workshops to hammer out a way forward for the Voltaire era. The reputable Dirk Hohndel was brought in as Chief Open-Source Officer.[727] Under Hohndel's guidance, a team was formed led by Johnny Nguyen as Director of what was called internally *Project Constellation*.

---

[722] IOHK youtube channel, youtube.com/c/IohkIo

[723] Catalyst Tracker, bit.ly/FundedProjectsReporting

[724] CIP 1694, github.com/JaredCorduan/CIPs/blob/voltaire-v1/CIP-1694/README.md

[725] A stiftung is foundation which exists to give effect to the stated, non-commercial wishes of its founder, as set out in a foundation deed and the articles of association (statutes).

[726] Ciampi, Karayannidis, Kiayias and Zindros (2020), 'Updatable Blockchains', iohk.io/en/research/library/papers/updatable-blockchains/

[727] Dirk Hohndel Joins Cardano Foundation as Chief Open Source Officer, cardanofoundation.org/en/news/dirk-hohndel-joins-cardano-foundation-as-chief-open-source-officer/

The first question was 'What is good governance?'. Charles Hoskinson explained in his ScotFest keynote that the answer was based on three different categories:

1. **The idea of representation** …did you consent to something? There is direct representation where you personally voted on something, and **delegated authority** where you hand someone else your vote. In CIP 1694, this role is called a **DRep, a delegated representative**. This concept was already introduced in a similar form in project Catalyst. IOG like to plant seeds and telegraph upcoming features. Wisdom comes from testing and experimenting with ideas in a live environment. IOG has learnt a lot from 2 years of Catalyst funding rounds.

2. Governance needs some notion of rules, usually called a **constitution.** These are the guardrails that provide some degree of stability. The exciting thing about a constitution, in a blockchain setting, is that it can be machine understandable. Formal specifications can be the blueprints for Cardano, which a computer can understand to the extent it can integrate with an update system. Once a voting system is in place, a constitution can be ratified, hashed and embedded into a transaction. You now have the option to sign a type of 'end user agreement' by signing a transaction.

3. **Institutions** are generally a target of decentralization. If we are 'killing the middleman', why would institutions matter? Institutions, at their best, set standards and provide a review process from domain experts. Institutions are essential for good governance as they are the custodians of knowledge and best practices. People can be biased, sometimes we need objective neutral bodies to provide guidance. After much consideration, it was decided the most important 'anchor' institute would be a **members-based organization (MBO)** which should operate similar to other open sources initiatives like the Linux Foundation, or the Cloud Native Computing Foundation (CNCF).

So, 2023 is all about implementing these three things via CIP 1674. The CIP is deliberately high-level, to stimulate discussion and feedback.

Who, or what is the MBO?

The MBO is a point of aggregation to bring together all the different groups: over 3,000 stake pool operators, the Cardano Ambassadors, the 1,200+ projects building on Cardano, open-source projects running on Cardano (the Node, Mithril, Hydra, dcSpark, TxPipe.io, ogmios.dev, etc), IOG, CF, Emurgo, all ada holders, etc. The members will own and run the MBO, staffing the steering committees. The goal of Voltaire is to bring these moving parts together. As Charles Hoskinson stated in his keynote: "IO is not running the show, we haven't been for a long time..."

The vision for the MBO, was outlined by Johnny Nguyen at ScotFest:

> *Serve as the aggregation point of the entire Cardano community and its members. The members-based organization aims to uncover the community's*

pains and desires, facilitating the development of strategies to address them, and attracting firms and individuals with a capacity and the capability to do so.

Member-Based Organization

One of the anchor institutions for continuing to build and maintain the protocol

Cardano Constitution

A statement of shared values and guiding principles for the governance of Cardano

On-chain governance

A on-chain governance process that further facilitates participation in voting on certain changes to the Cardano protocol

Liquid democracy

Unlocking maximum participation opportunities in governance and decision making

Figure 66: based on slide from ScotFest

The MBO is the anchor institution for Voltaire, but not the only one. IOG has been steadily building out its presence in universities all over the globe, as well as opening the Hoskinson Center for Formal Mathematics,[728] the Zero-Knowledge Lab[729] as well as announcing the Edinburgh Decentralization Index (EDI).[730]

---

[728] Carnegie Mellon Receives $20 Million to Establish Hoskinson Center for Formal Mathematics, cmu.edu/news/stories/archives/2021/september/hoskinson-center-for-formal-mathematics.html

[729] Cardano builder IOG and University of Edinburgh launch Zero-Knowledge Lab to drive greater blockchain scalability and security, iohk.io/en/blog/posts/2022/11/18/cardano-builder-iog-and-university-of-edinburgh-launch-zero-knowledge-lab-to-drive-greater-blockchain-scalability-and-security/

[730] Cardano builder IOG and University of Edinburgh to create first ever index to provide industry standard metric for crypto decentralization, iohk.io/en/blog/posts/2022/11/18/cardano-builder-iog-and-university-of-edinburgh-to-create-first-ever-index-to-provide-industry-standard-metric-for-crypto-decentralization/

Governance actions follow a process of on-chain and off-chain steps to update the Cardano protocol

Proposal	Review	Ratification	Endorsement (hard fork)	Enactment
Anyone can submit a proposal to the Cardano blockchain to initiate: 1. Hard forks 2. Parameter changes 3. Treasury Movements/project funding 4. New constitutional committee members 5. Constitutional changes 6. MBO modifications	**MBO** conducts **technical, impact,** and **feasibility** analysis of proposals but cannot veto proposals	**Constitutional Committee** confirms that proposals are in line with Cardano constitution (Y/N)	In the event of a hard fork, **stake pool operators** must endorse the hard fork (Y/N)	Ratified (and endorsed) proposals that are approved by the applicable requisite vote are automatically enacted on-chain by protocol

Figure 67: Slide from Michael Madoff's (Voltaire Product Manager) talk at ScotFest

Everyone should read the CIP and form their own views, as governance is highly subjective. The CIP is worthy of a book in its own right, and Hoskinson has often stated he would like to write a book on governance.[731]

CIP 1694 is a living document and will update and evolve with coming workshops and discussions. While constitutions have been written before, we are entering unchartered waters as I don't think anything on this scale has been attempted in the crypto space. Liquid democracy is not a new concept, but there are few examples of successful implementations. The following is my take on CIP 1694, as of February 2023.

CIP 1694's motivation is to bootstrap the Voltaire era, to integrate new and existing on-chain and off-chain components to self-govern the ecosystem. The ultimate goal is to have a governance layer on top of Cardano that is fully, end-to-end, on-chain.

Where we are – 5 out of 7 system

At time of writing, governance transactions (eg. Hard forks, parameter changes, etc.) require a signature from at least five out of the seven Cardano governance keys, currently held by the three founding entities. This process was always intended to be an ephemeral form of governance as we got through the earlier eras of the roadmap before Voltaire.

Terminology & Concepts

The CIP introduces some new terms. First there is a **governance action** which any ada holder can submit. Three individual groups then vote to ratify, or drop, the governance action.

---

[731] Charles Hoskinson - Book about Decentralized Governance, youtube.com/watch?v=kutZ41J-tTU

The three groups that form this tricameral[732] legislative body:

- A constitutional committee,
- DReps (same name but different role to Catalyst dReps).
- Stake pool operators (SPOs)

The **constitutional committee** will have a similar role to an upper house. Continuing the analogy, DReps would make up the lower house. A **DRep**, or **delegated representative**, can be any ada holder representing themselves, or other ada holders who have delegated their voting rights to them. **Stake Pool Operators** are the same group introduced earlier who run the nodes that power the network.

Ouroboros has been a huge success story, with ~75% of ada staked making Cardano one of the most decentralized networks. By leveraging the SPO network, the process gains a passionate Cardano user group who are educated and qualified to vote on crucial decisions.

The Cardano **Consitution** will be drafted in 2023 with as much input from the community as possible. This Constitution will contain the guardrails, the shared values, core tenets and guiding principles agreed upon by stakeholders. In these early days, it will just be a text document with its hash recorded on-chain. IOG's Chief Legal Officer Joel Telpner joined Charles Hoskinson for a fireside chat[733] at ScotFest to discuss the challenges of drafting a new constitution. Telpner described what a constitution is:

> *I think you can actually simplify a constitution and say it's a set of rules, but it's a set of rules to do what? It does three things. It establishes how you legislate; it establishes how you administer and establishes how you adjudicate. It creates this framework for those three functions.*

Each of the three bodies plays their role in ratifying governance actions. Roles may vary for each body in different circumstances. For example, the constitutional committee will always be in one of two states, either a **normal state**, or a state of **no confidence**. As you might expect, if it's in a state of no confidence, it cannot participate in governance actions. It must be replaced before any governance actions can be enacted.

The makeup of the initial constitutional committee is not confirmed, but likely to be the core members of the members-based organization. One of the first tasks will be to rename the MBO. My suggestion is GaaS (Governance as a Service).

There are two ways to replace the constitutional committee. If it's in a normal state, the committee itself, along with the DReps, can both approve a motion to replace the constitutional committee. The SPOs are not required in this scenario.

---

[732] Tricameralism is the practice of having three legislative or parliamentary chambers. It is contrasted with unicameralism and bicameralism, each of which is far more common

[733] ScotFest fireside chat with Joel Telpner, youtube.com/watch?v=YvTfSx6pv9Y

If the constitutional committee in a state of no confidence, the SPOs and the DReps can vote to replace it. If it's already in a state of no confidence, the assumption is the majority want to replace the constitutional committee.

The upper house generally has less members than the lower house, however, there is no fixed size (quorum) for the constitutional committee in CIP 1694. It can vary each time a committee is formed. The quorum size is the signature threshold, how many committee members need to sign to ratify something.

There are **six different types of governance actions**:

- A motion of no confidence in the constitutional committee.
- Change the members (and/or quorum) of the constitutional committee.
- Constitution updates
- Hard Fork initiation
- Protocol parameter changes
- Treasury withdrawals (small, medium or large)

As anyone can submit a governance action, there is a **governance deposit** required to prevent spamming. This deposit is returned once the governance action is ratified, dropped or expired.

Governance actions will be ratified by on-chain voting, with each of the six types of governance actions having different ratification requirements based on some, or all of the following:

- a set quorum votes of the Constitutional committee
- a set stake-controlled threshold of DReps
- a set stake-controlled threshold of SPOs

The chart below from CIP 1694 contains the different criteria for different governance actions to be enacted. At time of writing, there are many placeholders for threshold limits, etc. These will probably be set after much debate, workshops and contributions from interested parties.

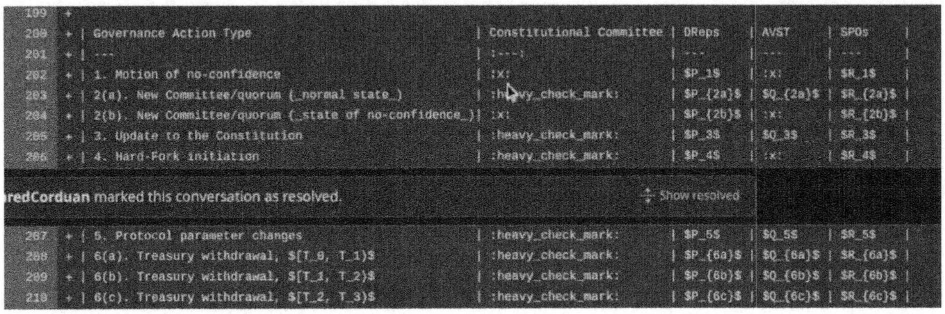

```
+
+ | Governance Action Type                                  | Constitutional Committee | DReps      | AVST       | SPOs       |
+ | ---                                                     | :---:                    | ---        | ---        | ---        |
+ | 1. Motion of no-confidence                              | :x:                      | $P_1$      | :x:        | $R_1$      |
+ | 2(a). New Committee/quorum (_normal state_)             | :heavy_check_mark:       | $P_{2a}$   | $Q_{2a}$   | $R_{2a}$   |
+ | 2(b). New Committee/quorum (_state of no-confidence_)   | :x:                      | $P_{2b}$   | :x:        | $R_{2b}$   |
+ | 3. Update to the Constitution                           | :heavy_check_mark:       | $P_3$      | $Q_3$      | $R_3$      |
+ | 4. Hard-Fork initiation                                 | :heavy_check_mark:       | $P_4$      | :x:        | $R_4$      |
redCorduan marked this conversation as resolved.                                    Show resolved
+ | 5. Protocol parameter changes                           | :heavy_check_mark:       | $P_5$      | $Q_5$      | $R_5$      |
+ | 6(a). Treasury withdrawal, $[T_0, T_1)$                 | :heavy_check_mark:       | $P_{6a}$   | $Q_{6a}$   | $R_{6a}$   |
+ | 6(b). Treasury withdrawal, $[T_1, T_2)$                 | :heavy_check_mark:       | $P_{6b}$   | $Q_{6b}$   | $R_{6b}$   |
+ | 6(c). Treasury withdrawal, $[T_2, T_3)$                 | :heavy_check_mark:       | $P_{6c}$   | $Q_{6c}$   | $R_{6c}$   |
```

Figure 68: Chart from CIP 1694

The **Active Voting Stake Threshold** (AVST) is the percentage used to determine if there is sufficient voting stake. Without going into too much detail, AVST is used to determine certain requirements. For example, if there is sufficient AVST, SPO approval is not required for a given governance action. Otherwise, SPO voter approval is required.

Governance actions will be checked for ratification on epoch boundaries. Only one governance action of each type can be staged for enactment, in any given epoch. A vote can be a **yes,** a **no** or an **abstain**. An abstaining vote won't count for active voting stake but if you want to change your vote, you can just vote again and it will superseded your early 'abstain' vote. A governance action's progress can be monitored on-chain.

Observations

A question that comes to mind is how to ensure a fair spread of voting power if the constitutional committee votes per person, while the DReps and SPOs vote by stake? Also, the three chambers are not always voting on actions. The DReps seem to be the most active voters. The constitutional committee is voting most of the time, but not for a no confidence motion, or if it's a new committee or quorum vote. The upper house is typically the most powerful, while SPOs sometimes vote only if the active voting stake threshold isn't met. You might see the SPOs as having the weakest position in the tricameral body if they vote least often. However, it is more nuanced than that because the DReps and SPOs can get rid of the constitutional committee.

Also remember the SPOs demonstrated another aspect of Cardano's decentralization when they effectively vetoed the original date for the Vasil hard fork.[734] Does CIP 1694 have any measures in place to stop the SPOs postponing a future hard fork by not upgrading to the latest node?

The CIP appears to favor voting by stake over votes per person. Voting per person requires some notion of identity verification, so there is proof someone is who they claim to be. The CIP explains that a fully decentralized solution for this is currently not possible. With regulation seemingly imminent, it is prudent to steer clear of any mechanism that can be construed as 'centralized' by willfully ignorant parties. That said, the CIP should be open to change in future as decentralized IDs (DIDs) evolve. The World Wide Web Consortium (W3C) announced that Decentralized Identifiers (DIDs) is now an official web standard in summer 2022. IOG Chief Scientist Aggelos Kiayias infers they will inevitably be part of the 4th generation of blockchains.[735]

The CIP states the makeup and role of DReps is subject to change. It will be interesting to see who the community deems to be eligible and how much, if any, domain expertise is required. The naming clash with the Catalyst dReps roel is confusing, especially for Cardano newcomers. As one of the first agenda items is to find a more fitting name for the MBO, perhaps a better name for DRep may also be voted on.

---

[734] @KtorZ 'delay is good', twitter.com/_KtorZ_/status/1538101313564811265?s=20&t=Kygsq-InxS6AO0XhjFfr8g

[735] First Principles: Research for the Future, youtu.be/MVuweooiXPI?t=2280

The initial DRep registration process, and delegation to them, will mimic the certificate system currently used for stake pools. Will this lead to a disproportionate number of SPOs acting as DReps also? As the constitutional committee's initial role is to bootstrap the framework, can they force an agenda if the community interest is too little, or too much? The vote needs a high participation rate in order for a system to be legitimate, but who decides these thresholds?

CIP 1674 is in its infancy, it's hard to be certain how all this theory will work in practice. For example, one of the benefits of the current (5 of 7 keys) system is it's relatively fast. What happens if there is a black swan event, and a major update is needed urgently? Will this apparatus of moving parts be able to affect change in timely manner? If 'Constitution updates' are one of the six governance actions, which part(s) of the constitution can be updated?

Can a malicious party slow it down? If only two of the three chambers will vote in certain scenarios, will there by legislative logjam as happens when a controlling majority of the US senate blocks the house of representatives? What measures are in place to prevent filibusters?

These are just some thoughts, and you can see from the ongoing discussion on GitHub,[736] that bringing this into effect will be non-trivial. That is to be expected. Wouldn't it be suspicious if such a drastic change was enforced quickly without community input? The CIP goes into greater detail on the plans to roll this out gradually in different phases. *Lace* light wallet is not mentioned in the CIP, but It's clear that IOG's new mobile wallet, and other Cardano wallets, will play a pivotal role in user participation and buy-in.

Where we are going

Preparations for implementing CIP 1694 are underway. The current proposal encompasses two new ledger eras. The first era will be called *Conway*, after the celebrated English mathematician John Horton Conway. The current plan for the Conway ledger era is to:

- introduce SPO voting for hard forks
- provide an on-chain mechanism for rotating the governance keys
- re-plumb the ledger rules involving governance as outlined in CIP-1694

Follow the latest updates from the different engineering teams on GitHub.[737]

If CIP 1694 is a success, then we should realize the vision laid out in the *Road to a Polyglot Ecosystem for Cardano* whiteboard video.[738] The governance mechanisms outlined above would allow for multiple clients, with different dev teams, different approaches, programming languages and commercial USPs. There would be no

---

[736] CIP 1694 ongoing conversation, github.com/cardano-foundation/CIPs/pull/380

[737] Ledger team updates, input-output-hk.github.io/cardano-updates/2023-01-19-ledger

[738] Road to a Polyglot Ecosystem for Cardano, youtube.com/watch?v=skcCg1WaedA

canonical[739] client or wallet for Cardano, just certified or uncertified. IOG have been working on this for some time, writing papers and building out expertise in formal methods, specifically with Agda.[740]

The idea would be that interested parties, such as dcSpark, would work with the MBO to form a team of *Cardano Technical Fellows* (CTFs) who maintain the reference architecture. This non-production code would be put through the CIP process, before a formal spec, in Agda, is drafted. This 'Agda core' spec enables code extraction to serve as a reference for testing. The CTFs can prove properties about the spec and also maintain a wallet certification, as well as the core cryptography of the system.

There would no longer be a canonical client of Cardano, just competing clients written in Rust, Typescript, Python and Haskell. The users would just be concerned with if it was certified or not. This creates a healthy 'survival of the fittest' marketplace where security is assured and there is more choice for the end user.

CH at ScotFest keynote:[741]

> So that's Voltaire ...it's deeply philosophical, it's the hardest thing I've ever done in my life, it's the hardest thing you're ever going to do in your life and we're going to get it done, because it needs to get done and I'm damn tired of our industry failing, and it's about time we can point to something and say 'you know what we did it the right way'. We have to tend to our own gardens first. That was a lesson of Candide. So we have to fix Cardano's governance before we have the right to complain about any other person's governance.

To get involved in the Age of Voltaire, you provide feedback on GitHub and participate in the MBO by registering at cardanombo.org

Special Voting Events

It's unclear when Catalyst will resume with Fund10 and how long it will take for CIP 1694 approved and implemented. In the first Town Hall of 2023, the Catalyst team introduced a new concept called *Special Voting Events* (SVE) that will take place using Catalyst tooling. A SVE is a vote held that's unrelated to Catalyst fund cycles. It is a stopgap measure for obtaining community consent on important decisions before CIP-1694 is live.

---

[739] Canonical, in computer science, is the standard state or behavior of an attribute. This term is borrowed from mathematics, where it is used to refer to concepts that are unique and/or natural.

[740] Agda is a dependently typed functional programming language. Charles Hoskinson referred to it as 'Super Haskell'

[741] IO ScotFest Keynote with Charles Hoskinson, youtu.be/tbtkClr3Y3I

Chapter 10: RealFi on Cardano

'Wealth consists not in having great possessions,
but in having few wants.'

— Epictetus

The DeFi Revolution

The number of ada users and software developers working on Cardano is steadily increasing. Sites like *CardanoCube*, *Built on Cardano*, *Building On Cardano*, and *Essential Cardano* are busy mapping a fascinating ecosystem with ~110 projects launched and ~1,100 about to deploy.

Cardano was designed to be a safe and reliable platform for developing blockchain-based assets, services, and systems. Decentralized finance, or DeFi, has risen in popularity in recent years, introducing a slew of new financial products ranging from practical to dubious. DeFi's ultimate purpose, as the market develops, is to assist people and businesses in conducting financial transactions without the need of a central, costly intermediary such as a bank, or in achieving greater returns on their assets in an era of inflation and negative interest rates.

Cardano has extended this further. The goal is to provide low-cost banking and insurance services to the millions of individuals throughout the globe who do not have access to such services. This would aid in the dismantling of barriers between developed and poor countries. This concept is dubbed 'RealFi' by IOG.[742]

Despite the spike in Cardano's popularity, general blockchain awareness and acceptance remain low. Not least, due to the mound of jargon that any crypto-curious individual must wade through. TradFi, DeFi, RealFi, DApp, DEX, liquidity, and other terms are synonymous with the most recent blockchain products.

Why do we need DeFi?

How can we utilize blockchain in everyday life? Why is it important? Blockchain is all about trading or exchanging funds under certain circumstances for an almost limitless variety of uses. Blockchain technology is already used by companies across all verticals.

	Traditional Finance	DeFi
Custody	Held by institution or custody provider	Held directly by users in non-custodial accounts or via smart contract
Unit of Account	Fiat Currency	Denominated in digital asset or stable coin
Execution	Facilitated via intermediaries	Facilitated via smart contract
Settlement	~3-5 business days depending on transaction, during M-F business hours.	Seconds to minutes depending on blockchain, 24/7 operating times.
Clearing	Facilitated via clearinghouses	Facilitated via blockchain transaction
Governance	Specified by exchanges & regulators	Governed by the protocol developers & users
Auditability	Authorized third-party audits	Open source code & public ledger, can be audited by anyone
Collateral	Transactions may involve no collateral, intermediates take on risk	Over-collateral generally required.
Risks	Vulnerable to hacks and data breaches	Vulnerable to hacks and data breaches of smart contracts

---

[742] John O'Connor, 'Welcome to the age of RealFi', iohk.io/en/blog/posts/2021/11/25/welcome-to-the-age-of-realfi/

Figure 69: Traditional Finance v DeFi, Courtesy of CoinYuppie[743]

What is DeFi?

Decentralized finance, often known as DeFi, is a blockchain-based type of finance that serves the same functions as conventional finance (TradFi). You may use cryptocurrencies to make and receive payments, pay for goods and services, and invest in projects rather than bonds or equities. DeFi, on the other hand, does not rely on a middleman and instead relies on smart contracts to settle transactions equitably. RealFi is created by combining an identification layer, such as Atala PRISM,[744] with a 'bridge' to the actual world.

Means of exchange

We traditionally pay for goods and services with money. The most common form of this medium of trade is coins or banknotes issued by central banks. The word fiat has become common among cryptocurrency users to denote real-world money. Fiat money includes the US dollar, the British pound, and the Japanese yen. Since governments no longer have to back their currency with gold, this term has been adopted. Instead, they designate their currencies to be legal tender by a formal decree known as a fiat.

On the blockchain, crypto assets are used instead of fiat currency.

How it all works together

Before we get into the nitty gritty of DeFi nomenclature, let's have a look at how it all works. Smart contracts are the driving force behind security and fair agreements. Assume you've downloaded a DApp and want to lend Bob 10 ada. We need to know that Bob will pay it back, and we'd want to be able to collect some interest if he does so later than expected. Traditionally, users sign contracts that include such terms. This is done on the blockchain as well but using smart contracts.

Smart contract: a code-based automatic digital agreement that monitors, validates, and executes the legally binding portions of a trade between two or more parties. When preset criteria are satisfied, the smart contract algorithm automatically executes the contract steps.

Smart contracts do not access particular data on their own. For example, let's assume we agree with Bob that he will repay us by February 23rd. The date, whether Bob completed a transaction, and whether the supplied amount equals the amount due are all required for a smart contract to execute. Smart contracts make use of oracles to do this.

---

[743] DeFi is innovating at 10 times the rate of traditional finance?, coinyuppie.com/defi-is-innovating-at-10-times-the-rate-of-traditional-finance/

[744] **Atala PRISM** is a decentralized identity solution built on the Cardano blockchain. It creates a new approach to identity management, where users own their identity and have complete control over how their personal data is used and accessed.

An Oracle is a tool for interacting with real-world data. Oracles link to trustworthy external data sources, allowing smart contracts to run by reference information like accurate time, weather, election outcomes, sports statistics, and cryptocurrency markets. Oracles guarantee that data is accurate, timely, and unaltered.

Broader DeFi ecosystem

Users leverage a variety of DeFi systems and apps for a variety of reasons. For example, asset management solutions (or simply wallets) allow customers to store, transmit, and receive cryptocurrencies. There is a plethora of decentralized apps (DApps) available:

With the fast-growing Cardano ecosystem, more and more DeFi goods are coming to Cardano. For their financial requirements, users may now utilize new DApps and platforms. As a result, IOG is focusing on the following to guarantee that users and the developer community can provide and consume high-quality products:

- The DApp Store is a user-friendly store where all Cardano DApps may be found. It will be available via the Lace light wallet, as well as a desktop browser extension. It will be a seamless on-ramp compared to the current experience.

- DApp certification: certification and assurance ensure items satisfy quality standards. While certification is optional (Cardano is open source and decentralized), it helps both developers and consumers since it contains security checks that aid in smart contract audits. There are three certification levels, each of which is useful in conjunction with the others.

DeFi systems and DApps are mostly used for financial transactions. These may be used for investing, lending, and borrowing in addition to funds transfer. In reality, on the blockchain, users may borrow crypto without paying interest:

- Flash loan: operates as a quick loan with no collateral (funds required to secure a loan of other cryptocurrencies or tokens) or know-your-customer (KYC) checks. The flash loan, on the other hand, requires payback inside the same block that it was provided to the borrower. The original transaction is rejected if the loan is not repaid, and the lender keeps the funds.

Let's have a look at a few more of the most often used phrases in DeFi:

Exchange: a cryptocurrency exchange that allows users to purchase and sell cryptocurrency. There are two different kinds of exchanges. A CEX (centralized exchange) is run by a distinct company or structure that is governed by rules and regulations. Users may purchase and sell their assets in a safe, peer-to-peer manner on a DEX (decentralized exchange), which has no middleman.

Another buzzword you'll come across is liquidity. It tracks the amount of circulating supply and trade activities on a particular DEX or CEX. Users' trade demands need the circulation of supplies. This is what liquidity refers to: having a sufficient quantity of coins or tokens to meet the needs of users.

Liquidity encompasses the following actions and concepts that go along with them:

- **Liquidity mining** refers to the practice of producing or adding new currencies or tokens to meet transaction demand. Liquidity miners (providers) are often compensated in order to sustain the user base and create liquidity pools. Yield farming is another name for liquidity mining

- **Liquidity pools**: a collection of deposited cryptocurrencies that serves as a source of liquidity for the network when the currencies are in high demand

- **AMM** (automated market maker): a pool of cryptocurrency that acts as a liquidity provider between 'trading pairs.' A trading pair is a match between two parties, such as Fred who wants to sell his bitcoin and Barney who wants to purchase it. AMMs are decentralized and rely on the liquidity that their users provide.

Decentralized exchanges are more than just handy trading platforms for cryptocurrencies. They may also be used to generate revenue.

Some key terms:

- **Return on investment** (ROI): the profit or loss on an investment, usually stated in percentages

- **Yield farming** is sometimes known as liquidity mining. Farming is a term used to describe a process in which rewards are exchanged for making funds available

- **Yield**: the amount of rewards earned by staking crypto or mining liquidity

- **Leverage**: the act of borrowing with the expectation of making a profit higher than the interest paid.

In a time where some banks are offering negative interest rates, the low-risk way to earn interest on your principal is just by staking, or delegating your stake on Cardano.

Each ada holder has a stake that is proportional to the quantity of ada they hold. A tech-savvy individual may create a stake pool and operate it to assist in the verification of Cardano transactions in exchange for rewards. To get a portion of these rewards, anybody may delegate their ada to a stake pool. There is no danger with this as no ada leaves your wallet. Ada may be delegated, or spent, at any point from your wallet.

August 30, 2020, DeFi 'network effect'. CH:[745]

---

[745] Surprise AMA 08302020, youtu.be/lIz3GnCHbOc?t=993

The reality is that the first mover advantage is actually a disadvantage in DeFi. Those network effects were ephemeral and often covered with mistakes, scars and explosions. You actually want to be in the imitator, the second mover category for DeFi, and I think we'll have a lot more luck than the first movers did in the space and there'll be a mass exodus because those first mover architectures and designs are just too inflexible, and Cardano is much better suited as a platform.

~~DeFi~~ RealFi for the Masses

The term *RealFi* was originally coined by IOG's African operations director, John O'Connor, in his blog in 2021.[746] The phenomenon that is DeFi (decentralized finance) is the focus of many outsiders looking at the crypto industry. Studies like the *SoK: Decentralized Finance*[747] paper from the Imperial College London lay out the core concepts.

RealFi is a superset of DeFi, proposing a regulatory framework made up of four additional features:

- identity,
- metadata,
- governance,
- standards and certification

Identity is the notion that a DApp itself would have some agency. It would have an ID, and its users would have IDs… not traditional IDs as we know them in Web 2,[748] but perhaps decentralized IDs (DIDs) that would still allow them to prove know your customer (KYC) and abide by anti-money laundering (AML) laws, etc. A user can retain some anonymity yet still be able to selectively disclose data when necessary.

Metadata is setting the context for transactions and actors in a system. It is the wider story of why a transfer took place, why certain data was or wasn't provided. It can be the terms and conditions, the end user agreement, signed before using a DEX, etc.

Governance is how the system is maintained. How does a decentralized community upgrade, update and change parameters in DeFi? Who, and by what means, implements change? What is the threshold for certain actions? Why is the threshold set differently for certain updates? Who decides what is a critical update? What mechanisms are in place? How automated should they be?

---

[746] Welcome to the age of RealFi, iohk.io/en/blog/posts/2021/11/25/welcome-to-the-age-of-realfi

[747] SoK: Decentralized Finance (DeFi), berkeley-defi.github.io/assets/material/defi-sok-ariah-2101.08778.pdf

[748] Web 2.0 allows anyone to create content but centralises authorities and gatekeepers, such as major search engines and social media platforms. Web3 enables peer-to-peer interactions without centralized platforms and intermediaries.

Standards and certification in RealFi are still emerging and to be agreed upon. These are the measures by which DApps and projects can be assessed in marketplaces. In a decentralized, open ecosystem, they can be optional but enable users to know more about a product or service provider.

These four features can be used to implement some form of regulatory structure that can be tailored for any jurisdiction. It is now inevitable regulation is coming to the crypto industry after the spate of debacles in 2022.[749] This framework goes some way to meeting the regulator halfway and forming decentralized regulation, aka dReg, aka 'reg tech'. There needs to be some form of overlay for the standard regulatory measures such as transaction reversals, asset freezing, etc.

The motives behind DeFi have too often been 'get rich quick' schemes, with bad actors using customer funds to pay for celebrity adverts, or vanity naming rights for sports stadiums.

There's rarely any intention of offering real loans to people who need them in oppressed regions, without access to basic credit or monetary system. The reason it's called *RealFi* is, beyond the fact that you have these four features above, you also have real use and adoption of an alternative to the traditional financial operating system. A blockchain-based, crypto-based financial stack built on protocols and egalitarianism, instead of centralized entities that repeatedly collapse due to human greed, incompetence, and corruption.

The rest of this chapter outlines some of the building blocks for RealFi. You'll notice that nothing is controlled by a single government, or federated entity.

November 24, 2020. Re: motivation behind Cardano. CH:[750]

> *So why does Cardano exist? I did a TED talk in 2014 and I have not deviated since I did it. I said I care about economic identity. Every day we wake up, there's three billion people who don't have economic identity. They're unbanked, they're outside of the global economy. They get screwed…they pay 85% interest on loans. When their kids go to London and work as maids and wire money back, there's a 15% charge for that. When they get money, they can't hold on to it. They have no insurance, so when a disaster happens, they've nothing to cover it with. So one bad event, one monsoon, one hurricane…they're done. That's the reality for three billion people.*
>
> *. . . So, what's the solution? You can be a bleeding heart liberal and go around donating…telethons don't work. You need an economic solution and the only way to have such a solution is to give people economic identity. You have to give them their own identity, banking system, insurance and lending systems. What are we doing? We are giving people stablecoins, exchanges, the ability to*

---

[749] Top 10 Crypto Scams and Hacks of 2022, u.today/top-10-crypto-scams-and-hacks-of-2022

[750] CROW..Live With Charles Hoskinson of Cardano ADA 11/24/20, youtube.com/watch?v=z3s6olBfbfA

securitize their business interests, peer-to-peer lending, the ability to quantify knowledge with oracles, new business models like decentralized media, decentralized content sharing, new venture capital models… that is what our industry is about at its core.

Atala Prism Decentralized IDs

Atala PRISM is a digital identity platform built on SSI (self-sovereign identity) core principles. It is IOG's suite of services for verifiable data and digital identity.

To define digital identity, we must first understand all that identity entails. A digital identity is data used by a computer to represent an external agent. This can be a person, organization, application, or device. A verifiable credential is a set of claims and metadata that cryptographically prove who issued it. They are similar to the physical documents you use like a driver's license or passport.

A digital entity might use a verifiable credential to share information online. This exchange of info poses some concerns about security, however, like how safe is the data you share once it's out there in the open. Who really controls the data? Is it really decentralized?

With social media requesting so much personal information, and centralized crypto exchanges behaving like banks, securing your own identity has never been more important. **Self-Sovereign Identity (SSI)** and decentralized IDs (DIDs) aim to solve this problem.

Self-sovereign identity is an approach to digital identity, based on a set of principles,[751] that gives individuals control over the information they use to prove who they are online.

Decentralized identifiers (DIDs) are a type of identifier that allows for verifiable, decentralized digital identity. A DID can be tied to any subject (e.g., a person, organization, thing, data model, abstract entity, etc.) as determined by the controller of the DID. The World Wide Web Consortium (W3C) DID Working Group defines a DID in its core specification:

- DIDs are controlled by the entities that hold them,
- They enable cryptographic authentication of the DID holder,
- They describe the discovery of information needed to launch secure and privacy-preserving communication methods.
- Give access to service-independent data portability.

In June 2022, the World Wide Web Consortium (W3C) approved the advancement of the DID core specification to the W3C *Recommendation* stage. This was a milestone as it

---

[751] SSI principles, github.com/WebOfTrustInfo/self-sovereign-identity/blob/master/self-sovereign-identity-principles.md

endorsed the continuous research of **digital identity,** and paves the way for identity platforms such as Atala PRISM. The approval of the specification, opposed by some big tech giants (Google, Apple, et al), gives the DIDs credibility and impetus for broader adoption.

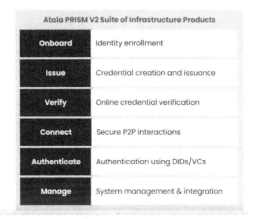

Atala PRISM V2: A suite of identity infrastructure products

PRISM V2 is Atala's next-generation SSI offering, based on the learnings of Atala PRISM V1.x

- Supports **global identity standards** that make Atala solutions more widely applicable across different ecosystems and use cases

- Improved architectural model to increase **maintainability** and **scalability**

- **Differentiates** through values and approach (privacy preservation, ease of integration into ecosystems, performance)

- Targeted towards two key stakeholders in the new data economy:
  - **Individuals** – by making verifiable data work in the form of seamless, trustworthy interactions
  - **Service providers** that need to meet compliance needs

Atala PRISM V2 Suite of Infrastructure Products	
Onboard	Identity enrollment
Issue	Credential creation and issuance
Verify	Online credential verification
Connect	Secure P2P interactions
Authenticate	Authentication using DIDs/VCs
Manage	System management & integration

Figure 70: Atala Prism V2, from Denitsa Bogoeva's talk at ScotFest.

The Atala Prism team have been working with DIDs for some time. They have implemented large scale solutions with the likes of DISH (dish.com) in the US, and the Ethiopian Ministry of Education. They also have a pioneers program, with two completed programs in 2022 and over 200 developers building on Atala.

Atala Prism V2 builds on the lessons of the past few years, and addresses issues like conforming to standards and compliance with laws such as the Travel Rule.[752] It is built for seamless integrations with partners like the *Lace* light wallet.

Babel Fees

Cardano is introducing a novel mechanism that allows the payment of transaction fees in user-defined tokens on Cardano. Babel fees are named after the Babel fish,[753] a creature in Douglas Adam's book *The Hitchhiker's Guide to the Galaxy* that enables you to hear any language translated into your own. Despite the galaxy's many varied languages, this vision of global translation provides for meaningful communication.

---

[752] The Travel Rule requires parties to obtain and exchange beneficiary and originator information with virtual assets transfers over a certain threshold.

[753] Babel Fish, hitchhikers.fandom.com/wiki/Babel_Fish.

Smart contracts allow for the creation of a wide range of unique tokens in the cryptocurrency sector. Babel fees are based on the idea of using your preferred token to interact with the platform. Similar to how you would interact with legacy financial systems, where you would use your local currency by just making a selection in a dropdown. 'Babel fees' convert the token you're using to the one required by the platform for transactions or whatever trade you want to execute on the platform. IOG's chief scientist, Prof Aggelos Kiavias,[754] was ahead of the curve when introducing this concept early in 2021. IOG also produced a video whiteboard walkthrough[755] on their 'IOHK' YouTube channel at the time. The paper 'Babel Fees via Limited Liabilities' was subsequently published in April 2022.[756]

In most blockchains, it's typical that a legitimate transaction must come at a cost to the sender. Without such a limitation, anybody may overwhelm the system with minor transactions, overflowing its capacity and leaving it worthless. On that basis, a common implication is that for any blockchain that supports user-defined currencies, paying transaction fees in such tokens should be forbidden. Instead, transactions should be charged a fee in the platform's native token, which is seen as valuable by all the token holders (hodlers[757]). It's arguable that such a limitation is bad for adoption and interoperability with other blockchains and legacy systems. How are IOG planning to work around this shortcoming?

EUTXO enables innovation

Cryptography and game theory[758] have a history of making the seemingly impossible achievable. Cardano's Extended UTXO (EUTXO) architecture enables a solution because of how native assets function on the platform.

Tokens may be generated using a minting policy, and they are regarded similarly to ada on the ledger. Creating a valid transaction requires the consumption of one or more UTXOs. On Cardano, a UTXO may hold more than simply ada; it can also handle a token bundle containing numerous distinct tokens, both fungible and non-fungible. It is therefore feasible to use a single UTXO to construct transactions that transfer many

---

[754] Babel Fees, iohk.io/en/blog/posts/2021/02/25/babel-fees/

[755] Cardano360 - February 2021, youtu.be/YXaK0cvgoFQ?t=2184

[756] Chakravarty, Karayannidis, Kiayias, Peyton Jones, Vinogradova (2022), 'Babel Fees via Limited Liabilities', iohk.io/en/research/library/papers/babel-fees-via-limited-liabilities/

[757] **HODL** is slang in the cryptocurrency community for holding the cryptocurrency rather than selling it. HODL can also mean 'Hold On for Dear Life' and refers to not selling, even during strong market volatility and poor market performance.

[758] **Game theory** is the study of mathematical models of strategic interaction in between rational decision-makers. It has applications in all fields of social science, as well as in logic and computer science. Originally, it addressed zero-sum games, in which each participant's gains or losses are exactly balanced by those of the other participants. Today, game theory applies to a wide range of behavioral relations and is now an umbrella term for the science of logical decision making in humans, animals, and computers.

distinct tokens. Ergo, underrated pioneers in the crypto space, have already delivered 15k outputs per transaction using EUTXO and rollups.[759]

The ledger's transaction fees are priced in ada, using a function fixed as a ledger parameter. The costs necessary for a successful transaction may be anticipated accurately prior to execution, which is a key strength of Cardano's EUTXO architecture. This is a unique property that other ledger configurations do not have.

How will Babel Fees work?

Babel fees enable a transaction to announce an ada-denominated debt equal to the amount of fees the transaction issuer is required to pay. A transaction like this would be rejected by the ledger. However, it might be seen as an open offer in which the debt is taken on. Why would someone accept such a burden? To make this attractive, the transaction may give some quantity of token(s) to whoever covers the debt. The assumption being the token bundle is already existing in Cardano. This would be a one-to-one transaction between ada and the given token(s) at a fixed rate.

Consider a block producer who notices a transaction like this. The block producer may generate a matching transaction and claim the tokens on offer by absorbing the debt and covering it with ada. The transaction with the debt, as well as its matching transaction, become admissible to the ledger as a group. The set of two transactions becomes priced in ada as a whole because of the debt absorption, and so it does not violate the ledgers' accounting requirements in terms of ada fees. Therefore, the transaction with the debt is settled.

Users can propose transactions priced in whatever token(s) they own and have them settle in the ledger as normal transactions if a block maker is ready to take them up on the spot trade.[760] This shows how native assets, the EUTXO architecture, and the small but powerful change of adding liabilities in the form of negative values in token bundles can handle Babel fees, allowing users to price transactions in any token that the system supports natively.

For the above concept to work, Cardano must have liquidity providers who have ada and are ready to issue matching transactions. The ecosystem of thousands of stake pool operators (SPOs) are obvious initial candidates to make the market by advertising exchange rates for their preferred tokens, etc.

Following the introduction of native assets with the *Mary* hard fork, the possibility of negative amounts in token bundles can be incorporated into Cardano's ledger rules. Aside from Babel fees, this opens up other use cases such as atomic swaps[761] for spot

---

[759] Roundtable with Charles Hoskinson and Alex Chepurnoy | Ergo Pulse, youtube.com/watch?v=k9a3SYV6FJA

[760] **Spot trading** is a continuous process of buying and selling tokens and coins at a spot price for immediate settlement. The trader usually intends to gain profits from market fluctuations.

transactions. It's just another example of how Cardano innovates instead of forking and copying first and second-generation blockchains.

A worked example

Below is an example transaction in human readable format. This is about Bill, Ted and Barney exchanging ada and a new native token, JohnCoin (JCN).

Transaction:
< Receive 20 ada from Bill
> Send 10 ada to Ted
> Send 9.66 ada to Bill
–Use 0.34 ada as the transaction fee

Bill has received 20 ada in the past, so has a UTXO worth 20 ada in Daedalus. He takes that UTXO, sends 10 ada to Ted, 9.66 ada back to himself, and uses the leftover 0.34 as the transaction fee. For it to be a legitimate transaction, the inputs and the outputs must be equal, ie. $20 = 10 + 9.66 + 0.34$

Now let's look at a transaction that uses JohnCoin, JCN as well as ada.

Transaction:
<Receive 20 JCN from Bill
<Receive 4 ada from Bill
>Send 10 JCN to Ted
>Send 10 JCN to Bill
>Send 3.66 ada to Bill
–Use 0.34 ada as the transaction fee

This time Bill wanted to send 10 JCN to Ted. He also had to include some 'extra' ada to cover the transaction fee. It worked fine, but it was inconvenient and not really sustainable if we were dealing with hundreds, or thousands, of transactions.

Here's how this same transaction would work with Babel fees.

Transaction:
<Receive 20 JCN from Bill
>Send 10 JCN to Ted
>Send 8 JCN to Bill
>Send -0.34 ada and 2 JCN to whomever takes on the debt
–Use 0.34 ada as the transaction fee

This poses some questions:

How can Bill pay the 0.34 ada fee if he didn't have any ada in Daedalus begin with? With

---

[761] An **atomic swap** is an exchange of cryptocurrencies from separate blockchains. The swap is conducted between two entities without a third party's involvement. The idea is to remove centralized intermediaries like regulated exchanges and give token owners total control.

babel fees, this isn't a problem. So long as the inputs equal the outputs, the transaction is legit. The negative and positive ada in the outputs cancel each other out.

How can Bill send a negative amount of ada to just anyone, as a valid transaction? It isn't a valid transaction until someone 'volunteers' to take on the debt. It has to be voluntary as no one can be sent negative ada without their permission. Why would anyone 'volunteer' to take on the debt? They would not only take on the debt, ie. the negative ada, they would also receive the additional 2 JCN.

So the first user to 'volunteer' to take on the debt, Barney in this example, will make a transaction as follows:

Transaction:
<Receive 4 ada from Barney
<Receive -0.34 ada and 2 JCN from Bill's transaction
>Send 3.32 ada to Barney
>Send 2 JCN to Barney
–Use 0.34 ada as the transaction fee

Barney has volunteered to take on the debt of -0.34 debt, in doing so validating Bill's transaction. All fees were technically paid in ada, however, the way Bill sees it, he only paid using JCN.

If Barney wants the 2 JCN, he must also accept the -0.34 ada. They cannot be separated. Note that since two transactions were needed for this process to work, the total amount of fees paid was double than normal, 0.68 ada.

This means that the amount of JCN that Bill pays has to be greater than or equal to 0.68 ada to make it worth it for Barney. Since fees are relatively small on Cardano compared to other chains, doubling them shouldn't be a major issue.

This system works as long as there are users who consider the asset 'JohnCoin' JCN to be of value. They will compete in a fair and open market to offer the best exchange rate for fees. Tokens not considered valuable are useless in this system and can't be used to pay fees, but that's the way it should be.

Research comes to life

Babel fees is just one area where IOG are bringing research into reality. IOG research engineer Paulina Vinogradova presented the elegant solutions being considered, competitive analysis of other chains' solutions, as well as some of the remaining challenges in this presentation.[762]

February 27, 2021. Re: Babel fees. CH:[763]

---

[762] Babel fees via limited liabilities, youtube.com/watch?v=iJEmRZ6leXE

[763] Surprise AMA 02/26/2021, youtu.be/6eD_rnII3ms?t=42

...basically, what that does is it gives every token issued on Cardano the ability to pay in the native asset, if there is a market for it. So it solves all the problems at the same time and you, as token issuers, now have your own network. It used to be that either you had to go borrow another network and pay in that network's fees, or you had to launch your own network and build a network effect behind it. This is the third option. The space currently does not allow that to exist. There are some clever hacks here and there, but for the most part, it's a new thing. It's an elegant thing and it's a thing that's brought uniquely because of Extended UTXO.

And that's the magic of doing things correctly. When you do things correctly, it's very easy to just innovate, and just add and say, 'here you go'. What that means is we're probably going to be the ultimate stablecoin platform for all the stablecoins because you pay the transaction fee in the stablecoin. You don't have to pay 100 of Eth to send a dollar of Tether.[764] you know that's the point, and that's what we've been looking for and that was just one of many things that came.

Stablefees

Cardano has a novel technique for making fees more equitable, stable, and predictable over time. Enabling transactions on cryptocurrency platforms runs afoul of the platform's underlying asset's dual purpose. Users may keep and trade it as part of their investment portfolios on one hand. On the other hand, it provides the 'gas' required for transaction processing. Because of this duality, the system should have a process for changing transaction prices so that they stay competitive and acceptable. The system should also enable users to identify the optimal fee for fast transaction processing, based on their particular demands.

Transaction fees are required for three reasons: For starters, transaction processing costs the system in terms or resources consumed. Allowing transaction processors, stake pool operators, to offset their expenses is only fair. Secondly, even with theoretically limitless capacity, transaction issuers must be prevented from flooding the network with worthless transactions in a DDoS attack. Thirdly, incentivizing transaction processors to deliver high-quality service is good practice.

The above issues may be addressed by charging transaction fees.

Learning from the past

The first system for pricing transactions on distributed ledger was introduced by Bitcoin. This system works in the same way as a first-price auction: transactions bid for a spot in a

---

[764] **Tether** (ticker USDT) is a cryptocurrency that is hosted on the Ethereum and Bitcoin blockchains, among others. Its tokens are issued by the Hong Kong company Tether Limited, which in turn is controlled by the owners of Bitfinex. Tether is called a stablecoin because it was originally designed to always be worth US$1.00, maintaining $1.00 in reserves for each tether issued.

block with a certain reward, and block producers choose which transactions to include. Block producers are also granted the power to mint new coins, meaning that their operations are funded by the whole community via an increase in the overall currency supply. Over time, inflation decreases linearly, and transaction fees become more prominent in the rewards. This process has been challenged for its inefficiency, despite the fact that it has allowed Bitcoin to function for well over a decade. Over time, transaction fees have also increased.

In the Summer 2021, IOG introduced a new mechanism that compliments the Babel fees[765] idea and expands on Cardano's approach to ledger rules and system assets. The goal is to make fees fair, consistent, and predictable over time. The mechanism is described in the context of Cardano but it may be applied to any other cryptocurrency with equivalent properties.

What are Stablefees?

Stablefees' central concept is to provide a base pricing for transactions by tying them to a basket of commodities or currencies. Stablefees include native 'decentralized reserve' contract which produces and administers a stablecoin tied to the basket.

The idea mirrors the workings of the International Monetary Fund's SDR (Special Drawing Rights)[766] which is a fiat currency that is evaluated against a basket of five currencies: the US dollar, the euro, the Chinese renminbi, the Japanese yen, and the British pound sterling. The stablecoin, or 'Basket Equivalent Coin' (BEC), is the currency that is used to pay transaction fees (and other pricing needs of the platform like Stake pool operator costs).

Ada has a dual purpose in this system: it serves as a reserve asset for the decentralized reserve and as a reward unit for staking. In severe cases when the reserve contract's liquidity is depleted, it may also be used as a fallback currency. The issuer will need to receive BECs before completing a transaction, either via third parties or directly by transferring ada to the decentralized reserve contract.

What criteria will the reserve use to distribute BECs? In return for ada, the reserve contract will also issue equity shares, referred to as decentralized equity coins (DECs). The decentralized reserve will often change the value of BEC to be tied to the underlying basket of commodities by leveraging the value of DECs. DECs will absorb ada vs. the basket fluctuations to keep the real-world value of BECs consistent. The AgeUSD[767] stablecoin has already been implemented on Ergo (sigmausd.io). Ergo (ergoplatform.org) is an innovative proof-of-work blockchain (also EUTXO-based) co-founded by the prodigious Alex Chepurnoy.[768]

---

[765] Babel fees - denominating transaction costs in native tokens, iohk.io/en/blog/posts/2021/02/25/babel-fees/

[766] Special Drawing Rights (SDR), imf.org/en/About/Factsheets/Sheets/2016/08/01/14/51/Special-Drawing-Right-SDR

[767] The AgeUSD Stablecoin Protocol, github.com/Emurgo/age-usd

[768] Alexander Chepurnoy, ergoplatform.org/en/hall_of_fame/

These three coins, which are issued by the system natively, will appeal to various groups. The security and liquidity of BECs (Basket equivalent coin) may appeal to risk-averse, transaction-heavy investors. DECs (decentralized equity coins) will get the most benefits if ada rises but will suffer the greatest losses if ada falls. DECs may be more appealing to long-term investors. Furthermore, since decentralized reserve pricing these currencies in ada, both BECs and DECs may make staking and governance easier. Returns may be provided at various rates, depending on the type of the coin. Ultimately, all rewards will be priced and paid in ada, which will continue to be the most adaptable of the three currencies.

Oracles

An on-chain oracle is at the heart of this system, determining the price of the basket in ada. This oracle may be implemented using stake pool operators (SPOs) in a decentralized fashion. From the fees received during BEC/DEC issuances, the reserve might award further rewards to all oracle contributors. This will guarantee two things: thousands of contributors from all over the world, and ledger rules that calculate a synthesized exchange rate in a canonical manner. For example, through a weighted median across all price submissions in an epoch. If oracle contributors misuse their contributions, their reputation and performance on-chain can be tracked, and they may be held responsible.

How does the pricing work?

How should transactions be priced, and block producers rewarded? Using the existing approach on Cardano, each transaction will be deterministically converted to a specific value denominated in BECs, using a formula defined by the ledger rules. The formula will consider transaction size as well as processing needs and may include runtime metrics like mean system load. The base fee will be the result, ensuring that the transaction will be executed by the system. End users will be able to raise the fee by applying a multiplier to the base fee and speed up processing. This will be important during periods of high demand.

When contrasted to the first-price auction model, this strategy has one advantage: the pricing mechanism is continually stabilized to a fair default value. If necessary, users do price discovery in just one direction to speed up processing. Furthermore, transaction issuers may hoard BECs to protect their future transaction-issuing capacity while avoiding ada price volatility.

Stablefees vs Babel fees

The Stablefees mechanism may be seen as an extension of Babel fees, and both mechanisms work well together and complement each other. Babel fees may be used in tandem with Stablefees with one caveat: instead of ada, BECs can be used to pay Babel fees. This means that all costs will be paid in ada (via a Babel fee liability convertible in

---

ada on the spot). As a result, the whole process is backwards compatible in that it won't affect casual users who just have ada and don't want to get BECs.

Regarding diversity, while the above scenario describes a single global BEC, the same technique may be used to issue regional BECs pegged to multiple commodity baskets with varied weightings. Such 'regional' BECs will be able to boost system inclusiveness while also allowing SPOs to have more fine-grained transaction inclusion policies.

Stablefees 'lite' alternative

The above approach necessitates the use of a decentralized reserve contract and the contract's issuance of BECs and DECs (decentralized equity coins) to purchasers. A 'lite' version forgoes the reserve contract and instead modifies the fee formula directly using the price oracle to peg it to the agreed-upon basket of commodities. The mechanism that results denominates transaction costs in BECs and instantly converts them to ada. The amount due varies based on the value of BEC. The process is otherwise comparable, with the multiplier allowing unidirectional price discovery.

The main drawback is that a potential transaction issuer does not have access to a native token that allows for predictable transaction processing; instead, transaction issuers must pay fees in ada. Nonetheless, the fees will adapt and hold steady in relation to the basket due to the pegging mechanism. Therefore, a transaction issuer will be able to properly structure their off-chain asset portfolio to suit their transaction requirements.

Research-driven approach

The granular aspects of the Stablefees mechanism are being researched by IOG. Charles Hoskinson mentioned in a recent update[769] that Tiered Pricing and Babel Fees are low-hanging fruit that needs to get implemented soon. It's likely Stablefees will follow around that timeframe also. The pricing oracle and the global BEC will very likely find more uses other than just paying transaction fees, extending the potential of Cardano DApps.

Tiered Pricing as the network scales

Cardano's adoption will keep growing as demand for decentralized finance grows. IOG's research team are continually reviewing methods to ensure that all users have equal access and throughput. The Cardano network will stretch and develop to fulfill the need for smart contracts and DeFi. Similarly, the transaction fee model used by Cardano will need to be upgraded.

The existing approach is straightforward and equitable: every transaction is processed equally, and users cannot change their priority by paying greater fees. This strategy works effectively as long as the throughput capacity is similar to the demand.

However, there are certain disadvantages. With more people using Cardano, there will come a point when not all transactions will be able to be included on the blockchain, even

---

[769] Surprise AMA 01/07/2023, youtu.be/djhKk-3rYhU?t=875

if the parameters are tweaked. Although boosting the mainchain's capacity and routing transactions to Hydra will help relieve this issue, the core system must always remain adaptable in all potential scenarios.

In the event of a denial of service (DoS) attack, this is significant. With the system as it is, an attacker may take advantage of the system's fairness and pass their harmful spam off as legal transactions, causing everyone else to wait longer. There are safeguards in place that make an attack like this impractical. However, for further security, the network should be able to raise the costs of such attacks without endangering the system's fairness and price efficiency.

In 2022, members of the IOG's research team began working on this issue. The solution presented preserves the cornerstones of Cardano transaction processing (predictability, fairness, and cheap access) while addressing the challenges that may develop as demand grows. For blockchains, IOG's method proposes an innovative transaction fee structure. The design's major feature is dividing each block into three 'tiers' depending on the use case. Each tier is intended for various sorts of transactions and accounts for a certain proportion of the maximum block size. The tiers, as well as the recommended division that IOG considered, are as follows:

- fair (50%)
- balanced (30%)
- immediate (20%)

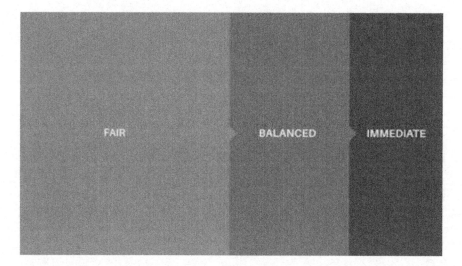

Figure 71: Tiered pricing: a block can be split into three tiers.

Going from right to left from the graphic above… 'Immediate' and 'Balanced' function by having a distinct 'fee threshold' for each. Transaction issuers would define the tier of service they need in order to be included in a block. This may be accomplished by imposing a transaction fee cap. Then, beginning with the 'immediate' tier, the 'balanced' tier, and lastly the 'fair' tier, each block would be filled. Within the same tier, similar transactions would be charged the same rate. To make this decision easier, each transaction would only be paid the smallest fee that would ensure its inclusion in the block. Fees for 'immediate' and 'balanced' tiers would be dynamically and deterministically adjusted after each block (using demand levels in prior blocks) to guarantee that each tier consumes its desired percentage of the block.

The distinction between 'immediate' and 'balanced' tiers is the manner in which fees are changed, notably the 'speed' with which they change given the present load. The 'immediate' service threshold would always be greater than 'balanced', reacting more quickly to demand and assuring that the transaction requesting it would be served as quickly as feasible. The 'balanced' threshold would be slower to adapt and more stable, making it inappropriate for time-sensitive transactions, but it would provide a lower, more consistent price in exchange for a longer, more variable waiting period.

The 'balanced' and 'immediate' tiers are designed to manage transactions with varying degrees of urgency, while the 'fair' tier is designed to handle everyday transactions. The 'fair' tier is meant to be an improvement of Cardano's present approach, keeping fees low (or even stable, by pegging to a basket of commodities/fiat, as discussed in IOG's blog[770] on stablefees) and eliminating any uncertainty for users. This tier would work similarly as Cardano does now (Jan 2023), as long as demand is minimal, and transactions fit inside half of the block.

However, if demand grows, a unique mechanism for 'fair' tier transactions will be activated. The approach would use a priority function to filter transactions in a fee-independent way. Giving precedence to transactions based on the age and quantity of their UTXOs is an example of this. The sum of the quantity of each input multiplied by its age, then divided by the total size of the transactions in bytes, would be the priority of a given transaction. This priority might be used with a threshold (updated dynamically after each block) to reject transactions with too low a priority. By constantly offering a cheap way into each block, such a method ensures **liveness** for each transaction at a low and predictable price, limiting the impact of a malicious attacker, or a rush in demand, on pricing.

The notion of the multiplier, which IOG established in the stablefees concept, is also extended, and clarified by the tiered pricing approach. As a result, each of the three tiers has a deterministically computed multiplier, whose value is determined by the congestion of the appropriate tier in prior blocks. The 'fair' tier always has a multiplier of 1.

This technique differs from existing pricing approaches, such as those employed by Bitcoin or Ethereum (even allowing for Ethereum Improvement Proposal EIP-1559),[771] in which each transaction must surpass a variable fee to be included in a block. The disadvantage of this strategy is that the fee that everyone must pay is determined by the 'richest' customers. Worse again, this is the fee that the wealthiest users pay to have it turned into a block 'immediately.' Furthermore, since the ideal bidding strategy is not obvious to users, these sorts of transaction fee mechanisms might unwittingly 'shape'

---

[770] Prof Aggelos Kiayias, 'Stablefees and the Decentralized Reserve System', iohk.io/en/blog/posts/2021/06/10/stablefees-and-the-decentralized-reserve-system/

[771] EIP 1559, cnbc.com/2021/08/04/what-to-know-about-the-ethereum-london-hard-fork-eip-1559-upgrade.html

demand or inadvertently raise prices, even if the fees are largely a function of supply and demand.

The multi-tiered strategy is more polished. It recognizes that not every transaction has the same requirements, allowing several use cases to take place at the same time and allowing users to easily choose the service they want. Tiered pricing allows for predictable and fair fees while reducing congestion on the main chain in this manner. Tiered pricing, when combined with design changes that concentrate on improving the main chain's raw throughput capacity and processing power, demonstrates how Cardano will be able to handle any transaction processing demand.

Djed stablecoin

Cardano's primary stablecoin is named after *Djed*, the symbol of 'stability' in ancient Egypt and the symbolic backbone of the god *Osiris*, the god of the afterlife and resurrection. Djed is the first stablecoin to remove price fluctuation via formal verification. One of the major roadblocks to cryptocurrency adoption is its volatility. Transparency, immutability of data, and proven security of financial transactions are all advantages of blockchain technology. It is, however, more difficult to forecast crypto market fluctuations compared to fiat currencies. This makes it difficult to use cryptocurrency in everyday life.

A stablecoin is a cryptocurrency that is pegged[772] to a basket of fiat currencies or a single fiat currency; commodities such as gold or silver; equities; or other cryptocurrencies. Stablecoins have built-in processes that maintain a minimal price variation from their target price, making them suitable for storing or exchanging value since the volatility is removed.

There are three main stablecoin types:

- Over-collateralized stablecoin backed by basket of other cryptocurrencies
- Algorithmic – the reserve (made up usually of one or more cryptocurrencies) is controlled by an algorithm
- Fiat-backed – a fiat currency reserve is used as collateral

---

[772] Pegging means attaching or tying a currency's exchange rate to another currency

Djed VS Other Stablecoins

	Overcollateralized (Djed)	Algorithmic	Fiat backed
Centralization	Decentralized	Decentralized	Centralized
Collateral	Exogenous collateral ($ADA)	Endogenous collateral	Exogenous collateral (fiat)
Collateralization	Overcollateralized – up to 1:8	Partially collateralized	Collateralized 1:1
Reimbursements	$DJED is always redeemable for the collateral ($ADA)	Algorithmic stablecoins depend on the value of the governance token	Fiat backed stablecoins depend on trust in the issuer
Stability	Djed stability is based on overcollateralization	Algorithmic stablecoins stability is based on trust on a governance token	Fiat backed stablecoins stability is based on trust in the issuer

Figure 72: Stablecoin Classification

The price stability of certain stablecoins is jeopardized due to a lack of transparency and liquidity in their reserves. To solve these issues, IOG has partnered up with Emurgo (another of Cardano's three founding partners) and the Ergo blockchain, which, like Cardano, employs the UTXO-based accounting model, to develop Djed, a stablecoin contract. The implementation was based on the Djed research paper.[773]

How stablecoins work underneath the hood

Different processes contribute to the coin's value stability and assist to minimize price fluctuations. The economic concepts of supply and demand underlie these systems. A popular technique is to back the stablecoin with a reserve of the pegged currency. If demand for 'buy' or 'sell' orders exceeds supply, the supply should be raised to minimize price swings.

Stablecoin reserves are not usually kept in cash. They are usually invested in financial assets that provide interest, such as bonds. The operator raises funds from the returns on these investments. Price stability is maintained as long as the stablecoin is fully backed by reserves in the currency to which it is tied — and the operator can respond rapidly to fluctuations in demand.

The Djed stablecoin is intended to be a fiat currency-pegged asset with a governing algorithm. This method ensures a steady flow of funds. Djed isn't only a dollar-denominated currency. It can function with any currency if oracles are available to provide the contract with the appropriate price index.

---

[773] Zahnentferner, Kaidalov, Etienne, Díaz (2021) 'Djed: A Formally Verified Crypto-Backed Pegged Algorithmic Stablecoin', eprint.iacr.org/2021/1069.pdf

Djed's reserve coin is called **Shen**, continuing with the ancient Egyptian theme. The Shen is said to be a symbol of both royalty and symmetry with a deep connection with infinity and permanence.

Risks

Investments are often connected with stablecoin reserves. Due to the lack of liquidity in these investments, the operator may be unable to respond quickly to demand. In the short term, this weakens stability. Fiat-backed stablecoins have the disadvantage of requiring faith in the parties holding the reserves. Tether stablecoin (USDT) has already fallen as low as $0.92 in 2017[774] due to a lack of reserve transparency and the 'full-backing' claim, as well as ineffective stabilizing safeguards.

When the underpinning asset is a cryptocurrency on a public blockchain, there are no transparency concerns. Furthermore, because of its automated and secure processes, the adoption of smart contracts allows the rapid and reliable implementation of stabilizing steps.

What category of stablecoin is Djed?

Djed is categorized as an over-collateralized stablecoin. The semantics are important because although Djed uses an algorithm, using an algorithm in itself is not a reason to be called an algorithmic stable coin. Djed uses external collateral (ada) which is unrelated to the protocol. Algorithmic stablecoins uses internal collateral, like in the case of Luna and UST. Djed is over-collateralized 4x to 8x, while algorithmic stable coins are usually only partially collateralized. Over-collateralized stable coins are traditionally less capital efficient, however, djed is different and actually fixes that with the Shen model with its symbiotic relationship. So djed is very capital efficient... one dollar worth of ada always equals one dollar worth of djed.

Another difference is djed is always redeemable for the collateral, which is ada. Algorithmic stablecoins are not always redeemable. They are dependent on the value of the governance token. Djed stability is based on over-collateralization and not on the trust on the governance token, which is what you need to have if you're using an algorithmic stable coin.

Djed is a crypto-backed algorithmic stablecoin contract which functions as an autonomous bank. It works by minting and burning stablecoins and reserve coins, as well as holding a reserve of base coins. The contract uses the reserve to buy and sell stablecoins and charges fees that accrue in the reserve to keep the price of stablecoins pegged to a target price. Holders of reserve coins, who contribute funds to the reserve while accepting the risk of price volatility, are the beneficiaries of this revenue stream.

Formal verification – the theory behind Djed

---

[774] Tether Price History and Everything You Need to Know, rain.bh/learn/tether-price-history-and-information-you-need-for-tether-trading

Djed is the first stablecoin protocol that has been formally verified. Djed's design and stability features are considerably enhanced by the use of formal methods[775] in the programming process. Mathematical theorems are used to prove the properties using formal methods:

- Maintain the upper and lower bounds: the price will not move above or below the given price. Purchases and sales are not restricted in the typical reserve ratio range, and users have no motive to trade stablecoins on the secondary market outside of the peg range

- Peg stability during market crashes: the peg is maintained up to a certain limit, which is set by the reserve ratio, even when the price of the base coin falls drastically

- There is no insolvency since there is no bank involved, there is no bank contract to go bankrupt

- No bank runs because all users are treated equally and honestly, there is no reason for users to scramble to redeem their stablecoins

- Monotonically rising equity per reserve coin: the reserve excess per reserve coin is guaranteed to rise when users engage with the contract under certain circumstances. Reserve coin holders are certain to earn under these circumstances

- No reserve draining: under certain circumstances, it is impossible for a rogue user to carry out a series of acts that would deplete the bank's reserves

- Bounded dilution: there is a limit on reserve coin holders and their profit can be diluted as a result of issuing more reserve coins.

Versions

Djed is available in two versions:

- Minimal Djed: This version aims to be as minimal, intuitive, and simple as possible while maintaining stability

- Extended Djed: this more sophisticated version offers greater stability. The adoption of a continuous pricing model and dynamic fees to further encourage the maintenance of an appropriate reserve ratio are the primary distinctions.

Implementations

---

[775] **Formal verification** is the act of proving or disproving the correctness of intended algorithms underlying a system with respect to a certain formal specification or property, using formal methods of mathematics. Formal verification can be helpful in proving the correctness of systems such as: cryptographic protocols, combinational circuits, digital circuits with internal Memory, and software expressed as source code.

IOG, Ergo, and Emurgo have been testing various techniques by implementing the Djed stablecoin contract.

SigmaUSD on Ergo was the first Djed stablecoin contract to be deployed. In Q1 2021, it was the first stablecoin to be implemented on a UTXO-based ledger. It contained a 1% charge for buying and selling transactions, as well as an hourly exchange rate update from an oracle. An unidentified user with a big quantity of ERGs (Ergo's native currency) launched a reserve draining attack against the first version but the attempt was unsuccessful, and the perpetrator is said to have lost $100k.

To deter similar attacks, the first version of Minimal Djed was replaced with a version in which the charge was set to 2%, the oracle updated every 12 minutes, and each oracle update could only affect the price by 0.49 % unless the price difference was larger than 50%. This increased resistance to reserve draining attacks.

The IOG team has also implemented Djed in Solidity. One version employs the Ethereum blockchain's native currency ether as a base coin, while the other can use any ERC20-compliant token as a base coin. These implementations have been launched to testnets for Binance Smart Chain, Avalanche Fuji, Polygon Mumbai, Ethereum Kovan,[776] Ethereum Rinkeby, and RSK testnets so far.

In addition, there is an OpenStar implementation. OpenStar is a Scala-based[777] framework for private permissioned blockchains. Djed's implementation with OpenStar is based on the concept of off-chain smart contract execution in order to create a stablecoin on Cardano that is not reliant on on-chain smart contracts.

Djed implementation on Cardano

Cardano's Alonzo upgrade made Plutus smart contracts possible. Plutus runs on Haskell, which ensures a secure, full-stack development environment. Djed's implementation has run in parallel, and assisted in, Plutus V2's development.

Stablecoins and reserve coins are native assets in this implementation that are uniquely recognized by the hash of the monetary policy that regulates their minting and burning via the Djed protocol. This approach also expects that oracle data, such as the exchange rate, be delivered to transactions as signed data rather than being posted on the blockchain.

See the Djed paper or Bruno Woltzenlogel Paleo's talk at Ergo summit 2021[778] for more information about Djed stablecoin.

---

[776] **Kovan** is a Proof of Authority (PoA) publicly accessible blockchain for Ethereum; created and maintained by a consortium of Ethereum developers.

[777] **Scala** is a general-purpose programming language providing support for functional programming and a strong static type system. Designed to be concise, many of Scala's design decisions aimed to address criticisms of Java.

[778] Ergo Summit 2021 - Entering The New Era - Announcing AgeUSD & The Hardening Upgrade, youtube.com/watch?v=zG-rxMCDIa0&t=8366s

COTI (currency of the internet)

COTI is a longtime partner of IOG. The cFund[779] for Cardano Developments made its first equity investment in COTI. It acts as a bridge between DeFi apps and the Cardano blockchain. COTI offers a solution called Ada Pay (adapay.finance), a payment gateway that allows retailers to accept ada payments with near-instant settlement. Unlike many financial products on the market, Coti's treasury has always had transparent proof of reserves.

Charles Hoskinson and COTI chief executive Shahaf Bar-Geffen revealed at the 2021 Cardano Summit that the COTI (coti.io) platform will be the official issuer of Djed.[780] Stablecoins, according to the COTI development team, are a 'killer app' that will be used by a huge number of crypto users to settle payments and cover expenses.

Terra UST 2022 collapse

Terra's UST algorithmic stablecoin[781] lost its peg[782] to the US dollar in early May 2022. UST plummeted to 9c forcing Terra to dig deep into its Bitcoin reserves (~$1.3 billion) from its confirmed Bitcoin address[783] in a desperate attempt to steady the ship. The dramatic collapse was summed up well by the Coin Bureau.[784]

Tether (USDT), one of the industry's oldest stablecoins, has previously received criticism for its lack of transparency[785] and reluctance to be audited. The suddenness of Terra's collapse renewed skepticism on the viability of existing stablecoins and drove many[786] to re-evaluate their views of Djed, and how it's designed to be more resilient to similar hazards. Shahaf Bar-Geffen confirmed in subsequent update[787] that Djed survived unscathed from the same tumultuous weekend for the crypto markets.

---

[779] A closer look at the cFund, iohk.io/en/blog/posts/2021/07/28/a-closer-look-at-the-cfund/

[780] Djed update, medium.com/cotinetwork/djed-development-update-421cea2c610b

[781] **Terra (LUNA)** is a Decentralized system focused on enhancing the DeFi space through programmable payments to drive adoption. The Protocol has a native Token, LUNA, and is backed by a host of fiat-pegged Stablecoin. By employing Stablecoin, Terra presents a payment infrastructure void of the shortcomings of traditional payment methods such as Credit card and old Blockchain-based payment systems.

[782] Terra UST collapse, coindesk.com/business/2022/05/09/ust-stablecoin-falls-below-dollar-peg-for-second-time-in-48-hours/

[783] Terra BTC address, bitaps.com/2c2daf15ff549f84faf3dde74da288727f4a63724c957bf83a2d263a97779f65/bc1q9d4ywgfnd8h43da5 tpcxcn6ajv590cg6d3tg6axemvljvt2k76zs50tv4q

[784] Crypto Market EMERGENCY: UST, LUNA & BTC - What Gives?!, youtube.com/watch?v=x5v67Larlx8

[785] The tether controversy, explained, theverge.com/22620464/tether-backing-cryptocurrency-stablecoin

[786] Cardana ADA: I was wrong, youtube.com/watch?v=ew-qrNFKWtA

[787] COTI updates by Shahaf Bar-Geffen, COTI's CEO, youtube.com/watch?v=453M7PjkIbc

Djed is launched

COTI have already signed 40 partnerships with DEXs in the buildup to the long-awaited Djed launch. The private testnet scalability issues were addressed. The public testnet was launched in May 2022 and was followed by a full regress audit. Two security audits were conducted, which is due diligence for such a financial token. The public mainnet was launched in January 2023. For the latest, visit the Djed website (djed.xyz).

Other Stablecoins on Cardano

In April 2022 WingRiders launched with their DEX also bringing wrapped stablecoins[788] (USDC and USDT) and liquidity through the Milkomeda bridge.

At the 2022 Cardano Summit, James Wager of Indigo Labs announced iUSD. iUSD is pegged to the median value of USDC (USD Coin), TUSD (TrueUSD), and USDT (Tether); this design allows iUSD to maintain its peg even if one of these three stablecoins depegs.

Also in Lausanne, Vineeth Bhuvanagiri (Director of Emurgo Fintech) announced *Anzens*, a product suite to bridge the gap between DeFi, RealFi and TradFi (traditional finance). The first product will be a dollar-backed stablecoin, USDA, launching in early 2023. In time, Emurgo will expand beyond the tokenization of dollars to other currencies and real-world assets.

In his talk,[789] Bhuvanagiri highlighted the savings in fees when using Cardano's native asset standard. By contrast, Ethereum's smart contract-based model requires more funds for gas (transaction) fees when moving funds around in USDC and USDT. USDC (USD Coin) and USDT (Tether) are centralized stablecoins, issued by private entities who charge hefty fees, primarily based on Ethereum.

Djed FAQ

Why do we need Djed?

The turmoil of the crypto markets in 2022 were a testament to why we need stability and trust from protocols, not humans. Djed will provide a safe haven enabling users to keep funds on-chain in times of volatility and transfer assets in RealFi DApps and lending protocols. Stablecoins bring a lot of TVL (total value locked) to the ecosystem. They are like a safe haven for assets that enable the system to function smoothly. The FTX exchange collapse, the major crypto story that reached mainstream attention in 2022, was one of human greed and corruption. Djed is a completely decentralized, autonomous

---

[788] $ADA: DEX WingRiders Launches, Bringing USDC and USDT Stablecoins to Cardano Mainnet, cryptoglobe.com/latest/2022/04/ada-dex-wingriders-launches-bringing-usdc-and-usdt-stablecoins-to-cardano-mainnet/

[789] Stablecoins: what Cardano needs to bridge the gap between traditional finance and DeFi, youtube.com/watch?v=XGAH-TYl600

stablecoin with no human middleman involved. It will be driven by the community with no institute involved.

In his fireside chat with Shahaf Bar-Geffen at Scotfest,[790] Charles Hoskinson suggested countries like El Salvador should look at the Djed as the only way to do a stable CBDC that isn't backed by Fiat. If governments want a stablecoin backed by crypto reserves, and live 100% in the cryptocurrency space, there's no other mechanism like Djed currently available.

What are the coins involved in Djed, and what is their purpose?

$DJED is pegged to the US dollar, backed by ada as its base coin. Its reserve coin is Shen ($SHEN). Shen keeps a healthy reserve ratio in the smart contract. Shen is there to incentivize users to put ada into the smart contract.

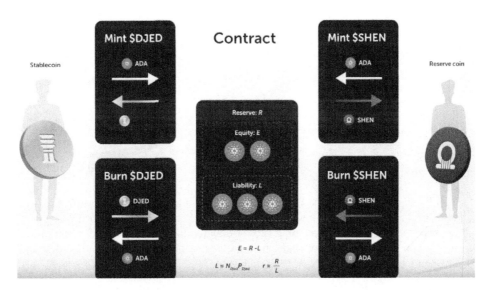

Figure 73: How does Djed work

What does over-collateralized mean?

The ratio between the reserve and the liability is always maintained at a range of 400-800%. For every dollar request, there will be a reserve of $4-8 worth of the reserve coin. Over-collateralized stablecoins are more secure, and fully transparent for inspection. There is no human involvement like with Luna where the network was halted when the price started collapsing.

---

[790] COTI Keynote & Fireside Chat, youtu.be/vyyUiT8NvaI?t=911

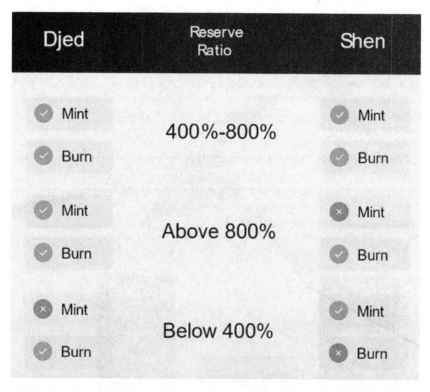

Figure 74: Djed reserve ratio.

How does Djed work?

At a high level, ada is backing the Djed stablecoin. Those who have Djed are the first to receive from the liability pool. They will always get back one dollar for their Djed. This is the safety mechanism in the system, it is over-collateralized, so Djed holders get the priority. On top of this, there is an equity pool created by those who provide liquidity and receive Shen in return.

I send Ada to the smart contract, I get Djed back in return. If I want my ada back, I can send Djed back to the smart contract and get back ada. If I want to enjoy some upside while accepting more risk, I mint Shen by sending ada to the smart contract and burn it when I want to take my upside out. The process is autonomous, managing itself without any human involvement.

400-800%

Within the ratio of 400-800%, ie. 4x – 8x worth of ada to dollar ratio, this is the optimum range. You can mint and burn Djed, you can mint and burn Shen…

Above 800%

Above 800% (8x), you can mint and burn Djed as much as you like, however, you cannot mint Shen anymore. For example, Shen holders are rewarded for the risk they take on early on. They are providing liquidity when needed. Otherwise, everyone might just wait until the ratio goes over 800% to mint Shen. The fact that you can't mint Shen over 800% effectively protects Shen holders who minted it earlier.

Under 400%

You can't mint Djed because there is not enough collateral. You can just burn Djed, and in doing so, raise the ratio. Within this range, you can send ada to the smart contract get Shen back. Under 400% (4x), you mint Shen but you can't burn it. This is the risk Shen holders take on, they can't burn it (withdraw) below 400%. Shen holders must wait until there is more ada in the smart contract and the reserve ratio rises above 400% (4x).

What is the roadmap for the Djed?

Coti have been deliberate and methodical with Djed's implementation. The date has been pushed back a few times due to audits over-running and some small issues rectified. This is the prudent approach with so many failings in the industry to date and Djed's success being pivotal to RealFi and DeFi adoption on Cardano.

Version 1.1.1 was the initial release in January 2023. It has the minimal Djed version. It's compatible with the Vasil hard fork, but it doesn't enjoy the full capabilities of Vasil. It will have an upgrade oracle with 6 external sources. There were two audits, including one by Tweag (tweag.io). There should be plenty of adoption right away with over 40 partnerships in place with all the main DEXs, NFT marketplaces, wallets, lending and borrowing services, etc.

The next version of Djed, V1.2 will fully utilize Vasil, ie. Plutus V2. It will be faster, approximately 4 transactions per minute.

Djed v1.3 will have 'extended Djed' with dynamic fees and prices and importantly, it will have staking support. You won't sacrifice staking rewards by using Djed. There is more detail in the white paper.

Djed will be part of Coti's Treasury. Coti's treasury is a system that hosts about 450m worth of Coti and a wrapped version of Djed can be provided to this treasury for rewards. Other wrapped assets will be supported also, so wrapped Bitcoin, Ethereum, etc.

Coming in 2023 is also 'Djed pay', an app and crypto gateway that will allow merchants, e-commerce platforms, non-profit organization and essentially anybody that would like to send and receive Djed as a form of payment easily.

Is there a risk to holding Shen?

Shen's purpose is to maintain a reserve ratio in the smart contract, in other words to provide stability to Djed. Shen is expected to be volatile, and you are not able to burn Shen (withdraw) below certain 400% (4x). Shen is the reserve coin for Djed, and the reserve has liabilities. Dollars need to be paid out to Djed holders on demand. Shen holders have greater upside, as they are eligible mint/burn rewards. There is a greater ada exposure, but you gain extra ada when ada price goes up. In a future release, Shen holders will also gain staking rewards.

What types of rewards are there for Shen holders?

As Shen is volatile, and Shen holders provide liquidity so there must be incentives to take on additional risk. Shen holders automatically receive rewards in the form of mint and burn fees from the system. This is subject to demand and adoption, however, initial estimates by Coti predict there to be approx. 10% rewards.

Once Coti enable staking (on the roadmap), Shen holders can also avail of staking rewards (additional 3-5%). Many of DEXs partnered with Coti will offer attractive yield farming rewards. They need to incentivize users to bootstrap liquidity on their various platforms. Shen holders who can avail of up to 15% rewards. So overall, there is a potential for ~30% returns.

There are more potential benefits. If you are bullish on ada long term, ie. you are taking a long position, then holding Shen can potentially be lucrative. For example, if ada is worth $1 when the user sends ada to the smart contract, they get back one Djed in return. Over time, ada price appreciates to $3. So, the Djed holder burns their one Djed and gets back their $1. The obvious question is where does the additional $2 go? This $2 automatically goes to Shen holders. It can rise by any amount. If ada rises at all, Shen holders receive the excess.

Is there a middleman?

There is no middleman, or institution involved. The system is autonomous, dynamically adjusting 'buy' and 'sell' conditions for Djed and Shen based on the reserve ration. Anyone can learn more from the paper on djed.xyz and review the smart contract.

Why is Djed better than Terra Luna?

2022 was a bad year for hacks and scams but the two big collapses, FTX and Luna, were due to human greed and corruption. The lack of self-regulation within the crypto industry was also a factor. Just as the crypto industry was tarnished by the FTX collapse, some are trying to tarnish Djed as guilty by association. Luna was also an algorithmic stablecoin, Djed also has an algorithm but that's where the similarity ends. Djed is categorized as an over-collateralized stablecoin.

There are years of academic research behind Djed's algorithm. It started as the product of formal methods and has been battle-tested in simulations. Ergo have also implemented their version, SigmaUSD, which has withstood huge market volatility (90% drop) and maintained its peg. The theory behind over-collateralized stablecoins has repeatedly shown its resilience in adverse market conditions.

Luna was not over-collateralized, Djed is over-collateralized by a healthy 4-8x ratio. Luna was backed by an asset, UST, which it had a direct correlation. The Luna 'death spiral' occurred because as UST lost its peg,[791] the solution was to sell Luna. So, Luna's price inevitably nose-dived creating a circular dependency. As the fiasco unfolded, the centralized entity behind Luna even tried to halt the network and add Bitcoin as an uncorrelated backing asset.

Djed is backed by Ada, which is uncorrelated to Djed. There is no dependency, ada can exist without Djed. Ada has its own utility and ecosystem with plenty of liquidity. Djed is autonomous and decentralized running on its own smart contract. There is no human involvement, no central entity adjusting the reserve ratio. The dynamic 'buy' and 'sell' conditions are all set automatically. The fees go to Shen holders, not to the centralized issuer.

How does Djed compare to other stablecoins?

Most stablecoins today are *fiat-backed*. There is typically a trust required in a centralized entity. You have to believe them when they promise to collateralize at a one-to-one reserve ratio. There is an onus on you to verify, read the audit reports, etc.

There is often a lot of FUD (fear, uncertainty and doubt)[792] floating around about such stablecoins from different vested interest groups. Another key drawback of holding a centralized stablecoin, such as USDC, is that your account can be frozen or seized by the centralized authority. With centralized, fiat-backed stablecoin, the community does not benefit from the protocol. It can be extremely lucrative for the issuer, especially if fiat lending rates are low.

Crypto-backed stablecoins have a dependency on the underlying crypto reserve asset. A quick look at *coincap.io* will show how volatile the markets have been. The risk goes up when the stablecoin is not over-collateralized.

What is the fee structure for Djed?

To review the latest fees, visit *djed.xyz*

How EUTXO copes with impermanent loss

Impermanent loss[793] is a downside to those providing liquidity to a DEX. It can be a confusing term for newcomers.

---

[791] The Death Spiral: How Terra's Algorithmic Stablecoin Came Crashing Down, forbes.com/sites/rahulrai/2022/05/17/the-death-spiral-how-terras-algorithmic-stablecoin-came-crashing-down/?sh=2e4307f371a2

[792] Crypto Biz: You can't stop the Tether FUD, cointelegraph.com/news/crypto-biz-you-can-t-stop-the-tether-fud

[793] In DeFi, **impermanent loss** refers to the loss in value when investing liquidity in a liquidity pool compared to just holding tokens. The event occurs when the price of a user's tokens changes compared to when they deposited them in a liquidity pool. The larger the change is, the bigger the loss.

The automated market maker (AMM) and order book are the most common architectures used to run DEXs (decentralized exchanges). AMMs are straightforward to build, and this architecture has subsequently become the standard for account-based chains. However, there are several drawbacks with this design, 'impermanent loss' being one of them.

Cardano employs the EUTXO model, which is deterministic, making it more predictable than the account-based model in terms of impermanent loss. The term 'impermanent' is a little deceptive because a drop in token price might only be transitory, and the price could climb again depending on market conditions. Because the price corrected upwards, the loss would be transient (impermanent). All that matters is the dollar price when you withdraw. If it's lower than the price you bought at, then obviously the 'loss' becomes permanent. Ada peaked at $1.20 in the 2018 bull run.[794] It plummeted then rose to an all-time high of $3.10 in Sept 2021. Volatility is to be expected in an immature industry, pricing emerging technology.

With light-touch regulation, it's arguable that 'impermanent loss' is an inevitable risk for liquidity providers[795] in the 'wild west' of crypto trading exchanges. If the loss exceeds the trading fees collected, the liquidity provider bears a loss, which could have been avoided if they had kept their tokens. It's also common that while liquidity providers may not lose money, their earnings may be lower than if you had simply retained the tokens.

AMM

The Automated Market Maker (AMM) DEX architecture offers smart contract-based automated trading of crypto pairs. With Ethereum being the dominant smart contract platform to date, naturally most pairs are between Ethereum tokens and stablecoins.

Liquidity pools enable users to pool their assets into smart contracts, which effectively power AMMs. The more liquidity in the pool, the more reliable the trading environment for traders on the DEX with which the pool is affiliated, and naturally, the more transaction fees the liquidity providers earn. Liquidity pools provide the liquidity on both sides of a trade. The pool uses an algorithm to determine the price of an asset based on its availability in the pool.

So AMMs are solely dependent on their liquidity providers to provide sufficient pool size to ensure trading is fair and reliable. Liquidity providers are more commonly known as 'market makers' in traditional finance.

---

[794] A bull market or **bull run** is a state of a financial market where prices are rising. The term bull market is often used in the context of the stock market. However, it can be used in any financial market including cryptocurrencies.

[795] A **market maker or liquidity provider** quotes both a buy and a sell price in a financial instrument or commodity held in inventory, hoping to make a profit on the bid-offer spread, or turn. The U.S. Securities and Exchange Commission defines a 'market maker' as a firm that stands ready to buy and sell stock on a regular and continuous basis at a publicly quoted price.

IOG has several papers[796] on the importance of the right incentives[797] in cryptocurrency space. Incentives are essential to motivate liquidity providers for DEXs to function reliably and fairly. Liquidity providers are incentivized by yield farming[798] in this case.

Order book

The mechanics of order book architecture should be familiar to anyone working in the world of economics. It's a simple model to understand. The order book basically stores all buy/sell (asks/bids) orders and organizes them according to the asset's price when the traders place their orders. The asset can be exchanged if there is sufficient supply and demand.

Order book architecture is much more suited for EUTXO-based ledgers, such as Cardano and Ergo, because its design, together with EUTXO features, mitigates the impacts of impermanent loss.

The number of tokens in a liquidity pool, and the number of liquidity providers contributing to it, are variables when it comes to predicting and avoiding impermanent loss. If there is regular impermanent loss occurring, then pools are not viable and liquidity providers will naturally go to a more profitable rival pool(s). It can be a vicious circle, as it can be too late to salvage once a 'crypto bank run' occurs like what happened with the Terra Luna debacle.[799]

To recap from earlier,

- UTXO-based blockchains don't have accounts holding a balance. Users' wallets keep track of a list of unspent outputs corresponding with all of the user's addresses and determine the user's balance. Remember UTXO transactions are analogous to 'cash in cash out'. The EUTXO model includes a datum, which is contract-specific metadata. This is significant because it allows Cardano to accommodate multi-assets and smart contracts.
- Account-based model holds a coin balance in an account (protected by a private key or a smart contract). Assets are represented as balances inside users' accounts, with the balances being saved as a global state of accounts. Each node

---

[796] Kiayias,Koutsoupias, Stouka (2021) 'Incentives Against Power Grabs or How to Engineer the Revolution in a Pooled Proof of Stake System', arxiv.org/pdf/2111.08562.pdf

[797] Judmayer, Stifter, Zamyatin, Tsabary, Eyal, Gaži, Meiklejohn, Weippl (2021), 'SoK: Algorithmic Incentive Manipulation Attacks on Permissionless PoW Cryptocurrencies', eprint.iacr.org/2020/1614.pdf

[798] **Yield farming** is a DeFi term for leveraging DeFi protocols and products to generate high returns that sometimes reach over 100% in annualized yields 'when factoring in interest, token rewards, 'cashback' bonuses, and other incentives.' Yield farming is a way for cryptocurrency enthusiasts to maximize their returns. It typically involves users lending or locking up their funds using smart contracts. In return, users earn fees in the form of crypto.

[799] Is Do Kwon going to get arrested after Terra's LUNA price collapse?, fxstreet.com/cryptocurrencies/news/is-do-kwon-going-to-get-arrested-after-terras-luna-price-collapse-202205191033

maintains its own state, which is updated with each transaction.

There are various major distinctions between the above models, but there is one that stands out. AMMs that operate on Account-based chains are more likely to employ the Constant Formula Market Maker (CFMM) pricing formula, which is one of the most widely used AMM algorithms. There are inefficiencies in this formula, such as it provides users with little to no privacy.[800]

Also, the Total Value Locked (TVL)[801] is dispersed throughout the whole price range, implying that an asset's price might be $1 or $100,000. CFMM pricing is unreasonable under this premise and does not represent actual market realities. Furthermore, deals with a low token volume tend to have a lot of slippage.[802] While CFMM is a common feature for AMMs, these inefficiencies may cause liquidity providers' earnings to be impacted. What's more, this liquidity is prone to impermanent loss.

EUTXO and order book DEXs mitigate impermanent loss

The key advantages of EUTXO architecture in terms of security, determinism, parallelism, and scalability were discussed earlier. EUTXO features make Cardano a suitable platform for DEXs that use order book architecture, since it provides greater resistance to impermanent loss. This design has a number of advantages, one of which is the concentration of liquidity allocated within a custom price range. This feature improves liquidity efficiency while reducing impermanent loss.

Global vs Local state

Unlike Account-based blockchains, where each transaction outcome changes the global state, EUTXO-based blockchains verify transaction legitimacy at the transaction level, with the balance equal to the total of remaining UTXOs. EUTXO works at the local level.

This is not the case with account-based blockchains. Smart contracts and other actors constantly interact and impact the global state, resulting in the use of assets and resources, as well as the volatile fluctuation of gas prices. Transaction fees can be very unpredictable because of this, even spiking between the time a transaction is submitted and the time it's verified. As a result, the chain may reject such a transaction, but the gas costs are collected nevertheless, potentially resulting in the user's wallet taking a hit. As

---

[800] Chitra, Angeris, Evans (2021), 'Differential Privacy in Constant Function Market Makers', eprint.iacr.org/2021/1101.pdf

[801] The **(TVL) Total Value Locked** into a smart contract or set of smart contracts that may be deployed or stored at one or more exchanges or markets. This is used as a measurement of investor deposits. It is the dollar value of all the coins or tokens locked into a platform, protocol, lending program, yield farming program, or insurance liquidity pool.

[802] **Slippage** refers to the difference between the expected price of a trade and the price at which the trade is executed. Slippage can occur at any time but is most prevalent during periods of higher volatility when market orders are used.

transaction volumes increase and enterprise customers consider using the platform, this is a critical flaw for the likes of Ethereum.

Extortionate 'gas' fees are not an issue with Cardano's EUTXO model, since transactions are verified and executed at the local state. This is made possible by adding a datum (supplementary contract-specific metadata) to the transaction. The datum is passed to the transaction's validation logic, ensuring that EUTXO remains deterministic. This essentially guarantees that transaction costs are fixed and will not vary in the future. Another advantage of EUTXO and determinism is that bad actors cannot reshuffle transactions, which is a danger with Account-based models.

A key benefit of transaction validation being local is that it allows for a high degree of parallelism. Account-based chains can't do this since transactions must be handled sequentially.

Cardano has met with some criticism for being too conservative by its competitors.[803] Rather than 'move fast and break things', Cardano has been implemented carefully with scalability and performance addressed only after a secure network and consensus protocols were established. As the enhancements introduced at Vasil take hold, expect to see a raft of DEXs flourish on Cardano such as ErgoDEX and Axo among many others.[804] Genius DEX is another who outlined their strategy in their medium blog and video.[805]

ERC20 Converter

Cardano's proof-of-stake network can accomodate Ethereum tokens like SingularityNet AGI[806] thanks to an ERC20 converter. Connecting blockchain protocols and partnering on applications is critical to realizing the promise of decentralized finance (DeFi) as a viable alternative to conventional banking.

Early in 2021, DeFi Pulse, a monitoring website, claimed that bitcoin worth more than '$75 billion is now locked up' in DeFi. Later the same year, Cision reported 'DeFi Total Value Locked Hits All-Time High of $236 Billion'[807] and reached the existing all time high of $256 Billion[808] in Dec 2021. The majority of this wealth is in the form of ERC20 token-based crypto-assets.

---

[803] Criticism from Solana founder, twitter.com/IOHK_Charles/status/1532360549857693697?s=20&t=YIDNMde_QXHGEURpgZj8UA

[804] CardanoCube DEXs, cardanocube.io/collections/exchanges-dex

[805] What is impermanent loss?, geniusyield.medium.com/what-is-impermanent-loss-2f03a90a8bcb

[806] **SingularityNET** (ticker symbol: AGI) is a decentralized marketplace for Artificial Intelligence.

[807] DeFi Total Value Locked Hits All-Time High of $236 Billion , prnewswire.com/news-releases/defi-total-value-locked-hits-all-time-high-of-236-billion-301412901.html

[808] Total Value Locked in Defi Nears Lifetime High, Ethereum's TVL Dominates by 54%, news.bitcoin.com/total-value-locked-in-defi-nears-lifetime-high-ethereums-tvl-dominates-by-54

Even since moving to proof-of-stake, Ethereum is fees are still high and unpredictable. Cardano facilitates the transfer of ERC20 tokens to its platform to broaden the range of use cases for application developers and businesses. Users of supported Ethereum tokens may migrate them from Ethereum's overloaded network to Cardano and benefit from its increased transaction capacity and lower fees, as well as improved security, and interoperability.

Why are ERC20 tokens so popular?

In 2015, Ethereum introduced the blockchain to the notion of smart contracts and 'programmable money.' Because of its value in ordinary business transactions, tokenization and the ERC20 token have grown in popularity since then. Tokens created by blockchain-based applications may be used for a variety of purposes, including:

- financial payments
- a unit of transaction
- means of access to digital services
- rewards / incentives
- voting rights
- a vehicle for investment

ERC20 tokens that are well-designed may meet a variety of requirements, and the more helpful they become, the more demand for them develops, and their value rises in tandem. That is why these tokens are so popular and supported by so many wallets and exchanges.

Eth v Ada

The ERC20 token standard was created for Ethereum, and there are now over 750,000 contracts (etherscan.io/tokens) based on it, including Binance coin (BNB), Tether (USDT) and Uniswap (UNI)[809] to mention a few.

Ethereum is a well-known and useful blockchain, but it is stagnating and growing more costly. The 'gas' fees charged for validating transactions are growing rapidly as more users engage with decentralized apps. A Cointelegraph study featured in *DeFi Adoption 2020*[810] also outlined the issues that Ethereum users are facing. This finding was corroborated by Morgan Stanley's report in 2022.[811] Ethereum has not yet overcome

---

[809] **Uniswap** is a Decentralized Exchange (DEX) built on Ethereum that utilizes an automated market-making system instead of a traditional order-book. It was inspired by a Reddit post from Vitalik Buterin and was founded by Hayden Adams in 2017.

[810] DeFi Adoption 2020: A Definitive Guide to Entering the Industry, s3.cointelegraph.com/storage/uploads/view/48c6c4e03f85bc722d76f88c2676478b.pdf?_ga=2.42938214.27041 8488.1602500005-1231871226.1593587737

[811] Morgan Stanley warns Ethereum could lose ground to Binance, Solana, and Cardano, making shift to 'proof of stake' even more urgent, fortune.com/2022/02/18/ethereum-smart-contracts-proof-of-stake-binance-solana-cardano-morgan-stanley

these obstacles, and it is unlikely to do so soon. Many companies will wish to look at other possibilities.

IOG's emphasis is on offering a value proposition that exploits Cardano's advantages over Ethereum by facilitating the transfer of ERC20 tokens to Cardano. Cardano's boasts greater transaction processing capability and cheaper fees, as opposed to Ethereum's high cost and often congested traffic.

What does the ERC20 converter do?

Cardano now supports ada and native tokens, millions of which have been minted.[812] IOG introduced the ERC20 converter in late 2021 to secure future compatibility and to build the groundwork for expanded commercial potential.

The ERC20 converter is a utility that will enable ERC20 token issuers and their users to migrate their tokens to Cardano. It's intended for token issuers (organizations that want to migrate their tokens to Cardano) and their users (token holders) when moving their ERC20 tokens to the Cardano network.

Users simply convert their Ethereum tokens in a few clicks, and these tokens will be 'translated' into a native token on Cardano that has the same value and functions similarly to an ERC20 token when transferred over. Additionally, if the user decides to do so at a later time, they may burn their tokens on Cardano and return them to the source network. Convertibility in both directions is built-in.

SingularityNET (singularitynet.io) were the first to migrate to Cardano. The SingularityNET AGIX token[813] was launched via the ERC20 converter, and its release represented the first step in the SingularityNET to Cardano migration strategy. The inaugural testnet let users evaluate the migration process while using AGIX tokens on the Cardano and Ethereum Kovan testnets.

Metamask (a Chrome browser plugin) was used to verify an account, and additional functionality followed. Users had to provide their Daedalus testnet address to move their tokens to Cardano and keep track of their balances and transactions.

Users can view SingularityNET coins listed and available for migration in their ERC20 converter account, as well as data such as token balance, by clicking on a token. They only need to choose the token, define the quantity they want to convert, and then migrate them to a Cardano address. When tokens are sent to the address, they may be used for Daedalus wallet payments and transactions. Both Etherscan (etherscan.io) and the Cardano Explorer display all of the actions.

---

[812] CardanoCube ecosystem, cardanocube.io/cardano-ecosystem-interactive-map

[813] SingularityNET Phase II Launch Sequence Activated: AGI token to be hard-forked to Cardano-compatible AGIX, blog.singularitynet.io/singularitynet-phase-ii-launch-sequence-activated-agi-token-to-be-hard-forked-to-10ede4b6c89

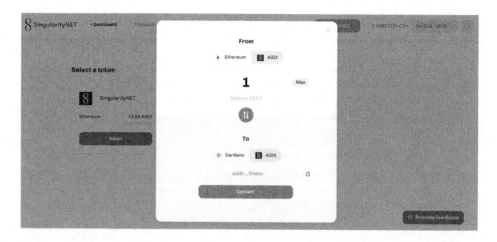

Figure 75: ERC20 Converter

Users will see various tokens on the dashboard as time goes on. Tokens that are eligible for migration will be displayed first, and if tokens are not yet listed, the user may subscribe for notifications on any changes.

IOG's purpose is to support many tokens to facilitate commercial transactions. So, in the future, the ERC20 converter will operate as a bridge across blockchains, allowing for successful cross-chain communication with a range of tokens.

AGIX ERC20 Converter

In December 2021, IOG revealed that the AGIX ERC20 converter testnet was online and available for community assessment.

This initiative's first partner was SingularityNET and the converter was an important step on IOG's budding partnership with the SingularityNET community. Users leveraged a permissioned bridge to transport SingularityNET's AGIX tokens from Ethereum to Cardano and back in the first testnet version. This was a huge step forward in promoting blockchain interoperability in order to create a functioning ecosystem for decentralized finance (DeFi). Users evaluated the testnet's capabilities and tested the transfer of AGIX tokens to take advantage of Cardano's greater transaction capacity, cheaper costs, and proven security advantages.

Bridge to interoperability

Interoperability is critical for growing blockchain adoption and growth across the board. Along with IOG's blanket open-source strategy, making blockchain solutions available to everyone, regardless of protocol, has always been one of their top goals. IOG is working on making it possible to migrate tokens from other blockchains and sidechains to Cardano in a safe and frictionless manner.

The AGIX ERC20 converter bridge went live on mainnet on 18 April 2022. See *bridge.singularitynet.io*

372

Certified DApps on Cardano

With the surge of new third-party apps comes the potential of improper or harmful information, as well as content that isn't up to par. As a result, addressing challenges like discovery and quality assurance is critical for early ecosystem development. At the 2021 Cardano Summit, IOG provided a deeper dive[814] into this crucial issue by introducing a certification program to examine apps built on top of Cardano. This will be integral to the DApp Store on Lace.

DApp discovery

The DApp Store, a prototype[815] of which was shown at the Summit, will allow developers to submit their Cardano-based DApps and make them accessible to the rest of the community. Developers will be able to publish their DApps without fear of censorship thanks to the store's trustworthy and democratized environment.

The Plutus DApp Store solves two particular entry barriers:

- There is presently no official DApp discovery mechanism. Almost all new products are discovered organically or by word-of-mouth, or through social media promotions.

- There is no aggregated picture of all DApps accessible in a given ecosystem for end users.

Through automated logic checks, human smart contract audits, and formal verification, a certification program provides consumers with certainty about the behavior of any applications they use.

Any DApp, certified or uncertified, may be found in the store, but Lace will give users clear information regarding a DApp's certification status. The DApp Store's goal is to serve as a platform for transparent user evaluation rather than acting as a gatekeeper or judge.

The importance of certification

The DApp Store is a storefront for DApps. It does not, however, provide any 'built in' guarantee except for community validation. This is when the second component enters the picture. IOG's certification procedure is responsible for preventing code-level security bugs, achieved by deploying several degrees of 'defense.'

There will be numerous levels to choose from. Automated logic checks, at their most basic level, will help identify some forms of harmful code. These will, for example, be

---

[814] Cardano 2021 Summit session on Certification, summit.cardano.org/sessions/smart-contract-certification-the-why-and-how

[815] Cardano 2021 Summit DApp Store demo, summit.cardano.org/sessions/redefining-dapp-discovery-bringing-dapps-to-the-mass-market

able to determine if the contract has a mechanism for recovering funds that have been locked up. Locked funds must be retrievable under a well-written contract.

Furthermore, manual smart contract audits will assist IOG in verifying the integrity of any DApp. In the end, thorough formal verification will test the mathematical model to establish that a smart contract's behavior matches the formal specification.

Any certification program, of course, is only as good as the people who put it together and operate it. As a result, IOG has partnered with some of the most well-known players in the functional programming field.

Certification and assurance

IOG demonstrated[816] automated testing of smart contracts, which are components of DApps rather than whole DApps, during the 2021 Cardano Summit. In the long run, IOG hopes to see user-designed tools, their deployment to the store, and the expansion of the Plutus DApp Store to incorporate additional features like upvoting, reviews, and Atala PRISM integration allowing users to provide feedback on the store's DApps.

When it comes to building and dealing with smart contracts, high assurance is essential. You want to know that the source code is of excellent quality, that the contract is secured and will perform as expected, and that it makes use of good attributes and behaviors. Certification guarantees that security tests be carried out prior to any deployment, and that smart contracts may be inspected as they evolve. It aids both smart contract developers and end users by assisting with the protection of user assets and reputation from code defects or exploitation.

IOG announced their intentions to offer higher levels of certification for decentralized apps (DApps) at the Cardano Summit 2021. This certification scheme will establish quality standards for DApps and associated smart contacts.

Three certification levels

Professor Simon Thompson,[817] technical project director at IOG, and Shruti Appiah,[818] head of product at IOG, are leading this endeavor. It will assist IOG in adhering to best practices seen in the industry. They're collaborating with companies like Runtime Verification (runtimeverification.com), Tweag (tweag.io), Well Typed (well-typed.com), Certik (certik.io), and others to launch this new certification program, which will be integrated to the new DAppStore. This will be available on IOG's new light wallet, *Lace,*[819] unveiled in Texas at Consensus 2022.[820]

---

[816] Smart Contract Certification, summit.cardano.org/sessions/smart-contract-certification-the-why-and-how

[817] Prof. Simon Thompson, iohk.io/en/team/simon-thompson

[818] Shruti Appiah, iohk.io/en/team/shruti-appiah

[819] Lace light wallet, lace.io

[820] Consensus 2022, coindesk.com/consensus2022/

What are the various levels of certification?

In terms of assurance and auditing, there are three levels of certification, each of which is complementary to the others rather than progressive.

LEVEL ONE	LEVEL TWO	LEVEL THREE
Automated tooling	**In-depth audit**	**Formal verification**
This level gives **continual assurance** about a range of properties for smart contracts.	This level involves looking at the technology and processes that led to it being produced.	This level is more **specialized**.
• It covers the discovery of different types of issues or bugs and is characterized as **low cost, low effort, accessible to everyone** while providing a **substantial level of assurance.**	• It is characterized by the fact that it involves a **manual audit** and **verification** of smart contracts within the DApp itself.	• We aim to provide **full assurance of critical aspects** of applications through formal verification of smart contracts.
• It can be **applied repeatedly** and **automatically,** so each time there is a release or a sub-release of an application, we can test to ensure that the application still has the properties that we expect.	• The audit is performed at a much more **in-depth level** and involves more manual effort that can **address a DApp in its entirety,** even if it is written in a variety of languages.	• Formal verification involves ensuring that a smart contract **serves the specific business or technical requirements** defined at the outset.

Figure 76: Levels of Certification

Benefits of assurance

Both application developers and auditors will be able to verify the validity, compliance, and consistency of requirements via certification. It will also ensure that DApps launched on Cardano are free of typical security flaws and offer a degree of resilience, stability, and upkeep. While certification will be heavily encouraged and the DApp Store will be curated, it will not be compulsory or operate as a 'gatekeeper,' ensuring a balance between user assurance and decentralized principles.

You can give assurance to the community and ensure that things will operate as planned by auditing the specs, design, and ideation stages. This evidence provides extensive documentation of requirements, which will serve as a future reference point.

Certification and the DApp Store

IOG intends to link this certification with their new DApp Store to produce cryptographically secure non-fungible tokens (NFTs) that serve as proof of the certification levels they will guarantee. The DApp Store will be part of *Lace* light wallet, where users will able to examine the certification status of each DApp as they browse through the categories and individual DApps. Users will have more confidence in the quality and safety of DApps if the required certification status is evident throughout the selection process.

At ScotFest[821] in 2022, Simon Thompson provided an update on the team's progress. Working with the community, the *Cardano Dapp Certification Working Group* is now in place along with the guardrails outlined in *CIP-52 - Cardano audit best practice guidelines*.

Also, at ScotFest was IOG's Head of Wallets & Services, Alex Apeldoorn, who previewed[822] what is coming with Lace. IOG's flagship wallet will touch every aspect of user experience going forward:

- use hardware wallet to secure your keys in Lace mobile app and browser plugin
- avail of out-of-the box DApp connector functionality for ease of use with other DApps, based on CIP standards
- send multiple assets to multiple wallets in a single transaction
- Lace's first partner is the governance team. Catalyst proposals and voting will move there from IdeaScale.
- multi-stake pool delegation will extend to delegating to multiple DReps
- audit features based on integration with Atala Prism DIDs and verifiable credentials
- Partnership with Pezesha on their RealFi Center

Oracles on Cardano

Using Plutus and Marlowe to develop dependable and transparent financial applications utilizing oracles and smart contracts lies at the core of DeFi and RealFi's promise. IOG announced an innovative strategic relationship with Chainlink[823] Labs at the 2021 Cardano Summit,[824] which will assist developers in creating smart contracts for Cardano DeFi apps.

Chainlink's 'decentralized oracle networks' will enable access to real-world databases, allowing 'smart contracts' to execute around data like election outcomes, sports scores, and cryptocurrency prices. Another example where this may be beneficial is the delivery of weather data. Chainlink Labs collaborates with a number of FinTech firms in Sub-Saharan Africa that are attempting to make parametric insurance a reality. Weather data that is secure, reliable, and resilient is a critical input for parametric insurance[825] contracts.

---

[821] DApp Certification Program, youtu.be/kSvfj1YZ1Oo

[822] IOG's light wallet platform Lace, youtu.be/KWulFbCSXus

[823] **Chainlink** (ticker: LINK) is a decentralized oracle network that brings off-chain data into an on-chain format, bridging the gap between isolated blockchains and real-world data.

[824] Cardano Announces Strategic Collaboration To Integrate Chainlink's Oracles, chainlinktoday.com/cardano-announces-strategic-collaboration-to-integrate-chainlinks-oracles/

[825] **Parametric insurance** is a type of insurance that does not indemnify the pure loss, but ex-ante (Latin for 'before the event") agrees to make a payment upon the occurrence of a triggering event. The triggering event is often a catastrophic natural event which may ordinarily precipitate a loss or a series of losses. But parametric

Across numerous blockchains, but primarily Ethereum, Chainlink delivers oracle services to fuel hybrid smart contracts. Smart contracts may connect to any external API via Chainlink oracle networks, allowing them to use safe off-chain calculations for feature-rich applications. Chainlink presently secures tens of billions of dollars across DeFi, insurance, gaming, and other important sectors, providing a universal gateway to all blockchains to global organizations and prominent data providers.

Developers utilizing the blockchain will be able to inject Chainlink's institutional-grade data into their smart contracts. Support for additional Chainlink decentralized services will come after market price feeds: sports data for betting markets, weather datasets for parametric insurance products, and verifiable randomness for gaming and non-fungible tokens (NFTs). This partnership between IOG and Chainlink Labs will provide access to a plethora of secure data, assisting DeFi in realizing its goal of creating a more cost-effective and equitable global economic system.

IOG state Chainlink is their preferred oracle option for Cardano, however, there are worthy alternatives as listed on Essential Cardano[826] and third-party sites like CardanoCube.[827] Charli3 launched the first Cardano native oracle at *Rare Bloom* in Denver.[828] Another EUTXO-based option is Ergo's Oracle Pools[829] who claim in their blog:

> The design of Ergo's oracle pools are more efficient and programmable than using multiple single oracle data points such as in Chainlink's oracle design. We build hierarchies of confidence using oracle pools, and pools of oracle pools, in Ergo. It's faster, cheaper, and more beneficial to the end user.

Ergo's claims should be taken seriously, having already demonstrated their technical prowess delivering 15k outputs per transaction using EUTXO and rollups.

Cardano in Africa

Cardano was introduced at the start of this book by citing its mission:

> Cardano is an open platform that seeks to provide economic identity to the billions who lack it by providing decentralized applications to manage identity, value and governance

---

insurance principles are also applied to Agricultural crop insurance and other normal risks not of the nature of disaster, if the outcome of the risk is correlated to a parameter or an index of parameters.

[826] Essential Cardano Oracles, github.com/input-output-hk/essential-cardano/blob/main/essential-cardano-list.md#oracles

[827] CardanoCube Oracles, cardanocube.io/collections/oracle

[828] Charli3 Cardano Native Oracle Launch at Rare Bloom, youtu.be/bGFMMs0oDZo

[829] Ergo Oracle Pools, ergoplatform.org/en/blog/2021-04-27-chainlink-oracles-vs-ergo-oracle-pools/

Despite technological advances, people still live in two different worlds, one for the developed, and one for the developing. The billions who lack economic identity are not currently in the developed world. The demand for Cardano is most pronounced in the likes of Africa, southeast Asia, the subcontinent of India, Mongolia, Latin America, amongst others, where the effects of globalization have not been so favorable.

Cardano is not just a cryptocurrency; it is a platform for governance, identity, and tokenizing digital assets. Countries without working infrastructure and systems are ripe for disruption. There is a wider gamut of possibilities for installing, or replacing, systems for voting, land ownership registries, payment mechanisms and supply chain processes.

There is precedent for this strategy. When Estonia left the Soviet Bloc, they had a blank slate to start over from. Their subsequent digital transformation[830] is seen by other countries as an example of how to overhaul your infrastructure.

Africa is not Cardano's sole focus, but it is an ideal launchpad for their technology. All the projects and initiatives discussed in this chapter can be reproduced in other jurisdictions, including the developed world. If a system can work for 5m Ethiopian students, it can work similarly for the country's 107m citizens. If a system can connect the unconnected in Tanzania, its model can be rolled out to neighboring countries.

Kenya's M-Pesa[831] (mobile money payments) success story is proof that 'necessity is the mother of all invention'. Since its launch in 2007, M-Pesa is now flourishing across Africa with millions of users and transactions every month, often on old mobiles discarded by users in the developed world.

Microlending platforms like Kiva (kiva.org) provide a profitable business model that is well-suited to Africa's expanding economy. Small loans may be life-changing for farmers, entrepreneurs, and anybody with the will to create and flourish in this environment.

It's getting easier and cheaper to get users online, and this continuing trend is key for infrastructure projects like World Mobile. While there are the old challenges like corruption and civil unrest in Africa, there is often no legacy system to replace, so decision makers are more open and forward-looking.

Demographics is another major consideration. Africa is the world's youngest continent, with a median age of 20 years and 60% of its population under 25. One of the reasons China has invested over $20 billion in Africa's infrastructure is they see it as an opportunity to shape geopolitics and world economics in the decades to come.

---

[830] 8 lessons from Estonia's digital transformation for Latin America and the Caribbean, blogs.iadb.org/administracion-publica/en/8-lessons-from-estonias-digital-transformation-for-latin-america-and-the-caribbean/

[831] M-Pesa: Kenya's mobile money success story celebrates 15 years, africa.businessinsider.com/local/markets/m-pesa-kenyas-mobile-money-success-story-celebrates-15-years/srp9gne

In the past, the likes of Silicon Valley were the primary drivers of innovation. This has changed with blockchain as it is permissionless, more accessible and built to enable social financial inclusion on a global scale. The model is becoming flatter, with less hierarchies, so now anyone anywhere who has an idea and drive can use blockchain platforms.

IOG's roots in Africa are deep as showcased during their 'Africa Special' in 2021. John O'Connor, Director of African Operations at IOG, provided an update on progress at ScotFest.[832] There are now 60 funded projects across 12 different countries across the continent. In 2021, there were just two projects in two countries, both with IOG involvement. Now there are many projects funded by Catalyst, Emurgo Africa and *ariob*, (ariob.io) an incubator scheme IOG runs in collaboration with iceaddis (iceaddis.com).

Ethiopian Ministry of Education

This was IOG's flagship partnership announced in 2021. The project was to implement SSI, leveraging Atala Prism system enabling 5m students and 750k teachers transition from paper-based systems to a DID-based solution. Tracking grades, education attainment and attendance are an ideal use case to pave the way for future partners. Verified credentials could then enable the graduates to prove their academic achievements and succeed in the job market. The *Tigray* civil war (2020-2022 ceasefire) did not help matters, but development is now complete and due to be deployed live in schools very soon.

World Mobile Chain (WMC)

Under the charismatic leadership of Mickey Watkins, World Mobile are trailblazers in bringing connectivity to the developing world. World Mobile runs on a mesh network[833] leveraging Cardano to deliver last-mile connectivity to the unconnected, or those who are being overcharged for it. Leveraging cutting-edge tech and aerostats,[834] WMC aims is to provide internet access at 50% of the price of rival networks. World Mobile has made rapid progress[835] evolving from 'smart cities' to 'smart countries' and are now launching their 'dynamic network technology' to areas of the US that don't have mobile coverage

Empowa

Empowa is as 'RealFi' as it gets. This decentralized funding platform delivers affordable housing across Mozambique and beyond. Empowa uses crypto-based liquidity on

---

[832] IOG & Africa, youtu.be/tHC80NFj4lo

[833] A mesh network is a local area network (LAN) where the nodes connect directly, dynamically and non-hierarchically to as many other nodes as possible. The nodes cooperate with one another to efficiently route data to and from clients.

[834] How World Mobile's aerostats work, worldmobile.io/blog/post/how-aerostats-work

[835] World Mobile: Building smart cities, building smart countries, youtube.com/watch?v=5ijAOa6VjzA

Cardano to provide financing for housing developers to deliver a 'lease-to-own' model. There is a dire need for such a project, with the absence of any real mortgage market across the continent. Empowa have already had a big impact, expanding from 1% access to housing, to 60% in Mozambique.

Pezesha

Pezesha is a fintech company based in Kenya for powering affordable working capital to small and medium businesses (SMEs) in Africa. Launched in 2016, its mission is to democratize financial services for the unbanked across Africa. Pezesha's founder, Hilda Moraa, went into greater detail in her talk at ScotFest.[836] IOG have previously invested in Moraa's dream and they will partner with *Lace* light wallet and Atala Prism to make their loans accessible to a wider audience. RealFi on *Lace* will be in the form of a 'marketplace of marketplaces', and one of those marketplaces will be Pezesha.

Charles Hoskinson often stated that his measure of success is if something like Pezesha could run on Cardano[837] as it would bookend his vision laid out in his Ted Talk[838] in Bermuda in 2014. I suspect there may be a demo in 2023 featuring Hoskinson issuing a loan on Pezesha using *Lace* and Atala Prism.

Figure 77: Image credit Pezesha

Outlook

Cardano has come a long way in a short space of time. The Byron era was slow and frustrating, but it led to the creation of the hard fork combinator and the steady release cadence we've seen since. It wasn't long ago when the idea of proof-of-stake was ridiculed, now it's self-evident. The extensive research and steady implementation of prior eras mean developers are building on granite.

---

[836] Powerubg affordable working capital, youtube.com/watch?v=2ZgOAduls7Q

[837] Charles Hoskinson explains how he will know that Cardano has achieved 'Success', cardanofeed.com/charles-hoskinson-explains-how-he-will-know-that-cardano-has-achieved-success-356.html

[838] The future will be decentralized | Charles Hoskinson | TEDxBermuda, www.youtube.com/watch?v=97ufCT6lQcY

Cardano has stayed true to its principles, even when it was inconvenient. The incentivized testnet (ITN) could have been a cryptocurrency in its own right, but it was just an *orderve* before Shelley mainnet. Cardano has approached development from a different angle to other 'build first, fix later' blockchains. With hacks and scams now weekly news in the industry, this methodical and sensible approach is a breath of fresh air.

There has already been the unexpected CNFT boom, a result of the right features and easy user experience. When I was studying for my masters (2018) I remember thinking at the time a term like non-fungible token (NFT) would never catch on. Now NFTs are on the verge of going mainstream. More programming languages are being accommodated, developer tooling is proliferating, and *Lace* light wallet will soon cater for on-chain voting and partial delegation. But it's just one wallet competing in a thriving ecosystem.

We are now in the Age of Voltaire, the most challenging and ambitious implementation of on-chain governance ever. Nobody else is attempting anything like this. Another differentiator is the Midnight sidechain, the only solution offering privacy-based smart contracts.

As you can see from the last few chapters, there are a lot of moving parts in their infancy. Yet as features like Mamba are released, earlier parts of the roadmap seem to make more sense in hindsight. While the mainchain has prioritized security and reliability, sidechains enable developers to have more flexible programming paradigms and faster consensus protocols. Adoption takes time, Ethereum had to wait more than two years before *CryptoKitties*[839] garnered significant user adoption.

No matter how impressive Cardano may be, there are dark regulatory clouds forming with the fallout of 2022's scams and hacks still unfolding. It's frustrating that something as principled and meticulous as Cardano is mentioned in the same breath as some of the actors now departing the stage. Let's hope it's just the trash taking itself out.

Regulation may be on its way, but it is not clear what form it will take or how it will be enforced. Most countries are now rolling out CBDCs (Central bank digital coins),[840] typically preceded by a regulatory crackdown on anything resembling competition. One case study of note is Nigeria where a third of the adult population use crypto, the highest adoption rate anywhere. When the government banned crypto in February 2021, the assumption was citizens would embrace the eNaira (Nigerian CBDC).

The reality was crypto couldn't be banned, and never went away. In October 2022, a Bloomberg report found usage of eNaira at just 0.5% of the country's population. In the past month (Jan 2023), the Nigerian government has placed a cap on ATM cash withdrawals, seemingly to force CBDC adoption, only to perform a full U-turn passing a

---

[839] Guide to Ethereum, medium.com/coinmonks/pauls-guide-to-ethereum-280be582653

[840] CBDCs by country, cbdctracker.org/

bill legalizing cryptocurrency. *The Nigerian Capital Market Master Plan*[841] claims it's only interested in creating a 'vibrant capital market'. Whatever the motive it shows how supposed regulatory headwinds can turn to tailwinds very quickly.

In any case, Cardano continues marching to beat of its own drum, with the last eras of the roadmap coming to fruition. While some competitors are trying to bandage failing infrastructure, and others just implode, Cardano is already looking toward '4th gen' technologies[842] like multi-resource consensus, privacy-based smart contracts, etc. *Midnight* was originally to be a separate proof-of-work blockchain but it's likely the *Minotaur* and *Ofelimos* research papers will resurface somewhere in Cardano's future.

This book started by explaining the origins of Bitcoin. It is ironic that Cardano is now leading the way in realizing the vision outlined by Satoshi Nakamoto in the 2009 Bitcoin whitepaper. CH:[843]

> *We realized the vision of Bitcoin. For Colored coins, (we have) Cardano native assets. Lightning is basically what Hydra has achieved. Inclusive accountability means that everybody has a copy of the blockchain, even without having a copy of the blockchain. So, you're your own node, you're your own bank. When you look at input endorsers, it creates a network that can scale to billions of users eventually, and tons of things going on, without sacrificing decentralization, the system gets more decentralized over time ...and then Voltaire, that one CPU-one vote notion ...that idea that everybody can contribute in governance, I think we will be there. So, all the things that Satoshi outlined, we finally realized, in some way or another, in this project with this community, and we're just getting started in that respect.*

Whatever unfolds next, one thing is for certain, there will be plenty to write about in the next edition of *Cardano for the Masses*.

---

[841] The Nigerian Captial Market Master Plan, sec.gov.ng/wp-content/uploads/2015/10/Opportunities-in-the-Nigerian-Capital-Market.pdf

[842] First Principles: Research for the Future, youtube.com/watch?v=MVuweooiXPI

[843] Let's Talk Basho, youtu.be/fhVo-2QUjLM?t=1938

Printed in Great Britain
by Amazon